Contemporary Authors®
Autobiography Series

ISSN 0748-0636

Contemporary Authors

Autobiography Series

Shelly Andrews
Editor

volume **23**

GALE

an International Thomson Publishing company I**T**P®

EDITORIAL STAFF

Shelly Andrews, *Editor*
Linda R. Andres and Motoko Fujishiro Huthwaite, *Associate Editors*
Marilyn O'Connell Allen and Sheryl Ciccarelli, *Assistant Editors*
Cindy Buck, Mary Gillis, Heidi J. Hagen, Kevin Hile, Laurie Collier Hillstrom, Carolyn C. March,
Thomas McMahon, Lori J. Sawicki, and Diane Telgen, *Contributing Copyeditors*

Victoria B. Cariappa, *Research Manager*
Corporate Research Information Service, *Research*

Gwendolyn Tucker, *Data Entry Supervisor*
Civie Green and Nancy Sheridan, *Data Entry*

Hal May, *Publisher*
Joyce Nakamura, *Managing Editor, Children's and Young Adult Literature*

Mary Beth Trimper, *Production Director*
Deborah Milliken, *Production Assistant*

Barbara Yarrow, *Graphic Services Manager*
C. J. Jonik, *Desktop Publisher*
Randy A. Bassett, *Imaging Supervisor*
Robert Duncan, *Imaging Specialist*

Theresa Rocklin, *Manager, Technical Support Services*

Library of Congress Catalog Card Number 86-641293
ISBN 0-8103-9330-1
ISSN 0748-0636

Printed in the United States of America

ITP™   Gale Research, an ITP Information/Reference Group Company.
ITP logo is a trademark under license.

10   9   8   7   6   5   4   3   2   1

Contents

Preface   vii
A Brief Sampler   ix
Acknowledgments   xi

Preface

A Unique Collection of Essays

Each volume in the *Contemporary Authors Autobiography Series (CAAS)* presents an original collection of autobiographical essays written especially for the series by noted writers.

CA Autobiography Series is designed to be a meeting place for writers and readers—a place where writers can present themselves, on their own terms, to their audience; and a place where general readers, students of contemporary literature, teachers and librarians, even aspiring writers can become better acquainted with familiar authors and meet others for the first time.

This is an opportunity for writers who may never write a full-length autobiography to let their readers know how they see themselves and their work, what brought them to this time and place.

Even for those authors who have already published full-length autobiographies, there is the opportunity in *CAAS* to bring their readers "up to date" or perhaps to take a different approach in the essay format. In some instances, previously published material may be reprinted or expanded upon; this fact is always noted at the end of such an essay. Individually, the essays in this series can enhance the reader's understanding of a writer's work; collectively, they are lessons in the creative process and in the discovery of its roots.

CAAS makes no attempt to give a comprehensive overview of authors and their works. That outlook is already well represented in biographies, reviews, and critiques published in a wide variety of sources. Instead, *CAAS* complements that perspective and presents what no other ongoing reference source does: the view of contemporary writers that is shaped by their own choice of materials and their own manner of storytelling.

Who Is Covered?

Like its parent series, *Contemporary Authors*, the *CA Autobiography Series* sets out to meet the needs and interests of a wide range of readers. Each volume includes essays by writers in all genres whose work is being read today. We consider it extraordinary that so many busy authors from throughout the world are able to interrupt their existing writing, teaching, speaking, traveling, and other schedules to converge on a given deadline for any one volume. So it is not always possible that all genres can be equally and uniformly represented from volume to volume, although we strive to include writers working in a variety of categories, including fiction, nonfiction, and poetry. As only a few writers specialize in a single area, the breadth of writings by authors in this volume also encompasses drama, translation, and criticism as well as work for movies, television, radio, newspapers, and journals.

What Each Essay Includes

Authors who contribute to *CAAS* are invited to write a "mini-autobiography" of approximately 10,000 words. In order to give the writer's imagination free rein, we suggest no guidelines or pattern for the essay.

We only ask that each writer tell his or her story in the manner and to the extent that feels most natural and appropriate. In addition, writers are asked to supply a selection of personal photographs showing themselves at various ages, as well as important people and special moments in their lives. Our contributors have responded generously, sharing with us some of their most treasured mementoes. The result is a special blend of text and photographs that will attract even the casual browser. Other features include:

Bibliography at the end of each essay, listing book-length works in chronological order of publication. Each bibliography in this volume was compiled by members of the *CAAS* editorial staff and submitted to the author for review.

Cumulative index in each volume, which cites all the essayists in the series as well as the subjects presented in the essays: personal names, titles of works, geographical names, schools of writing, etc. To ensure ease of use for these cumulating references, the name of the essayist is given before the volume and page number(s) for every reference that appears in more than one essay. In the following example, the entry in the index allows the user to identify the essay writers by name:

> Auden, W.H.
> Allen   **6:**18, 24
> Ashby   **6:**36, 39
> Bowles   **1:**86
> etc.

For references that appear in only one essay, the volume and page number(s) are given but the name of the essayist is omitted. For example:

> Stieglitz, Alfred   **1:**104, 109, 110

CAAS is something more than the sum of its individual essays. At many points the essays touch common ground, and from these intersections emerge new patterns of information and impressions. The index is an important guide to these interconnections.

For Additional Information

For detailed information on awards won, adaptations of works, critical reviews of works, and more, readers are encouraged to consult Gale's *Contemporary Authors* cumulative index for authors' listings in other Gale sources. These include, among others, *Contemporary Authors, Contemporary Authors New Revision Series, Dictionary of Literary Biography,* and *Contemporary Literary Criticism.*

Special Thanks

We wish to acknowledge our special gratitude to each of the authors in this volume. They all have been most kind and cooperative in contributing not only their talents but their enthusiasm and encouragement to this project.

A Brief Sampler

Each essay in the series has a special character and point of view that sets it apart from its companions. A small sampler of anecdotes and musings from the essays in this volume hint at the unique perspective of these life stories.

Fleur Adcock remembers being sent with her sister, Marilyn, to Wiltshire during World War II: "This was the second occasion when Marilyn and I were separated from our parents. I was enchanted with this taste of normally forbidden squalor: we lived in a two-roomed cottage with feckless, earthy Mrs J. and her toddler, carrying all our water in buckets from the village tap, getting lice in our hair and mysterious sores on our feet, and learning rather belatedly that there were adults in the world who drank, swore, quarrelled with their neighbours, and engaged in other, more interesting activities with soldiers from the nearby camp. Mrs J. herself was sober and faithful to her absent husband, but she liked company and chose me to provide it, setting the clock outrageously fast or slow several times a week so that I'd miss the bus to my school. As this was a huge and terrifying coeducational establishment in distant Chippenham . . . I didn't mind. It all came out in the end and our mother swooped and removed us to be with her in more hygienic accommodation in Chippenham. . . ."

Norman Levine describes a Sunday morning when he was on weekend leave in London: "I would cross the road to go and hear the soapbox orators at Speakers' Corner in Hyde Park. The war was coming to an end. There was talk and speculation, in the papers, on the BBC, of what peace would be like. Most of the speakers had heavy European accents. But spoke with eloquent gestures. Their arms punctuating their words. I was walking towards a speaker who had the largest audience. I could hear laughter from the crowd. And astonishment from the speaker at this reaction to what he was saying. He was finishing another short passionate speech. When, triumphantly, he ended with: *'Vat the pipple vant . . . und vat the pipple get . . . ist piss.'* He brought the house down. And he could not understand why."

Sandra McPherson speaks for the budding poet of her youth: "As far as I knew, my kin saw poetry as rhymed innocence, just a hobby. I don't know how or when I perceived that it was more important than that to me. I do know that in high school I set out to write one hundred poems. And I did write that many. When the trauma of social dancing in the high school gym was the antithesis of poetry to me, I would go home, lock myself in the bedroom, and supply poetry out of privacy, pain, secret joy, and language. A few friends and Lucile Eastman, my senior English teacher, wanted the poems, said the poems meant a lot to them, and called me 'Poet Laureate of T-101.'"

Marilyn Nelson shares memories of pre-Civil Rights days: "On one of those cross-country trips, which we made driving all night, stopping at dusk-to-dawn drive-in theatres where Mama and Daddy snored while we children watched movies until we couldn't help giving up, Daddy drove as we slept and parked the car on the edge of the Grand Canyon. We awoke to that grandeur at dawn. Daddy was like that. He loved the sound of rain on the car's roof at night, and once or twice he invited me to sleep in the car so I could hear it. I slept in the backseat, he in the front. Rain sounds like wren's wings beating against a parked car's roof at night. Or like a cascade of coins made of moonlight. Or like a raging stampede of chipmunks. Daddy could pull coins out of our ears. I remember thinking as a young child that as long as he could do that, we would never be poor."

Gibbons Ruark remembers his father as a man of deep faith: "I think perhaps the hours closest to the center of his nature were those spent composing his sermons by hand or reading Paul Tillich or Jeremy Taylor or the *Little Flowers of St. Francis*. He was at home in his study. Sometimes the door into the rest of the house would be open, but often it was closed, of course, and we children were taught to creep by it, especially on Saturday nights when he would be working on his sermon. Memory tells me that he wrote it out in longhand first and then rather quickly typed it up, since his writing was small and crabbed and he at least claimed that he often couldn't decipher it himself once it was stale. Then he would memorize the sermon. We could hear his low voice reading it over and over, the words a mystery but their cadences carrying a meaning of some kind under the door. The next morning at eleven, not to tempt fate, he would lay the typescript on the pulpit before him, but I don't recall seeing him from my second-row vantage point ever look down at it once. His delivered sermons were vivid, but what haunts me more is the hidden murmur of the night before, the narrow gleam of light at the threshold of the door, something coming from in there which might be described by Robert Frost's phrase about birdsong in the Garden of Eden after Eve's arrival, a 'tone of meaning but without the words.'"

Richard Tillinghast, poet on pilgrimage to Asia: "My first day in India, two things happened: war was declared, and either I lost or someone pinched the pouch that held my passport, my shot record and other travel documents, and eight 100-dollar bills. I arrived in India broke and without any legal identity. Mysteriously, the pouch turned up in a small town eighty miles from Delhi. Word from the chief of police in the town reached me where I was staying in Delhi, and I took a car there. The chief of police, whose name told me he was a Muslim, invited me to his house, where a good lunch was served on the lawn. Then, as I watched in amazement, he handed over everything from the pouch, including the hundred-dollar bills, whose serial numbers he wrote down on an official form that he asked me to sign. I returned to Delhi feeling as if some strange morality play had been acted out for my benefit."

These brief examples only suggest what lies ahead in this volume. The essays will speak differently to different readers; but they are certain to speak best, and most eloquently, for themselves.

Acknowledgments

Grateful acknowledgment is made to those publishers, photographers, and artists whose works appear with these authors' essays.

Photographs/Art

Fleur Adcock: p. 1, © Caroline Forbes.

Larry Eigner: pp. 19, 49, 55, 56, 60, Beverly Eigner; p. 30, Nina Zurier/*Poetry USA*; p. 32, Jesse Beagle.

Christopher Fry: p. 63, © Jane Bohn; p. 70, © Karsh/Camera Press Ltd.; p. 72, Enitharmon Press; p. 74, AP/Wide World Photos.

Douglas Glover: p. 96, Geof Isherwood.

Robert Gurik: pp. 99, 106, André Le Coz; p. 108, Jacques Grenier; pp. 110, 111, Studio Lausanne Inc.; p. 114, Candia Maris.

Rachel Hadas: p. 125, Nick Romanenko/1992 Rutgers; p. 128, Dorothy Alexander; p. 131, © Miriam Berkley.

Norman Levine: p. 165, K. Beaty/*Toronto Star;* p. 165, National Archives of Canada/PA-70984; p. 168, David Noble; p. 169, Thelma Mason; p. 172, P.E.C. Smith; p. 172, AP/Wide World Photos; p. 173, Clive Capol; p. 175, © 1980 Jane Brown.

Naomi Long Madgett: p. 193, John L. Prusak; p. 199, Elmer Dandridge; p. 203, Robert Moseley; p. 210, © Patricia Beck/*Detroit Free Press;* p. 212, Ernest L. Harden, Sr.

Sandra McPherson: pp. 215, 226, 230, Walter Pavlich; p. 219, Gwen Head; p. 222, © Mary Randlett; p. 223, Henry Carlile; p. 229, Layne Evans; p. 232, Susan Kelly-DeWitt.

Marilyn Nelson: p. 248, George A. Hill Studios.

Gibbons Ruark: pp. 269, 286, Kay Ruark; p. 281, Anne Wright; pp. 282, 284, 287, Gibbons Ruark.

Alan Shapiro: p. 298, Patricia Evans.

Richard Tillinghast: p. 301, © Talbot; p. 303, Rolland Studio.

Text

Larry Eigner: Essays "Rambling in Life," "'The Bible Told Me So' or '. . . Said by Mother," "A Note Detailing Tags," and "Method from Happenstance," from *areas lights heights: writings 1954–1989,* by Larry Eigner. New York: Roof Books, 1989. Copyright © 1989 by Larry Eigner. Reprinted with permission of James Sherry/Segue Foundation./ Poems "loneliness, existence," "The wandering mosquito," and "live / , bird which," from *another time in fragments,* by Larry Eigner. Fulcrum Press, 1967. Copyright © 1967 by Larry Eigner./ Preface "statement on words" and poems "so the fine green arm" and "the pastorale" from *The World and Its Streets, Places,* by Larry Eigner. Black Sparrow Press, 1977. Copyright © 1977 by Larry Eigner. Reprinted with permission of Black Sparrow Press./ Poems "Imagine that was the," "how apparent, cloudy," and "Listening to the wind," from *Things Stirring Together or Far Away,* by Larry Eigner. Black Sparrow Press, 1974. Copyright © 1974 by Larry Eigner. Reprinted with permission of Black Sparrow Press./ Poem "A Wintered Road," by Larry Eigner. Originally published in *Dartmouth Quarterly,* February 1954. Reprinted with permission of Larry Eigner./ Poems "Letter for Duncan," "The bird / of wire like a nest," "Occasionally," "From the Sustaining Air," and "Again dawn," from *Selected Poems,* by Larry Eigner. Oyez Press, 1972. Copyright © 1972 by Larry Eigner. Reprinted with permission of Larry Eigner./ Poem "B," from *From the Sustaining Air,* by Larry Eigner. Coincidence Press, 1953./ Poems "the strange the familiar," "Take it," "anything," "Rembrandt Life Takes," "How much you believe in," "an original," and "Remember," from *Anything on Its Side,* by Larry Eigner. Elizabeth Press, 1974. Copyright © 1974 by Larry Eigner.

Christopher Fry: Excerpts from letters written by Laurence Olivier to Christopher Fry, 1949–50. Reprinted with permission of Harbottle & Lewis Solicitors of the Estate of Laurence Olivier.

Rachel Hadas: Lines from James Merrill's "Mirabell," from *Selected Poems 1946–1985* by James Merrill. Copyright © 1992 by James Merrill. Reprinted by permission of Alfred A. Knopf Inc./ Tribute to James Merrill originally published in *PN Review,* July-August 1995. Copyright © 1995 by Rachel Hadas.

Naomi Long Madgett: Poem "Poets beyond the Blues," from *Exits and Entrances,* by Naomi Long Madgett, Lotus Press, 1978. Copyright © 1978 by Naomi Long Madgett. Poem "Silence" from *Phantom Nightingale: Juvenilia,* by Naomi Long Madgett, Lotus Press, 1981. Copyright © 1981 by Naomi Long Madgett. Poem "Newblack" from *Pink Ladies in the Afternoon,* by Naomi Long Madgett, Lotus Press, 1972, 1990. Copyright © 1972, 1990 by Naomi Long Madgett. All reprinted with permission of Lotus Press./ Selected poems from *Octavia and Other Poems,* by Naomi Long Madgett. Third World Press, 1988. Copyright © 1988 by Naomi Long Madgett. Reprinted with permission of Third World Press.

Sandra McPherson: Poems "1943," "Open Casket," "Studies in the Imaginary," "Childish Landscape," and "On Coming Out of Nowhere," from *The Year of Our Birth,* by Sandra McPherson. Copyright © 1973, 1974, 1975, 1976, 1977, 1978 by Sandra McPherson. First published by The Ecco Press in 1978. Reprinted by permission./ Poems "Ode Near the Aspen Music School," "Helen Todd: My Birthname," and "Geasters, Birthparents' House," from *Patron Happiness,* by Sandra McPherson. Copyright © 1979, 1980, 1981, 1982 by Sandra McPherson. First published by The Ecco Press in 1983. Reprinted with permission./ Poems "Yellow Sand Verbena," "The Feather," and "From My Notebook, Cape

Contemporary Authors®
Autobiography Series

Fleur Adcock

1934-

Fleur Adcock in London, 1991

I

Any brief outline of my life has to begin with the words "I was born in New Zealand," almost immediately followed by "but." That "but" leads to the question of my national identity and how it has influenced, infected, and to some extent distorted the course of my adult life. I did not choose to be born in New Zealand; nor to be taken abroad at an early age and imprinted with an indelible af-

fection for England; nor to be torn tearfully away from there at thirteen ("like Juliet from Romeo," as I once said) and required to become a New Zealander once again. I did, quite definitely, choose to leave New Zealand when I was at last free to make a choice, and England has been my home ever since. But by then there was another "but."

First, though, the background. I shall resist going into great detail about my early ancestors (although I have spent years researching

1

them—part of the colonial need for "roots," no doubt, and of my particular need to establish British credentials). Three of my grandparents immigrated to New Zealand from Manchester, Sam and Eva Adcock in 1914 (with my ten-year-old father, Cyril John), and my maternal grandfather, Alfred Robinson, some ten years earlier. He was a widower with a small child; very soon he met and married Jane ("Jinnie") Brooks, who was a New Zealander by birth but only just: her parents had sailed from Northern Ireland in 1874 and Jinnie was conceived on the long sea voyage.

All these people could be called pioneers; to emigrate at all presupposes an adventurous nature, but they also had, or acquired, the versatility and practical skills necessary for survival. Sam Adcock had been a packing-case manufacturer, with a sideline in barbering to earn extra money for the venture; he found himself creating and running a small dairy farm in wild, empty country near Pirongia in the North Island (my young father had to milk the cows before riding to school on his pony). Richey and Martha Brooks were of farming stock, but they had had a general store in Londonderry and opened another in Drury, near Auckland. Alfred Robinson was a housepainter, but he combined this with poultry farming when he too settled in Drury. Unlike his wife Jinnie, who was mystified when their eldest daughter took up music as a career, he had an enthusiasm for the arts; he taught himself French, read Shakespeare, and named my mother Irene after his favourite actress, Irene Vanbrugh.

The Adcocks shared this admirable Lancashire tradition of self-education (Sam had studied chemistry at the Mechanics' Institute), but access to universities was beyond their means; as far as I know, none of my father's direct ancestors had attended one since the seventeenth century. For him, too, this ambition was out of reach. He had a passion for science, but this would have meant a full-time course with access to laboratories. Instead he became a "pupil teacher" at the tiny local school, learning on the job, until he was old enough to train at Teachers' College in Auckland. After that, teaching in remote country schools, he gained his first degree by extramural study; he was never inside a university until he got to London at the age of thirty-five.

He married my mother in 1931. By then Sam and Eva had had enough of backblocks

Fleur and her sister, Marilyn, 1939

life; they sold the farm and settled near my other grandparents-to-be in Drury. This little township was the family base—the nearest thing to a home—but my parents were always on the move, to one sole-charge or two-teacher school after another. I was born in February 1934 and my sister Marilyn twenty-one months later. I came to full consciousness at about this time in Kuaotunu, in the Coromandel Peninsula; my earliest memories are of rackety journeys in ancient cars on precipitous dirt roads, and of the schoolhouse with the baby in a cradle. The fireplace in the main room had a guard made of blackboard; I tried to chalk a face on it, but all that came out was a round mass of scribble—my first failed creative endeavour.

After Kuaotunu, Palmerston North—a town, for a change; then Rangiwahia; then Tokorangi, where I turned five and the world opened up for me: I went to school, I learned to read and write (in the infants' class, with a woman teacher—my father taught the older pupils), and I met poetry. Our mother had always sung to us and recited little verses (some written by herself, about us), but at Tokorangi our bedtime reading was from a Georgian anthology: Rupert Brooke, John Drinkwater, Harold Monro. This was not in a bedroom but in a shelter-shed beside the grassy school playground: there was no house available, it was summer, and we were used to camping out; the school itself had plumbing and a stove for cooking; while my father spent the evenings working there at a classroom desk by electric light, my sister and I snuggled down in our campbeds and listened to "Grantchester" or "Overheard on a Saltmarsh"—"Nymph, nymph, what are your beads?—Green glass, goblin. . . ." One of the older girls let me try on her necklace of glass beads (blue, not green); they tinkled in my soul for forty years until they surfaced in a poem.

In 1939 we sailed for England. This move happened to coincide with the outbreak of a world war, but by September 3 we were on the water and it was too late to turn back (except that our ship did, in the literal sense, turn back from its approach to the Suez Canal and take us the long way round Africa to Southampton). The object of our trip was for my father to do a Ph.D. in psychology at the University of London. Not surprisingly, this took longer than planned—he spent most of the war working in the Civil Defence Ambulance Service as well as giving lectures for the WEA (Workers' Educational Association).

We stayed in England until 1947 and, for reasons which have since been explained to me with perfect logic but which at the time I hardly even enquired into, I went to a total of eleven schools in seven-and-a-half years. Sometimes there were three or even four in one year; sometimes, when neither the threat of bombing nor the demands of my father's work made it necessary to move on, the same one for several years at a time. I didn't much like the changes (even now I have to suppress faint twinges of school phobia when I enter a strange school to give a poetry reading), but I got used to being a newcomer—as a New Zealander I was that already—and at least my sister came to some of the schools with me, and our mother was usually at home waiting for us.

However, there were exceptions to this, the first of them in 1940. My father was deputy-in-charge of the Ambulance Station in Sidcup, on the outer fringes of London, and my mother working different shifts at another. I had already experienced two local schools (the first had closed because so many children had been evacuated), and the Blitz was getting closer. An offer arrived from distant cousins in Leicestershire to take Marilyn and me as "unofficial evacuees" (the alternative being "official" ones, with their reputation for lice and filthy habits). It seemed a good idea.

Uncle George and Auntie Eva, as we were to call them, had a farm in the village of Scalford, near Melton Mowbray. They had two daughters of their own, older than us, and the farm was crammed with delights: a cowshed, pigsties, orchards, fields full of this and that, a huge mysterious barn haunted by cats, a house which was really two houses joined together, with a Grandma and Grandpa living in one part. Water came from a pump, lighting from gas (downstairs) and candles (upstairs); cooking was done on a coal range; horses pulled the plough and the farm cart. We were there for nine months, going to the village school (even Marilyn, who was technically too young) and picking up the local accent. In our free time we explored the woods, barn, and outhouses, watched the cows being milked, wore out our knickers by sliding down stacks of straw, rode on the cart to haymaking and to market; as far as I remember I was perfectly happy.

Our parents came to visit us when they could, which with their work and wartime restrictions on travel was not very often; in between, we wrote to them—Marilyn in pictures, I in words. Not just letters, either: stories, too; even a book. The "book" was one folded sheet of paper with its title ("The Blue Flower") on the outside and an illustrated story inside, but to me it was a significant advance. It was at Scalford, too, that I composed my first poem— "Hurry up and come to bed. / All through the night you cudle [*sic*] Ted" (later expelled from the canon when I blushingly realised that "Ted" could refer to a boy as well as a teddy bear).

Early in 1941 my mother left her job and took us to Surrey, to lodgings in an unromantic street with the fairy-tale name of Honeycrock Lane. There was a forgettable school, and an unforgettable public library, a little tin-roofed hut the size of a garage, with rows of children's stories in dark, sturdy bindings. I plunged in. Fairly soon (a matter of weeks, perhaps?) we had moved a mile or two along the road to Outwood. Our house was called Top Lodge, and was one of two gate houses at the entrances to a country estate (its twin still stands, I believe, but Top Lodge has disappeared to make way for the M23 motorway: a secret demolition company moves around the world destroying houses I have lived in). Once again we had woods to explore, but we were not alone in them; a few days after we had moved in Mother noticed noises and traffic she had not expected in such leafy surroundings, and was informed that a Searchlight Battery was camouflaged in the woods just up the road. Doris, who looked after us when Mother was out on her bicycle collecting insurance, often had uniformed visitors to afternoon tea, and a soldier called Johnny came for walks with us and made Doris giggle.

I went to another village school, alone at first because Marilyn was recovering from whooping cough at what I considered unnecessary length. This was my sixth school, and the staff had no reason to expect that I would stay there any longer than at the others; for the first few days they let me sit around and read, but no doubt I eventually had lessons. I don't remember them; what I remember of Outwood School is terror and poetry. The terror was inflicted, as so often, by boys: in a routine tickling raid on the girls they had discovered that I was abnormally afraid of being tickled—I was convinced I would lose my breath and die—so they tended to lie in wait for me. To avoid them I lurked in the playground shed and wrote poetry.

Sometime in 1941, while I was still seven, we moved again: my father (whom we scarcely ever saw—when he was not on duty he was driving around the country lecturing on economics and liberal studies for the WEA) had bought us a house of our own. It was between Salfords and Earlswood, a 1930s semi in a street called Woodside Way which began at its junction with the main London to Brighton road, turned a couple of corners, and petered out at a ploughed field fringed with a smallish but adequate wood. On the other side of the wood was the railway line, and beyond the railway line (which we were not allowed to cross but did) more woods.

We stayed in Woodside Way for nearly three years, far longer than anywhere in my life un-

til then. We could no longer date events by "When we lived at . . ." but had to find other pegs to hang them on. This makes for a less crisply sliced-up ordering of memories; it suggests, in fact, a blur of contented normality. There was still a war on—when had there not been?—but for more than two years we seldom heard an air-raid siren, and did not have to be hustled out of bed and down to the cupboard under the stairs while bombs fell, as once at Outwood. Our father was still away, but so was everyone else's, and at least ours came home one weekend in three and was not (we falsely imagined) in danger of being killed. Our mother was at home all day like an ordinary mother (she had resumed her former occupation as a music teacher, now that we had a piano); Marilyn and I settled down to be ordinary children, the kind who had friends.

I still wrote poems, but that was OK: we were beginning to do poetry at school; I won a gold star for my epic on the Pilgrim Fathers. I read a lot of books—Mother gave me her copy of *Gone with the Wind* because I was so besotted with it (a year or two later, as my taste improved, she did the same with *Pride and Prejudice*). I made a succession of transitory friends, and one fairly durable one called Edna. But she and the others lived too far away to be easily accessible out of school hours; mostly Marilyn and I went around with the kids in our street, or just with each other. We spent as much time as we could in the woods. In spring they were full of wild flowers—primroses and celandines at first, followed by a sea of bluebells—and in autumn there were blackberries and hazelnuts. We made dens in the undergrowth, and I climbed the trees until I knew them almost by heart. For years afterwards I dreamed about those woods, and was desolated to hear, in my twenties, that they had gone. (In this case the demon demolition team left my house alone and struck at what had been my spiritual home.)

Our other chief resource was the common: Earlswood Common, with extensions into Redhill and Salfords. It stretched for miles between the built-up areas, a rambling hilly paradise furred with bracken and long grass and full of hidden dingles where anything might happen. We brought home tadpoles; now and then we saw snakes; once I found a brilliant fly agaric toadstool and took it to school for the nature table. School was St John's in Earlswood, on the edge of the common: a church school, firmly segregated except for the infant classes. The boys' half was back-to-back with ours, but cut off by a high wall; we never saw a boy older than six. Our half was ruled by a stout headmistress with powdered moles on her face. When I was nine she castigated me publicly in assembly for coming second in my class instead of top (Edna, who was usually second, had beaten me).

My class teachers were tolerable, though; one, in fact, was actually kind—she lent me books to take home and read. New books were in short supply, with the paper shortage; I was usually given one for Christmas or my birthday, and I got two (an early Puffin and a guide to wild flowers) when I had my tonsils out. Once my mother found a copy of Yeats' *Fairy and Folk Tales of the Irish Peasantry* in a junk shop and bought it for me; I read it until the pages came loose. (It's the first edition, 1888.)

Most things, indeed, were either scarce or rationed. Sweet rationing was no great hardship to me, but I resolutely ate all of mine so that Marilyn wouldn't get them; our standards of justice had an Old Testament rigidity: *exactly* half each, the rule was. Eggs appeared at intervals of perhaps three weeks until we acquired four ducks; oranges were extremely rare, lemons nonexistent. And once we saw a banana: a girl at school was sent one by her father, and it was reverently displayed in assembly and raffled for the benefit of the Red Cross at sixpence a ticket. Then there were clothes. Our clothing coupons sufficed for the dull basics (shoes, underwear, socks). Most of the rest was secondhand: strange coats inherited from people's cousins or brothers; outgrown or shrunken cardigans; droopy crepe dresses cut down from the gifts of kind old ladies. I went to school one winter in a 1920s cloche felt hat.

At ten, with my slightly older classmates, I sat the 11-plus examination (the selection process for grammar school admission). Before I knew I had passed there came another upheaval: the doodlebugs arrived. Officially known as V1s or flying bombs, they chugged up from the coast towards London, falling wherever their fuel ran out; we were in their flight path. Off we went again, first back to blissful Scalford but then, as Auntie was not well, to a village in Wiltshire.

This was the second occasion when Marilyn and I were separated from our parents. I was enchanted with this taste of normally forbidden squalor: we lived in a two-roomed cottage with feckless, earthy Mrs J. and her toddler, carrying all our water in buckets from the village tap, getting lice in our hair and mysterious sores on our feet, and learning rather belatedly that there were adults in the world who drank, swore, quarrelled with their neighbours, and engaged in other, more interesting activities with soldiers from the nearby camp. Mrs J. herself was sober and faithful to her absent husband, but she liked company and chose me to provide it, setting the clock outrageously fast or slow several times a week so that I'd miss the bus to my school. As this was a huge and terrifying coeducational establishment in distant Chippenham (Marilyn, being younger, was at a local school—I'd sampled that too, to add to my list) I didn't mind. It all came out in the end and our mother swooped and removed us to be with her in more hygienic accommodation in Chippenham; Marilyn and I slept in an attic, sang carols in the dark, unlit streets at Christmas, and shyly begged passing American soldiers for "Any gum, chum?"—which was the thing to do.

After one more move, to the village of Frant near Tunbridge Wells, and two more schools (a small and brutal private one which Marilyn had to endure for the whole term while I escaped to the Girls' Grammar) we were told that we were going to our own house at last. Back to Woodside Way and our friends? No such luck: that house had been sold. We howled and grieved, but there was a reason, although no one explained it to our satisfaction at the time: our father had been appointed regional organiser for the WEA in Kent, and a convenient base for his work was Sidcup. The house he bought there was rather grander than we were accustomed to, but to compensate for this it had a shifting population of somewhat unpredictable tenants in the rooms we didn't need for ourselves. It also had a large, half-wild garden, full of fruit trees and rambling roses, with space at the end for a new batch of ducks. There were woods nearby, to which I could go on my bicycle with my friends (yes, I acquired friends again), and I kept caterpillars and joined the Guides and was a relatively normal eleven- and twelve-year-old.

I went to Chislehurst and Sidcup County Grammar School for Girls, where the initial impression I made was not good. It was my twelfth school—my fifth in that academic year alone—and I had had enough. I was the youngest in my class again, and perhaps also slightly disturbed. Although I eventually settled down and quite liked being there, my conduct was always viewed with some disfavour: innocent enough stuff (a certain amount of illicit tree-climbing, snowball-throwing, and mild teacher-baiting), but juvenile.

However, I caught up with the curriculum, did well enough academically, and began writing poems again. On the whole life was stable and not too bad. The war ended shortly after we moved to Sidcup, and my father was at last free to live at home with us and finish his thesis. Rationing and shortages continued ("Don't waste bread! Eat potatoes instead!" said the posters, until potatoes were suddenly scarce too), but we were used to all that. The barbed wire was removed from the beaches and we had our first seaside holiday, camping on the coast of Kent. We made a trip to Ireland, and were promised France next.

I should have known it would never happen. Instead my father was appointed to a university lectureship in Wellington; after all, he had his interrupted career to pursue, and it didn't occur to him that to leave England would break his sentimental daughters' hearts. (My mother had some notion of it; she still feels slightly guilty.) For weeks before our departure in March 1947 I walked through the sparkling, frozen landscape of that record-breaking winter saying goodbye to everything: our wonderful garden; the den I'd constructed there, with its painstakingly woven latticework of twigs; the trees encased in rattling shrouds of ice; the ducks; the black cat we'd adopted; my friends. Marilyn and I sang sad Vera Lynn songs as we packed our most treasured belongings in one tea-chest each for the journey. It was all over.

II

Long-distance travel in those days was still by sea, which at least made the transition gradual. We sailed on the *Arawa,* in stormy weather; for a few days I lay in my bunk haunted by seasick, delirious dreams of being whisked back to England on a 'plane. After that I kept a diary, read more than half of the Bible (there was not much else), learned to swim at last,

and fell in unrequited love with a young half-Italian steward who asked me to write a poem about friendship for him and his cabin-mate, Bob. There were stops at Curaçao and Panama, seductively foreign, where we bought greedy heaps of oranges and bananas. It was all pleasantly unreal.

Reality awaited me in New Zealand, but it took some time to reveal itself. At first there was my grandmother's house in Drury, so deeply familiar to me from early memories that I felt as if I'd walked into one of my nostalgic dreams (like those of being back in Scalford, back in Wiltshire, back in any place I thought I'd lost forever); there were Grandma Robinson herself, and my Adcock grandparents, and uncles and aunts and great-uncles and great-aunts and cousins and second cousins: a bewildering access of instant family; there were the unlikely-looking towns, with their sun-baked wooden houses, brightly coloured tin roofs and Wild-West-style verandah-fronted shops; there were the quaint accents, the casualness of manner, the untroubled prosperity, and the general air of plenty: meals oozed richly with cream, butter, and meat, and the war seemed never to have happened.

All this was in and around Auckland, where Marilyn and I drifted from one family household to another while our father sorted things out in Wellington and tried to find somewhere for us to live. Houses were hard to come by because of government restrictions on property sales; our first home in Wellington proved to be a flat over a small sweet factory in Newtown, with no furniture but beds, packing cases and a deck chair. Eventually we found a house of our own in Miramar, but because the original plan had been that we should live near the university I was enrolled at Wellington Girls' College (rather than Wellington East, the newer school which served the eastern suburbs). I was at Katherine Mansfield's old school, Robin Hyde's old school. Later the history of the creaky, elegant wooden building impinged on me, and I delighted in it, but when I first arrived it was merely yet another school (my thirteenth), and one where they laughed at my English accent— "Say apple." "Apple." (Hysterical false laughter from my audience.) "Say it again."

Thirteen is not a good age at which to undergo culture shock: it has shocks enough of its own built into the machinery of puberty. I was small and immature for my age, and it was a year or so before periods and pimples arrived, but the emotional swings and mood changes of adolescence were already shaking me. I was still desperately in love with the English countryside—its woods, its wild flowers (there were none to speak of in New Zealand), its weather and seasons. The only poems I remember writing in the first year of my exile were on such topics as spring in Surrey, contrasted with the boring imperceptibility of spring in Wellington, where there was no frost or snow to melt and most of the trees had been green all winter. These were hardly calculated to go down well at school, had I been so rash as to reveal them.

But my classmates were more interested in swimming, tennis, and clothes than in poetry or, needless to say, in me. It was not until I was fifteen, and in the sixth form, that I made friends suited to my bookish temperament and was able to sit with them after school in Annabelle's milk bar in Molesworth Street discussing Literature and Life. By now I was writing a good deal; after a lull, poetry had flowered again—as is its way in adolescence: the creative urge is often merely a hormonal surge. My style tended to be modelled on that of *The Waste Land,* and my subject matter was cosmic despair, featuring me alone in a desolate landscape; but the landscape had begun to incorporate the hills and sea of Wellington (together with its devastating wind). I loved the sea, and spent hours wandering around the local bays (Lyall Bay, Moa Point, Worser Bay) or along the beach at Paremata (where we had a boat house for weekends and holidays), but I was remarkably slow to notice the astonishing physical beauty of Wellington as a whole—the hills and the harbour; my usual aesthetic focus was set at close-up, not long-range.

School became more tolerable. I passed all the exams which came my way (exams were easy; sport and social demands were what I couldn't face) and eventually won a university scholarship. My sixth form subjects were English, French, Latin, and German: I had developed, almost by accident, a passion for languages—the basis for an enduring fascination with language itself. Most writers are able to point to an eccentric, sympathetic, and inspiring English teacher who set them on the path to literature. My English teachers were unremarkable; it was Ingeburg Garai, my teacher of Latin and, later, German, who influenced

With her husband, Alistair Campbell, Wellington, 1953

me. She was herself German, and as well as giving after-school tuition in that language to several of us who took it seriously despite its tiny niche in the timetable she bullied me into working hard at Latin and persuaded me to concentrate on that and Greek at the university. English literature, after all, I'd be reading anyway, and modern languages would be better learnt in the countries where they were spoken.

I followed her advice. The Classics Department at Victoria University was excellent; I learned Greek (from the alphabet to Sophocles in two years), and I also learned, among other things, two useful truths: that translating from or into another language is a profoundly illuminating way of learning to use one's own; and that Latin poetry is literature and not just some kind of word game. For this latter insight and much else I am indebted to Kenneth Quinn, who as well as introducing me to Greek and making grammar and syntax almost fun was my tutor for my special M.A. subject (on the poetry of Horace).

I had other lessons to learn. My later teens coincided with the 1950s, of all dreary decades, but before I left school I had managed to meet a few boys, at the church social club, and once I was a student my options widened. I hastened, however, to narrow them. Soon after my eighteenth birthday I astonished my friends by becoming engaged to a poet, Alistair Camp-

The author with Alistair and son Gregory, 1954

bell, and married him six months later, half-way through my second year. He was seven years older than me, broodingly handsome, half Polynesian, and training as a teacher. My parents gave their consent, on condition that I should finish my degree (the subtext being, although such things were not mentioned, that they'd rather see me married than risking the scandal of premarital pregnancy to force their hands).

So I had my wedding, looking about fourteen in my prim-collared white dress, and Alistair and I set up house in our wooden cottage in Tinakori Road, where I read the books he read (a valuable education in modern poetry) and drank in his conversations with poet-friends (Louis Johnson, James K. Baxter, Denis Glover). I managed not to get pregnant for nearly a year—our son Gregory was born in March 1954, by which time I had duly achieved my B.A. Three years later we had another son, Andrew. By then my university education was finished (I had spent two years, instead of the usual one, on my M.A.); but so, in effect, was the marriage. It would have been more surprising, per-

haps, had it lasted, given the fact that I was so ridiculously young, romantic, and ignorant when it began.

I should prefer to forget most of 1957, as well as parts of 1956. Everyone concerned behaved badly to some extent—certainly by the standards of puritanical New Zealand society—and yet we were filled with floundering aspirations to be generous, tolerant, and just. In the end the people who had to sort out the mess were Alistair and myself, with the aid of Alistair's new partner, Meg (who was even younger than me). We were all friends, and wanted a swift, stress-free divorce, which duly came about. There were to be no battles over custody of the children; we agreed that I should keep Andrew, while Gregory stayed in the family home with his father and Meg.

In my naivety it never occurred to me, then or for years to come, that I might receive anything but credit for this agonizing sacrifice. I was convinced, incredible though I now find this, that it was my clear and obvious duty. I was as much to blame as Alistair for the failure of the marriage; he was a good father, who, while I was a student, had shared in the parenting far more than was then usual. I could not bear to deprive him of both his children (justice and fair shares, the principles I had been raised with, seemed to forbid that). Gregory loved both his parents equally, and would suffer relatively little disruption if he stayed in his familiar, secure surroundings, with the same father but with Meg and her imminently expected baby instead of me and Andrew, rather than sharing an uncertain future in a one-parent family.

Or so I thought. In fact things went wrong within a few months, when Meg was taken into hospital with a severe case of postnatal depression, and this was to be a recurring pattern after her next two pregnancies and beyond. My attempts to regain possession of Gregory were discouraged by various professional advisers who convinced me that to remove him would endanger both the stability of the marriage and Meg's precarious mental health, as well as confusing the child himself.

There's no point in rehearsing the list of complications and miseries. It was not all bad: Gregory and the other children survived, apparently unscathed; Meg, Alistair, and I are good friends now, after all; the wounds are more or less healed. But under the scar tissue there is, for me, a constant tingling pain which I have always found difficult to write about or even mention. Endlessly though I analyse the motives of my younger self I can never really forgive her. I missed most of Gregory's childhood; he grew up without me, and my two sons without each other. Years later, after we had all found each other again, I imagined that my remorse might fade. It does not.

Back to chronology: in January 1958, after my decree nisi, I packed up my essential belongings—clothes, baby gear, and the few books which were mine and not Alistair's—and moved to Dunedin, in the South Island, to become a junior lecturer in classics at the University of Otago. For someone with residual school phobia this was not the ideal job, but what else did a degree in classics qualify me for? A year later, after various ups and downs, I resigned, spent several weeks vainly hunting for jobs and

With sons Andrew and Gregory, 1958

several more working in a coffee bar while Andrew went to a grim day nursery, and then by accident and good fortune found myself back in the university as a librarian. A bit of a come-down, I thought, issuing books to the students instead of marking their Latin proses, but it meant that I could stay in my university flat, pay a proper child minder for Andrew, and keep us both alive until I decided what to do next. (In fact I qualified as a librarian, and remained one until Andrew was capable of keeping himself.)

The next three years were crucial in my apprenticeship as a writer. To begin with, there was suddenly time to read again—librarians don't have work to take home in the evenings; instead I took home large quantities of the library stock (loan records showed that I borrowed more books than anyone in the university, with one exception) and read my way through literature of all kinds in several languages. Then there was time to write; I sat in front of my coal fire night after night deliberately trying out styles and techniques. Also I made friends—friends of my own at last, not Alistair's friends and their wives; a few of them, I confess, were semialcoholic medical students (I had some catching up to do), but as time went by more and more were writers, or students who like me wanted to become writers. We had a discussion group, with Charles Brasch, founder and editor of New Zealand's only literary magazine, as its father figure, where we read our work aloud and listened to criticisms of it. Occasionally Charles would say, in his discreet way, "Would you send me a copy of that? I'd like to consider it for *Landfall.*" Slowly my poems began to appear in print.

Apart from these literary evenings, though, and a few others differently spent, I was mostly alone in the flat after Andrew's bedtime. This was the other bonus: solitude. It took me long enough to recognise it as a benefit—I had spent my first twenty-four years living with other people, and there were times when I longed to be interrupted by the telephone or a knock at the door—but I came to cherish it, and am now so addicted to being alone that I find it hard to live with anyone for more than a month or two. As a writer, and also by temperament, I flourish best without the presence of another demanding adult day after day (children are a different matter).

However, this realisation sank in a little too slowly. In January 1962 I met Barry Crump, a best-selling author of picaresque, anecdotal sagas about deer-culling, rabbit-shooting, and life in the bush or the pub, told in the casually colourful Kiwi male vernacular: not my kind of literature at all, nor my kind of man. A month later, when he was twenty-six and I not quite twenty-eight, we were married. This was lunacy, as all our friends told us in the brief space of time before the wedding (if they had been less violently opposed to it I might have been readier to see the massive drawbacks myself; at the time I seized on it as an escape route from an intolerably painful and clearly doomed relationship with someone else). A year of confusion and melodrama followed. We moved to Wellington, where I somehow managed to hold down a job in the Turnbull Library, even when I had my arm in plaster. (This was known as "the time when Crump broke Fleur's arm"—although in fact it was dislocated, not broken, and unlike my occasional black eyes, bruises, and chipped teeth Barry had not caused it.)

The Turnbull had a fine collection of early printed books and editions of seventeenth- and eighteenth-century poetry; cataloguing these offered a soothing refuge from my increasingly chaotic life outside the library; but by the end of the year I had given my notice, signed a separation agreement as a first step towards extricating myself from what could no longer be called a marriage, and booked a passage for myself and Andrew on a ship to England.

Fleur Adcock and Barry Crump, Wellington, 1962

Once again, I was running away, and this time it was permanent. Thirteen years were to pass before I could bear to set foot in New Zealand again.

III

I arrived in England at the tail end of the worst winter since 1947; it was almost as if the country had been kept on ice for my return. Sylvia Plath had taken her life the week before. London was just emerging from freezing smog. None of this could bring me down from my euphoric high. I was twenty-nine, with a few trunks and tea-chests of possessions, no money, and a child who, disoriented by the move, had temporarily forgotten how to read. (He was nearly six, only a few months older than I had been when I arrived in 1939.) We'd both have to start again.

This was easier than it might have been. By sheer chance my mother was in London on holiday; she found me a child minder for Andrew and a room in East Finchley (where I was awakened each morning by bacon fumes drifting under my door from the communal gas cooker on the landing outside where two Irish bus conductors fried their breakfast). And these were the sixties: there were jobs. Within a few days I had strolled into a temporary one, at the Northern Polytechnic, and by October I was in permanent, pensionable employment with the Civil Service in the Colonial Office. In fact the library was a joint one, combined with that of the Commonwealth Relations Office, and as the years went by it merged with and subsumed the Foreign Office Library, but throughout all the changes of names and status I worked in the same building in Great Smith Street, Westminster, for a total of fifteen years.

This was the day job: it paid the bills and kept us alive; it also occupied vast areas of my time and energies, involved me in friendships and office politics, and taught me certain skills which I have now forgotten. But I never in any sense thought of it as a career, and after my first swift promotion to a level at which I could afford to live in tolerable comfort (with Andrew taking over the bus conductors' room) I refused to apply for any further advancement. My essential preoccupations lay elsewhere.

I have always been subject to obsessions (for the first few years Italy was one—I learned the

In London, about 1970

language, pored over art books, and took Andrew on holidays to Florence, Urbino, Siena, Venice, and Ravenna; later I had phases of total absorption in, for example, medieval Latin literature, twelfth century history, gardening, learning to drive, Romania, and genealogy). All the time, though, the central thread was poetry. If 1961 had been my breakthrough year, when I wrote the first poems I still stand by, 1962 with all its turmoil brought my writing to a standstill, and in 1963 I was faced with a whole new set of adjustments: culture shock once again. It was brought home to me that I had, after all, become a New Zealander. The most minor aspect of this was my accent, which I hastily proceeded to modify. More serious was the realisation of how sheltered from harsh political and social realities had been the society from which I came. The starving children in the Oxfam posters distressed me (no one had told us about them in cosy "Godzone"); we knew about the Bomb, of course, but here there were marches and protests to express what previously I had put only into poems; the newspapers contained solid international news and

Four generations: Fleur Adcock holding her granddaughter Lily Campbell,
with daughter-in-law Elizabeth and mother Irene Adcock, Wellington, about 1982

informed comment, unlike the provincial chit-chat I was used to. For a few months all this stunned me into writing naive banalities or nothing at all.

As for British poetry, I was reasonably *au fait* with recent developments—the excellent University of Otago Library had subscribed to many literary magazines, and I had ordered some of the books they reviewed—but that was no substitute for being on the spot, surrounded by bookshops full of new publications. Soon I met actual poets. One evening I went to hear William Empson read, and saw a familiar face in the audience: Hubert Witheford, a New Zealander settled in London. He introduced me to the Group, which met weekly at Edward Lucie-Smith's house. Hubert was a very intermittent attender, but I became a devoted regular for the next few years, while the Group lasted. There I met George MacBeth, Peter Porter, Anthony Thwaite, Alan Brownjohn, and a large but shifting population of other poets now well-known to the historians of such matters. They

were mostly men; to be a woman poet was still slightly freaky (I had to wait for the late seventies before the exciting surge of British women poets really began).

These contacts were just what I needed. They helped me to overcome my diffidence about submitting poems to British magazines, and the strict but friendly criticism enabled me to look at my own work more clearly, and encouraged me to produce more of it. I began to get published. Knowing the right people is of no use if they don't like one's poetry, but enough editors liked enough of mine, it seemed. After a few setbacks I had a collection accepted by Oxford University Press. It was called *Tigers,* and combined new poems with a selection from my New Zealand book, *The Eye of the Hurricane,* which had appeared there in 1964 but had no overseas distribution. I was on the way.

In the same month as *Tigers* came out (May 1967) I bought a house, three doors along from our lodgings: a late Victorian end-of-terrace with a leafy garden: my own bit of the earth. For the first five years we shared it with two friends from New Zealand, Alex Guyan and Meg Sheffield (a writer and a radio producer), who became almost members of the family. After my nomadic childhood and the upheavals of my twenties I was ready to reverse the pattern and put down roots. Although I have lived in other places since, for periods ranging from a few months to two years, East Finchley has remained my base; I am not sure whether it is inertia, timidity, or some kind of loyalty which prevents me from leaving this increasingly traffic-congested suburb now imprinted with so much of my history.

There have been excursions, however, and not just trips abroad for poetry festivals, conferences, or holidays. The most emotional was my first return visit to New Zealand, at the end of 1975—thirteen years after I left. Practically speaking it had taken me that long to accumulate money, opportunity, and sufficient annual leave to go for two months (the minimum time to make it worthwhile). But I also

had to overcome a deep dread of how I might react to the place. "Ambivalent" is too mild a word for my feelings towards New Zealand, then or now. After I escaped in 1963 I had recurrent nightmares of finding myself back there, trapped, with no return ticket and a weight of smothering guilt. In my waking life the guilt persisted, but so did something of the panic.

Leaving out the emotions, the brief record of that visit goes like this: I met the grown-up Gregory (whom I hadn't seen since my mother brought him to England in 1966)—we went on holiday together to my old haunts in the South Island, talked and laughed and drank in pubs and got to know each other; I met Marilyn for the first time in thirteen years, and her two new daughters and new husband; I spent time with my parents (whom I had seen in the interval), and Alistair and Meg (whom I hadn't), and dozens of old friends. I travelled all over the country, variously accompanied, and indulged my nostalgia for childhood places; I spent hours, often in the middle of the night,

Three generations: sons Gregory (left) and Andrew, with their father, Alistair,
and grandfather John Adcock (right), about 1982

re-reading old letters and weeping for dead friends. And then came the farewells.

"Did you enjoy your holiday?" asked my colleagues back in London. Holiday? Pilgrimage, perhaps; a sacred duty. I felt mangled. I even toyed briefly with the thought of trying to live in New Zealand—but then sobered up and dismissed it. My ecstatic reception had been for a returning absentee; the novelty would have worn off, on both sides, had I stayed. Amid all the warmth of family affections and the seductions of the place itself (landscape, clean air, beaches, cheap wine, fresh fruits), I'd been homesick for England. I had no function in New Zealand; I felt foreign; I missed things which it seems snobbish or elitist to mention: the BBC; decent newspapers; medieval churches— indeed any buildings more than a hundred years old; different accents in every county; and snow, spring, bluebells, autumn, fog. These sound trivial and superficial, but exiles have died broken-hearted for less.

It will be clear that I have a pronounced susceptibility to places. I had spent most of my childhood yearning for the place we had just left, or the place before that, even while attaching myself enthusiastically to the one we had just arrived in. Later I flirted with other countries: Italy, Holland, Ireland, Nepal (where I visited Alex and Meg when they were based there in 1973). The act of travelling, or the process of adjusting to new surroundings, released sensations in me which often led to poems. In 1976 I gave a poetry reading in the Lake District, and was enchanted by this taste of the English countryside in a relatively unspoiled state. The following year a literary fellowship at Charlotte Mason College of Education in Ambleside was advertised; I applied and got it. My head of department, suspecting that if thwarted I'd resign altogether, scanned Civil Service regulations for a clause which permitted me a year off, and I found myself transformed into a new creature: healthy, non-metropolitan, with new friends, a new function (the college was small, but I also ran a writing group for people from the village and surrounding area), and time to read, write, walk, gaze, study the flora and fauna, and exult in weather and seasons.

Going back to London and my job felt like being jailed a second time for a crime I had already served one sentence for. I lasted barely

another year in the FCO, and in 1979 left forever. This was not "early retirement"—the tiny pension I had earned was put on ice until I reached sixty—but dropping out. By choosing freedom I was choosing poverty, but that was nothing new, and I could no longer juggle the conflicting demands of writing and a full-time job. Andrew was at the London School of Economics and fairly independent; during my absence in Ambleside he had shared our house with fellow students, to help with expenses, and was happy to do so again.

But I was not about to plunge straight into the hazardous waters of freelance life; the immediate reason for my resignation was another fellowship, equally exciting but longer: two years, funded by Northern Arts, at the Universities of Newcastle upon Tyne and Durham. It took me back to the north of England, where I had discovered I felt at home, and to a city which was a stimulating centre for literature and publishing. I lived in Newcastle, in a university flat occupying the whole first floor of what had once been the Vice Chancellor's house: four enormous rooms plus kitchen, bathrooms, and entrance hall, all totally empty. I went to auction sales for cheap furniture, and had fun setting up my encampments under the high ceilings. There was a garden (tended by university gardeners), and a few minutes away, on the Town Moor, cattle grazed and skylarks twittered and soared. All this was within walking distance of the city centre and the university.

My duties were not onerous (Northern Arts paid its writers to write): one day a week of sitting in my office waiting for customers to bring me their poems and problems, another day (Tuesdays) in Durham, delightful to visit but a bit too precious for actually living in, and various readings, workshops, and less formal events. I enjoyed having students around me (a compensation for the absence of my own young people) and being able to provide a foil to the more official elements in their courses. I liked the city, with its genuinely indigenous population (Geordie accents and not a tourist in sight). Once again, as in the Lakes, I read up on the local history and took the whole area to my heart.

The literary fellowship had a musical equivalent; when I arrived the Composer in Residence (then in her second year) was Gillian Whitehead, a New Zealander. We became close friends, and she asked me to write the words for a com-

Fleur Adcock in England, 1980s

mission she had received, a piece for soprano and orchestra. As it was to be performed locally we chose a local subject; the result was *Hotspur: A Ballad for Music,* sung in the persona of Harry Percy's wife Elizabeth Mortimer (not, as Shakespeare calls her, "Kate"). This was the first of a series of collaborations with Gillian: from the fourteenth century we moved back to the twelfth, and I wrote first a song cycle and eventually a full-length opera libretto on Eleanor of Aquitaine.

My other large enterprise, also derived from that remote and fascinating era, was an assortment of translations of medieval Latin poems taken from the *Carmina Burana* and other texts which I explored in the two university libraries. This project was pure self-indulgence; I'd sit up until the early hours of the morning twisting and hammering my English versions to match the intricate metres and rhyme schemes of the originals. I had no expectation that anyone would actually wish to publish these, but they were snapped up by my friend Neil Astley, the young founder of Bloodaxe Books. In 1979 he

was still technically a postgraduate student at Newcastle, running the firm from a bed-sitter and the English department's telephone, but I watched it grow into one of the two or three most thriving and eminent poetry publishers in the country. *The Virgin and the Nightingale* came out in 1983, with parallel Latin and English texts. My own poems, meanwhile, had been appearing every few years in slim collections from my regular publishers, Oxford University Press, who in 1983 issued what they chose to call my *Selected Poems* (to me it was more in the nature of a *Collected,* containing everything I could still stand the sight of).

By then I had reluctantly left Newcastle, where I should have been happy to settle if that had been a realistic option. London held fewer attractions. In 1980 Andrew had gone on a Commonwealth Scholarship to New Zealand, where he still lives. I followed at the end of 1981 and spent five months there, editing an anthology of contemporary New Zealand poetry and escaping before the inevitable hail of missiles could descend on me—who did this Pommie woman think she was, to pronounce on *their* literature? I had grandchildren by now (Gregory and his wife Elizabeth had already produced two), and my visits to New Zealand to see them became more frequent. My other excursions included a term in Norwich as Writing Fellow at the University of East Anglia in 1984 (which coincided with my beginning work on another controversial anthology, the *Faber Book of Twentieth Century Women's Poetry*), a similar term in Adelaide in 1986 (I was rather surprised to find how much I liked Australia), and several brief but unforgettable visits to Romania, both before and after the revolution. These led me into friendships with Romanian poets, mostly women; I learned the language and published translations of work by two of them, Grete Tartler and Daniela Crăsnaru. This was a completely different exercise from translating medieval Latin poetry, which had up to a point been just a means of showing off my technical skills; with the Romanians my duty was to present their poetry as straightforwardly as I could, without allowing my own voice to intrude.

Trips and travels aside, the life of a freelance writer tends to lack drama. When people ask what I've been doing, it's easier to give a list of the places I've been to for readings, festivals, or courses than to describe what has been happening at my desk. The balance there has altered over the years: apart from whatever long-term project is on hand, I now do less reviewing and radio work, but sit on more committees and judge far more competitions. The humdrum elements of my working life are governed by what comes my way—I see myself as the passive recipient of commissions.

And then of course there's my personal life. Not all of my passions have been for places; however, having eventually learnt discretion (an English quality, perhaps—my Kiwi outspokenness got me into a certain amount of trouble in the past) I am not going to name names. Yes, I had a good many love affairs, some more casual and transitory than others; but the two men who were most important to me, one in the interval between my two marriages and one much later, were both married. These matters are not secret—I was often far from discreet at the time—but private. So, no names or teasing hints; instead, some wise-after-the-event reflections. Given my needs for solitude and independence, it is perhaps no accident that I was

drawn towards men who were not free, or far too young, or geographically remote, or a combination of more than one of these: anything that would save me from the risk of a full-time relationship.

This did not always mean, though, that nothing durable came of such affairs: several of my male friends are ex-lovers (if we were friends once, why abandon it?). I am only intermittently gregarious, but friendships, together with family affections, persist over time and distance—which in view of my history is just as well. One great bonus of writing poetry is the way it brings you into contact with fellow poets and other enthusiasts for the craft. By no means all my friends are poets, or even interested in literature, but for the fact that I have lived and been befriended in such widely disparate places as Ambleside and Adelaide I can thank poetry.

My family has expanded happily in several directions (with one sad contraction): I now have four grandchildren—Gregory's Oliver, Lily, and Julia, and Andrew's little Cait; three of my four nieces also have children. Marilyn is still my best friend, and we now manage to spend time together most years, in one hemisphere or another; she is a novelist, which means that we share interests and professional patterns of life without competing. My mother, spirited as ever, travelled alone across the world to visit me last year at the age of eighty-six. She and my father were divorced in the traumatic year which led up to my own first divorce, just missing what would have been their silver wedding; he married again, and spent thirty contented years with Ngaire, another member of the Psychology Department in Wellington. In 1987, just before she was due to retire, he died suddenly of a heart attack.

He was a very private man, in contrast to my more chatty and outgoing mother; but I am grateful that he lived long enough for me to get to know him better than in my youth. Sorting through his mass of papers after his death I found letters from several generations of Adcocks and some old photographs I hadn't seen before, including a mystery bundle of glass negatives. I had these printed, and there he suddenly was: a young teenager on the farm at Te Rauamoa seventy years before, with his parents and visiting cousins. All these discoveries revived my enthusiasm for family history, which has since then flared up until it threatens to oust poetry from the forefront of my concerns. The two go hand in hand—I write poems about my ancestors—but there is a more general point to be made here. For much of my life poetry was an illicit activity, something for which I stole time from my "official" duties. Now that poetry itself is my job, the rebel in me sometimes needs to turn elsewhere for secret satisfactions. I love facts: digging them out, fitting them together, solving puzzles. To find a clinching piece of evidence in a parish register can give me as much of a buzz as hitting at last upon the exactly right word or the perfect rhyme. I want to bring those buried lives back to the light, grim and circumscribed though most of them were, and present the record to my descendants.

They may not be interested—but then they may not think much of my poetry, either. To have a mother/grandmother who bears the label of "poet" must feel strange. A student in a school I once visited remarked, after I had described the activities which make up my working life, "It sounds like a rather selfish way to earn a living." Perhaps he was right; perhaps I should have pursued the ambition I briefly entertained at eight years old and become a doctor. Well, it's too late now.

—London, August 1995

BIBLIOGRAPHY

Poetry:

The Eye of the Hurricane, Reed (Wellington, New Zealand), 1964.

Tigers, Oxford University Press (London), 1967.

High Tide in the Garden, Oxford University Press, 1971.

The Scenic Route, Oxford University Press, 1974.

The Inner Harbour, Oxford University Press (London and New York), 1979.

Below Loughrigg, Bloodaxe, 1979.

Selected Poems, Oxford University Press, 1983.

The Incident Book, Faber, 1986, reissued, 1990.

Hotspur: A Ballad for Music, music by Gillian Whitehead, monoprints by Gretchen Albrecht, Bloodaxe, 1986.

Meeting the Comet, Bloodaxe, 1988.

Time-Zones, Oxford University Press (Oxford, England, and Auckland, New Zealand), 1991.

Editor:

(With Anthony Thwaite) *New Poetry 4,* Hutchinson, 1978.

The Oxford Book of Contemporary New Zealand Poetry, Oxford University Press, 1982.

The Faber Book of Twentieth Century Women's Poetry, Faber, 1987.

(With Jacqueline Simms) *The Oxford Book of Creatures,* Oxford University Press, 1995.

Translator:

The Virgin and the Nightingale: Medieval Latin Poems, Bloodaxe, 1983, reissued, 1988.

Grete Tartler, *Orient Express,* Oxford University Press, 1989.

Daniela Crăsnaru, *Letters from Darkness: Poems,* Oxford University Press, 1991.

(And editor) *Hugh Primas and the Archpoet,* (Cambridge Medieval Classics 2), Cambridge University Press, 1994.

Larry Eigner

1927-1996

EDITOR'S NOTE: *It saddens me greatly to report that on January 30, 1996, Larry Eigner was hospitalized with a severe case of pneumonia and died February 3. The videoconference conducted to help compile this essay was the last public interview he did. Therefore, I am truly honored to not only have had the opportunity to meet such an extraordinary poet "virtually enough" (as he wrote recently), but also to know that he was able to be a part of this series. I would like to extend very special thanks to Larry's brother and sister-in-law, Richard and Beverly Eigner, and to Larry's good friend Jack Foley for their enthusiasm and support. This essay would not have been possible without their assistance.*

The various pieces that follow are comprised of Larry Eigner's prose, poetry, and interviews. Primary sections include "Rambling in Life: another fragment another piece," an autobiographical essay written by Larry Eigner, dated from February 28, 1986 and published in areas lights heights: writings 1954–1989; *Jack Foley's interview with Larry Eigner, for KPFA-FM, recorded March 9, 1994 and broadcast August 8, 1994; transcript from the film "Getting It Together: A Film on Larry Eigner, Poet (1973)," transcribed by Jack Foley and published in* Poetry USA, *Issue no. 24, 1992; and a videoconference I conducted with Larry Eigner, Richard and Beverly Eigner, and Jack Foley on December 29, 1995. Together these pieces give insight into the life of a poet unbound by structure or convention.*

Larry Eigner

RAMBLING (IN) LIFE

another fragment another piece

This being a universe of happening and coincidence ranging from immediate to ultimate and huge to minute, I was born in August, the elder of my two brothers two Julys later, on the same day of the month, and so when I was thirteen in 1940 and had a Bar Mitzvah which I was hard up to doing as I felt out of control and wild as ever—in the sun-parlor facing the small audience, my first one, in the living room—the Bible passage I somehow got through was Isaiah chapter 40, not the whole chapter but maybe the first ten or twelve verses, the first third of it, first half of the portion (I wasn't given, shown, the pre-

ceding section of the reading, from Deuteronomy, at all, come to think of it forty-five and a half years afterwards):[1] the beginning of Handel's *Messiah* anyhow: "Comfort ye, comfort ye my people . . . Make plain in the desert / A highway for our God. // Every valley shall be lifted up."[2] As powerful and singing a page as there is. I now wonder when I first heard the Handel—very likely not before FM radio came

---

[1] The Haftorah (conclusion), Isaiah 40:1–26, the Sedrah (portion), Deuteronomy 3:23–7:11.
[2] Isaiah 40:1–4.

Larry (center) with his brothers, Richard (left) and Joe, about 1940

to Boston when I was past twenty-six or so. Nobody suggested any of the Bible as an actual model of writing to emulate or match, say, and the Bible was a remote thing from age or (sectarian) religion or something, anyway not to be rivaled, Henry W. Longfellow, whom my mother read to me, was the person to match or outdo by equaling a good part of his output before I grew up, my own idea, and during my teens I kept trying to rhyme as I had rhymed before, from the age of five or six to eleven, when I went to stay at the Massachusetts Hospital School (MHS) in Canton near Great Blue Hill south of Boston, for the sixth, seventh and eighth grades, till I was graduated from the eighth grade at the top of my class it seems and came back home to Swampscott on the north shore of Massachusetts Bay. It has borders with Marblehead and Salem, where my mother's parents lived (first I knew directly opposite the House of the Seven Gables a little ways back from the sea wall overlooking the beach at the end of Turner Street, then a couple of blocks inland on the same street in a build-

ing with a corner store just at the intersection) and where she grew up (for many or few years on the site of the Salem Post Office or Telephone Exchange, parked in front of which, in 1951 or '52, I got the mostly tetrameter poem "Parts of Salem") after being carried stateside at about age one from a village in Lithuania near Bialystok not far from the Polish borderline

—now there's really a somewhat eastern
place name, Slonim—

as well as Lynn, which has shoe factories and a GE plant and where my Eigner grandmother lived (widowed when I was four). Most of one or both summer vacations I must've spent at the school. Time has never passed slowly, I'm nosy in all directions, curious, what with enough things beyond sight and/or hearing, out of reach, so, willy-nilly and indiscriminate as I am, I've never known boredom. Nor idleness, not till recently anyway, as I was always trying to make out, in physiotherapy and at other times. Helping others help me. And, my left arm and leg pretty wild till I had cryosurgery about six weeks into my thirty-sixth year, I had to keep my attention away from myself to sit still, yet not too far away either. Egotism and altruism, how do they go together in, by now, billions of people (and when? in the phrase I once heard Martin Luther King say he got from Hillel, 2000 years back)!? In a while after I was there MHS was extended to include high school, with two or three new buildings, so it went from Grade 1 to Grade 12. At graduation in '41 I got a copy of *Bartlett's Quotations,* and what with the *Reader's Digest* too, already known, with its "Quotable Quotes" column, I went through high school, the town sending a (substitute) teacher to my house and then in my senior year three or four teachers, keeping an eye out for colorful phrases, lines, when I read a play or book called great, while going on and waiting for something great to happen at the end. And I took to geometry especially, even while I took all the subjects as attentively as I could and enjoyed that, and went looking for a rule, certainty, safety, as to how to begin a paragraph, say, and where to end it and begin the next, should there be a next. Or I did put off more rhyming, just about, till I got through high school. I thought to make a part of a living sometime in the future. Holiday-greeting-card verse. I brought off a sonnet or two. Conventional- and open-minded at once, because extroverted, I tried to think of reason(s) why Shakespeare should be of greater import, more relevant, than a ballgame. As I was told. A man should think for himself. I wanted to see. I'd like to be able to walk alone for instance. I couldn't rhyme really, not frequently at any rate, quatrain on quatrain, couplet after couplet—anything has to be easy enough to do, feasible. At one point while I was in high school a local poet (I heard she was a poet, did I actually meet her once?) wrote or told me only a "master" would attempt blank verse, you had to rhyme. There was a block. And I of course believed it, it came from a veteran, an adult. I was too over-eager in schoolwork if not simply reading to learn much at all, tried too hard to get things "under my belt," as my thought was, my aim—in general I was out to learn as much as I could about everything, so that in an emergency in case he didn't know I could advise a companion how to fix a flat tire for example. Summers I was "good to myself" and every day waited for the baseball game to come on the

radio—and you wanted the Red Sox to win today and win tomorrow whether they did or didn't today. In some way I can't now remember, baseball records, first-time-ever feats, in their variety or number, yes, provided enjoyable "arithmetic."

I added, subtracted, multiplied and even did some long division in my head—there was no other place to, I guess, though I've used a notebook and pencil off and on, since whenever, likely, anyway, at first in bed—visualizing the numbers that changed as I worked on them, or it might have been just relying on memory, and while I did visualize words all right when it came to spelling them, and at Boston's Children's Hospital where I was found to have a high IQ or somewhere else it was said I had a "photographic memory"—maybe you're surprised when you forget to the extent you depend on your memory. My father, who grew up in Haverhill next to Lawrence, Jack Kerouac's home town, hailed from Boston, my grandmother and grandfather perfect strangers till they got to this country, she from Galicia and he from Austria, its Hungarian part, as I heard my mother say when Anselm Hollo on his way with Bob Hogg to or (back to Buffalo?) from Charles Olson in Gloucester came by our place and they got to talking. I'm the oldest of three brothers. From a forceps injury at birth (August 7, 1927) I have cerebral palsy, CP. The doctor, Richard Williams, Mother says, apologized for not measuring her right. If he had, she's said, I would have been delivered in the

Remember
  sabbath days to
  keep time still
    how multiple   clothe
    the past   it's
     not bare but
    it takes time
     to look   eat
    and prepare   darkness
     among the stars

(From *Anything on Its Side*)

                    how apparent, cloudy

          big ideals

            the worth

              something then

        what the

            madness

                and blood

                    the warmth of families

                      is earth   held home

              someone far away

                a stretch

                  within walls

                      sky   rain   sun

                by the sea

                    cossacks

                      down the steps

                    silence

                        this side

                    (From *Things Stirring Together or Far Away*)

Caesarean way. The doctor told my folks they could sue him for malpractice, but considering the thing an accident or something they didn't, anyhow they let it go. Reading, the beach and everything else was like vacation compared to physiotherapy, which was tough, scholarship was something to look forward to. Either my mother was too small or I was too big. Today, February 28, 1986, the Prime Minister of Sweden was shot dead coming out of a Stockholm movie theatre with his wife. The self is some head you can't go around, back, nor in front of. How far might it go? What do questions mean? Curiosity too led me to try reading the billboards on the way to Boston and the physiotherapy clinic at Children's Hospital three times a week, before I was eleven, beside my mother behind the wheel of our Model T. "An Apple

a Day Keeps the Doctor Away" was like one of the Ten Commandments, something as significant or whatever, or the 23rd Psalm, as was "Look for the Silver Lining" and all the other songs and maybe whatever was on the billboards. It was the Depression, whoever knew about it, and there were a number of cheerful songs. And what my mother read me of Eugene Field, and Robert Louis Stevenson's *A Child's Garden of Verses*, besides Longfellow and Poe. Hitler taking over Danzig (G'dansk now), on the radio by the bed shortwave crackle seashell echo hollowing land and rough water across to the sunny network here. For some months I was an in-patient on about the top floor of Children's Hospital to get exercising the afternoons one room we took steps past having a small desk or two with a blackboard, and mornings in the

Imagine that was the
last Rom
eanov   Hvns help

us   King
John/Charles

the story goes

as Grampa dodged
the draft,no kosher
mess   or whatnot

my uncle
born in the woods

apprenticed to a
cabinet-
maker

who used no nails I
recall

Bleeding Trouble   Rasputin   etc etc

the wife
hit with ideas

Ceas ar

No uncle
would take the throne

(From *Things Stirring Together or Far Away*)

---

ward there were the soap opera programs fifteen minutes apiece by which one was on it was pretty easy to tell the time, mystifying enough for one thing the same two companies one of them mostly but different brands of sponsoring suds which was better and a couple times Mussolini in Abyss in i a[3] Ethiopia and talk in the waiting room about Shanghai and gunboat in China. Thirteen and a half, five or six months before graduating eighth grade, two cortex operations deep then deeper, exercises after or between them, the second especially taking hours, whichever started with an awful dream going faster and faster and more and more of the thinning humming louder edge of crack-

ling effervescent checkerboard squares, black and red alternate with some chorus "Thou art our Monarch" many times and three or four clunk scrapings, maybe the surgery did a little good, no one could quite tell, my first hardons from the jacket illustration on Mark Twain's *Prince and Pauper* a while before reading it—into mid or late teens I smelled ether apparently in the air off and on and gagged more and more, there was this girl up the street too. Main idea to control, to live, mind over matter. I recall an FM station or two before "Educational Radio," come to think now, and there was Toscanini on NBC, but that hardly got to me at all, while Saturdays during World War II and maybe before as well as after it I listened to the Metropolitan Opera broadcasts, mesmerized by the gentleman announcer and the quiz and opera

---

[3]Abyssinia.

characters and all, looking up to and trying to appreciate "Grand Opera" to get beyond or grow to see the good in the spectacular singing etc. I used to try to see through factory walls, just about, to see how machines, say toy guns, worked and how shoes were made, and how rooms in a house I'd be taken into fit together, and it figures if TV had had an earlier advent or if I had stopped creeping indoors and out and got up on wheels earlier than I did my curiosity wouldn't have got so exacerbated as it did. About when I was eighteen or nineteen my brother got a record player with 78s of a few pieces like Tchaikovsky's *Pathetique Symphony,* Strauss's *Til Eulenspiegel,* Prokofiev's *Classical Symphony* and *Peter and the Wolf,* and maybe a couple of others. They were enough all right. I enjoyed them.

There was Norman Corwin's "On a Note of Triumph" celebrating Hitler's end and the war's. My father wasn't up to playing anything at all much, playing cards or records or anything. You'd ask him to play a record and he'd dive into the phonograph sitting atop the record cabinet in our bedroom at the back of the house, in its south and east corner with the kitchen and back hall and stairs beyond the closet, with his hands and fumble with the knobs or something. I couldn't see what. Up the stairs my left and right Grmpa counting *eins/zwei/ drei/vier* . . . I got a "walker" with its four swivel wheels and a seat in the back end of the frame, had it at the Hospital School, useful on clear enough paths and fields as well as floors and paved walks, despite a drawback or two, and when I returned home, within three or four years anyway, I got a wheelchair to replace it, metal sides and footboards with folding-up fabric seat, one of the first such wheel-

chairs to be manufactured; besides which I had, from about the year I got back, a big straight-backed wood-and-wicker carriage to go around the neighborhood in—though none too speedily or easily, as my feet didn't reach to the ground in it and so I could only push on the right wheel (my left hand useless), and keep a fairly straight line, avoid going in a circle, by pulling back on the wheel, without the chair going backwards, scrunching, turning the wheel in one spot, making a small rut or hole, dotting the ground or street with a line of them, as much as I pushed forwards. Still must've gone down to the beach sometimes, though every so often mother remarked too bad I'd got so heavy she couldn't any longer take me, pushing the old small sagging straw carriage the shortcut five minutes through the woods or the other way up the hill and along the sea road—while I said I had been there enough for all times, had a lot of it in memory—as her sister was there too, besides their mother and father, less often, who after a bit I heard was, with his chicken store, a black marketeer, profiteer. Biology walks around with all of us every day. You'd ask him (my father) to get a station on the bedside table radio, and he'd go and switch rapidly back and forth across the dial and ask, as if you could see through him, *Is this it, is this it, is this it?* In France during World War I, in a drill, he got his gas mask on wrong, and after recovering from that or from flu or both stayed on at the hospital as a bookkeeper. My mother has a good nose, whereas he couldn't smell a thing, maybe since the winter day he fell into a pond and pretty much froze. My mother did bookkeeping in a Boston Italian bank. He went to Dartmouth College in Hanover, New Hampshire, graduated

---

How much you believe in

whatever

God

so many people

(From *From the Sustaining Air*)

23 Bates Road, Swampscott, Massachusetts, 1959: (from left) Larry, his parents,
Israel and Bessie Eigner, and his brother Richard

in 1916, and then learned, majored in, account-ing at Tuck School, the business school there. Must have been after he got out of the army he went to Northeastern U in Boston at night and took a law degree. Maybe after he got married in 1924 on the Fourth of July along with one of his brothers. He tried to make out as a lawyer for some while but then got his job with the IRS. He drove the car with-out accident, cautiously inching out of the drive-way while on the other hand shooting or rather forgetfully riding past roads we were to turn off on—this was one of the things exasperat-ing mother, that she could never take in stride (I heard he once backed his father's Pierce-Arrow into a plate glass window, intent on go-ing forwards, though), went to the golf course with his bag of clubs I don't know how many times and one morning went fishing. He sat in the low deep living room easy upholstery-armed chair much of the time. "Go ask your father, he went to college," but somewhere else, blocked out somehow, anyhow later as I re-member, he always started as if in the first

grade and couldn't ever get far towards what I didn't know without running out of steam, babytalk talking to a neighborhood kid, exag-gerated pronouncing anyway. Before we learned to read we'd ask and ask till he got to read-ing us the funnies, comics, Sundays, even though at some point there was Mayor La Guardia on the radio reading some of them from New York, but in a minute or two he'd stop, forgetting, and we'd have to nag him all over again. One afternoon in his late seventies or so on the front porch glassed in by then after an hour or two he got a thermometer affixed upside down. How near did my brother and I come to death laughing? In '69 or '70 I read that only in man are difficult births sometimes, so far as is known, this being due to his outsized braincase. A price exacted for the human brain sort of. While since Caesar or before his time it's been avoidable on occasion. The quicker the delivery the less brain damage from low oxygen supply, and CP too or for that matter stillbirth comes from a long enough delivery period. Nothing was said about stroke, though,

anything
        has to be easy enough
                to get done

(From *Anything on Its Side*)

on this radio program about a Johannesburg doctor trying out a decompression belt on expectant women patients to in effect give them fourteen more pounds of push and unexpectedly finding the babies when nine months old had eighteen-month-old IQs, a radio program in 1964 or so, the night before my nephew was born in St. Louis on Hallowe'en. "O wld to God the giftie gie us / To see ourselves as others see us," mother quoted (Robert Burns) pretty often. Circumcision delayed till I was three weeks old instead of eight or nine days for some reason. The doctor said I needed bacon so usually we had it when we had eggs, though never of course pork. Mother had it in life or death matters any of the old injunctions were off, I think she got it from her mother. Sure were impressive those stories of people refusing to eat pork whatever happened, being faithful. Salami, baloney, ham, eggs. Usually my father burnt the toast, it smoked and then it had to be scraped. He was the second of eight kids, one of them died very young. Grandpa was a baker and then financed and maybe otherwise built three apartment houses besides quite a few two- and three-family buildings, lost a lot in the '29 crash. We had one of the two-family, two-story places, and my zany aunt who kept saying aggravating astoundingly stupid and callous/selfish things my mother kept repeating as monumental had another next door. My eldest uncle came around sometimes and did repairs as on the other properties in paint-stained overalls or looked at things and sent the carpenter or plumber or phoned one or the other to come. Mother had an older sister and two older brothers, the older one who was eighteen when he and "Zaidee" (Grandpa) emigrated and who spoke with an accent had in Lithuania been apprenticed to a cabinetmaker and the younger one was an electrician. My

brother [Richard] went to Dartmouth and when he came home on his Xmas vacation brought cummings's *Collected Poems* but there was also the modern anthology and wasn't that a (senior year) high school book too, before, in two volumes, British and American, instead of one big one? He recited two or three poems now and again so now I looked at cummings seriously or singly enough to see for one thing punctuation can be actually part of a piece. One Saturday night before New Year's, besides, it happened he got Cid Corman on the radio and called me over to hear, there was W. B. Yeats's "Fisherman," maybe it was CC's first program end ("This Is Poetry," WMEX Boston). Maybe his sign-on.

I finished up the last correspondence course from the University of Chicago Home Study Department three to four months before. I took seven, yes, somehow not all in pairs, two by two, but three a year and the last just by itself, my mother typing up my reports or anyway theme papers. In the Versification course one time I asked the instructor what "free verse" was, or what was there to it really if anything, something I was puzzled over for some years, and he called it meretricious, there was nothing to it. I felt an obligation to support or advance poetry, a constructive or good thing in the world, and wrote Corman at the radio station, for one thing anyway, about his nondeclamatory way of speaking lines, objecting to or disagreeing with it. More or less. Take up swords. How many games? Corman proposed I take to and I guess try emulating, besides cummings, Williams and Pound—anyway, in the next year I started writing again. He had Creeley on one program and then substituting for him one or more Saturday nights, so I got to have a correspondence with and try to read Creeley, who recommended D. H. Lawrence, Dostoevsky's

August 1964

Notes from the Underground, Robert Graves's *White Goddess,* and things I didn't get around to too, and there was a blind guy for a stretch subbing on the program, with whom I exchanged letters and visited once in Watertown west of Cambridge and Boston with my parents, past them up the Charles River, Al Gazagian; also a fellow listener up in Friendship, Maine, A. McFarland, we still write each other sometimes. First night this FM station that carried the Boston Symphony broadcast there was *Hamlet,* three and a half hours or something, and from then I got to Shakespeare, while some Shakespeare plays you had before in school.

Big ideas from Tin Pan Alley (pop songs, Torch Songs). And Keats too sometimes and some Shelley, besides Shakespeare, I took it in stride enough when the plays came on the radio more naturally. Skimpy stage directions, I never had much imagination, and I figured G. B. Shaw was easy to read like a novel, because of such long directions, for quite a while too long. Shaw's celebrated as well. It was bad, wrong, to be homesick, and easy

not to be, so I wasn't, but mother, considering I was, came to the hospital twice each weekend, with a few exceptions I think, and brought me cookies, apple pie maybe and chocolate cake. Thin skin it seemed going with being a cripple no good either, just the same, or not right. "Sticks and stones may break my bones / but names will never hurt me." The school south of Boston besides, Sundays I think. Or else Saturdays. Brothers at Harvard different times and then one or two years together, the two in an upstairs apartment, there was an elevator there, I can barely remember, and we went there twice or maybe once a week, Saturday afternoons, Sundays. She typed up the theme papers to send to Chicago, one at least I had in the composition course, quite an argument we had about one word's spelling, and she'd've been glad, it looked like, to pay for all 400 courses in the catalogue, or a lot of them, you got credits and if you came to Chicago for some while you could have a degree, but anyway I quit, after seven courses. I figured I might as well read on my own. Once I finished with school, anyway after therapy and the doctor, I was her responsibility and just about anything I told her about or said was idealistic and impractical, foolishly not making sense, or self-centered. I was it turned out way behind, I guess something like my father, I was stubborn and demanding and forgot things done for me. "Don't worry." "Have I ever let you down? Trust me." She was worried. I was. Gloom anyway inside me before we started for physiotherapy outpatient. Rainy enough, thunder, lightning, sunshine, blowy at the clothes reel out the bedroom window, dark; sheet hanging to dry hurled around the back porch corner post above the steps, dirty clouds move fast, the railing was pulled away at last once and the reel was moved to the back end of the porch bolted then to that post. Mother kept trying to get my father to have the garage moved over and round to face the street from the shoulder of the driveway. Writing first and foremost was to be understood, had to be clear, while then I figured immediacy and force take priority, too bad but you can't be both or all three too often, not long before I read Olson's "Projective Verse" essay in the 1950 mag *Poetry New York.* In a year or two she thought she couldn't understand poetry and I was the poetry expert. Still sort of my scoutmaster. Like OK, so far, so good; Forward, March. 🐦

Occasionally

Well, they're used to it
   in those days we
didn't have floors
like now, no
electricity   no telephone
radio   no vacuum
cleaner   But don't you think it's too bad
that college isn't nearer home?
You could get bread for five cents
I came here   no faucets
a pump in the yard

Grandma raised a family
one room over there
                        The Two Old Men
born in one bed

            What are you talking about

Eskimoes, even they who remember
slightly better times?
                        while they live
they barely balanced their land

No consequence
                Remember now

ALL I CAN ADD IS
from where the war is
and more hardship

you'd be surprised
said grandmother
                    after seventy years
      after a hundred years

(From *From the Sustaining Air*)

REMBRANDT LIFE TAKES

to see
dark   the
invisible

time's
long enough you
remember

you thought it was
as it is

(From *From the Sustaining Air*)

Take it

every atom of me

belongs to you

across distances

one space

a photograph of a dam

or a morgue

or hospital

or anything

on its side

(From *Anything on Its Side*)

s t a t e m e n t   o n   w o r d s

Amid increasingly palpable news rather than rumor of scarcities (to be
hugely euphemistic about it), abundant moments in various places persist
and keep on in high or ultra high frequency, and a poem can be assay(s)
of things come upon, can be a stretch of thinking.

(From *The World and Its Streets, Places*)

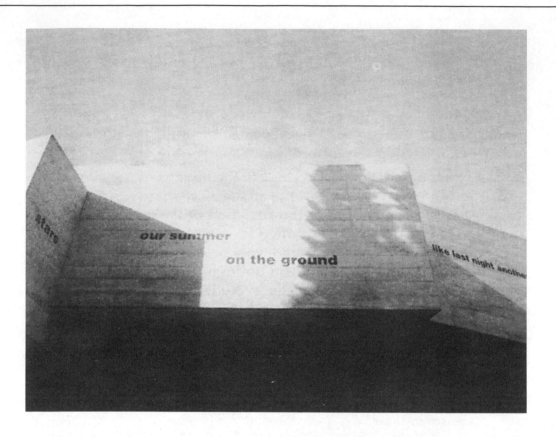

During the summer of 1993 the University Art Museum of the University of California at Berkeley paid tribute to Larry Eigner by exhibiting his poem "Again dawn" on the building's facade while the interior of the museum was undergoing renovations

Again dawn

    the sky   dropped
         its invisible whiteness

        we saw   pass out
               nowhere

        empty the blue

           stars

       our summer
            on the ground

     like last night another
                time

       in fragments

Larry Eigner in front of the museum's main entrance

OMNIPRESENT TO SOME EXTENT

Jack Foley's Radio Interview with Larry Eigner
Recorded for KPFA-FM's Poetry Program, March 9, 1994

JACK: This is Jack Foley with the Poetry Program. My guest tonight is Larry Eigner. Many of you probably saw the wonderful poem beginning "Again dawn. . . ." which was recently exhibited on the outside walls of the University Art Museum in Berkeley. That poem was originally published in 1967, in Larry Eigner's book *another time in fragments*. . . .

Larry's the author of a great many books. His first, *From the Sustaining Air,* was edited and published by Robert Creeley in 1953. There was a second expanded edition published in 1967 by Toad Press, and then a reprint of the original edition by the Coincidence Press in 1988. Other books include *On My Eyes*, 1960, edited by Denise Levertov; *another time in fragments*, 1967; *Flat and Round*, 1969; *Selected Poems*, 1972, edited by Samuel Charters and Andrea Wyatt; *Things Stirring Together or Far Away*, 1974; *Anything on Its Side*, 1974, republished in its entirety by Leslie Scalapino in her *O One / An Anthology*, 1988; *The World and Its Streets, Places*, 1977; *Country / Harbor / Quiet / Act / Around*, 1978, which was selected prose, edited by Barrett Watten; *Earth Birds*, 1981; and *Waters, Places, A Time*, edited by Robert Grenier, it won the San Francisco State Poetry Award in 1983; *areas lights heights: selected writings 1954–1989*, edited by Benjamin Friedlander, appeared from Roof Books in 1989, and Black Sparrow Press will be bringing out a new book, also edited by Robert Grenier, *Windows / Walls / Yard / Ways*. Ron Silliman's large 1986 anthology of L=A=N=G=U=A=G=E poetry, *In the American Tree*, was dedicated to Larry Eigner. . . .

*   *   *

JACK: . . . [Referring to Larry's poem "Again dawn"] That was from 1967.

LARRY: Yeah.

JACK: A long time ago. I love that book, though. The book that that comes from takes its title from that last line, "another / time / in fragments." You liked it, too. A lot of people suddenly discovered a lot of your poems from that book.

LARRY: Yeah. When I forget what a line meant I'm disappointed, I guess. You know, my mother said, "To communicate, you must be clear, first of all" though I soon realized that immediacy and force take priority.

JACK: You've said that it bothers you if you forget what a line means long after you've written it. Your mother said that clarity was the thing. She kept at you to be clear.

LARRY: And I wanted to be clear but immediacy and force have to take priority, I soon realized. Footnotes are distracting but when someone reads in public he can preface with a few words. Like, for an example, you could say "All toes enough stepped," but if it were "All toes enough stepped *on*" it would be clearer. But without the "on" it seems to work better. So you play it by ear, "slow or fast past mind insist." That's most of the poem. There are a couple more words that I forget.

JACK: You were born near Swampscott, Massachusetts, which is where you grew up. Right? And you came here, to California, pretty late. You were born in 1927, and you came here in '78. So you were fifty-one.

LARRY: Fifty-one. Yep.

JACK: And that was right after your father had died.

LARRY: Yeah. In March.

JACK: Was that part of the reason?

LARRY: Yeah. Well, my brother Richard wanted me to move near him, and my mother finally agreed after my father's death. My mother was

Larry Eigner and Jack Foley reading in Petaluma, California, summer 1988

always afraid I'd be a burden on anybody else but her. And too much of a burden.

JACK: Your mother wanted you to be independent and to help adults help you.

LARRY: She would worry about me. I was always trying to help people help me. I'd go haywire every time they'd try to exercise me.

JACK: When you say you went haywire over the exercises, you mentioned in one of your books that you didn't like being physically exercised so much when you were a child.

LARRY: It was the hardest part of my life. Everything else was like vacation. But I was also doing schoolwork and Hebrew classes until I was about twelve years old. I remember a few words from back then.

JACK: Well, you still read a little Hebrew.

LARRY: A few other words I picked up . . . Anyway, I was always trying to help adults help me. I was unable to keep up with other kids.

JACK: Wait. Let's backtrack a bit. The reason you got the cerebral palsy was itself a birth accident. Right? The doctor mismeasured your mother.

LARRY: I should've been delivered by Caesarean but the doctor measured her wrong. The doctor said afterward that she could sue him, but she said, "What's the use in doing that?"

JACK: I guess the answer to that is money, but your parents seem to have had enough money.

LARRY: My grandfather got to be a millionaire and then I guess he lost a great deal of it during the 1929 crash. I never knew how much exactly.

JACK: You mention your grandfather a lot in some of the prose you wrote.

LARRY: My father's father died when I was four. But my other grandfather I remember better—

the grandfather on my mother's side. They were from Lithuania.

*   *   *

LARRY: The best I can do for people is to share poetry and other good things. I was still ego-altruistic because I was trying to help people help me. Now especially I wonder what to say to kids about the future. I once started a piece of prose, "Optimism itself, like the sun on the floor, or rug"—actually it was the floor of a hospital where I was an in-patient for a while. I went to a clinic in Boston, Children's Hospital, two or three times a week. My mother brought me in there for physical therapy. Nowadays I wonder about the future, how people are gonna get along, especially kids. The best thing I can think to tell kids is that the long run is always made up of the short ranges. I only realized that fully last year, although maybe in 1971 or so I wrote a little four-line poem, four stanzas, "The forest / trees / together / how?" How does the forest go together with the trees? Early this year I realized after listening to Paul Ehrlich—he sounded over-optimistic—I realized then, if a picture is big enough, has enough detail to it, if you try to look at the whole thing it's just as much of a specialty as anything else. If it's big and/or complicated enough, you don't get enough of the detail so you can appreciate the present.

JACK: One of the things you've said, actually, which is kind of interesting and like that: "A poem," you said, "can't be too long, anything like an equatorial superduper highway girdling the thick rotund earth, but is all right and can extend itself an additional bit if you're sufficiently willing to stop anywhere" (from *Waters / Places / A Time*). And you made that as a discovery, that you could just stop a poem.

LARRY: Well even Robert Frost (I wish I could rhyme like that), even he said no surprise in the writer, no surprise in the reader. A poem extends itself like you're walking down the street. And you extend the walk sometimes, unexpectedly.

JACK: You say in one of your essays, "If you're willing enough to stop anywhere, anytime, hindsight says, the poem can be like walking down a street and noticing things, extending itself without obscurity or too much effort."

There is a poem here I want to put on the radio because I think most people familiar with your work will never have heard this poem or come across it. It was written, you said, in 1951 or 1952 and then published in the *Dartmouth Quarterly* in February 1954 and it's a very different poem from the kinds of poems that you usually write now or have written since. It's called "A Wintered Road."

A Wintered Road

Rain and the cold had made the street
Clear, metallic; like a plate's
Stems, animals, and incident
Held abstract in one element—

Except this was all around,
Out the window, hedge, fence, ground,
Rough reality within
The supernatural discipline.

Maples stood unassuming then,
Frozen water budding them,
Bud piled on bud   each opening
Awake to this fierce whitening.

Tall grass, weighed over, matted, lined,
Was tangled in a quick design
And a stringent thatch of frost
Which let no spore, no seed be lost.

Only the houses and telephone poles
Were ample, wooden, free, almost
Their spring, fall, summer selves.
                              Slack wires
Spaced windless air with their firm
                              layer

And outdoor cripples, elbow-oared
In the road lurched slowly homeward,
                              towards
Where they could witness this alone
And ring up neighbors on the phone.

LARRY: I never know whether a poem is good or bad, but I think that's less powerful than something by Dr. Williams.

JACK: I think that sounds a lot like some of Hart Crane. And it's kind of interesting the way in which you're using language here. Because Hart Crane would write like that sometimes.

LARRY: Early Hart Crane.

JACK: Hart Crane was an early influence on you. "Praise for an Urn." Poems like that.

LARRY: Yeah. I remember that one.

JACK: And he would rhyme something like this. These are off rhymes, an interesting one "opening" "whitening." I think it's an interesting poem. And you were maybe what, twenty-five, twenty-four?

*   *   *

JACK: Your mother began reading Longfellow to you. Is that right?

LARRY: Yeah. "Life is brave and life is earnest." Right now I don't know what isn't a powerful poem. My mother read me Eugene Field, as well, "Winken, Blinken and Nod." That's pretty much like Edward Lear.

JACK: Did your mother like your poetry?

LARRY: She thought it wasn't clear enough. Then when I got to be pretty successful, she said I'm the poetry expert and she kind of became resigned to my not being clear.

JACK: You complain sometimes about not being able to understand some of the poetry you read.

LARRY: Writing is like playing one game at a time and doing your best at it. Reading is like trying to compare all the games you ever saw and then watch one of them, trying to figure out which one it is. And there are a lot of things in poems now, . . . I feel conscientious to read them. I try to be constructive and write people back, but I don't understand it.

JACK: Actually, you said something about yourself. You said, "I'm scatterbrained, for whatever reason. I can't keep much in my head for long, can't really understand much, and can't follow ideas of any abstruseness or complexity, and when I do see what people mean, am like that considering caterpillar in the face of a few differing viewpoints, baffled and all. There are quite a few poems/poets I definitely like, so I'm not utterly indecisive after all." And then you say, when you're talking about

J. H. Prynne, "His comments seem penetrating, but I wouldn't know exactly, being so fragmented myself that I can't take a survey (can't see much into the verse of Prynne himself, for instance)." Fragmented. That word comes back.

Is that maybe why most of your books have been edited by other people?

LARRY: Maybe most of them. I forget.

Letter for Duncan

just because I forget
to perch different ways
            the fish
     go monotonous

         the
     sudden hulks of the trees
       in a glorious summer

you don't realize
   how mature you get
     at 21

     but you look back

     wherever a summer
       continue 70 seasons

     this one
       has been so various

       was the spring hot?

every habit

   to read

nothing you've done you have

     older

       the fish
     can't bother screaming

     flap by hook

     the working pain

         jaws by trying a head   bodies

    you'll always go to sleep
    more times than you'll wake

     (From *another time in fragments*)

*   *   *

LARRY: What you read about being willing enough to stop anywhere—along about 1970, I got to write being willing enough, not too ambitious, so then I got clearer, like the stuff in *Anything on Its Side*—more understandable to myself and the reader.

Here's a poem I did after 1970.

the bird / of wire like a nest

the bird
of wire like a nest

is all through the air

        still, minutely
          simple

dead in its way,   the material
    take in the eyes,   time

    we can waste on a piece of music
    while hours may tick by

you remember from childhood

    a bird
depending on the weather

        flight was a brief
        impenetrable keen breast

    doubling lives

    sleep   peace in various light

the lark a little further beyond
        the countryside

(From *another time in fragments*)

so the fine green arm

of the phone truck

    the line-men are birds,they

        might ride to the trees

        that
          cross-piece now is precise

    it takes two

    the fresh pole there
        for days

        plenty of oil share
          what

    bright yellow

    over the tires

           up north and east

can make a sound

when did we turn the lights

    them carried too

    O it is, huh

    and nothing can bring it back

(From *The World and Its Streets, Places*)

*   *   *

I seem to remember this as having to do with people leaving their motors running . . . Before that I was kind of on to environmentalism. I felt bad about the waste of gas and oil. I forget if it was real pollution by that time or not. . . . Before I wrote this I wrote quite a few ecological poems. The third one is in *Anything on Its Side*, published in 1974.

JACK: You always refer to your books by the dates. You say "my 1974 book."

LARRY: That's right. . . .

JACK: There are a lot of trees and birds in these poems. And "air" is another word that shows up a lot in your work.

*   *   *

JACK: Your poems have a lot of subtlety and they're a little bit like, people have noticed this before, haiku. . . .

I want to read a statement you made, it's a little long, but I think it's a very good and important statement and it's something that's an interesting one. And maybe also to talk about your poetry in translation. There's a very interesting French translation of one of your poems here:

> . . . I'm cautious, and come onto things by under-statement. Wary of exaggeration. Sotto voce has resulted in the suppression of words. Don't like to begin with a big B, as if I was at the Beginning of all speech, or anything; which may also have something to do with why usually I've had an aversion more or less to going back to the left margin after beginning a poem, but otherwise than in hindsight I just tried to do the best I could, the simplest and most immediate thing being punctuation,[1] once words were forceful enough—a matter of getting the distances between words, and usage of marks to conform as well as might be to what there was to say, as spoken, then these typographical devices entering themselves into the discovery and the initiation of attention. As with any other detail, after dispensing with a routine duplication device—e.g. a period as well as a capital letter—a new thing immediately (neither period nor capital results in sentence splice, a poem without very explicit rests, if that's what seems good), then, the availability of the device for vital use in some other connection that may crop up, possibly. Oaks from small acorns. Forests of possibility. But they can't reach the stratosphere or leave the ground. In the stratosphere

you get very stark claustrophobia. Now that I've met up with a good number of things and people I'm less able to keep open and give everyone the benefit of the doubt than I used to, which was the only way I found of getting along, just about, and it still is practically my only way—kind of a bootstrap affair.

(A limitation is, that though I seem to do all right al fresco, later when my nose is out of it two inches away the stuff is more doubtful and apt to go flat. Many lines flush with one another can go more permanently flat, on the other hand, and bill boards seem heavy).

Parodying Socrates a little, you might say I know enough to feel naive.

("Method from Happenstance,"
from *areas lights heights: writings 1954–1989*)

"I know enough to feel naive." I like that very much and it makes you a little bit like le Douanier Rousseau. I want to also read a mistranslation into French of a poem of yours. But it's an interesting mistranslation. Joseph Guglielmi translated many of Larry Eigner's poems into French. This is the sixth poem in Guglielmi's *L'éveil* (1977):

> vent
>
>   léger
>
> à dos d'oiseau;
>
>   sa forme
>
>   dans le contour
>
>   des branches

LARRY: I translated Guglielmi, not the other way around. I tightened it up.

JACK: Oh, *you* translated it. Oh, I see. It's even more interesting that way.

This is Larry Eigner's translation of Guglielmi's poem:

> wind
>
>   light
>
>   bird back
>
>   branches

A literal translation would be: "light wind at the back of a bird; its form in the contour of the branches." In the English both "light" and "back" are ambiguous; they are not in the French.

---

[1]"From a confrontation, first, with work by e. e. cummings, then by Williams and others."

Both poems were published in *Moving Letters* #11. You left out a lot. You translated only certain key words. And it's interesting that way too. I thought it was a translation back of you.

I want to read the first poem in your first book, your second book really, but your first as Larry Eigner, and it is called "B."

B

    Is it serious, or funny?
    Merely?

          Miasma of art
               The

    more the merrier is my view

    seeing the levels of the world

    and how easily emptied space

                 is

    Here they made the perfect pots
    on the beastly floors
    the spoons and knives randomly dealt

    and tread on the pine-cones
    bare-footed
    to cut wood

    and here, the women went undone
    till noon, plaiting

     Once this happened
    and the cooks brought food to their seniors in wigs
    in dressed-stone mansions;

    I am omnipresent to some extent,
    but how should I direct my attention

    sufficiently to what I desire, to
    stop, to
    what is charging on the roadbed, what
        going away, the

    fire-gong, people and buses

      and even in my room, as
    I know
           the waving sun
              the

    constant ephemerals

          (From *From the Sustaining Air*)

". . . the constant ephemerals." I don't know how ephemerals can be constant, but I love that phrase. The sun doesn't wave, it rises and sets. But that's all right. It's a waving sun in this poem.

LARRY: I don't know either, but it reminds me of Gertrude Stein's eternal present.

JACK: "I am omnipresent to some extent," you say. I love that line. But the first thing you say to the world is "Is it serious, or funny? / Merely? / Miasma of art." And it's kind of funny sometimes and sometimes it isn't. I think "I am omnipresent to some extent" is kind of funny. At least in some contexts. It sounds like Walt Whitman suddenly taking himself up short, "I am omnipresent, to some extent." . . . Larry is very much a poet's poet. And I think that's clear from some of the poets who have been associated with Larry. Robert Creeley, Denise Levertov, Robert Grenier, and Ron Silliman. Quite prominent poets. And Robert Duncan was a fan of Larry's as well.

Cid Corman once said,

> The random quality is often due to the brevity of the poet's attentions, acute and wandering. Finding every distraction a focal point and in the alert mind mingling ideas, facts, as wires, hinges, bolts, and sometimes just flashes. Glimpses and glances, queer connections of the most familiar.

Larry, I want to ask you one other thing. You mention, in one of the quotations from your book *areas lights heights,* you say that at one time you were a workaholic, and you believed in a work ethic, but you say no longer—"every hour or two is a new day around the world, but by now I opine you can have overkill in anything, for example there's no shortage of any kind of writing that I can see. Nor is Work any longer a very great good—life or living is its purpose. Career or profession seems obsolete in enough ways by now, and now I think of a return to amateurism." Do you regard yourself as an amateur?

LARRY: An amateur is a lover of a subject. What's the use unless you really feel like it? Spontaneity. What's the use of keeping up with a specialty for a whole lifetime? Once a poet always a poet. But I don't agree with that.

JACK: Do you think of yourself as a poet still?

LARRY: Nobody's a poet when he's asleep, and so forth. I was going to read one more poem.

                    the pastorale

                 symphony

              the snow is
                          white   white

                    in the yard

                       sunshine

                          the wind   sheep

                    what do the clouds graze

                 in safety as

                    a child feels

                       heedless

                          of indoors

              positioned   slow   like the aerial

              half blown down

                 by the freak blizzard

              what this place may be

                 unreally cold and wet

                 when the music was conceived

                              (From *The World and Its Streets, Places*)

                              JACK: Thank you, Larry.

This interview was broadcast on KPFA-FM August 8, 1994, the day after Larry Eigner's sixty-seventh birthday.

"The Bible Told Me So" or ". . . said by Mother"

It's hard to say what unrealities may not enter the real, and there's as much in the spectrum from real to unreal as, say, between here or the zenith and the antipodes. Reality isn't likely to be all black and white—gray— or black or white. Man's bootstraps, his imagination, is quite a part of reality, or when that element fails, is unattained, or has no points of application, a stonier reality closes in, like death. Often enough it's a question that never can be answered with absolute precision, how much imagination can penetrate a reality already present, and how much it has to for there to be a notable interaction or change. To be alive is to be chemically active—no ideas in a dead man's head—and the more points of interaction perceptions have with things in spaces other than that occupied by the head, or nowadays maybe the more they interact with such things, the faster they do, the greater correspondence, correlation, cross-reference, then the truer they'll be.

Don Quixote, an imaginary figure, finds stimulus to cover a considerable range in as many books, an uncertain number (within a chosen area), as he reads, trying to live by them as people before and since Cervantes' time have tried to live more or less by the Bible or Koran—extensions of their experience anyway in any books of tradition. A Confirmation, very often, a stabilizing activity. Or how much of a peg should a text be, how hard can the Bible be hammered without detracting greatly from reality, and thereby truth (reality inclusive of imaginative perceptions), itself? Then by now we have what seems a good deal of anarchy, for instance the Theatre of the Absurd (I hardly pick up much spirit for a fast whirl from a page anyhow), which *Don Quixote* already is, pretty much, random and disjointed enough, and for one thing piling the learned Moor, Cid Hamete, purported author of the "history" (Cervantes says he got another Moor to translate it for him)—cited in various spots—on top of everything else. Or to say one thing or another is overdone becomes a fine point, in view of Cervantes' whole, the combination he makes;

but he's only less fragmentary than a present-day kaleidoscope, perhaps, in being slower. This as regards plot, the sequence of things that happen. Maybe a more human, less grueling pace—in some senses. Thematically there's this traveling back and forth between the ideal, absurd and fantastic, and the beginning of reality (everyday—the communal view—as distinct from where men start from, individually, in childhood). And how much literary or traditional basis is there for the Theatre of the Absurd (B. Brecht deriving from Shakespeare, as well as John Gay and musical theatre et al.)? The Book of Nature, which has been opened more and more since Dante and Giotto and Leonardo, has gotten very weighty by now, bigger than the Library of Congress. How pure would it be nice to have escapism and the hermetic be? Lucky that biologically we're still the same, at least that we sleep at night and so other things—it's a consideration. Don Quixote considered the knights of old to have been fairly similar to himself at that, with the same bodily needs; although it was or "is a point of honor . . . to go for a month at a time without eating." Some peg is needed, based on likeness, it seems, before you can have extension, which would require difference. (Don Quixote gained wisdom in applying his texts and/or personal experience, in the process of course developing his own commentary. Though too much interaction between imagination and a given reality breaks down the body, and too little results in bad falls, catastrophes, likely as not disastrous. Such is life.)

You also have the illiterate, the layman, like Sancho Panza, or the naturalist (Thoreau, W. H. Hudson) or backwoodsman. Well, friends and peers. An oral tradition is at the least adequate to some things. It's unknown, too, if there were any long-time hermits before there were any books.

—Larry Eigner

(From *areas lights heights: writings 1954–1989*)

GETTING IT TOGETHER

A Film on Larry Eigner, Poet (1973)

Film made by Leonard Henny and Jan Boon
Poetry by Larry Eigner
Read by Allen Ginsberg
  [and Larry Eigner—Eigner's note]
Text by Michael F. Podulke

With commentary by Larry Eigner (1989)
Transcript by Jack Foley

ALLEN GINSBERG:

    loneliness, existence
            this is the fine flower   and
        the bodies in a ring
                the geometry

        some substance given the stuff of
            the earth, imitable
                    air
                the graces in a car   *June 1978*
                    gun
        and exhaust   the word is familiar now and the curves
        perfect as straight lines

            Barefoot to match
                the atmosphere, a
            plain for the distance, the
                    slung horizon

(another time in fragments #19)

NARRATOR: This film is about Larry Eigner, a poet living in Swampscott, Massachusetts, almost completely paralyzed by injuries received at birth. He cannot walk[1] and can only just speak and use his hands. He gets his poetry down on paper by dictating it to his mother and his brother [Joe,] who are able to understand him. In recent years he has mastered one-fingered typing, a technique which unfortunately cannot keep pace with the speed of his thinking or poetic invention. Larry is getting it together on pure will power.

[1]*Walk unless someone holds him or he holds onto a bar or railing, one hand is useless and his speech isn't good. He remembers he made up bad rhymes as a child and had his mother write them down. His brother J was seven and he was thirteen years old when he began typing in earnest (with one finger) while he did a few strokes on a toy typewriter before.—Eigner's note.*

GINSBERG: Ah, obviously[2] the form of the verse is dictated by his physical condition of slow hesitancy and difficulty in maintaining his hand steady to write words. And as the words come swiftly through his mind he has to stop his whole thought process to write down a word while thoughts are going on still.

[2]*Obvious maybe but not too good a guess.—Eigner's note.*

GINSBERG, FOLLOWED BY EIGNER:

Birthday[3]

<pre>
Every-body was supposed to be enthusiastic   it
  was a big hall with lots of corners
    though 4-square simply, stating the case
     simply, and letting it go at that
     and the girl who looked disgusting, almost in bed,
     or was she disgusted, was
     polite, as might be under such
                              circumstances
       she said, you're not in the way

I had thought I was,   with
her permanent small expression,
                          and
eyes,   the wheelchairs had to
keep on the go,   and we were all 30 or 45,   time
always went by,   Till all the
               eyes were turned
the true surprise, a man as a
hectic native .. doing
a strip-tease

     down to a "censored" in black

  letters, and many
were doubled, as well, by age

       and bits of mistletoe were strung up
       by the idea man with no fingers
       who had only time for that

     as it turned out
                    being volatile
     which was about as far as we got
</pre>

(On My Eyes #41)

[3]*i.e., Xmas party of the "Indoor Sports" at the Jewish Community Center in Lynn, Massachusetts, December 1952, possibly '53—Eigner's note.*

EIGNER: I was thinking that your way there was kids and marriage, and so forth, you know . . . idealism, all right. I wanted . . .[4]

[4]*Nervous distracted and bewildered, Ei . . . was thinking (again) that a "normal" life isn't really an ideal goal to aim for, dancing for example—but anyhow, for instance, no one maybe was ever out to do ballet inside of a wheelchair, after all.—Eigner's note.*

QUESTION: How do you write a poem?

EIGNER: I used to try very hard, I used to go around all the time thinking of the . . . trying to write poetry. . . . But, ah, I forget how it was . . . you know, it was often by the skin of my teeth like that . . . you know, oh "what's the [bellyache?]." Comes in awkward. I did satisfy the inawkward thing and I tried to get most of it anyway, nagging, hoping sort of, like, you know, hoping against hope, maybe, you know, egotistical, and anyway, like I used to try and walk, you know, hoping in a sense a lie, turned out what seemed to me pretty awkward but I know I did it to the best I could, and all.

GINSBERG:

      live
     , bird which
       sings
           above
       and underneath

       or two birds, may
          all

        go   subtly

          we are

          in the air

     feet

             on the ground

          the air goes
          thin then
          budding relieve
          the branches like
          fresh children

            leaves
        die, fitful
          mass of voices, curled, in
           continuous air

(another time in fragments #72)

GINSBERG, FOLLOWED BY EIGNER:

> eyes, eyes
>   the hurt
>   is not the blind
>
>   staring
>   birds sing
>
>   day or night
>
>   how
>   the trees grow
>
>   branches
>
>   rounds of the sky**

> [Eigner's typescript: Mrch 23 69 #297]

JACK FOLEY'S NOTE: The text of this poem, both in Eigner's typescript and as read by Ginsberg, differs from the subtitles in the film. The subtitles read: "eyes, eyes the hurt is not the blind staring birds sing day and night how the trees grow birches lining the sky."

GINSBERG:

> *The wandering mosquito*
>
> into my face
> among the masses
>
> When does he go to sleep
> I forget he's irregular
>
> Is there any sleep, at all, for him,
> before death?
>
>   he wanders miles and miles and
>   becomes aware of the window
>   where the moon is
>
>   in a short time
>
>   the peg-board
>
>   and it's raining outside
>
>   94 humid
>
>   he hasn't hurt me yet
>
>   I have to open the window
>
>   his head is a constant drop of blood

> *(another time in fragments #56)*

GINSBERG:

       I ride I

          don't believe in planes

                what purpose there is

        various principles

        tremendous craft

         until my end

              the surface gets easy

               infinite air circuits

                merging

            clouds like our wing

            out the lined window

            maximum length every

            light spreads

                [Eigner's typescript: June 30 . . . July 2 70 #405]

At Golden Gate Park, San Francisco, during the "Summer of Love," 1968, with Robert Duncan (standing left of Larry) and Larry's brother Richard (standing behind Larry)

EIGNER: I've got some, maybe just a descriptive poem. This is it. "Whitman's Cry at Starvation in a Land of Plenty." Maybe I'd rather have it down here, Frank.

    Whitman's cry at starvation
     in a land of plenty

        prison camps the mean
           South

            six ways
                  of saying it
      the big problem is

      consumption and conservation and population

       population consumption conservation

        conservation population consumption

        population conservation consumption

      or what about
       bringing others in

         conservation consumption population

          consumption population conservation

      I could have watched for a week
       the able horsemen
       with no nonsense

      put the sick with the strong

    eighty thousand to a hundred thousand
     of the wounded and sick
        critical cases
     I generally watched all night

         was with many from the
            border states

         bedded down
       in the openwork of
        branches and stars

      must not and
          should not be
       written perhaps

      marrow of the tragedy
       one vast central hospital
       with fighting on the flanges in
       the flesh—

      how much of importance is
       buried in the grave
       in eternal darkness

              [Eigner's dating: April 7f 66 # k L]

                  I didn't do that too bad, did I?

GINSBERG:

Listening to the wind
how it may change
a bird opens to fly
the other side of the world
is pulled down

the car pool burning

(*Things Stirring Together or Far Away,* p. 80)

[Eigner's dating: Feb 17f 68 #172]

QUESTION: Larry, how would you effect your idea that the world one day wouldn't go hungry? You've written about a hunger strike.

EIGNER: I think of it as . . . I thought of it as a weekly fast or a frequent enough fast to get people to realize that living like Thoreau . . . sort of a regular . . . ME! Like "I had a great few years." And also to be aware of limitations, the possibility, the likelihood, whatever it is, of bad harvests, and also the limitations there ought to be because if you use too much fertilizer and grow too much food it's bad, you know, too much nitrogen in the water and the air, and all sorts of things go together, it kind of goes together, the awareness of limitations and one kind of brain, just fear, a lot of fear, and when people all [?] it's because of fear so I have this idea of a fund drive in conjunction with the fast. Sounds like The March of Dimes. Have food, budget, money . . .[5]

[5]*Food-budget money saved in fasting go towards supplying people without enough or an equal share of food or whatever with more.—Eigner's note.*

COMMENT: This is less like a form of resistance or recalcitrance ["resistance or recalcitrance" is the phrase in the subtitle but the man seems actually to be saying, "political recalcitrance"] than it is a form of prayer almost, abstinence as a form of prayer almost.

EIGNER: Yeah, getting things together. Yeah, yeah, abstinence wouldn't be good unless you could also have giving along with it . . . yeah . . . because just restraint by itself would be . . . pretty much get people down.[6]

[6]*bring fear and hostility.—Eigner's note.*

GINSBERG:

clouds move
shadows move   some

smokes invisible

here to there

roofs top

fire escapes

the bottoms drawn up

[Eigner's dating: July 12 70 #411]

JACK FOLEY'S NOTE: This transcript—like, evidently, the subtitles in the film—is only an approximation, though I listened as carefully as I could to the soundtrack and tried as hard as I could to make out the subtitles. Ginsberg's reading—and sometimes Eigner's reading—departs slightly from Eigner's text; the subtitles are at times a condensation of what is said rather than what is actually said; there are some words in the subtitles which are not heard on the soundtrack (e.g., the question, "How do you write a poem?"). These are inevitable difficulties in the shift from the oral/aural to the written. As Larry puts it at the end of *another time in fragments:*

> there is everything to speak of
> but the words are words

JF 7/26/89

```
an original
            eye
a reverent
            eye
    wild
    discipline
            eye
            eye
what you
    see you
    settle
        on                          CEZANNE A
            moves                       CATHOLIC
    do something
    feel                                    UP
        a                               OLD
        victory                         HILLS
    or mountain
                what
            you can't
                go through
                    nor replace
                    a road
                        a like
                            curve
```

(From *Anything on Its Side*)

A Note Detailing Tags

It must've been a couple or about three years after I started trying poems again from listening to Cid Corman's radio program and corresponding with him and Creeley et al. that I began labeling em so I could in short shrift record what I submitted where, but since I might best or could only pencil in a notebook lying in bed (nor cd I take a sheet out of book or binder to type on, insert it afterwards) I just figured to keep the labels as brief as I could for as long as possible, hence once I'd numbered verse pieces 1 through 99 I used tags, a, a1 through a9, b b1 . . . y9 then 1a . . . 9z and then ab, ac and so on. I reserved AA, BB etc. for prose and had wariness, presence of mind not to go in for z7 for instance wch in penciling cd easily be the same as 27, but didn't think to avoid 2i through 9i, z1 through z9 and others. (I cdn't say when I first typed a record on a loose sheet—early on, it seems—nor since when I've done this regularly, sometimes penciling there, too. Not too bad an idea to have as much as possible in sight at once, no matter how reliable memory is, in a small space or on one page.) Also about as soon as an editor took anything I reused its tag, though never more than once or twice, seldom perhaps without adding an apostrophe, and later when I'd been 5½ yrs putting more than one poem on a page (at first for a while copying a poem once or maybe sometimes twice over again below the initial typescript in triplicate or often as otherwise quadruplicate), for instance I had four different poems (ih/ih'/ij/ij') on one page, three on another (iw/w/iw') and, like, jm/jm'/j"/j'm on another, sort of thing I carried on for at least 15 months ('65–'66), maybe any time space allowed, also I see now I repeated de within a month somehow or other and ab in 5 days (the four poems in early '62 and late '61 all

writ I guess on the 6th floor of Massachusetts General Hospital but of course typed up at home). Kind of lucky I began dating things as a regular thing in October '59 after Don Allen sought for dates to things he took for *The New American Poetry* when he asked me to show him stuff and I did; before that I considered luck might more than likely run out, I might be jinxed and get writer's block if I dated, it'd be overconfidence, counting chickens before they hatched, laying claim to lasting fame, though one or two things I did date and besides I remember what I wrote in the Summers of '53 and '54 and (so too) "After 2 Years" in July, August, September or October of '56. En through ez or so are from '64, the f's and early e's from '63. From lack of recall and in some haste I on one occasion used xyz for instance and 101, 105–8 and 5L2 through 5L9 for things at some time after I wrote them, guessing at their chronological position or maybe to indicate I cdn't determine it. Some, like "Letter for Duncan," I never got to label, thinking their whereabouts would stay in my head. A few such aren't dated either, at least one of em likely anyway from before 10/59, likely as not.

Whew! So a good bit before June 15 '66, when I exploited kv, the system had in large part become chaotic. A week or so later I flew to San Francisco to stay with my brother for two months, and he got me to start all over again with #1 (June 25th), and with a few repeats (#913a, 913b, 913c and 913d could form a group or series, 984' I guess I was thinking might well be so-so by comparison with 984 directly above it) I last month (May '89) reached 1650.

—*Larry Eigner*

(From *areas lights heights: writings 1954–1989*)

"VIRTUALLY ENOUGH"

Videoconference with Larry Eigner &
Richard and Beverly Eigner, Jack Foley, and Shelly Andrews, December 29, 1995

[It should perhaps be noted that, at this point in his life, Larry was somewhat weakened and less forthcoming than he was at other times, though he was still able to communicate.

—Jack Foley]

SHELLY: What are your earliest memories?

LARRY: Pine Street when I was four years old. I was taking a nap in the front parlor near a railroad crossing. A plane went by often and the noise bothered me.

RICHARD: We lived at two addresses, Pine Street for about two years, whereas Larry spent approximately fifty years of his life at 23 Bates Road, Swampscott. That's the principal address. That was a tract of land. It was land on which a house was built. Most of it was undeveloped. Over the years, the lots in that tract of land were sold off almost exclusively to Italians. We were completely surrounded at 23 Bates Road by houses most of which had been built by Italian immigrants. Up to when he was eleven years old, Larry went to Boston for physiotherapy sessions three times a week. Then he went to the Massachusetts Hospital School for sixth, seventh, and eighth grades. It was a statewide,

partly public, partly private school. Larry graduated top of his class.

SHELLY: What was it like going away to a school for these years?

LARRY: At first I was thin-skinned, sensitive. Then I got to have thick skin. I became pretty popular. I think they liked me.

RICHARD: That school was a very rough place. Some of the children were pushed around on wheeled carts. Others were being treated for tuberculosis. He returned to Swampscott after the Massachusetts school and had a substitute teacher come into our home to school him. She was very interested in literature.

LARRY: First Mrs. Blodgett, and then a math teacher as well, who was principal of the high school.

RICHARD: This arrangement was worked out with the public school system. Larry also spent summers at Robin Hood's Barn, in Vermont, a summer camp for handicapped children which was run by two New England ladies. They dressed up as characters, and the staff played parts like Maid Marian. It was my mother's campaign to have Larry educated as much as he was. At that time, it was thought that children like Larry could not be educated. That was followed by correspondence courses in versification from the University of Chicago, which I think was suggested by this Mrs. Blodgett.

*　　*　　*

SHELLY: What do you remember about your Bar Mitzvah in 1940?

LARRY: It was in my front parlor at Bates Road, I had stagefright and was scared of giggling.

JACK: Larry giggles when he gets nervous.

Curiosity

LARRY: Curiosity keeps me going. I might have less of it now, but I had enough of it earlier.

JACK: "Curiosity" is a big word for Larry. He uses it a lot. Anything anybody said he took very seriously.

LARRY: I was both conventional and the opposite.

JACK: Were you "subversive"?

LARRY: I don't know what you mean. My mother read things out of the paper she thought I might get a kick out of and I tried to reciprocate. Mother would tell me to go to my room if I wanted to say them out loud.

RICHARD: When did you begin to write poems?

LARRY: Very early. I used to be in bed. My mother would come and take down the poem.

RICHARD: Or Father would. I remember being in the same bedroom with you and sometime in the course of the night you would wake saying, "I've got a poem." They used to rhyme in those days. Some of them were sonnets.

LARRY: I don't remember this.

JACK: I have an early poem of Larry's that reads like Hart Crane. It's called "A Wintered Road" [see page 33].

RICHARD: I remember a sonnet called "The Disciplinarian," the last lines of which were "ephemeral and worthy to be erased / if ever wind was sung or sunset traced."

LARRY: My eighth grade graduating class at the hospital school had a print shop. They published a book. The first book listed in my list of poems is this book, *Poems* (1941). It's not in any of my regular books. I was fourteen years old. Juvenilia.

*   *   *

LARRY: I never get bored. And this poem is a good example of my lack of boredom.

        the strange   the familiar
          headlights   eyes

        we loved riding
      the back of the truck

        the sleigh on its course
      coming down the hill
      spilling so many ways

          we could never jump

      a flying start

          it was
          always
      suppertime

          the bells at
          sunset
            there

        the horses

      every night the power
          sleeps   wakes up
            in the morning

          (From *Anything on Its Side*)

RICHARD: My mother's father used to sell vegetables from an open truck. It used to be horse-drawn. He was the much more plebian member, he was all-earth, and one of his activities was giving the grandchildren what he called a "back ride." He'd back up the truck on a quiet street at what seemed like a rapid rate. The house was situated in an area where houses were being built. And there were a lot of vacant lots. You walked through a woodsy path and came to a beach. We could hear the ocean from the house.

JACK: You'll notice that Larry's extremely careful about line spacing.

*   *   *

JACK: Your father was technophobic, I gather. He couldn't work the radio.

RICHARD: According to my mother my father was technophobic. In fact, according to my mother, we all are. My mother was the stronger parent.

*Larry Eigner with his brothers, Joe (left)
and Richard, and parents Bessie and
Israel Eigner, early 1950s*

*   *   *

LARRY: After my two brothers moved away, usually you could hear a pin drop. My father, very absentminded, and my mother thought by turns I was either impractical or idealistic or self-centered. I was to be seen and not heard. So you could hear a pin drop and I got stagefright. But otherwise I had plenty of time to concentrate on typing, keeping up with the mail, writing two or three poems a week—I type often enough and/or fast enough with just my right index finger, my thumb on the spacebar, lifting it and coming down with every stroke on a key, so I hardly need to look at the keyboard.[1]

---

[1]This paragraph was excerpted from a letter from Larry Eigner, dated January 3, 1996.

Influences

SHELLY: How did your correspondence with Cid Corman begin? You were listening to his radio program and you wrote him a letter?

LARRY: My brother was listening to the radio and called me over. Cid Corman was reading Yeats. I wrote a letter to Cid Corman objecting to the way in which Corman was reading Yeats. I felt that Yeats should be more declamatory. Corman responded and this began our correspondence. I also discovered Pound, William Carlos Williams, and Robert Creeley through Cid Corman. Charles Olson, too. Creeley substituted for Corman on the radio station. Hart Crane was another influence. I discovered him on my own, somehow.

JACK: Creeley used to read Hart Crane. One of Creeley's first poems in *For Love* is about Hart Crane.

LARRY: Another influence was e. e. cummings.

RICHARD: That was the beginning of the emphasis on spatialization.

SHELLY: Are there other poets who've influenced you?

RICHARD: Robert Kelly, Jonathan Williams. Williams was a publisher and poet.

LARRY: My 1960 book. Denise Levertov wrote the preface. *On My Eyes.*

JACK: She wrote in the preface that she can't tell if a Larry Eigner poem is good or bad. She also happened to be the editor of the book.

*   *   *

BEVERLY: Larry, would you like to tell about visits to the house by William Carlos Williams and Charles Olson?

RICHARD: We visited Charles Olson in Gloucester. He was at least 6′5″ and a Viking. He was a postman in Boston. Lived in a fisherman's part of town on a promontory, up a rickety flight of stairs, and Olson came down and carried

Larry up the stairs to his den, in which he had, among other things, the works of Alfred North Whitehead. Olson saw that Larry was reading Whitehead and said, "Stonecutting all the way."

BEVERLY: That was August of '64.

LARRY: Before you got married.

JACK: Larry's major influences are William Carlos Williams, Hart Crane, and Charles Olson. Larry's also read lots of other people and lots of Language poetry, but it isn't fundamentally an influence. The former are poets he goes back to. Larry told me once that he was a little afraid sometimes that the Language poets would find out that he didn't understand their work. And I told this to Lyn Hejinian, who is a Language poet. She said to tell Larry that the Language poets started seminars and readings in order to understand each other's work.

Robert Duncan is another poet who was interested in Larry. I don't know if you have *another time in fragments,* but there's a wonderful statement by Duncan about Larry's work as a development of Williams's line:

> . . . *his phrasings are not broken off in an abrupt juncture but hover, having a margin of their own* . . .

RICHARD: When did you first meet Duncan face to face?

LARRY: The summer of '68.

*   *   *

SHELLY: Could you talk about your correspondence courses at the University of Chicago?

RICHARD: Larry started taking the University of Chicago correspondence classes right after high school. They used to come in the mail every other week. They taught very traditional verse forms. Our mother loved poetry, especially when it was in recognizable meter, even if it wasn't rhyming.

SHELLY: Did these versification courses help you with what you've written since?

LARRY: No.

RICHARD: I disagree.

SHELLY: Was that reason to drop out?

LARRY: I bet my folks would've paid for all 400 courses.

Clarity

LARRY: I once made an effort to write long poems. When I stopped that, around 1970, I was willing to stop at any word. When I got that way, I think my stuff became clearer.

JACK: It's hard to find exact examples of this. We tried. But he feels that that was a very important moment for him. It's like walking down the street and being able to stop at any time. He's talking about openness and tentativeness.

LARRY: Five words . . . ten words.

JACK: One of the questions that arises from Larry's work is "What do these words have to do with one another?" They're all there on a page, and that means that you tend to experience them with some degree of unity. And then you have to make the connections between the words. And you can stop at any place. He's not committed to, say, fourteen lines, as in a sonnet.

RICHARD: He makes the reader work.

LARRY: That's like Language poetry, right?

JACK: What Larry's hearing when Richard says that are certain statements made by Language poets which have been used to justify Language poetry. And Larry hears that because he's familiar with those statements. Ron Silliman dedicated his book *In the American Tree* to Larry. Larry is thought of as a sort of father figure to Language poets.

LARRY: I'd rather be clear and communicative. Immediacy and force take precedence.

RICHARD: There's some subversion there, of clarity.

JACK: Subversive. It's a funny word because in the '50s to be subversive was a negative thing. Now it's positive. Every third woman writer has been called subversive, "of the dominant paradigm," or whatever.

LARRY: After that I read Olson's projective verse. Energy goes all the way across from the writer to the reader. Before that I thought of the idea of immediacy. Immediacy and force.

JACK: Olson sort of made me leave graduate school. This goes along with a story I tell. I won't tell the whole story. But at a certain point in the story I go over to a library shelf and take down Olson's *Maximus IV, V, VI*. They had a profound effect on me. And when I told Larry that I went to the library and took *Maximus IV, V, VI* off the shelf, he said "Uh oh." I didn't have to say any more.

Allen Ginsberg

BEVERLY: [To Larry] Wasn't the summer of 1968 when you met Allen Ginsberg?

JACK: Ginsberg did the narration for a film about Larry.

RICHARD: Ginsberg at one time visited Bates Road, not alone, but with his entourage, which was quite a bit for my mother to take, her having grown up in Salem, Massachusetts, influenced by Henry Wadsworth Longfellow . . . then to be visited by Ginsberg and entourage.

LARRY: My mother was apprehensive about meeting or welcoming in the house Ginsberg because he's gay—maybe what to say to him. I didn't think of who might be with him. I guess she didn't either. He had slipped on the ice on his farm in New York, so he was on crutches and sat down on the floor to play his portable organ. Gregory Corso came with him.[2]

RICHARD: But she let them in the house and was very considerate to them.

LARRY: This was two years before 1968.

Jack Foley

SHELLY: Jack, when did you first meet Larry?

JACK: In 1986. I was doing a poetry series in Berkeley. I'd admired Larry's work for many years but I hadn't met him. And I was given

his phone number, not his address, his phone number, to ask him to do a reading, so I called him. And the first thing Larry did was to clear his throat. Something like *Aaaa-UUUUh-ha*. And I thought to myself, what am I going to do? I knew he was disabled but didn't realize the disability extended to his speech. And it was sink or swim. I didn't know this but there was someone else on the line listening in case I needed help. I decided to understand Larry. And so I understood him.

I had him do a reading at the series and it worked out very well. In fact, Larry liked the idea so well he said, "Here's my two bucks, I'll come every week." So I brought Larry for three years to the series every week. So he was there for all the people who came. Also, we've done a lot of readings together.

We wanted to do a radio show for a long time, but we were unable to figure out quite how to do it. Then we figured a way. We had a microphone above Larry. And we actually videotaped it as well.

Oh, hey, do you know about this? One of Larry's poems, from *another time in fragments*, the title poem, was exhibited on the walls of the University Art Museum.

BEVERLY: The director at the University Art Museum in Berkeley put one of Larry's poems on the exterior walls of the art museum.

JACK: It appeared for about six months. They should have left it on permanently. They were doing a renovation on the inside and space was available on the outside walls. "Again dawn" is also in Larry's *Selected Poems*.

It was wonderful. Usually when you read a poem you have to look down. There you had to look up.

SHELLY: Did they get the spacing right?

JACK: Yes. More or less. They had to redo the spacing, but they went over it with Larry.

Serendipity

SHELLY: Do you set certain times aside for your writing, Larry?

LARRY: No. I can't concentrate on the keyboard enough so other people work for me.

---

[2]From Larry Eigner's letter, dated January 3, 1996.

It's very difficult for me now. I make a lot of mistakes.

JACK: Also, he condenses words, so that "could" for example will be "cld." And if you're making a lot of typos *and* condensing at the same time, it becomes pretty impenetrable. Larry even has difficulty making it out later. But people help and he memorizes. He has his poems in his head before they're committed to the typewriter.

LARRY: Partly anyway. Reading or listening is harder because you have to get at what they really mean.

JACK: He has more difficulty reading other people, it's harder because he has to get at what they really mean. For him writing is easier. And he's uncertain of the meaning of lots of texts. Especially since a lot of the texts that he reads are Language poetry. And these are difficult texts and he's uncertain about what these texts mean.

LARRY: I understand some things, but there might be something I'm missing. And I worry about that.

RICHARD: Are you onto any new direction? Are you going to be changing your style?

LARRY: Serendipity.

JACK: "Serendipity" is another big word for Larry. I mean, what happens is, I'll come over and he'll say "I got a poem on Friday." It's the same thing that used to happen when he was a kid. It's just "I got a poem." Something comes to him.

SHELLY: I was going to ask how you maintain a fresh perspective, Larry, but serendipity seems to answer that.

JACK: For Larry, it would be hard to maintain a *jaded* perspective.

* * *

JACK: Larry sort of regards himself as semi-retired, but he has for many books, for many years. But there was a point in his life where he felt that at one time he was working very hard all the time, and then there is a point where that doesn't happen anymore and the work ethic doesn't have as much of a sway upon him. That was something that happened in his life. When did that happen exactly? Was that after the operation? Larry had an operation on his left side. At one time his left side was wild.

LARRY: A few years ago. After I got to Berkeley.

JACK: Larry used to tell me that his whole left side was wild, which means *this* used to happen all the time [he waves his arm upward]. And the way he controlled it was *not* to think about it. But if he forgot it totally, it would go wild. But if he thought about it too much, it would go wild. So he had to maintain a balance between not thinking about it but thinking about it just enough to control it. And that kind of thing changed after the operation. His left side is no longer wild. But some of that seems to have affected his attitude about his poetry. He was less pushy about getting the poems out. Not that Larry's ever been pushy. And now words like *serendipity* become very important to him.

RICHARD: Do you have to control the poems in the same way you control your left side? Do you have to think about it in some middle ground?

LARRY: No.

JACK: The poems have a feeling of control about them. But I think for different reasons. And sometimes one finds things in them that Larry's forgotten he's put in. Ambiguities. Larry will sometimes not see the ambiguities in the poems which he may have seen at the time he wrote them. I have a friend, Jake Berry, a very powerful experimental poet whose poems are much more obscure than Larry's, but in some shorter poems, the word he used to describe them was the word "flash." And these words were in a space like Larry's, having nothing to do with one another, rather short and intense. And he saw them in a flash. And I think some of Larry's poems come to him kind of like that. In a flash.

Larry rarely edits his own books. Individual poems are worked on by Larry, but the books often are edited by someone else. And the order is determined by someone else. Larry approves of it, he looks at it.

*   *   *

SHELLY: What are some of the themes that you find yourself returning to time and again?

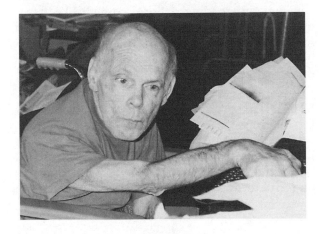

LARRY: Hindsight. I see different things in each poem. "Only the imagination is real."[3] I don't know.

JACK: He's not reflective about his poetry in that sense. It just happens, he says. Imagination is a big deal to him, though. Music is something that keeps coming back in your poetry.

SHELLY: Mostly classical?

LARRY: That's right.

JACK: Classical music primarily. Larry doesn't listen to jazz. Also, he will collage passages from other writers. There's a poem he wrote about Whitman that is mostly Whitman. "Whitman's Cry at Starvation" [see page 45]. The last lines to that. Anyway, that's a technique of Larry's too. He takes quotations from other writers and works them into the fabric of his verse. He

---

[3]This is a quotation from William Carlos Williams's poem, "Asphodel, That Greeny Flower," in *Pictures from Brueghel.*

sometimes acknowledges them and sometimes not.

*   *   *

SHELLY: Larry, can you recall one of your happiest memories?

LARRY: Quite a few, I guess. Reading Shakespeare.

RICHARD: Do you remember when you went to Maine and lived out on the promontory? Do you remember Robin Hood's Barn?

LARRY: Yeah. That was good.

RICHARD: What about Massachusetts Hospital School?

LARRY: After a while.

JACK: He hated physical therapy.

LARRY: Miss Trainer would get me up on rollerskates.

JACK: Her name was Miss *Trainer?* It sounds like an allegory.

RICHARD: Rollerskates?!

LARRY: I would feel guilty if I didn't work hard.

RICHARD: I guess that wasn't a happy moment then.

LARRY: I used to kick her in the shins . . . with the rollerskates.

BEVERLY: I thought it was a happy moment when you moved to Berkeley.

JACK: Incidentally, moving to Berkeley over his mother's objections. She felt that Larry would be too much of a burden and that he shouldn't do it.

RICHARD: My mother felt that Larry was her responsibility. She died in January 1993.

BEVERLY: After the death of Larry's father in 1978, Richard and I moved Larry from Massa-

chusetts to Berkeley and he has been living on McGee Street since then.

JACK: I should add that Richard and Beverly have done an enormous amount for Larry, in setting up the kind of house for him. They added a ramp for him.

Cerebral Palsy

SHELLY: What has been the biggest drawback about having cerebral palsy? Difficulties communicating? Being dependent on others?

LARRY: I don't know. Being jerky in my movements.

JACK: Larry likes to talk and at the poetry series he would talk to people. We would have arguments and one time the argument was about e. e. cummings. Well, Larry and I both love cummings but a lot of people reject cummings—they read him at sixteen and when they reject their sixteen-year-old selves they reject him. Also they don't get the Greek puns. The argument was getting pretty heated. And in the middle of it Larry said, it was amazing, "anyone lived in a pretty how town / (with up so floating many bells down)." Which is a couplet. The conversation suddenly stopped. I knew he was quoting a poem. But it's the most complicated sentence I've ever heard Larry say.

*   *   *

LARRY: Dependent as I am, all of my life, with little self-confidence/reliance (although for instance, I even pick up pencils off the floor)

being apt to make unexpected wrong moves, I expect people to make fewer mistakes or get things wrong than I do. And with me, ego/ altruism is a pretty thin coin. It's two sides close together, it sure seems to figure.[4]

*   *   *

JACK: Larry believes his cerebral palsy causes him to have a limited attention span. So when you or I are reading a book, and dislike it, we blame the author. Larry's not sure. It might not be the book. It might be him. It puts him in a relationship to a text that is different than other people's.

LARRY: I *think* I'm not getting something when I really am.

JACK: We will sometimes read something and talk about it. And Larry will tell me he doesn't understand it when it's clear to me that he does. But again that's part of the cerebral palsy, his uncertainty.

RICHARD: I think Larry has accepted the world as framed by his condition. I don't think he's capable of comparing what life would be like without cerebral palsy.

JACK: Remember he's had it since birth.

RICHARD: Although it was a disability, my mother was determined that he would not remain in the category of "uneducable."

JACK: He was on the floor until he got his wheelchair.

RICHARD: And it was a long time before he got his wheelchair.

LARRY: My goodness.

BEVERLY: They used a wheelbarrow, didn't they?

RICHARD: The Massachusetts school was a very primitive place and they did use wheelbarrows. Tuberculosis of the bone. There were all kinds

---

[4]From Larry Eigner's letter, dated January 3, 1996.

of disorders. One got the impression there was no other place for them to be.

BEVERLY: Larry's education would not have happened without his mother's philosophy.

JACK: His mother really pushed him. She deserves an enormous amount of credit.

RICHARD: My mother came with an immigrant family to Salem, Massachusetts. They lived very close to the landing from which the clipper ships sailed. She was the star pupil according to her account, which I believe, in Salem High School. And she completely absorbed the Puritan ethic and the work ethic and the high valuation of literary culture. My mother, and my father too, really connected with literary culture.

*   *   *

SHELLY: Larry, what are you working on now?

LARRY: I'm going back to the old stuff. New versions of the old stuff.

JACK: The last poet I saw him reading was W. H. Auden. It's funny, too, because there's an odd Olson connection. Auden edited the *Portable Greek Reader,* which Olson admired tremendously, and Olson actually recommended Auden as a poet.

LARRY: Corman and other people are against him.

JACK: So was William Carlos Williams.

RICHARD: Do you want to say something about Corman? He might just be your longest standing literary friend.

LARRY: Corman and Creeley. I've kept up with Corman all these years.

JACK: You correspond actively with Corman still.

RICHARD: Corman lived for many years in Japan. He published the magazine *Origin.*

JACK: He still lives in Japan. Larry has through his whole creative career been associated with the Black Mountain poets, which would be *Origin* magazine and *The Black Mountain Review* essentially, and Olson, Corman, Creeley, and others mentioned. All those people were perhaps more famous than Larry because they were able to push their careers more than Larry's been able to do. But all of them love his work.

RICHARD: You were published in *Poetry* magazine quite a bit in the 1960s. One editor in particular.

LARRY: Henry Rago.

RICHARD: He was the editor for several years.

JACK: Larry's poetry has an appeal that crosses over schools. Language poets and others. Duncan hated the Language poets, but he loved Larry's poetry. He manages to cross over a lot of different ways of writing, of thinking about poetry.

RICHARD: Can you say something about the Beat poets?

JACK: Have you heard the Kit Robinson story? Kit Robinson, because he'd seen Larry's work in *The New American Poetry,* thought he was an incredible hipster. He thought he was a Beat poet. When he met him he was quite surprised. They thought you were a street poet and a hipster, Larry.

LARRY: Colloquial way of writing.

*   *   *

SHELLY: Do you have a philosophy you'd like to share with your readers?

JACK: Larry is very concerned about what to say to the young. He's also very concerned about ecology.

LARRY: Without short term, there'll be no long run. We have to be concerned about these things.

JACK: Who would you tell young people to read?

LARRY: My favorites. Hart Crane—he's magic. William Carlos Williams. Ezra Pound. Maybe Wallace Stevens.

JACK: Larry was reading Olson. Olson writes long poems using space. Larry writes short poems using space in a very similar way. You can see connections between the way they use space. All of this ultimately goes back to Mallarmé, "Un Coup De Dès," which is the great ancestor of this "field" verse.

*　　*　　*

SHELLY: Do you have any closing remarks, Larry?

LARRY: Since I've been at Berkeley I've had two hearing tests. I think there's a correlation between palsy and some kind of trouble hearing.

RICHARD: Here's your chance at final words.

JACK: But you have to be able to stop anywhere.

LARRY: Thank you. 🐛

---

from the sustaining air

fresh air

There is the clarity of a shore
And shadow,　　mostly,　　brilliance

summer
　　　　the billow of August

When, wandering, I look from my page

I say nothing

　　when asked

I am, finally, an incompetent, after all

(From *From the Sustaining Air*)

Manna　　What is?

Virtual bread?
　　Daily? Angel food?

it takes some imagination
　　–some–to turn
crowds into company
　　and so much too
　　　　that I can't try

[150 copies of this poem were made. 100 were distributed at foodbanks in Berkeley, California, and Charleston, Illinois. tel-let, Bread and Poetry, 2, November 1995.]

Readiness / Enough / Depends on

Mankind is so numerous by now, and enough of us are more active than ever, hopeless or just hyperactive, people are getting farther and farther from being able to get together enough to stop global warming and its consequences, doomsday or just about, for instance, yet the long run is made of many short terms, never could there be next week without tomorrow, and the momentary is maybe about as meaningful as what lasts for some generations. The more you do the less you see, too, the narrower is your tunnel of vision (vision is itself the more blurred the more you're in motion), as well as vice versa, and while doing anything you're more or less specializing, even when you try to see a whole it may be like the biosphere it's so big and/or complicated you can't get enough detail to be realistic about it. So, all in all, enough is enough. It's great enough to keep your head in the air while your feet are on the ground.

—Larry Eigner, February 1995

P.S. And, after all, it seems a good many people, more than a few, have done about all they could about the environment, for instance, before and after Rachel Carson.

In late March '95 came some news of biological evidence of global warming in addition to the physical evidence, i.e., El Niño every year lately instead of just every three years or so, increase in malaria from more mosquitos due to more rainfall.

Late March '95

(Statement forthcoming in *Poetry USA,* 1996)

Larry Eigner, 1996

Eulogy

In his own deftly-chosen words my brother was "palsied from a hard birth." The severity of his injuries set the frame and shaped the course of his life. The qualities which set him apart from other victims of misfortune were quite different from conventionally "good" qualities. Rather, they were a strong will; a determination to be a giving as well as a receiving person but on his own terms; the insight, coupled with a healthy irreverence, which enabled him to perceive the ironies of life; an ear for hearing and an eye and mind for seeing the sounds, sights, and patterns of his world.

My brother was able, by an alchemy as wonderful as would be the transformation of lead into gold, to transmute the spasticity which framed his earthly existence into the binding forces which became the fields and fires of his poetry. I choose to believe in his realization that he had created out of the materials of the human spirit a current which flowed into the river of humane culture which is deathless and immortal.

—*Richard Eigner, February 6, 1996*

BIBLIOGRAPHY

Poetry:

From the Sustaining Air, edited by Robert Creeley, Divers Press (Mallorca), 1953, Coincidence Press, 1988.

Look at the Park, privately printed, 1958.

On My Eyes, preface by Denise Levertov, Jonathan Williams (Highlands, North Carolina), 1960.

The Music, the Rooms, Desert Review Press, 1965.

Six Poems, Wine Press (Portland, Oregon), 1967.

another time in fragments, Fulcrum Press, 1967.

The- / Towards Autumn, Black Sparrow Press, 1967.

air / the trees, illustrated by Bobbie Creeley, Black Sparrow Press, 1968.

The Breath of Once Live Things: In the Field with Poe, Black Sparrow Press, 1968.

A Line that May Be Cut: Poems from 1965, Circle Press, 1968.

Flat and Round, Pierrepont Press, 1969, corrected edition, 1980.

Valleys / branches, Big Venus (London), 1969.

Over and Over, ends; or, As the Wind May Sound, Restau Press, 1970.

Poem Nov. 1968, Tetrad Press, 1970.

Circuits—A Microbook, Athanor Press, 1971.

looks like / nothing / the shadow / through air, illustrated by Ronald King, Circle Press, 1972.

Selected Poems, edited by Samuel Charters and Andrea Wyatt, Oyez, 1972.

words touching / ground under, Hellric Publications, 1972.

What You Hear, Edible Magazine, 1972.

shape / shadow / elements / move, Black Sparrow Press, 1973.

No Radio, Lodestar Press, 1974.

Things Stirring Together or Far Away (poetry and prose), Black Sparrow Press, 1974.

Anything on Its Side, Elizabeth Press (New Rochelle, New York), 1974.

suddenly / it gets light / and dark in the street: poems 1961–1974, Green Horse Press, 1975.

My God the Proverbial (poetry and prose), L Publications, 1975.

the music variety, Roxbury Poetry Enterprises (Newton, Massachusetts), 1976.

watching / how or why, Elizabeth Press, 1977.

The World and Its Streets, Places, Black Sparrow Press, 1977.

cloud, invisible air, Station Hill Press, 1978.

Flagpole / Riding, Stingy Artist, 1978.

Heat Simmers Cold &, Orange Export, 1978.

Running Around, Burning Deck, 1978.

lined up bulk senses, Burning Deck, 1979.

time / details / of a tree, Elizabeth Press, 1979.

now there's / a morning / hulk of the sky, Elizabeth Press, 1981.

earth / birds (forty-six poems written between May 1964 and June 1972), illustrated by Ronald King, Circle Press, 1981.

Waters / Places / A Time, edited by Robert Grenier, Black Sparrow Press, 1983.

A Count of Some Things, Score Publications, 1991.

Windows / Walls / Yard / Ways, edited by Robert Grenier, Black Sparrow Press, 1994.

Other:

Murder Talk. The Reception. Suggestions for a Play. Five Poems. Bed Never Self Made, Duende Press (Placitas, New Mexico), 1964.

The Memory of Yeats, Blake, DHL, Circle Press, 1965.

(Contributor) *Free Poems among Friends,* Detroit Artist's Workshop, 1966.

Clouding (short stories), Samuel Charters, 1968.

Farther North (short stories), Samuel Charters, 1969.

(Contributor) *Panama Gold,* Zero Publications, 1969.

Andrea Wyatt Sexton, *A Bibliography of Works by Larry Eigner, 1937–1969,* Oyez, 1970.

Country / Harbor / Quiet / Act / Around (selected prose), edited by Barrett Watten, THIS Press, 1978.

areas lights heights: writings 1954–1989, edited by Benjamin Friedlander, Roof Books (New York), 1989.

Irving P. Leif, *Larry Eigner: A Bibliography of His Works,* Scarecrow Press, 1989.

Eigner's work appears in more than thirty anthologies, including *New American Poetry,* Grove Press, 1960; *Anthology of Contemporary American Poetry,* Doubleday, 1965; *Poems Now,* Kulchur Press, 1966; *Inside Outer Space,* Anchor Books, 1970; *The Voice That Is Within Us,* Bantam, 1970; *Postmodern American Poetry,* Norton, 1994; *From the Other Side of the Century,* Sun Moon Press, 1994. Contributor to numerous periodicals, including *Black Mountain Review, Chicago Review, Origin, Paris Review, Poetry,* and *Poetry USA.*

Christopher Fry

1907-

The Early Days

Two days before I was going to have a birthday for the eighty-eighth time on my eighty-seventh anniversary, I reckoned (if my calculation isn't hopelessly wrong) that I had used up 31,668 days of life, or 760,032 hours, which really doesn't seem very much. And of those hours I suppose I have slept about 253,344, leaving me 506,688 hours in which to make the best of things. Unfortunately, it seems to me, at a moderate estimate, that I have also frittered away or misused about 380,016 of those, leaving me no more than 126,672 well accounted for. I am being very lenient with myself even so. What an improvement there might have been if I had really got on with it. Got on with what, you may ask? Well, let us suppose there really is something called a Vocation—or even, to be more serious still, a Calling—not something which simply interests us, or rouses our enthusiasm (though it may, perhaps, begin with that)—but a kind of innermost instruction, which we are aware of even when we are ignoring or even deliberately stifling it. At the end of it all, at the end of the 31,668 days, or whatever it may be, it's salutary to look back and see by what linkage of events or interposition of other lives, and to what extent, we have been persuaded to follow the inner instruction, or have failed to keep it. "The persuasion of our days" I called it in a very early play, *The Firstborn*, where Moses says: "We must each find our separate meaning / In the persuasion of our days / Until we meet in the meaning of the world."

What might be called the initial sound of the Calling came very early on, while I was still at my kindergarten. I've been told I wrote a little play for the other seven- or eight-year-olds to perform. I don't remember anything about it, but forty years later the vice principal of that kindergarten quoted to me an unforgettable line from it, which I have now forgotten. And all through my teens I was scribbling away; useless, untutored stuff—the teaching of English at school was confined pretty much to rules of grammar and analysis. I didn't properly know what poetry was—neither did any of my schoolmasters, I fancy, except perhaps the French master—though as I approached seventeen something in the nature of it began to emerge, enough to get me into the *Public School Book of Verse* alongside verses by another adolescent called Bernard Miles, who became Lord Miles of the Mermaid Theatre. Sometimes it seemed that the words were forming themselves

Christopher Fry, 1993

The author in 1909

almost without my volition—as, for instance, when I was writing some verses about the school field, I wrote "And heard the crack of bat and ball contesting / Cold as an iceberg on our warm content," and then bringing my mind to it changed it to "And heard the crack of bat and ball contesting / Cold as an icedrop on our warm content." But I should have understood better what I was doing if someone had had the sense to advise me not to give up Latin (which I had rather enjoyed, as far as I enjoyed doing any work at all) to take up German, which unfortunately I soon lost patience with. The Calling was still trying to make sense of me, not helped by the indiscipline of my mind.

I wrote three plays in my school years: one in blank verse, I forget about what, another called *Armageddon,* about a group of men and women who had escaped from a devastated world

onto a rocky island (almost as though I were imagining the aftermath of the atom bomb twenty years before it was invented), and a comedy in the style of—in fact slightly satirising—J. M. Barrie. And in my penultimate year I put on a musical, for Speech Day as we called the prize giving: it was the time of Nigel Playfair's great success at the Lyric, Hammersmith with Gay's *The Beggar's Opera*. It was also the time when Oxford Bags, flannel trousers about twenty inches round the turn-ups, were in fashion. So I called the musical *The Baggers' Uproar*. The hero of the piece refused to follow the fashion, and the girls all deserted the Oxford Baggers and made a set at the chap who wore narrow trousers. A role in which I had cast myself. The following year we performed a sequel, which, since the sequel to *The Beggar's Opera* had been called *Polly,* was titled *Golly!*

And so schooldays came to an end. A time of take-whatever-turned-up followed. It would all have been fairly disastrous if it hadn't been for Amy Walmsley, the principal of the Froebel Teachers Training College, of which the kindergarten had been a part, who out of sheer anxiety for my welfare invited me to be a supernumerary member of the staff. She paid for me to have shorthand lessons, a skill I never mastered, and recommended me as a temporary tutor to Lord Ampthill's nephew when his prep school closed during a polio epidemic, and from this I went on to do a holiday-time tutoring of the grandson of the Persian explorer Sir Percy Cox. It was all pure bluff on my part. So how was the Calling prospering? Very poorly. Going back to the Froebel Training College, among all the smells and sounds of my childhood, where any writing I did was read and criticised by the head English teacher, seemed to send me back ten years, and to sap what little confidence I had managed to attain during my last year at school. But then Amy Walmsley saw an advertisement for a post at a kind of theatre and social centre at Bath called Citizen House run by a forceful redheaded lady called Consuelo de Reyes. Here I was office boy and occasional actor. My last job of the day was to take the office mail to the post office to catch the midnight post, and my attendance at rehearsals was spasmodic. In consequence when I appeared as the Bo'sun in the opening scene of *The Tempest* I dried completely, and the noise of the stage thunder and roaring wind made a vain hope out of the prompter. I could only bellow any nautical terms that I happened to know, which were few, such as "Heave-ho" and "Pull up the slack!" As the rest of the actors depended on me for their cues the ship and the scene sank in record time, the audience with it. But I was at least slightly back in pursuit of the Calling. The Nine Muses, though rather down-at-heel, hovered in the doorways of Citizen House. There were the Radcliff sisters, part of a literary family quite well known before the 1914 war. A middle-aged poetess called Lady Margaret Sackville asked me to show her how to work the hot-water geyser in the bathroom, and I acted in one of her plays, called *Alicia and the Twilight,* in which I played a character called The Poet, capital *T* capital *P,* though I have no memory now of what the play was about, even if I knew then. The writer of drawing-room ballads, Fred Weatherley, appeared—author of *Friend O' Mine,* which I knew from my brother's rendering of it in our musical evenings at home, so it felt rather like rubbing shoulders with the great.

Edith Craig, Ellen Terry's daughter, came and went. I shook hands in the Pump Room with G. K. Chesterton. There was also a visiting elderly (or so she seemed to me) actress called Sybil Ruskin who had played at the Old Vic. She directed me in a one-act play about people in a railway carriage. My part was a supercilious upper-class businessman, as I remember, and I was astonished when Miss Ruskin told the other actors to notice how delicately restrained my performance was—which as I well knew was because I hadn't the faintest notion what I was supposed to be doing.

Then came a moment when two possible directions presented themselves at the same time. Sybil Ruskin was joining a comedy company which was going on a tour of the Riviera, and she had suggested that I should join them. If I had done so she would quickly have found out why I had given such a delicately restrained performance. But at the same time there came an invitation to join the staff of a prep school in Surrey. Sir Percy Cox was an old friend of

"Pierrots" (Fry is on the left), 1919

the founder of the school, and had mentioned my name to him, and he had passed it on to the headmaster. The year was the end of 1927, or perhaps the beginning of 1928. It was an eccentric world then, or perhaps the devious workings of Fate were less scrupulous. I had never sat for an examination in my life (my headmaster had thought I would do better to spend my time reading in the school library). I don't even remember that I went for an interview. I believe I simply turned up on the day appointed, which was in the spring term, 1928. There followed two and a half to three years trying to keep up with the brighter boys.

And how was the Calling getting on? Well, it was making faint amateurish efforts to keep going. I wrote a couple of plays for the boys to act: the first was in verse, I think—a kind of imitation mediaeval morality play; the second was a comical piece called *The Tragedy of a Retired Admiral.* I also wrote the words for a choral work to the music of a fellow member of the staff called Michael Tippett. But I had begun to feel cornered; I even began to feel that I had taught myself almost as much as the boys were ready to digest. Besides, I found I had £10 in the bank (my salary was £120 a year) and thought the time had come to launch myself into the adult world. The poet W. H. Davies, and a journalist called Rodney Bennet, presently to be the father of the composer Richard Rodney Bennet, had given me a letter of introduction to St. John Adcock, editor of a magazine called the *Bookman,* who in desperation to get me out of his office (I hadn't known how to leave politely) had given me two books to review: one a new translation of the poems of Francois Villon, the other Evelyn Waugh's *Vile Bodies,* which I gave an unenthusiastic notice. But almost at once St. John Adcock died, and the new editor had his own tribe of reviewers.

Here I must retrace my steps a little. Something else had happened, before I left the prep school, which had made some effect on the pursuit of the Calling. I had met Robert Gittings, and what follows is part of the obituary which I wrote for the *Independent* after his death:

At the beginning of 1929 the matron of the prep school I was teaching at lent me a copy of a literary magazine called the *Bermondsey Book.* In it were three poems by

an eighteen-year-old schoolboy called Robert Gittings. He had asked for criticism, but the editor thought printing them was comment enough. I was twenty-one, thought myself a schoolmaster, and wrote a letter to him about the poems. He took the letter to his English master, George Mallaby, who later became high commissioner in New Zealand, and they decided the writer was a retired Oxford don of about seventy. It took a few more letters and a brief visit on his way home from the St. Edward's School, Oxford, OTC [Officers' Training Corps] camp ("Having a ripping time," he wrote on the postcard giving the time of his arrival) to settle to a friendship which lasted for the next sixty-three years, and almost immediately made for exchanges of thought my schooldays hadn't provided. The following Easter we made a walk together from Stratford-upon-Avon across the Cotswolds, calling on W. H. Davies, his wife Emma, and their cat Pharaoh, for tea at Nailsworth (I had met Davies the year before), and continuing through the Forest of Dean to the Wye Valley, where at Tintern Abbey Robert led me deeper into Wordsworth than so far I had ventured.

In 1930 he went up to Jesus College, Cambridge, and won the Chancellor's Prize for poetry with a poem called *The Roman Road,* as Tennyson had done a hundred years before with *Timbuctoo.* Quiller-Couch recommended it for publication to the Oxford University Press with thirty shorter poems. In the summer vacation of 1932 he was lent an empty Victorian rectory in Somerset and invited me to join him there, suggesting that a month trying to write something of my own was not really much riskier than the odd-job sort of life I had been leading since I gave up being a schoolmaster. He was correcting the proofs of *The Roman Road* and writing a play about Aesop. This good example, his scholarly mind (he became a research fellow the next year), and the copy of *The Waste Land* which he had taken with him, all helped to give me the sense of direction I had lacked, though it would be another five years before I began to make anything of it.

I did begin a verse play about Aucassin and Nicolette during this time in the Somerset village. It contains one immortal line which I stole from the village woman who "did for me" before I was married. There had been a report in the newspaper of an elderly man being enticed away from his wife by a young girl. I said, "Really, Mrs. Ashby, he's old enough to know better." She replied: "Huh! While they has the strength to crawl a leg over a piece of straw they'll keep on to the last." (It seems to me a more bloodcurdling line than anything by John Webster.)

The £10 I had started with soon vanished, and the next five years were such an eccentric salmagundi of doing whatever turned up that I can't give you an orderly sequence. It included staging productions at Tunbridge Wells—which included the English premiere of Shaw's *Village Wooing.* Shaw, who had never heard of me, incomprehensibly gave me the rights to produce it when, as soon as I heard he had written a new play, I cheekily wrote to ask if I might. I wrote a couple of pantomimes in aid of the Kent and Sussex Hospital, and three other musical amateur shows, and then (I hardly knew how) found myself writing the lyrics and music for a piece called *She Shall Have Music* at the Saville Theatre in London; and soon after directing an even worse musical comedy which I regret to tell you was called *How Do, Princess!* A disastrous failure. The composer ended up in jail for bigamy; the producer ended up running a chain of lucky-charm stalls on the south coast; and the ancient stage director (he had worked with Henry Irving) was given a new set of false teeth by the British Legion, who also set him up in a mushroom farm where he died almost as quickly as the mushrooms grew.

The Calling, as you can imagine, had little chance against all this. However, an unexpected turn of events pointed me in what proved to be a helpful direction. I had a second cousin called Gwendolen who organised Dr. Barnardo's Young Helpers League in Tunbridge Wells. She persuaded the Barnardo Council to pay me a small salary to give lectures up and down the country about the work of the Homes, and to edit a magazine for schools, using work from the school magazines. I found at Christ's Hospital the poet Keith Douglas, who was killed so soon after in the war. They were good, footloose days in the early thirties, even if not exactly what the Calling intended—driving a none-too-roadworthy car along the almost empty roads—putting up where I could find. I remember one place, not much more than a shack on the seashore, almost like Daniel Peggotty's upturned boat on Yarmouth sands. And another

In Clapham Fields, 1926

tiny cottage, where I was given a huge supper, a night's sleep, and a cooked breakfast, and when I came to pay was told the price was nine pence, less than four pence in modern money. When I said "That can't be," the cottager said "Well, you're working for a good cause and I like to scatter me roses, botheration." I like the diffidence of "botheration." Then there was a bungalow at Whitstable. A rather genteel landlady this time, who stood looking through the window at my muddy car and said "Sometime I 'ave a £500 car stand h'outside 'ere. And one day Gladys Cooper come 'ere and said 'Can you put me h'up for the naight?' and I said 'Well, I 'ave faive people sleeping in my double bed already.'"

Out of all this came a commission to write a play about the life of Dr. Barnardo. By now I was in fairly poor shape to answer the stern voice of the Calling calling me to order. But I wrote the play, which was in prose, though it had a verse prologue and a few linking passages in verse, such as two lines describing the street arabs the young Tom Barnardo encountered: "They thieve their boyhood from the purse of time / And horde it against the cold and open skies." I directed this in various towns up and down the country. One of the performers when we did it at Bristol was a delightful sixteen-year-old called Deborah Trimmer, who turned into the film actress Deborah Kerr. Encouraged by the little regular income, I married. But everything depended now on some *deus ex machina* making the right move. And move he did, in the person of the vicar of the village where we lived, the Reverend Lilford Causton, who (knowing I suppose about the Barnardo play, this is how the linking goes) came to the door to ask me to write a play for the village to perform for the church's jubilee year. What is more he provided the subject in the story of St. Cuthman; and I wrote *The Boy with a Cart.* We performed it in the summer of 1938, and the following year Bishop Bell, George Bell of Chichester, invited us to do it in his palace garden. It set a number of other bells ringing: Oxford University Press published it, the director E. Martin Browne asked me to write a play for the Tewkesbury Festival, I met T. S. Eliot. In a very small way it was almost like Cuthman in *The Boy with a Cart* finding the kingpost swinging into place so that he could go on building his church at Steyning, though I couldn't then have imagined that fifty-five years later I should be listening to American drama students performing it in Florida.

Here is that speech of Cuthman's:

Gradually I was aware of someone in
The doorway and turned my eyes that way and
  saw
Carved out of the sunlight a man who stood
Watching me, so still that there was not
Other such stillness anywhere on the earth,
So still that the air seemed to leap
At his side. He came towards me, and the sun
Flooded its banks and flowed across the
  shadow.
He asked me why I stood alone. His voice
Hovered on memory with open wings
And drew itself up from a depth of silence
As though it had longtime lain in a vein of
  gold.
I told him: It is the kingpost.
He stretched his hand upon it. At his touch
It lifted to its place. There was no sound.
I cried out, and I cried at last "Who are you?"
I heard him say "I was a carpenter" . . .
There under the bare walls of our labour
Death and life were knotted in one strength
Indivisible as root and sky.

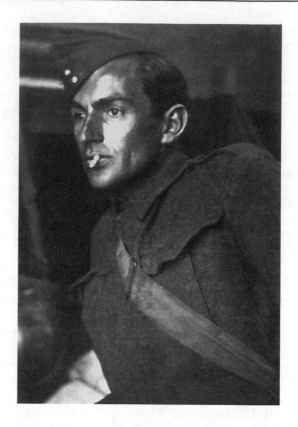

1942

The play I started to write for the Tewkesbury Festival was about the release of the Israelites from Egypt—this was 1938 and our minds were full of the only too little we knew of the Nazis and anti-Semitism—but then the Tewkesbury organisers asked instead for a pageant-play about the history of the Abbey. Martin Browne wrote the scenario and I filled in the words. It was called *The Tower* and no script now exists. About that time, too, in July 1938, I wrote some sonnets: a few of them survive and I've included one of them, because of the trouble the world still has from the Serbs' ambition for a Greater Serbia. I wrote this on August 4—date of the outbreak of the 1914 Great War—August 4, 1938: a sonnet addressed to Gavrilo Prinzip, the student who assassinated Archduke Ferdinand of Austria and his wife, which led to the horror of World War I. After his arrest Prinzip had said: "I hope that the fatal revolver shots will open the way to the Serbian army to march and occupy Bosnia, for the land is destined by its inclinations and traditions to belong to Greater Serbia."

Gavrilo Prinzip

At first when your living days were lifting you
To reach the human measure of the bone
You did not guess that all the time you grew
You carried other deaths beside your own.
But as the lethal hour swung into view
And your hot pulse knocked noisily between
Boyhood and manhood, then at least you knew
Three deaths now pressed where your one
  death had been.
You never knew the millions which you bore
Even in your childhood body while you played,
Or in your early tears what tears were piled,
Or when you fell what falling. Your huge core
Was never felt by you. But when she prayed
How heavily your mother stooped with child.

Well, only a month more than a year after I wrote that, the *second* World War began, on September 3, 1939. That summer we had performed *The Boy with a Cart* at Chichester, and *The Tower* at Tewkesbury. By the time the war started my wife, Phyl, and I had moved from Sussex to Oxfordshire. I was writing a series of children's plays called *The Tall Hill* for Geoffrey Dearmer of the BBC. And then by one of those unlikely twists of fate, the awful *How Do, Princess!*, like a ham-fisted conjuror producing a rabbit out of a hat, performed a good trick. The leading man in *How Do, Princess!* had been the actor Leslie French. (In 1929 I had seen him playing Ariel to Gielgud's Prospero at the Old Vic.) And now I found he was directing at the Oxford Playhouse. I went to see him and he asked if I could write some funny sketches for Pamela Brown, which I did, funny or not. When French went off to make a film he suggested to the Playhouse that I should take over his job. It meant riches—a salary of £6 a week, directing a different play each week. So though the typewriter was idle a different kind of answer was being made to the Calling: a greater knowledge of the theatre. For the six months of 1940 when Britain seemed so near to defeat I worked at the Playhouse. In December I was called up into the noncombatant branch [NCC] of the Pioneer Corps. The other Calling for a time fell silent, though the colonel let us rehearse and perform as much as I had written of *The Firstborn*, with the actor Michael Gough, who was in the same NCC company, playing Moses. What the sergeant major thought of it is hard to imagine. For a time, when we were stationed at Derby, a little woman called Miss Bott let me use her sitting room, to read in quiet away from the canteens, and something of that reading became useful to the Calling when the war was over. (It was Miss Bott who chanted to me her parody of a verse from Tennyson's *In Memoriam*. Instead of: "I hold this truth, whate'er befall / I feel it, when I sorrow most; / 'Tis better to have loved and lost / Than never to have loved at all," Miss Bott's version was: "I hold this truth, whate'er befall / I heard it from an old Welsh bard / It's better to have hummed and haa'd / Than never to have hummed at all.")

One of the books I was reading in her sitting room was *Holy Living and Holy Dying*, by Jeremy Taylor. In it he recounts the story of the widow of Ephesus, which he in turn had read in Petronius. And at the end of the war, after I had completed *The Firstborn*, I used the story to make a one-act play which I called *A Phoenix Too Frequent*. Done first at Martin Browne's Poets' Theatre, the Mercury in Notting Hill Gate, and then at the end of 1946 revived at the Arts Theatre Club, with Paul Scofield playing in London for the first time, I think. It led Alec Clunes (who had made such an invigorating place out of that little theatre during the last of the war years) to make me staff dramatist for a year, which altogether silenced me for those twelve months. Phyl and I had made a winter crossing of an irritable North Sea to attend the opening of *Phoenix* in Gothenburg, where I had my first unpromising taste of international fame. We came fraily down the gangplank to a group of newspapermen who in the cold early morning light eagerly asked me to give them my opinion of Swedish literature. I wished it had been Norway (Ibsen) or Denmark (Hans Christian Andersen). Strindberg had deserted me. And so, for a few months while I directed two plays at the Arts, I had the Calling, though I was now being paid to pursue it. But then, in the bitterest of all winters, 1946 to 1947, Phyl and I had been lent a flat in Landsdowne Crescent, Holland Park, as a refuge from our primitive cottage on an exposed hill in the Cotswolds where I had just begun to write *The Lady's Not for Burning*.

The flat turned out to be pretty exposed too. There was no heating except a two-barred electric fire, and very soon all the water pipes in the house froze. We had to carry a bucket down to the water hydrant in the pavement outside Holland Park tube station. That has always seemed to me why the first act of *The Lady* doesn't flow as happily as I should like. I'm always thankful when the audience comes back after the first interval. One day I will pare Act I down to make the play into two acts instead of three.

I had written the character of Jennet for Pamela Brown, and a rarer actress for the part there could never be. She had to withdraw from playing it in the first production at the Arts Theatre Club because rehearsal dates of an Aldous Huxley play, which she had agreed to do, started sooner than she had expected. I had to wait for 1949 when she played it with Gielgud at the Globe, or as we should now say, with Gielgud at the Gielgud. So here I was in 1949, the Calling placated for the time being with a play in the West End. And why had it turned out to be the play it was? Well, remember how soon after the war it came. The play, though dressed as though after the Hundred Years' War, was for me about the aftermath of the war we had just emerged from. Thomas Mendip was like the tramps I used to see after the 1914 War walking the roads in their old army greatcoats. It was a comedy, but how could we go back to laughter after the devastation, the striving, the pain, the horror of the Holocaust? That was what I believe it was about. John Gielgud said after the end of the run that he wished he had done it in a kind of modern dress. And at the University of Berkeley, California, a few years ago, the set was a house that had been bombed, the windows askew, looking out onto the springtime heavens or the vast night sky.

A few weeks ago I was sent the programme of a concert reading of *The Lady,* which the American actress Uta Hagen had recently put on in New York. In the programme she had reprinted a wireless talk I had given in 1948, in which I was making an early effort to put my point of view:

> The inescapable dramatic situation for us all is that we have no idea what our situation is. We are plunged into an existence fantastic to the point of nightmare. . . . We get used to it. We get broken into it so gradually we scarcely notice it . . . and yet the only believable thing is nothing at all . . . but then I see my hand lying on the table in front of me, and that one thing alone, the first impact of a hand, is more

In 1952

dramatic than *Hamlet.* What can I think then when the rest of creation comes to me, when the full phantasmagoria of the commonplace breaks over my head? . . . Poetry is the language in which man explores his own amazement. It has the virtue of being able to say twice as much as prose in half the time, and the drawback, if you don't happen to give it your full attention, of seeming to say half as much in twice the time. And if you accept my proposition that reality is altogether different from our stale view of it, we can say that poetry is the language of reality.

When rehearsals for *The Lady* started at the Arts Theatre Club in February 1948 I was already letting things get out of hand, as no sensible follower of a Calling should do. I had undertaken to write and direct a play for the Canterbury Festival which would have to go into rehearsal in May, and so far I had only roughed out a few pages of it; I was taking classes at the Central School of Speech Training in the little room behind the organ at the Albert Hall, though what exactly I was supposed to be teaching wasn't altogether clear to me; and I was discussing with Martin Browne the casting of *The Firstborn* for production at the Edinburgh Festival. It had been quite hard to think up a story for the Canterbury play. Canterbury had run out of dramatically suitable Archbishops. At the last moment I concocted a piece which I called *Thor, with Angels,* about the coming of Christianity to the Jutes of Kent. Jutes and early Britons aren't the most exhilarating characters to write about, so I also threw into the cast list the Arthurian magician Merlin, who would have been, I think, about two hundred years old at the time. And I gave him a long speech, to mark the passage of time dividing the two halves of the play, a speech which is perhaps pertinent to this matter of a Calling. In it I tried to speak of the human mind's pursuit after some comprehension of the creating power; the evolution of purpose, perhaps it could be called. Here is just the opening of it:

> Welcome, sleep;
> Welcome into the winter head of the world
> The sleep of Spring, which grows dreams,
> Nodding trumpets, blowing bells,
> A jingle of birds whenever the sun moves,
> Never so lightly; all dreams,
> All dreams out of slumbering rock:
> Lambs in a skittle prance, the hobbling rook
> Like a witch picking sticks,
> And pinnacle-ears the hare
> Ladling himself along in the emerald wheat:
> All dreams out of the slumbering rock,
> Each dream answering to a shape
> Which was in dream before the shapes were
>   shapen;
> Each growing obediently to a form,
> To its own sound, shrill or deep, to a life
> In water or air, in light or night or mould;
> By sense or thread perceiving,
> Eye, tendril, nostril, ear; to the shape of the
>   dream
> In the ancient slumbering rock.
> And above the shapes of life, the shape
> Of death, the singular shape of the dream
>   dissolving,
> Into which all obediently come.
> And above the shape of death, the shape of
>   the will
> Of the slumbering rock, the end of the
>   throes of sleep
> Where the stream of the dream wakes in the
>   open eyes
> Of the sea of the love of the morning of
>   the God.

As I remember, we rehearsed the play in May 1948 and played it in June, and early in July the BBC sent me off on a journey down the Rhine, from Holland through Germany: to write a programme about the devastated towns and cities I found there. (When it was broadcast no one heard it through, because soon after it started it was interrupted by the announcement of the birth of Prince Charles.) I was back from Germany in time for rehearsals of *The Firstborn* and its production at the Edinburgh Festival, followed by a tour, I think. And by then John Gielgud had started on the casting and Oliver Messel on the designing of *The Lady's Not for Burning.*

Laurence Olivier & "Venus Observed"

It must surely have been early in 1949 that Laurence Olivier asked me to write a play for the opening of his management at the St. James Theatre (of blessed memory), though I can find no letter to give us a certain date. *The Lady's Not for Burning* would have been on its pre-London tour—that was the play which was of some assistance to Margaret Thatcher's speech writers. It came into the Globe Theatre (now happily to be called the Gielgud) on May 11 of that year, so it is likely to have been shortly after this that I started to work on *Venus Observed.* At any rate, in a letter dated June 9, 1949, Olivier was writing: "I thrill very much at the implied possibility in your message; great brains stirring; wondrous thoughts flashing like lightning; the Muse beaming on you like a sunlamp. . . ." Perhaps I should tell you before we go any further that his epistolary style was not given to understatement, either in saying what he felt or in the affectionate warmth with which he addressed his friends. But things were not to go as aboundingly as either of us had hoped. Soon after I had started work Peter Brook asked if I would translate a play by Anouilh called *L'Invitation au Chateau.* I explained that I was enclasped with *Venus.* But then I had a creative block. Peter heard of this and said it would be good to take my hands off her for a bit, and then I could return to her refreshed. This led to the translation *Ring Round the Moon,* and to my running very late with the play for Olivier. By August 17, he was keeping up a brave front though he had every right to be feeling anxious. The play was tabled to open his new management at the St. James's Theatre in mid January. So far he had seen only a small part of Act I. By September 5 there were signs of strain. He wrote: "It sounds the most churlish thing ever, but really, if you wouldn't mind, I would enormously appreciate having *Venus* finished as soon as possible, as the soonest possible moment we can get on making plans for it will not be too soon for me in the situation in which I am at present." You will notice that some of his sparkle had left him, and the letter was typed by his secretary. He even began to think of doing an earlier play of mine, *The Firstborn,* as a kind of safety net. I evidently must have reassured him, though it isn't until October 22 that he was able to write: "I am really overjoyed to hear of the approaching finish of your play . . . you won't fail to send [it to] me the moment it's finished, will you; act by act, if you like. I've never been so excited about anything." I can't say that I felt the same; there were things in the play that I was unhappy with, and one character who was insisting on being a great

trouble to me, and continued to be so. I had written to Olivier to say that I would type out Act II, and post it to him before the end of the week. But by then I had got carried along into the third act, and dared not stop while it was in some kind of flow; so the second act remained untyped and unsent. I received a parcel. In it was a large typewriter ribbon, far too big for my 1917 Corona portable; a brush to clean the keys, and a round flat eraser. With them was an undated note saying "Dear fellow, Let me know if there is anything else you need won't you? I'm not making you nervous, am I? I do hope I'm not making you nervous. My prayers and affection are with you and for you. L." Was there ever such tolerance and restraint? I evidently got the completed script to him by the end of October, hardly more than a month before rehearsals were due to begin. At any rate on October 24 Vivien Leigh wrote to us to thank us for a message we had sent her for the first night of *A Streetcar Named Desire.* She said "Do please come and see me before I look and feel too old for the part!!

Christopher Fry and his wife, Phyl, with Jig, their Yorkshire terrier,
in the London house "Little Venice," mid-1950s

Oh, how exciting about 'Venus' having been observed." And on October 29 came the first of three telegrams, one for each act (we had no telephone), of an enthusiasm, each one more than the last, which left me astonished and nervously unconvinced. I was anxious to discuss the difficulties of the play, but when my wife and I went over to Notley Abbey for luncheon on Sunday, November 6, Olivier came out to welcome us, opened the door of the car, and said "Kit; tell me, what sort of nose do you think the Duke should have?"

It must have been very soon after this that he decided to read the play aloud to Vivien, with me there to hear him do it. My heart sank. I have to tell you that, great actor though he was, he was the worst reader, unrehearsed, of anyone I had ever listened to. My depression increased as the play went on. Vivien had sat silent throughout; not a muscle of her face had so much as twitched. At last it came to an end, and Vivien said in the tone of someone who had just been dissuaded from jumping off Beachy Head: "It's so beautiful—and so funny."

On December 8 he wrote saying: "I forgot to tell you, we had a reading last night, quite a private one, with nobody there except the Company, so that they could get to know each other a bit." That shows me what a short time I had given them for casting and for Roger Furse to design the sets, because the play opened on January 18, 1950, a week before the opening of *Ring Round the Moon.*

To provide a brief notion of some of the characters in *Venus Observed,* I've included the two opening pages of the play. The scene is a room at the top of a ducal mansion, once a bedroom, now an observatory. The Duke is in argument with his son Edgar whose mother had died when he was born. Also present Herbert Reedbeck, the Duke's agent:

DUKE: Anyone would think I had made in fact
  how natural it is.
  Aren't you my son?

EDGAR: Yes, father, of course I am.

DUKE: Then it's up to you to choose who shall be
  your mother.
  Does that seem to you improper, Reedbeck?

REEDBECK: No,
  Your Grace; it's not, perhaps, always done,

But few parents consider their children as you do.
I don't dislike the plan at all.

EDGAR: I sweat with embarrassment.

DUKE: You have been
  Too much with the horses. This, that I ask you
    to do,
  Is an act of poetry, and a compliment
  To the freshness of your mind. Why should you
    sweat?
  Here they will be, three handsome women,
  All of them at some time implicated
  In the joyous routine of my life. (I could scarcely
  Put it more delicately.) I wish to marry.
  Who am I, in heaven's name, to decide
  Which were my vintage years of love?
  Good God, to differentiate between
  The first bright blow on my sleeping flesh,
  The big breasts of mid-morning,
  And the high old dance of afternoon—
  Value one against the other? Never, not I,
  Till the eschatological rain shall lay my dust.
  But you, dear boy, with your twenty-five impartial
    years,
  Can perform the judgement of Paris,
  Can savour, consider, and award the apple
  With a cool hand. You will find an apple
  Over there by the spectroscope.

EDGAR: But why must you marry?
  Or, if that's an impertinence, why do I have to
    have
  A mother? I've been able to grow to a sizable boy
  Without one.

DUKE: Why? Because I see no end
  To the parcelling out of heaven in small beauties,
  Year after year, flocks of girls, who look
  So lately kissed by God
  They come out on the world with lips shining,
  Flocks and generations, until time
  Seems like nothing so much
  As a blinding snowstorm of virginity,
  And a man, lost in the perpetual scurry of white,
  Can only close his eyes
  In a resignation of monogamy.

EDGAR: Anyway, it would be an impossibly hasty
  Judgement. Honour you as I may, I don't
  See how I can do it.

DUKE: If Paris had no trouble
  Choosing between the tide-turning beauty,
  Imponderable and sexed with eternity,
  Of Aphrodite, Hera, and Athene,
  Aren't you ashamed to make heavy weather of a
    choice
  Between *Hilda, and Rosabel, and Jessie?*

So there, you have the name of six of the characters. It is Rosabel, incidentally, who was such a trouble to me. The summer before last I gave her a drastic going over; she is now a thoroughly reformed character, forty-two years too late.

I must include just a few lines from the end of the play, when the Duke's house has been burnt down and he is sitting with his agent, Herbert Reedbeck, in the garden temple, having watched his son, Edgar, and Perpetua walk away together. He says:

> Shall I be sorry for myself? In mortality's
>   name
> I'll be sorry for myself. Branches and
>   boughs,
> Brown hills, the valleys faint with brume,
> A burnish on the lake; mile by mile
> It's all a unison of ageing,
> The landscape's all in tune, in a falling
>   cadence,
> All decaying. And nowhere does it have to
>   hear
> The quips of spring, or, when so nearing
>   its end,
> Have to bear the merry mirth of May.

I include this for the line "brown hills, the valleys faint with brume," because on April 4, two months or so into the run of the play, I received a note from Olivier which said: "Dearest boy, Tonight I said 'The VARREYS FAINT WITH BLOOM'—I'm damn sorry—I can't say more. (They were spellbound by the way.) Love L." I replied with a telegram: "Try saying the O'Malleys quaint with brougham. That should keep them quiet."

Venus ran at the St. James's for most of the year, and then early in 1952 he was in America with Vivien Leigh appearing in the two Cleopatra plays, Shaw's and Shakespeare's, and as though that wasn't enough Larry also directed a production of *Venus Observed* there, with Rex Harrison as the Duke and Lilli Palmer as Perpetua. He wrote a mammoth letter from New York after the play had opened, over thirty pages long, a fascinating document, which takes us back-stage into all the difficulties of casting, the moves and performances, and the short-comings in his playwright. A cable came from him after the opening night dated February 14, 1952. It said, "Dear boy wonderful reception last night: press which am sending you is mixed with unhappy implications that I am to

Laurence Olivier, 1959

blame for faults / I don't honestly think you would agree however / writing fully next week when a bit clear." But it was two weeks before he started to write the promised letter, sitting in his theatre dressing room after Antony had died, and Vivien was left to go on with the play alone. This is what he says:

My Dearest Kit,
    Here at last, at long last. It is not going to be easy, first because I am now a bit tired out with it all, and then because it is rather like a boxer being asked to describe a fight in which he feels he has been knocked about a bit, and consequently feels a bit disheartened about making the full report on it; however darling Boy, such is the least that you are due, and so here is the best I can do. . . .
    Now before I start discussing my job I know you are most anxious to hear about the crits. They are *not*, I think, savage, and knowing that you must realise that universal opinion holds that your plays are prone to be too verbally rich for the modern ear,

it is to be hoped that you may appreciate that, though cutting may not do you good service as a poet, it may as a dramatist. . . .

For instance the first baby cut is when [Rex] introduces Hilda to the others: "There will only be the appearance of people being near to us." Rex thought he could never get over to the audience what that was meant to say—and why bemuse them, or make them feel unintelligent, and I must say I agree with him.

No change now, except that Edgar piles a second apple onto Rosabel which goes better for "plying Rosabel with Fruit."

When things were good-and-panicky just after the N.Y. opening, I tried a cut in the Duke's speech from "the dark tree with the nightingale at heart" to "one not unattractive beam." It seemed to take all the brilliance out of the speech and I couldn't stand it and so put it back.

After trying it in and out we finally did make your suggested cut in Rosabel's 1st Act speech. I didn't like the cut because it seemed to diminish her case as well as leaving out an important exposition of the Duke's character, but without moving her around during it, which she tried but didn't do very convincingly, the thing does seem rather a set speech, and the act is better for it being trimmed.

We tried also cutting "So Rosabel believes," but it wasn't to be borne and so is right back. (I cannot for the life of me get your explanation that the Duke has an instinct that "love is a whole state of being—not an explosion between individuals etc etc" from "Rosabel why pick on me etc"; to me he is just arguing Rosabel down on a perfectly callous and minute piece of logic; you will have to explain to me how otherwise the actor could make it understood when we meet!)

Nothing else textual to report in this act.

In Act II Sc. [1] we took out the little image of "the year, whose arrow Singing from the April bow" etc. Going from "and do what I tell you" to Perpetua:—"Show me."

I used to enjoy it vastly myself, but Rex found it too difficult to convey, and (now this is a point which will explain to you a little of what is lacking), did not *enjoy saying it,* which means you see that the Duke who is not only in love with words for their own sake, but who is even more in love with his own use and manipulation of them is not there as he should be. Please under-

stand there is a wealth of stuff that is. He is the most attractive actor imaginable, has a style, presence and personality, that is most original, brilliantly amusing, extraordinarily winning in its individuality. I really love his performance and I know you too would be captivated by it. If one wished to be scathing which I really do not–the worst one could say would be that it smacks of Berkeley Street rather than St. James's Street. The wine in his blood is champagne-like rather than the *more* fruity kind that I myself felt in it. His lack of vocal range and equipment makes it very hard for him to keep the sound of the part rich and always refreshing in tune and tonal idea. Repetitious inflections, sheer running-out of vocal ideas cause some of the highest flights of poetic imagery to flatten out into tired shallow cadences that have fallen weakly away to one side of the rip-roaring torrent that should be hurtling them ever changeably along.

(This is all very poetic but what I really mean is at times it's a little boring to listen to.)

I didn't use all your cut in the Rosabel-Hilda scene—(it's rather sad isn't it that whenever cuts are thought of the first person we leap at is the wretched Rosabel?)

We just snip from "it's coming again" to "God knows where."

And Jessie just "the way a thing is" line. She has to say *"work* yourself up"—*"Knock* yourself up" means something highly improper in this country!

Rosabel then goes straight from "curious thoughts" to "The girl Perpetua" leaving out the intervening four lines.

That's all in this scene.

Classical reference being such a tease to these audiences, I cut Perpetua's Noah—Charlemagne and Roland. She says

"And alone so long . . .

Alone so long and now casually" etc.

The *Sentence.* . . .

Now I must break off to explain about the Sentence. In the second act the Duke invites Perpetua up to the observatory room, ostensibly to look at the night sky through the telescope, but with the thought of love in his mind. Perpetua says "With your mind so full of enquiry, I'm surprised / You've had any time for love." The Duke replies "It takes no time. It's on us while we walk, or in mid-sentence, / A sudden hoarseness, enough to choke the sense. / Now isn't that so?" "Not so with me," Perpetua says. "You must try to use longer sen-

Christopher Fry seated behind his 1917 Corona portable typewriter (the portrait on the wall is of Alastair Sim; it was given to Fry by Sim's widow Naomi after the actor's death in 1975)

tences," says the Duke, and Perpetua embarks on a sentence forty-three-and-a-half lines long. I'd like to explain what I was up to in that sentence. It's true that it was, as one critic called it, "a stylistic joke." But it was also a lighthearted dig at the critics who reproved me for overelaboration. It seemed to me that if we were to convey something of the extraordinary profusion of the natural world, and the universe that contains it, of which we're a breathing part, we can't always be so economical and well-mannered in style and still be telling the truth. And it's not so farfetched to believe in the music of the spheres when we see in the autumn hundreds of starlings in the sky, looking like a great scarf of fine material, sweeping and turning and weaving back and forth like one single changing thought in the sky. In the London production Olivier had moved Perpetua about, which I thought took away from

her determination to keep her breath going for as long as possible, which is why he said earlier "Yes, standing quite still."

The *Sentence*—standing stock still is very successful and Lilli pulls it off brilliantly with only a little too much gesticulation and she is cutting this down all the time.

I'm not really sure that I am entirely happy about the stillness—it is even more blatantly a tour de force, but when my beloved author says do something I certainly will do it unless it kills me.

By the way I do remember at our first reading in London during Heather's *Sentence* turning to you and whispering "alright to move her around?" and you nodding your head in vehement approval.

Darling boy! I bring this up in no recriminatory vein—just a point of interest, I don't see why you shouldn't change your mind if you want to!

But here was the difficulty. Perpetua's speech—stock still—set piece. The Duke's Halloween speech also stock still—set piece: The scene becomes a goddam spelling bee you see. I tried moving the Duke around— it was horrid—didn't suit the Duke or the speech—it makes it pixilated and unconfident—all wrong. The way we had it in London did work alright—Perpetua swishing around and then the Duke stock still rang a change and the audience was held— anyway until the "rigid winter" which was too much for them. I cut that bit anyway for N.Y. because I *knew* it would be too much for them and poor Rexie was frankly dismayed by it. . . .

To digress a little. You know darling boy if you would act some of your roles, which I am sure you could as well as any of us, you would find out so much that would cause you some constructive pondering. *Please* don't think I am being impertinent enough to preach at you, it is only my duty as a "theatrician" (which they call me here!) and as a devoted friend, to offer you any conclusions that experience has brought me to. It cannot ever be right or desirable in the theatre that we should *lose our audience. Sound* for its own sake can be a property I know, but a very esoteric one; to be sparingly used in my considered opinion *only* when the audience is *fresh*. Their intellectual receptiveness gets tired as the evening wears on. W.S. was brilliantly conscious of this, and I think that is why he always manages to excite.

All the tragedies show him gradually relaxing his call upon the intelligence as the evening progresses until he finally says "alright, you see it's quite easy now" and sometimes "here you are groundlings—here's a damn good *fight.*"

The *Emotions* of the audience last the longest of the contributions that they bring to the theatre. *Intellect* wears out quickest. After all they have paid their money to enjoy themselves.

Time and Time again in *Venus,* in London, I would have the brutes in my hand like baby mice, and then out would come something *difficult* again, or obscure, or too clever, and it would be suddenly like playing in a hospital for croup—impatience had seized them and they were gone for a while. And they get more and more sensitive during the evening. When the play was really over after the general exit when I was alone with Georgie Relph, there would be the most sublime atmosphere of glowing emotional quietude, and then even not so difficult a word like "desuetude" would send them crestfallen back to their bronchitis.

Be a bit easier on them cockie will you? Don't *tease* the poor bastards too much. Exercise is good for them but they've paid mostly for relaxation.

Enough may be something too much—de ça. . . .

Now the Fire Scene.

Ah yes, the fire scene. It goes on for three pages at the end of the second act, and it had been the cause of worry to Olivier when he directed it in London, and continued to worry him in New York. Perpetua and the Duke are trapped by the fire in the observatory room, and Reddleman the butler and Bates the footman appear on the scene to rescue them: each wishing to do so in his own way—Reddleman, who had been a lion tamer who lost his nerve, now wishes to show his courage by carrying them down the smouldering staircase; Bates, an ex-burglar, wants to get them out of the window and down a ladder which he has brought to the rescue. I had thought of it as a tug of war between these two. So back to the letter:

I couldn't keep them all quite still shouting at each other, Kit, I'm sorry but I couldn't do that, it was altogether too agonising for the actors.

When you say the London production was too realistic for the quality of the scene you are *right.* But when you remove this scene from realism, what do you bring it to? *Farce.* Quite frankly it can take on no

other form. I wonder if you ever realised that quite graphically? Not *terribly* funny farce takes place.

In spite of our abominably poor Reddleman (which is a crippling disadvantage) I have managed to produce his "tragedy" much more clearly than before—he and Bates *are* on two sides of the stage and the other two more or less in the middle and there is a reasonably beguiling moment when all four are huddled in a tug of war—*Reddleman* trying to push them to the door and *Bates* to the window on *"Your Grace"* as he pounces on them. But the truth is that the audience don't give a damn about Reddleman (half of them in this place are still streaming in long after his first exit) and they can't make out why it goes on so long. Their spirits are led to expect a "punch" curtain (a long established requirement for a second act here) and the punch just fails to connect.

The whole thing is much less fussy—it's clearer, cleaner but to save my life and God knows it has exercised me as if that were the necessity—I cannot make the thing go.

I've never really liked the scene, I do believe there's something radically wrong with it. Possibly it's misguided dramaturgically— is it too capricious—too impish to let the most minor of sub-plots take over from the main protagonists at this point? I don't know. I only am certain that with the most brilliant performances at full length, or with inferior ones cut to ribbons the scene goes on too long. Like the witch hunt in the "Lady" only much more so, this fire in *Venus* is far too strong an element to expect the audience to be readily distracted from. I have cut the noises, the lighting effects, the smoke all right down to the mildest minimum, tho' this only gives the impression that nothing much is happening. In sheer desperation I introduced music as a palliative, a preparative and an excusing element for the change in dimension. It's alright—it helps fill in a bit and romanticizes it. But I don't really like it. But without it it's desperately flat. I tried *all* the dialogue back in except for "Snakes and ladders" a game they've never heard of here. And it just—just hangs fire. I tried playing Reddleman myself full out with the others— and it seemed there was no way of staging it that wasn't agony for everybody. You see Kit, there has been nothing particularly *unrealistic* about the scene up to now or the rest of the play—except the language and the audience has completely accepted that by now.

It seems to me that you have intrigued and provoked *basic* emotions, a) by the love scene and b) by the fire and then you say now listen to these *words* and get a kick out of *them* for your curtain and I think you have asked too much of people in a place of entertainment. The situation you've introduced is amusing enough—their quarrel I mean—and it's piquant at this point, but it somehow don't do no good boy. The words aren't strong enough (though I can't think *any* words could be better than your) and the jokes aren't funny enough to win over this occasion, and the spectators feel cheated and unsatisfied and your little friend feels frustrated and defeated. . . .

I have a really sound idea for the next piece we do together, and that is that we should *do* it *together,* right from its inception, through the designing period and right up to opening—Don't you think that might be nice? . . .

I must stop I am being called.

We are having rather a tough time in N.Y.—will tell you all when home—on the whole and are so dying to get home we dare not speak nor think about it. See you dearest Kit not too dreadfully far ahead—all love from Vivien to you and Phyll, and from Your

Larry

And What Followed

The Calling took a bit of a battering through 1949—the year which had started with Richard Burton leaving the cast of *The Lady* to play the part of Cuthman in *The Boy with a Cart* at the Lyric, Hammersmith—a battering, I mean, in the struggle to get *Venus* finished in time for the opening at the St. James Theatre in January 1950. And in 1950, we were moving into a London house, with all the excuses for not working which that provided. But once we had settled in I took things for a while more sensibly. The Religious Drama Society had commissioned a play for the Festival of Britain year, and I concentrated on writing *A Sleep of Prisoners.* One great regret I have is that in 1951 there was no such thing as video recording, to perpetuate that production at St. Thomas's, Regent Street, with the performances of Stanley Baker, Denholm Eliot, and Hugh Pryce and Leonard White—a production as near to my thoughts as human endeavour could come. It's just as well that there is no room left to explain how I strayed from the true path in the years that followed. You may have noticed that everything done so far had been because someone had asked me to do it. I have so little belief in my ability to put one sentence in front of another, it's only when I find I'm committed to try that I can break through my reluctance. What is worse, any wavering of confidence could be stilled by translating somebody else's work, or doing a kind of committee job on a film. So between the years of 1952 and 1986, instead of writing twenty or more original plays, learning more clearly the intentions of the Calling as I went along, I wrote only four. And for the rest of the time, say 10,950 days or 87,600 working hours, I relapsed into five films, six television plays, and six translations.

The plays were *The Dark Is Light Enough* (1954), written for Edith Evans, who was followed in turn by other actresses who dazzled me: Katherine Cornell in the States, Paxinou in Athens, Madeleine Renaud in Paris, Bodil Ipsen in Denmark, and very recently, Lilo von Pluskow in Germany—no man could complain about that; then *Curtmantle* (in which I believe I got nearest to what the Calling was after, though after a six-year errancy); and *A Yard of Sun* about the first Palio in Siena after the war, which José Ferrer directed in the States.

Nine years ago I thought my eightieth year was a reasonable time to down pens and give the daughters of Zeus no further trouble; but then I was put back to work by the BBC and Chelmsford Cathedral, and called the play *One Thing More, or Caedmon Construed.* If I ever write another it will have to be called *And Another Thing.* Or perhaps *I Forgot to Mention.* The play is about the first English religious poet, Caedmon, who was so fearful of using words that he hid himself away whenever the harp was passed round at the farm labourers' singsongs. When writing a play it's an advantage to start off with a fellow feeling for the main character.

I can only end with the words that I give to Caedmon towards the end of the play:

> I've been shown such a universe. These not-so-many years, what vastness has filled them, though I made so little of it. Before I am lost and found in God's love I should like to make one thing more, a song or half-song or no song, but one thing more in thanksgiving for having seen and known and lived and died.

BIBLIOGRAPHY

Produced plays:

(With Monte Crick and F. Eyton) *She Shall Have Music,* London, 1934.

Open Door, London, 1936.

(Author of libretto) *Robert of Sicily: Opera for Children,* 1938.

(Author of libretto) *Seven at a Stroke: A Play for Children,* 1939.

The Tower (pageant), Tewkesbury Festival, Tewkesbury, England, July 18, 1939.

Produced and published plays:

The Boy with a Cart: Cuthman, Saint of Sussex (also see below; Coleman's Hatch, Sussex, England, 1938; Lyric Theatre, 1950), Oxford University Press, 1939, 2nd edition, Muller, 1956.

Thursday's Child: A Pageant (London, 1939), Girl's Friendly Press (London), 1939.

A Phoenix Too Frequent (also see below; Mercury Theatre, London, 1946; Broadway, with "Freight," 1950), Hollis & Carter, 1946, Oxford University Press, 1949.

The Firstborn (also see below; broadcast on radio, 1947; Gateway Theatre, Edinburgh, Scotland, 1948), Cambridge University Press, 1946, 3rd edition, Oxford University Press, 1958.

The Lady's Not for Burning (also see below; Arts Theatre, London, 1948; West End, 1949; Broadway, Royale Theatre, 1950), Oxford University Press, 1949, revised edition, 1973.

Thor, with Angels (also see below; Chapter House, Canterbury, England, 1948; West End, Lyric Theatre, 1951), H. J. Goulden, 1948, Oxford University Press, 1949.

Venus Observed (also see below; St. James Theatre, London, 1950; Broadway, Century Theatre, 1952), Oxford University Press, 1950.

A Sleep of Prisoners (also see below; University Church, Oxford, England, 1951; St. Thomas's Church, London, 1951), Oxford University Press, 1951, 2nd edition, 1965.

The Dark Is Light Enough: A Winter Comedy (also see below; West End, Aldwych Theatre, 1954; Broadway, ANTA Theatre, 1955), Oxford University Press, 1954.

Curtmantle: A Play (also see below; Stadsschouwburg, Tilburg, Netherlands, 1961, West End, Aldwych Theatre, 1962), Oxford University Press, 1961.

A Yard of Sun: A Summer Comedy (Nottingham Playhouse, Nottingham, England, 1970; West End, Old Vic Theatre, 1970), Oxford University Press, 1970.

(Adaptor) *Paradise Lost* (produced in Chicago, 1978), Schott, 1978.

One Thing More, or Caedmon Construed (Chelmsford Cathedral, England, 1986; broadcast on radio, 1986), Oxford University Press, 1985, Dramatists Play Service, 1987.

Produced and published plays; translator:

(And adaptor from *L'Invitation au Chateau* by Jean Anouilh), *Ring Round the Moon: A Charade with Music* (West End, Globe Theatre, 1950), Oxford University Press, 1950.

(And adaptor) Jean Anouilh, *The Lark* (West End, Lyric Theatre, 1955; Broadway, Longacre Theatre, 1955), Methuen, 1955, Oxford University Press, 1956.

(And adaptor) Jean Giraudoux, *Tiger at the Gates* (also see below; West End, Apollo Theatre, 1955), Methuen, 1955, 2nd edition, 1961, Oxford University Press, 1956, (produced as *The Trojan War Will Not Take Place,* London, 1983), Methuen, 1983.

(And adaptor from *Pour Lucrece* by Jean Giraudoux), *Duel of Angels* (also see below; West End, Apollo Theatre, 1958; Broadway, Helen Hayes Theatre, 1960), Methuen, 1958, Oxford University Press, 1959.

(And adaptor) Jean Giraudoux, *Judith* (also see below; West End, Her Majesty's Theatre, 1962), Methuen, 1962.

(And adaptor) Henrik Ibsen, *Peer Gynt* (Chichester Festival Theatre, Chichester, England, 1970), Oxford University Press, 1970, revised edition, 1989.

(And adaptor) Edmond Rostand, *Cyrano de Bergerac* (Chichester Festival Theatre, 1975), Oxford University Press, 1975.

Published play collections:

Three Plays: The Firstborn; Thor, with Angels; A Sleep of Prisoners, Oxford University Press, 1960.

(Translator) Jean Giraudoux, *Plays* (contains *Judith, Tiger at the Gates,* and *Duel of Angels*), Methuen, 1963.

(Translator) Sidonie Gabrielle Colette, *The Boy and the Magic,* Dobson, 1964, Putnam, 1965.

Plays (contains *Thor, with Angels* and *The Lady's Not for Burning*), Oxford University Press, 1969.

Plays (contains *The Boy with a Cart: Cuthman, Saint of Sussex, The Firstborn,* and *Venus Observed*), Oxford University Press, 1970.

Plays (contains *A Sleep of Prisoners, The Dark Is Light Enough,* and *Curtmantle*), Oxford University Press, 1971.

Selected Plays (contains *The Boy with a Cart: Cuthman, Saint of Sussex, A Phoenix Too Frequent, The Lady's Not for Burning, A Sleep of Prisoners, Curtmantle*), Oxford University Press, 1985.

(Translator with Timberlake Wertebaker) *Jean Anouilh: Five Plays,* Heinemann, 1986.

Screenplays:

The Canary, BBC-TV, 1950.

(With Denis Cannan) *The Beggar's Opera,* British Lion, 1953.

The Queen Is Crowned, Universal, 1953.

Ben Hur, Metro-Goldwyn-Mayer, 1959.

Barabbas, Columbia, 1961.

(With Jonathan Griffin, Ivo Perilli, and Vittorio Bonicelli) *The Bible: In the Beginning,* Twentieth Century-Fox, 1966.

The Tenant of Wildfell Hall, BBC-TV, 1968.

The Brontës of Haworth (also see below; four teleplays), BBC-TV, 1973.

The Best of Enemies, BBC-TV, 1976.

Sister Dora, BBC-TV, 1977.

Star over Bethlehem, BBC-TV, 1981.

Other:

(Contributor) Kaye Webb, editor, *An Experience of Critics and the Approach to Dramatic Criticism,* Perpetua, 1952, Oxford University Press, 1953.

(Author of libretto) *Crown of the Year* (cantata), 1958.

(Contributor) *The Modern Theatre,* edited by Robert W. Corrigan, Macmillan, 1964.

The Boat That Mooed, Macmillan, 1965.

(With Jonathan Griffin) *The Bible: Original Screenplay,* Pocket Books, 1966.

(Contributor) *The Drama Bedside Book,* edited by H. F. Rubinstein, Atheneum, 1966.

The Brontës of Haworth, published in two volumes, Davis-Poynter, 1975.

Can You Find Me: A Family History, Oxford University Press, 1978.

Death Is a Kind of Love (drawings by Charles E. Wadsworth), Tidal Press, 1979.

Charlie Hammond's Sketch Book, Oxford University Press, 1980.

Genius, Talent and Failure: The Brontes, King's College, 1987.

Looking for a Language, King's College, 1992.

Also author of *Youth of the Peregrines,* produced at Tunbridge Wells with premiere production of George Bernard Shaw's *Village Wooing.* Author of radio plays for *Children's Hour* series, 1939–40, and of *Rhineland Journey,* 1948. Contributor to the anthology *Representative Modern Plays: Ibsen to Tennessee Williams,* edited by Robert Warnock, Scott, Foresman, 1964. Contributor to *Theatre Arts* and *Plays and Players.*

Douglas Glover

1948-

THE FAMILIAR DEAD

Douglas Glover

Let's be candid. I am forty-six and just at the beginning of my writing life. Whether that means one more book or twenty or none is immaterial. I have spent forty-six years getting to the point at which I begin to understand the art, something about myself, and what might be essential to put down. So the idea of writing this memoir is unsettling. I'm not being coy. I feel as if I am standing my life on its head, or that like Tristram Shandy I will write a whole book in the process of which I will have drifted further and further from my subject.

I have always been a writer in this sense—I relate to the world through writing. I didn't always know this, but it's true. People confuse me; I cannot express myself well in the spoken word. Growing up, I was never the wit, the raconteur, the charmer, the authority—all people I would like to have been. At university, where I studied philosophy, instead of participating in seminar discussions, I was apt to fall asleep. Later, alone with my typewriter and my books, I would come alive (and awake), begin to think, tracking the ideas through the words as they appeared on the page.

But this is a trivial example. Most of what I write comes from a place so private, painful, and mysterious that I cannot write about it except as fiction. So that my attempt here to write a memoir cannot but produce something ancilary and reductive—not a mirror but a shadow work, a vague presence distinguished mostly by what it is not.

Most of what life throws in a writer's way (and most of what he throws in his own way) counts only as interference. Knowing when and where I was born won't help a reader understand why I write or why I write what I write. But it might explain some of the difficulties I have writing—the inhibitions, the blocks, the boredom, the self-doubt, the torturous spells of inactivity. So that a memoir (once again) is far more likely to explain the act of not-writing than the writing itself—which is why writers' memoirs are often tedious or uninformative or simply untrue (the best kind). The truth is, as a writer, I have spent most of my life overcoming my life.

I was born at 3:30 in the afternoon on a Sunday, November 14, 1948, in Simcoe, Ontario (the family farm is just outside Waterford, ten miles away). I was due October 25. My parents had spent the intervening days waiting together

With his father, Murray Glover, May 1949

With his mother, Jean Ross Glover, January 1950

on the chesterfield in the sitting room, listening to the World Series on our old Rogers Majestic radio. Lou Boudreau was the hero of the hour. For a while, my parents joked that they might call me Lou Glover—somehow this seems significant. What if I had been called Lou? What famous writers have been called Lou? Lou Tolstoy? Lou Flaubert? Lou Hemingway? I probably wouldn't have been a writer; maybe I'd have been a happier man.

Friday the twelfth they thought I was finally coming, so they drove to Simcoe to the hospital where my mother was taken up to the obstetrics ward. There was a woman already in labor, and they could hear her screams. My father winced or made a face and said something, variously reported as: "I hope you don't scream like that," or "I hope you don't get like that." My mother thinks he was censoring her: "He always frowned on any expression of physical pain or disaster." But when I think of it, perhaps he only meant he hoped she wouldn't be in that much pain. This was one of those misunderstandings couples have, though I suppose it's not really a misunderstanding, that kind of misunderstanding requires a will to misunderstand. Forty-six years later, my mother is still simmering over my father's ill-considered remarks.

But at the time, all the fuss amounted to a false alarm. I may have wanted to be born, but nothing was happening. The doctor sent my mother home to her mother's house, about five blocks from the hospital. Saturday she returned to the hospital. Sometime Saturday my mother felt a jump, that is, I jumped; she felt me turn, and she believes it was at this point that I got my shoulder stuck in the birth canal and things started to go badly.

My mother lost heart. She remembers deciding there would be no baby after all, that it was never going to come out. She was naturally disappointed but began planning how she and my father would go away for a vacation once she got out of the hospital. The doctor even let my father into the delivery room to try to comfort her—a practice unheard of in those days. Then Sunday afternoon, the doctor threw his gloves in the air and said that's it.

They wheeled my mother into a room to prep her for the operation. She was jerking around on the bed with pain as the nurse painted her belly with red disinfectant. She lost control of her bowels. (My grandmother walked into this room shortly after my mother had left for the operation and saw the bed soaked red and covered with shit and had, as my mother says, a fit.) Then they wheeled her to the operating room, and I was out before you could say Lou Boudreau.

I emerged kicking, shouting, and flailing the air. By the time they carried me past my father and grandmother on my way to the nursery, I was beating my chest with my fists. I then proceeded to make such a pest of myself, keeping the other babies awake, that again, contrary to custom in those days, I was left most of the time with my mother. She rubbed my head to calm me, though she was half off her rocker herself. At one point, she dreamed or hallucinated that she was a pie plate someone had dropped and had broken into three pieces. She so alarmed the night nurse that the nurse went through the motions of looking under the bed and all around the room for the pieces of plate so they could put my mother back together again.

I think, on the whole, I gave my parents more trouble than they gave me. I can see a pat-

Riding "Rainbow," made by Jacob Glover for Herschel Glover, ridden by Murray and now Douglas, April 1950

tern here. I have two sons now, and they are carrying on the family tradition of wrecking the house, destroying social occasions, embarrassing other restaurant patrons, making their parents feel guilty and incompetent, and incurring dire medical expenses. Freud, for all his insights, missed the inverse of the family romance, which is something like a seventeen-month-old standing in front of the new $300 VCR with a lump of blue chalk in one hand, a claw hammer in the other, and joy in his heart.

My father was a farmer and a local politician—county warden, chairman of the school board, that sort of thing. His story is littered with regretful narratives, and I remember those long years at the end, a lot of time spent hugging himself to a TV he could barely see. He stayed at home, a training officer in the militia, when the men of his generation went overseas to war. He would have loved a career as an academic, and, after graduating, taught briefly at the Ontario Agricultural College at Guelph where John Kenneth Galbraith had been one of his classmates (Galbraith figures in several of my father's photographs of student hijinks). But a doctor told him he had better find work where he wouldn't be so dependent on his eyes, and his father needed him to help run the family farm, so he came home. Later, he became legally blind, though even then he could discern vague shapes and read with a magnifying glass.

He was always waiting for his life to begin, or he had seen it begin and sputter out. He once told me about the day he left Guelph. He drove the powder blue Ford his mother had bought him to the top of the hill going out of town and pulled over to the side of the road and got out and looked back on what for him was a golden world and wept.

I don't know how much of this is true. I do remember the annual Guelph reunions, the parties and dances and the pretty daughters of the other alums, that gifted, witty, happy gang of brothers, which then gradually began to die away for my father, so that by the end there wasn't much to go back to. My brother John later enrolled as an undergraduate in what had by then become the University of Guelph, then did a massive life-detour to play for years in a bluegrass band, crisscrossing the province with his guitar and mandolin, a brilliant, careless soul who once bit a bar patron on the bare buttock for mooning a young woman during one of his songs. Shortly before my father died, John returned to the university and restarted his life (at least in my father's terms), and it was a question of John's that sent my father off across the snowy yard that March night years later when he died.

At my father's funeral, a former classmate of mine reminded me how all the children in our country schoolhouse knew he was blind yet conspired to keep it a secret from their parents. The whole time I was in elementary school, he was chairman of the school board (this was his way of taking care of my brothers and me). There was no school bus, so often on rainy or snowy days he would drive over and take four or five of the students home. He stopped at every intersection, and the children in the front seat always knew to look for oncoming cars and shout, "It's okay, Mr. Gubber!" when the coast was clear.

When I began to write, my father appeared in two early stories, and then disappeared until *The Life and Times of Captain N.,* which is about a father who kidnaps his son and forces him to join an army in which he does not wish to fight. The son responds by covering his body with tattoos—words, signs, and messages—and becomes a writer in order to sew up the split in his soul.

My mother was a housewife, but she also had a degree in psychology and did volunteer testing and counselling for the local schools. She would practice testing my brothers and me, which was not a good idea. I had a tendency to chafe and get bored. One night I came out of the I.Q. sweepstakes with a score of 80. Both my brothers beat me—I was seven, Rodger was five, and John was three—a result from which I have never quite recovered.

My mother was an enthusiast and socially ambitious—she grew up in the bygone days of Norfolk County's "one hundred families" and two-day black-tie bridge parties. She would make a practice of coming to my softball games in jodhpurs. She made us join the Anglican Church in Waterford, though there was a brief schism when she got in a tiff with the altar ladies and we

The Glover family farmhouse, 1950

transferred allegiance to the United Church in Wilsonville in a huff. Church seemed to have everything to do with her and nothing to do with us. But I am still surprised when I leaf through my *Book of Common Prayer and Hymnal* at how much of the liturgy and how many hymns I recognize. For a while, she seemed almost to disappear from our lives—this coincided with her brief fling with curling, then the winter sport of the local elite. Her enthusiasms could be quite bizarre. I recall the year we all had to take doses of vinegar with our meals. I even had to feed vinegar to the poor horses in the barn. Only my mother seemed to think we were all better for it.

She was a competitive soul—it was always important that my brothers and I do things earlier, faster, better, and more often than anyone else. She used to take my school yearbook and pencil in my classmates' grade averages next to their heads in the class picture. She pushed Rodger and me into school a year early, then saw to it that we accelerated through another grade. By the time I reached high school, I was two years younger than my classmates. Life has always had a breathless, catch-up quality for me.

But I remember this: my mother was always reading to us. She would read us to sleep at night; she would read to us till she fell asleep herself. I think I taught myself to read picking up the books as they fell from her hands and trying to go on, puzzle out the words myself. She even read over lunch or at the dinner table. She always said a dollar spent on a book was never wasted. (She also says you can stop a cold by snorting cayenne pepper—I have never tried it.)

She was always telling stories: V-E Day in St. John's, Newfoundland, where she was a radio operator in the air force; the day when she was two and she fell out of the car as her father sped around a tight corner; the night my father proposed to her at the Officers' Mess in Simcoe; the year her entire high school class partied too much and flunked out; nights at the rooftop bar at the Sheraton in Montreal when the Ferry Command pilots would crack the tension by ordering whole table tops covered with Singapore Slings; summer weekends spent with her grandmother and elderly aunts Maggie and Emma in St. Williams by the lake; the night she was eating hot dogs with friends at the Arbor in Port Dover and news that Canada

had declared war came over the radio and all the boys piled into cars and drove straight to Simcoe to the armory to enlist. She even told my father's stories, which means he must have told them to her at some point, and I am glad he had someone to tell them to.

My mother still owns and operates the tobacco farm where I grew up. In the years before my father died, he used to take me aside and remind me that he had named me his executor because my mother was terrible at managing her money and would need considerable guidance and correction. And he was right. She did need a good deal of help—for about three months. Then she fired his accountant, hired a new sharegrower, gambled by buying quota when the bottom was falling out of the tobacco market, expanded her acreage, rented neighboring farms to get the land she needed, and ended up with her picture on the cover of a book the federal government produced on women in farming.

I started my first novel when I was sixteen. It was a revenge story called *Udon Thani*, set in Vietnam during the war, heavily researched in one issue of *National Geographic*. It begins with the massacre of a peaceful farming family. My most recent novel, *The Life and Times of Captain N.*, also begins with the massacre of a peaceful farming family in upstate New York during the Revolution—a clear line of development.

We were a peaceful farming family living on 150 acres on which we grew strawberries, asparagus, rye, and tobacco. I remember playing in the sandy laneways with Iroquois children when I was very young, in the days when my father hired Indians from the nearby Six Nations Reserve to dig his strawberry plants. When I was two, my parents bought me a Dalmatian pup named Pepper to give me someone to play with while they paid attention to my baby brother, Rodger. We had a barn bridge for sledding (a barn bridge isn't a bridge at all but a sort of dirt ramp) and 40 acres of woods at the back of the farm for exploring. There was a pretty and mysterious copse of cedar trees my father called Hernando's Hideaway and a swamp with great blue herons, snapping turtles, muskrats, red-winged blackbirds, and itinerant ducks.

As my brothers and I grew older, my father would carve us swords and guns out of scraps of wooden tobacco lath so that we could prosecute our endless wars, ambushes, invasions, and last stands. Winters he would flood the old greenhouse foundation behind the house so that we had a rink big enough for a dozen boys to play hockey till the moon came up. We had a huge fifteen-year excavation project in the backyard—a vast amoeboid complex of ever-changing galleries, tunnels, land bridges, and sinkholes. My parents were slow to buy a television—I remember going next door to the sharegrower's house to watch Fess Parker play Davy Crockett and die swinging his Kentucky long rifle on the Alamo parapet. The first television show we watched on our own set was "Wild Bill Hickock." I had a coonskin cap and, by the time I was six, a miraculous fringed buckskin jacket, the money for which I had saved by myself, helping with household chores and yard work.

We always had animals around the place, and my father was always grumbling about them. When I was very young, my father kept riding horses for show—Black Diamond was the mare and Chip was her colt. My father wanted Chip to be a show jumper, but he was a nasty-tempered horse. One of my earliest memories is of standing by the barn one evening and watching Chip throw my father headfirst into the stony driveway. I remember watching in hushed quiet from my upstairs bedroom window as the neighbor men carried my father into the house and waiting for the doctor to examine him and the weeks of convalescence and the quiet disappearance of the horses.

We also had rabbits that ate their babies, barn cats that ate their kittens, bantam roosters and hens, a black house cat called Sambo, and a pair of Belgian workhorses named Nell and Topsy. We bred Pepper to a nearby Dalmatian bitch and acquired one of the females and called her Cleo. I saved my allowance and chore money to buy a horse. My father may go down in history as the world's worst judge of horse character. Roscoe proceeded to drop me headfirst on every available piece of real estate. His most spectacular exploit consisted of catapulting me into the concrete barn foundation, then spinning around and kicking back into the wall before I hit the ground. This made such an impression on me that I eventually wrote a story about it.

I skipped kindergarten and started grade one when I was five—eight grades in a one-room fieldstone country schoolhouse built in the 1880s, belfry on the roof, sagging carriage barn attached at the back, and a huge oak tree in the yard. My teacher was a gorgeous Jehovah's Witness named Miss Smith. Every morning we said the Lord's Prayer and sang "God Save the Queen." Once a week a very Methodist-looking young woman would come to school with a felt board on a tripod and tell us Bible stories, deftly setting scenes and shifting figures with her blunt-nailed fingers. I played Tiny Tim in the Christmas pageant. My father made me a crutch and a leg brace out of tomato soup cans and harness remnants. Keith Rainey carried me across the stage, and I shouted, "God bless us everyone!" School never got better than this.

In the seventh and eighth grades, I had a teacher named Larry Woods who drove a black MGA ragtop, built model airplanes, and stayed after school to play chess with the kids. I remember painstakingly constructing my own control-line models and flying them to their doom in the school parking lot (nights I would lay in bed visualizing my hands, the lines, the rudder positions). I remember racing around the countryside, squeezed behind the bucket seats of the MG, chasing Larry's escaped

Douglas, with his Dalmatian, Cleo, 1965

radio control planes. Briefly, I became the center of a theological dispute between Larry and Bob Krug, a supermarket manager from Brantford who was married to our sharegrower's daughter. Bob was a glider fanatic, disdaining Larry's electrical gadgetry. I remember endless summer afternoons standing in rye stubble with a lit cigarette smoldering between my fingers (sinful frisson), waiting to light the fuse and launch his huge tilt-winged masterpieces. Later, I flirted with model rockets but gave them up after one day lighting a fuel pellet in my bedroom and burning a hole through the hardwood floor.

Summers we swam every day in a nearby gravel pit, warm, treacherously deep in places, with the machines and pyramids of sand and gravel looming just beyond. Over the years, two of my classmates drowned there. My brother Rodger suffered from hay fever that regularly transformed itself into asthma and pneumonia. So my mother and my brothers and I often fled pollen season, heading north to the Muskoka Lakes in August and early September. Several years in a row we rented a housekeeping cottage in a little place called Dwight on Lake of Bays just outside Algonquin Park. Later, we bought a tent, my mother became more adventuresome, and our summers in the north turned nomadic. One August I fell in love with the girl who ran the camp-site snack bar in Martin River and learned to jive to Del Shannon's "Runaway" played over and over on the jukebox after nightfall.

My father, of course, spent most of the summer at home nursing his tobacco crop. Tobacco defined his days, from greenhouse preparation in the spring to planting to harvest in August and September to grading and baling through the fall. A tobacco plant stands about shoulder height with broad, lush leaves stretching from a tough, woody stalk. The flowers emerge at the top, a spray of pink-and-white trumpets. The leaves are always slightly lighter underneath, so when a wind comes up and the leaves begin to toss, the effect can be startlingly beautiful, like a squall moving across a lake. Mornings after a heavy dew, or after a rain shower, you can stand next to a field of tobacco and hear the soft tump-tumping of water drops falling onto the lower leaves—just silence and that sound of water hitting the leaves.

Growing up outside Waterford in the 1950s and 1960s seemed ineluctably interwoven with the growing of tobacco. Tobacco farmers were considered smart operators, substantial individuals. We had our own language: "primers" for pickers; "boat," as in "boat-row"; "boat-driver," a high-sided sled dragged by horses between the rows during harvest; "kills" for kilns. Everyone worked in tobacco, or aspired to work in tobacco. It was a rite of passage: you started as a boat-unloader and worked up to primer (the most strenuous) or kiln-hanger (the riskiest). Children were let off school to help get in the harvest each September. And every girl would come to class in the fall with snapshots of a new boyfriend whose name was always Jean-Pierre or Michel or Antoine.

When I was young, we hired southerners to cure the crop for us. The first expert my grandfather hired was a South Carolina hillbilly with overalls and a big felt hat. The story is that he couldn't even read the numbers on the thermometer—he cured by smell. Growing up, I was to know several of his successors, elderly curemen with deep accents who were always reminiscing about coon hounds and possum hunts. Once one died in his sleep in the tiny one-room cureman's shack by the kilns, and we had to ship his body home.

I remember my father coming north to get me the year my parents decided I was old enough to work in tobacco harvest. And I remember my sense of excitement and self-importance on the long train ride home, my feeling of leaving childhood behind. All the subsequent summers spent working on the farm run together—one year I worked the boat-row (I could run fast enough to catch the horse if it ran away) on the last field gang in the area to use a horse. One year I worked two farms and primed tobacco for forty-two straight days without a break. I remember a Seneca boy who boxed with me behind the kilns one year and swimming at the gravel pit after work and drinking Molson beer evenings at the Hotel Syracuse in Waterford, playing Creedence Clearwater Revival and the Band on the bar jukebox.

But what I remember best is waking up in the mornings before work with my aching, swollen hands curled against my chest, and the terrible pain of the cold dew on my hands late in harvest, those chilly September mornings with the sun just coming up, and the smell of horse manure and sweat and the jingling of the harness, and being so tired that I could drop down in the dirt at the end of a row and sleep for thirty seconds, cradled in the earth, before the boat-driver raced up.

I was too small and too young when I started high school. The first day my mother convinced me to wear a white short-sleeved dress shirt and a blue clip-on tie. I don't believe I have ever recovered from the shock of being the only person wearing a white shirt and tie among six hundred standing on the gym floor for the introduction of the new teachers. (Two years later, when it was my brother Rodger's turn, he fainted.) I wanted to play football but was trampled by several huge farmboys the first practice and retired. I asked a girl to the Christmas dance. Then, to be on the safe side, I asked a half-dozen others as well. Apparently, this was a faux pas. My mother had to arrange a date for me with a girl who was still in elementary school.

I wanted to stand out, I wanted glory. Come spring track season, I discovered that my natural born pigheadedness, my unwillingness to give up, was an advantage in the long races. Thus began my career as a distance runner. Night after night, I would step off the yellow-and-black school bus, throw my books on the kitchen table, and lope off around the farm. At first, I wore my school clothes. In the winter, I ran wearing galoshes and an overcoat, slogging through snow drifts up to my thighs, a little boy, solitary, running through the snow in the darkness.

No one coached me. My father discouraged me. I just ran and ran. Later I bought books by famous coaches and tried to adapt their methods. I also bought running shoes and shorts, which was a big step up in the personal hygiene department. I became a high school track star, with letters and honors and all the paraphernalia of jockdom. By the time I finished high school, I was taking the train to Toronto every few weeks for track meets, racing, then wandering around the city in a strange delirium of youthful freedom. These were the sixties and Yorkville, Toronto's Haight-Ashbury, was in full swing with topless go-go dancers, hippies, bikers, and great music bars like the Riverboat.

In 1966, my mother had me registered to go to Trinity College, the Anglican college at the University of Toronto—nurturing ground of Canada's Anglo elite: Bay Street lawyers and future prime ministers. But at one of those twilight track meets, I met the cross-country coach at York University—then a suburban red-brick school just emerging from the mud of an old cow pasture far from the city's center. I fled tradition and the stodgy elitism of Trin-

ity for a half-built, inchoate institution with no identity.

Toronto is built on a grid of squares with one-and-a-quarter-mile sides. I roamed that city for three years, loping fifteen or twenty miles at a stretch, all the way down to the lake and back, or north past the rail yards at the top of the city and into the farms beyond, threading the golf courses and parks along the city's ravines. Mostly by myself, but also with a series of running buddies—some of the most carefree and loveable spirits I've ever known.

In the summer of 1967, on Canada Day, the country's one hundredth birthday, my brothers, Rodger and John, and I ran in a track meet early in the evening, then headed down to Yorkville, and suddenly found ourselves caught up in a joyful riot that took place that night. Surging out of Yorkville, down Yonge Street, we snarled traffic and roared "We Shall Overcome" and the first verse of "Oh Canada" over and over like mantras. Hookers sat on the seat backs of convertibles and boys stood in line for kisses, and people laughed and shrieked and wept. Every time the police tried to cordon off the street to stop us from going on, the crowd would somehow slip by and surge again. I can remember Rodger and me shaking our heads at the sight of our little brother, John—the irrepressible one—leading the charge on a police barricade that somehow miraculously melted away at the last moment. We were a happy gilded nation that night, and my brothers and I were an intrepid band of heroes at the center.

A few weeks later, out of nowhere (since I'd been sidelined with a leg operation in the spring), I came in third in the Canadian marathon championship in Ste.-Hyacinthe, Quebec. It was a boiling hot day, and the streets were lined with boisterous crowds offering water, spraying us with hoses. We had to run five laps through the streets of the city. The biggest problem for most of the runners was just staying on their feet. I remember I hardly passed anyone, but every lap there was a voice at the finish line yelling my place, and I kept moving up. When I came to the beginning of the last lap, my club coach ran for a hundred yards, dodging the crowd, screaming, "You're third! You're third!" He couldn't believe it. I couldn't believe it. I was just a kid. I had just had this tumor removed from the bone of my thigh. And no one was going to pass me.

A week later I tore the cartilage in my knee during training—I always trained too hard. I had a death wish for success. I went to Germany the next summer, summer of 1968, to train with a coach in Freiburg to try to make the Canadian Olympic team. I ran three times a day and danced every night in the discos and bars around the cathedral square. I roamed the Black Forest on foot and learned to drink Rhine wine. I fell in love with a German girl and wrote my first published story—the result of homesickness and reading Hemingway in the American Library every morning. Then I flopped at the Olympic trials and went back to real life.

Later in Edinburgh, where I went in 1969 for an M.Litt. in philosophy, I ran with the university harriers and shared a flat with a pale, wiry steeplechaser who had been thrown off the Scottish national team twice for drinking excessively. Saturdays we raced, then hit the pubs on Rose Street—the Abbotsford and Milne's—then bought carryouts and found a party to crash. I remember, mostly through a drunken

Winning the Canadian twenty-kilometer road race championship, Saskatoon, Saskatchewan, 1979

haze, wandering the stone staircases and Gothic closes of the old town, the dismal winter rains and the long summer nights, the fogs, and the stupidity of sheep. At nine o'clock Sunday mornings, we'd meet again and ramble twenty miles in the Pentland Hills, sweating out the beer, retching, moaning, in love with the pure pleasure of motion.

After Edinburgh, my injuries and operations got the better of me. I taught philosophy for a year at the University of New Brunswick, then found a job as a cub reporter on the *Evening Times-Globe* in Saint John's. This was 1972. I bought checked polyester trousers with two-inch cuffs, shaved my beard and cut my long hair, worked seventy- and eighty-hour weeks on speed and adrenaline, drifted from paper to paper, gained weight, wrote a lot of mostly unpublishable stories. Then, when I was working as an overnight subeditor at the *Montreal Star,* I started running again, out of vanity mostly, popping, for my knees, the human version of the Butolozodin they use on horses.

I finally quit the newspapers in 1976 to be a writer, drifted back to Edinburgh and my old running cronies, wrote a bad novel, started another one. Always running—a hundred miles a week in those days, up to thirty miles at a stretch. In the winter of 1978–79, I fled to Florida with the typescript of my third failing novel, *Precious,* nursing a sore foot. In Cedar Key, I found a quack who shot my foot full of cortisone and got me running again. I drank and played pool and ate huge plates of steamed shrimp at the L & M Bar and the Island Hotel and hung out with an animal behaviorist from Rutgers who was studying the long call of the laughing gull.

A week after I returned to Canada that spring, I picked up the mail and found a novel, a story collection, and three separate stories rejected simultaneously. I sat at the bottom of the step and cried. My father was there—he gave me his handkerchief. He could be caring and gentle when a person hit bottom. Maybe that's where he expected to meet me most of the time. I packed my car and headed west to a job as a subeditor on the newspaper in Saskatoon, vowing never to write again—my equivalent of a Victorian romance gone sour and the jilted lover slipping off to join the French foreign legion.

I was running again, still gingerly after that foot injury. I made friends with a pharmacy professor who ran marathons. I slipped like a shadow along the unpaved concession roads out on the prairie, rain or shine—sometimes they were troughs of gumbo mud that sucked my shoes off. I did laps at Diefenbaker Park overlooking the river, raced trains across the railway trestle bridge above the Mendel Art Gallery. I drank in an Indian bar on Twentieth Street, felt lonely, read and read. In July, Saskatoon hosted the Canadian twenty-kilometer road race championship. I won going away. I still have my gold medal with the enamelled red maple leaf on a white ground.

After that, I quit my job, moved in briefly with my girlfriend, ran through part of the Saskatoon winter (thirty-five degrees below zero was a balmy day), helped save a drowning blind man whose guide dog had led him into the South Saskatchewan River. In January I drove south to Santa Fe, hoping again to try for the Canadian Olympic team—but my legs were gone. My knees felt like the ends of two two-by-fours knocking together.

In Santa Fe, I started to write again, got a job selling running shoes in a shopping mall, danced with Spanish secretaries to a Panamanian salsa band at La Fonda, drank in a bar called the Green Onion on St. Michael's Drive where I met a woman who made her living sitting with the dying. That fall, fall of 1980, I went to the Iowa Writers Workshop. A year later my first book of stories, *The Mad River,* came out. Somewhere, in the turning of that year, I stopped running for good.

But what had been going on beyond all this running, this frenetic travelling? It seems clear that I was trying to escape the frustrations of my writing apprenticeship. Running wasn't my only escape. I showed an earlier draft of this essay to an old friend. He wrote: "You evade a lot, of course. Your Don Juan career, for example. The all-consuming, all-devouring attention you paid to the woman of the moment, the obsessive need to bend her to your desires." I think that the early writing, the travelling, the running, and the lovers all tied together in some mysterious way, that they formed a pattern. At the center of the web was the lust for glory, a desperate fear of failure, and my sense of myself as a callow farmboy in a larger world (always the little boy with a clip-on tie in a crowd of strangers). By glory, I don't mean love and fame. I mean first the

glory of control and mastery, the beauty of a line, the mysterious complexity of words properly organized, and the amazing rush when you throw a sentence into the void and it finds another and another. I'll probably never know why my lust for glory took this particular shape. But when the writing was bad, I would do anything to avoid the shame, the boredom, the dreadful emptiness.

I remember driving home to the family farm after running errands with my father in the spring of 1984 just after my first novel, *Precious,* was published and went out of print in a month, and me saying, choking, really, how a person had to take the long view, and my father saying that, well, he didn't have time to take the long view and that basically I was lazy, that I used writing as a way of shirking life's larger responsibilities— and then he died that night when I was already two hundred miles away, driving away angry.

This was eleven years ago. He left the house to walk over to the tobacco sharegrower's house next door to ask about something in regard to a research paper my biologist brother was doing, and a few minutes later the sharegrower found him lying in a snowbank next to the garage with his hand in his pocket reaching for his heart pills, already far away himself. The sharegrower carried my father into the house and put him on a couch in the sitting room, where, all the years I was growing up, he would nap and listen to the radio in the evenings, ball games and hockey games mostly, and where he sat listening to my Latin declensions and French conjugations, peering at the textbook through his magnifying glass.

He was dead then, and for a while everyone left the house, and my mother lay down next to him and sang him a song she remembered from when she was young: "I'll see you again / whenever spring breaks through again. / Time may lie heavy between, / but what has been is past forgetting." I turned around and drove back the next day, and we—my mother, my two brothers, and I—held this fine, barbaric funeral. For three days we kept my father in the front living room, with people coming to and fro, and my brothers and I going for long walks on the farm alone or together. I had a fanatical impulse to carry him, whenever the coffin had to be moved, myself, with the help of my brothers. And I remember just talking, talking, talking to him—sitting with him in the small hours of the morning, partly drunk,

Peggy Gifford and Douglas Glover, Iowa City, 1981

exhausted, yet holding this endless intimate colloquy with the dead.

During the days leading up to his funeral, I went through my father's desk, sorting the strange objects he had collected: old coins, a War of 1812 medal, the barber scissors he used to cut the ears off fox carcasses when he was warden and hunters would come to claim their bounty, his fifty-year Lions Club pin, a little stone baboon my middle brother, Rodger, had given him one Christmas—all these things I have hidden away in a locked trunk along with the clothes he died in. For a while I sat just looking out the window, thinking that this was what he looked out at, while reminding myself that he couldn't see, really, beyond the end of the desk. (Depression was the normal weather of my father's soul—a friend of mine once said something beautiful about the relationship between depression and the inability to see clearly.)

We buried him in a churchyard a few miles away, next to a rural Methodist church his grandfather had built. To get there we had to drive country roads past the farms where his father

and mother grew up, the ancestral acres—his father bought the present Glover farm in 1900 for $7,000, though his wife, my grandmother Bertha, who had something of a mind of her own, refused to move that far away from her own family (about two miles) for another year or so, and he had to drive back in the democrat whenever he wanted to see her.

I went back to my father's grave this summer mostly because my sons, Jacob and Jonah, have inherited the family obsession with the familiar dead and wanted to see where Grandpa Murray was buried. So we drove out to the Glover plot and dusted the dried grass clippings off the flat granite marker stones. There are two rows of graves with my father, the last but one in the first row. My mother kept the end space for herself, though I remember her grumbling about always having to sit in the aisle seat. Somehow death seems to her like sitting in the Strand Theater in Simcoe through a long double feature with my mother having to stand up again and again to let people out to the popcorn stand or the bathroom.

Douglas (second from left) with brothers, John and Rodger, and Rodger's former wife, Merilee Olson, Ancaster, 1986

The boys looked, but then got more interested in two Jacob Glovers at the other end of the row, the carpenter and the son who died young. It was a moment for them, not for me. I am still empty when it comes to my father and resent all the sentimental rubbish that gets written about fathers and sons, about conflict and reconciliation. I don't foresee any reconciliation for my father and me; we will walk down the stony road to Hell together, him calling me lazy and me thinking fuck you, and why did you give up when your eyes went, why did you? (But the thought occurs to me: What will my sons say of me when I am gone? In what failures and lapses will I be implicated?)

Americans grow up with stories of George Washington, Valley Forge, and the Gettysburg Address. I grew up with an equally romanticized but very different set of cultural fairy tales—Sir Isaac Brock dismounting at Queenston Heights to lead his men on foot against the American gunners dug in at the top, falling as he rallied them for a charge; the first Jacob Glover, born in 1735, arriving at the Niagara Frontier in 1787, a Tory refugee from the Revolution, with, according to contemporary records, "one Woman, 1 son, two daughters, 2 cows and two horses"; the murderous day-long battle at Lundy's Lane when the Canadian militia and a small army of English regulars fought an American army to a

standstill and then fell into exhausted sleep on the field with their arms when the Americans retired; my mother's memories of summers at the family place on Lake Erie, the construction of which had been delayed a year for fear the Fenians would burn it when they invaded from Buffalo in 1866.

Lorenzo Sabine records an anecdote about a Sgt. Jacob Glover who helped capture an American general on Long Island. The Pettits, my grandmother's people, operated a tavern in Trenton, New Jersey, called the Blue Moon, locally famous for its cockfights before the Revolution. My mother's ancestors—the McInnes and the McCalls—energetic, turbulent, and Scotch. The McInnes women were great horsewomen, drank too much, and were often born with six fingers, which was a sign of the second sight. One of the McCalls led a crack rifle company in the War of 1812, then either became a mercenary or simply ran off to Mexico. Years later, he returned to find that his wife had had him declared legally dead and married someone else. A great-uncle took the money meant for his McGill Medical School tuition, ran away to Europe, and ended up a doctor in Argentina. My great-grandfather committed suicide with laudanum the day before he was to appear in court to defend himself against an alienation of affection suit.

My great-great-grandfather Daniel Abiel McCall started the family general store and furniture, boat-building, and shipping business in the mid-nineteenth century in St. Williams, Ontario. He built a lake schooner called the Bay Trader and was deeply involved in cutting down all the timber on the north shore of Lake Erie and shipping it off to Buffalo and Cleveland. The acme of his business success coincided with the peak of the worldwide capitalist expansion in about 1870, then started to decline with the Great Depression of the mid-1870s. Now the store is gone, a flyblown Foodland sits on the lot. Daniel's descendants reputedly burned the family boat and furniture factory twice for the insurance. All that's left to us is some elegantly clunky furniture, some old photographs, and an anxiously unstable sense of middle-class superiority frozen in the nineteenth century.

In 1987, the woman I was living with began to tell people at parties that I had gone to bed for a year, reading nothing but Canadian history. In 1988, I went to Fredericton to be writer-in-residence at the University of New Brunswick where I managed to lose myself in the somewhat cluttered and Borgesian Loyalist Archives (along with microfilm troves from the Lyman Draper Papers and the Public Archives of Canada). This, on top of the year in bed, put an end to my relationship. After eight years of irresolution about marriage and children, the woman fled me and her shaky poetry career in the arms of a Toys R Us store manager to start a chain of beach clothing stores in the South where, I am told, she is highly successful.

But what had been going on beyond the reading, the sloth, the dusty monkish library haunting? There were obdurate structures in my life, mysterious and irreducible. Why the compulsive desire to stay away? What was the burden of family and country it seemed necessary for one to escape? Why write? Clearly, a part of me was little more than a processing station for messages the provenance of which I was at best dimly aware. When you are on a search with all your heart, answers drop off bookshelves (I think by fishing in bookstores, libraries, and arcane bibliographies). In a secondhand bookstore in Montreal, I found R. D. Laing's collection of Canadian Broadcasting Corporation radio talks, *The Politics of the Family,* and *Blackout,* a novel by the late great French-Canadian writer Hubert Aquin.

From Laing I took the lesson that family (country, culture) constructs consciousness unconsciously and secretly, that habits, ways of speaking, relations, and forms of thought are passed on through generations with the same indifferent determinism and purpose as genes on strands of DNA. From Aquin I learned difficulty and revolution. It occurred to me that his frenzied rhetoric, his baroque inventiveness based on the endless proliferation of levels and linkages, his obsessive misogyny—his difficulty, in short—were nothing if not signs of a tremendous effort to coin a new language, to achieve break-out velocity against the gravitational forces of family, country, and culture. Aquin failed; he shot himself to death in 1977. But not before he had written: "There is only one possible law of style: write to the maximum of intensity and incantation."

Laing thrust me back into time, into history, genealogy, and folklore in a restless search for threads, for clues to the mental DNA operating (in) me and the people around me.

Aquin affirmed my own baroque tendencies, the playfully self-conscious mode of high modernity, the rhetorical stance of the failed poet, for which I had already developed an affinity. But he also projected me into an arena of political and rhetorical speculation: satire in the mode of Juvenal, Swift, Celine, and Nathaniel West, and formalism in the mode of Viktor Shklovsky (which led, yes, down another rabbit hole—orality and literacy—via Vladimir Propp, Eric Havelock, and Walter Ong to, of all people, Marshall McLuhan).

My writing apprenticeship ended when I began to write *The Life and Times of Captain N.* It ended with the realization that I could see my country, its history, its politics, and my own life as a universal metaphor, that my life was less a problem than a riddle and a dance, that the old family (national, cultural) stories were not simply repressive signatures but ancient songs singing themselves endlessly. This reversal of vision is rhetorical; I am one of those people who has a difficult time distinguishing the personal from the rhetorical. Whatever can be said with force and beauty must be true. At the same time, I think my apprenticeship ended with the realization that the goal of literature is not simply truth, which is bourgeois and reductive, but a vision of complexity, an endless forging of connections that opens outward into mystery. To put it simply, the universal plot reads: Life is never what it seems, truth is always other (or the Other).

I am a nomad, an expatriate, a wandering Canadian. The region I come from is called southwestern Ontario, but the arts and university crowd have an affectionately derisive name for it—Sowesto—a play on Soweto, the black urbanized township at the edge of Johannesburg, South Africa. We live, the story goes, in the cultural fallout of Toronto and the United States. Everything dies, or seems to die, in the dragon's breath. The psychological effect of this fallout and the history of the people—the Tory refugees from the American Revolution combined with the violently reactionary and racist Orange Irish immigration of the 1840s, the two cloaked in a comfortable miasma of complacent Victorianism—is one of emptiness, ennui, self-satisfaction, and envy. A Vancouver sociologist named Tony Wilden wrote a book called *The Imaginary Canadian* to describe this effect—one is always being spoken for and never speaking, someone else tells you who you are and you go crazy or die trying to approximate the definition.

The trick is to understand that the victim who speaks is no longer a victim but a tragic hero or a clown or a culture critic. Reconstructed this way, the position of victim, the marginal and irrelevant—Canadians—suddenly becomes artistically and intellectually invigorating. It also just happens to coincide with one of the classic rhetorical stances of high modernism, the stance of the failed poet, the writer who cannot write. It is the stance of a Samuel Beckett, say, or Franz Kafka or Christa Wolf or Thomas Bernhard or Milan Kundera, writers who see both the comic and tragic possibilities of marginality, and who see marginality as a metaphor for the self in the modern age— that self that everywhere feels somehow exterior and irrelevant to its own destiny.

Marginality and exile are complex liminal states without forced allegiance or territory to defend, where translation (between languages, races, ideologies, and histories) is a natural form of thought, where difference is being. *The Life and Times of Captain N.* tells the story of three real people who began in the Mohawk Valley of upstate New York not far from where I live today and ended up Tory refugees after the Revolution, settling the part of Canada where I was born. The woman on whom the Mary Hunsacker character is based, for example, was kidnapped by Mississauga Indians near Fort Plain, New York, in 1780 and lies buried in a little

Stepdaughters Taber (left) and Morgan Ward, Cancun, Mexico, 1995

pioneer cemetery four miles from the Glover farm in Ontario. And my themes are translation, difference, history, and redemption.

In 1990, I married Helen Edelman, a beautiful, energetic Jewish girl from Scarsdale who has a career as a marketing and communications executive for a hospital in Troy, New York, and publishes academic articles on medical anthropology on the side. Possibly I could not have found a partner more different from myself, but in difference there is discovery. We live in a brown saltbox house on the tenth tee of a suburban golf course just outside Saratoga Springs. I have a Dalmatian dog again; her name is Nellie. In the summer, there is a constant, dreamy thwacking of golf balls beyond my study window, which sometimes makes me think I am living in a Walker Percy novel.

I have two graceful stepdaughters, Morgan and Taber Ward, from my wife's previous marriage. And we have two sons of our own— Jacob and Jonah—both named for men in the Bible who argue with God and angels (may they live up to their names, may their lives be lived at that pitch). Jacob is four, handsome and lean, a painter by inclination. Early on, he did what he called "ravish paintings"—he would cover the paper with swirls and flames of brilliant red, yellow, and orange, then paint everything over black, leaving windows, cracks, and pinholes so that everywhere the fire was burning beneath and through the gloom. I buy

Helen Edelman, 1990

swords by the dozen at the Dollar Store to keep him supplied with weaponry.

My second son, Jonah, is like me. He sees a hill, and he wants to run up it or down it. No half-measures. He gets this look in his eye and he grins. An obstacle is something to try, to test, to make yourself against, not something in the way. He may fall down, get a scrape, but he knows he's alive. He's only eighteen months as I write, doesn't talk much, plays the piano for his own pleasure, bangs a snare drum I bought Jacob, dances in preference to any other form of movement, loves dogs, and likes to watch the bats dipping over our yard at twilight.

Of my brothers: John is a postdoctoral fellow in gene biology at the University of Chicago and spends his spare time playing in blues bars or camping with his wife and daughter. Rodger finished a Ph.D. in physics at Stanford, published papers on the motions of very small particles, then became a family practice doctor in Oakville, Ontario. They are both brilliant, gifted, gentle men. Both have been married twice. Both were runners. Both share the family talent for finding the rocky pathway to the beach.

My relationship to writing is mysterious, mystical, romantic, and compulsive—still. I haven't taken proper care of things, have no perma-nent job, no pension plan. What might it mean to say I have spent most of my life overcom-ing my life? Walker Percy once said that nov-elists are ex-suicides, a view that Hippolyte Taine anticipated in the nineteenth century when he wrote: "To have a true idea of man, or of life, one must have stood himself on the brink of suicide, or on the doorsill of insanity, at least once." (I love that last phrase "at least once"—Hippolyte had a sense of humor.)

I am writing a novel about my great-grandfather who killed himself with an over-dose of laudanum in 1914. He kept the family store in St. Williams, wrote poetry, called him-self the Bard and the Possum, had a dog named Gyp, lived in his wife's house with her mother and her spinster sisters and his two daughters, and died of shame. The night he died, the men of the village gathered at the house and took turns walking him up and down the hall, trying to revive him. At the last, as he lay dying, my grandmother, then eighteen, climbed into bed with him, held him in her arms, and pleaded with him to try to live.

A year ago, I tracked down his suicide let-ter, missing since the day he died. (R. D. Laing would have appreciated this—how the messages are hidden away only to emerge at the proper time.) He wrote: "Life is sweet, but not worth

Sons Jonah (left) and Jacob, ages one and four, on the Glover farm in Waterford, 1995

while after having to go through a trial of this kind. I cannot stand such publicity and cannot take my wife and family through this vile thing. It is hard to part with my dear wife and girls, I hope they will survive the shock of my death. God protect them, those who have driven me to this receive their just reward, I have no fear of Death."

In the Ontario archives, I found the letter books belonging to the lawyer who was handling the case against him. So far as I can tell, there wasn't a shred of evidence on which to base the lawsuit. The wronged husband was a drunk and a failure; he suffered Nietzschean *ressentiment* in spades. But was my great-grandfather nevertheless guilty? And what might have been happening off stage, as it were, that made his death inevitable? The world was on the cusp. Modernity, the whole thrust of the bourgeois nineteenth century, was about to spin violently out of control. In the future, *ressentiment* would propel Hitler into power and fuel the Holocaust. Mass man and totalitarianism would submerge the individual. We would learn the fatal meaning of shamelessness.

The author at the Doublehook Bookstore, Montreal, 1991

My father was an orator. I haven't mentioned that. It made an impression. I remember the slightly quaint, orotund formfulness of his speeches and his jokes. I remember sitting with him once as he wrestled with a speech for the annual Man of the Year banquet, shaping it around a Shakespearean trope on the Four Ages of Man.

My mother still tells stories.

The saddest story she tells is about the pilot she fell in love with when the war broke out. There were several training bases around Simcoe; my mother's mother made it a practice to invite as many boys over for home-cooked meals as she could. Somehow she heard about this Newfoundlander, a bomber pilot in the Royal Air Force, who would stand at the gate as servicemen went on leave, making sure they had enough cash to get home, lending them money, taking care of them. He was huge, dashing, and kind; my mother was pretty, scattered, and energetic. They fell in love; maybe would have gotten married. He gave her a claddagh ring and went to war.

My mother was in Toronto at the university in the spring of 1942 when she came back to her room and found her mother and sister waiting for her. She didn't have to ask. She had dreamed a dream a few nights before. Her pilot was calling to her from far far away, telling her not to worry, that he would always be with her. He had flown a bomber in one of the first raids over Berlin, been hit by antiaircraft fire coming home, had nursed his crippled plane as far as the North Sea, trying to get home, before crashing. The Germans found him, buried him in a little cemetery near Lubeck looking toward Britain.

He must have had a premonition. Shortly before he died he wrote my mother telling her not to be too heartbroken if something happened to him. He also wrote to my grandmother asking her to watch out for Jeannie. I have never read such brave, manly, gallant words. My mother went to work in a factory making radios for tanks, then joined the air force herself. Years later, travelling in Europe with my father, she nearly went to see her pilot's grave, but some sentiment prevented her.

My mother's stories are overpowering, as is the memory of my father's public eloquence. I am still struggling to come out from under. But, grumble as I might, rue and regret, I think this is the way things should have been. I am a creature of stories and words. I am not much besides the words and stories.

But, oh, the beauty of the words, and the sound of my mother's voice droning on sleepily into the night.

Only now it is my voice.

BIBLIOGRAPHY

Novels:

Precious, Seal Books, 1984.

The South Will Rise at Noon, Viking, 1988.

The Life and Times of Captain N., Knopf, 1993.

Short-story collections:

The Mad River, Black Moss Press, 1981.

Dog Attempts to Drown Man in Saskatoon, Talonbooks, 1985.

A Guide to Animal Behaviour, Gooselane Editions, 1991.

Robert Gurik

1932-

LOOSE ENDS

(Translated from the French by Joel Miller.
Original French version follows.)

Robert Gurik

One of my earliest memories: holding hands with my mother, we bring provisions to my father, a lithographer occupying his print shop with striking colleagues. Through the fence, he slips me a few chocolates, chocolates filled with a liqueur. It is the first time in my life I taste it . . . I am four or five years old.

Was that moment perhaps the reason I have always associated class struggles with pleasure?

What motivates a career as a playwright? What motivates mine?

Born in France of Hungarian parents, I remained aloof from the French because in France one is always a foreigner. Therefore I found myself in the position of spectator, observer—an ideal position for a writer.

Because of the war, my generation was old young. Undoubtedly, one ages quickly when facing death. Often I have been asked why I

"My parents before my birth, near Marseilles," 1926

never wrote about the Second World War, considering that I lived through it as a Jewish child in occupied Paris. It is because I loathe sensationalism, I loathe romanticizing war.

I was a child; Jews were being hunted down. My twelve-year-old cousin Georges, whose parents had pushed him from the second-story window just before being led away themselves, crossed the entire city of Paris on foot to find us. My eight-year-old cousin Jean was snatched from the camp at Drancy by my mother. I wore the yellow star for a while, and then, for obvious reasons, stopped wearing it. My father buried himself in the so-called free zone. My brother, my two cousins, and I, shepherded by my mother, hid in a number of different anonymously rented apartments. We would live in one for a few months, and then, during the night, we would slip into all our clothing at once, layering each piece on top of the other. We would gather our meagre personal effects and clear out, our arms full of sacks and hastily buckled suitcases. However, because of my youth, nothing surprised me; it was neither

adventure nor game: it was the only reality I knew.

Perhaps it was because of the war that I have remained stamped with this apparent paradox: I have an absolute need for security—a roof over my head and food on my plate—and, at the same time, I truly attach no importance whatsoever to earthly possessions.

I was an average student, one of those of whom it is said "He could do better." As an adolescent, like many others, football and girls were my main attractions. Also, like many adolescents at the time, I wrote poetry, pseudo-Prévert. I vaguely thought I wanted to be a journalist.

I have never desired money, commodities, or power. In fact, everything in general interested me, and nothing in particular. My elder brother studied engineering. The first unrest in Algeria began. Once again there was talk of conscription. My brother left for Canada. It was decided that it would be best for me to follow in his footsteps. As did the rest of the family a little later. Or, being of Hungarian extraction (therefore a little Gipsy-like), perhaps I had the genes of a nomad.

After the war we continued to live in poverty to one degree or another. Just prior to emigrating, I was overcome with a passion for opera and the theatre, a feverous onset all the more surprising because I had not been—nor am I now—an aficionado of the theatre. With the exception of these few noteworthy months, the theatre has always bored me. During this initial theatrical convulsion, I was particularly struck by a production of *Diable et le bon Dieu* (*The Devil and the Good Lord*) by Jean-Paul Sartre, directed by Louis Jouvet and starring Jean Vilar, Maria Casares, and Pierre Brasseur. I remember to this day how I left the theatre full of enthusiasm, exhilarated and transported by that play. So much so that I immediately began to draft a socio-philosophical dramatic text, which quickly reached more than thirty obscene pages. So obscene in fact that my mother, who was running short of toilet paper like everyone else, cut up my immortal pages and dedicated them to this less than radiant purpose.

With my first dramatic efforts literally down the drain, I quickly forgot the whole affair and immersed myself in my preparations to leave. I was thousands of miles away from what awaited me.

". . . we wish you a happy stay in Montreal."

He awoke with a start.

"We are beginning our descent into Dorval Airport. The temperature is thirty-two degrees Fahrenheit under cloudy skies. Please ensure that your seat belt is securely fastened and that your seat back is in an upright position . . ."

Through the window, he saw the plane thread its way through the clouds, descending toward a new country, toward a new life, plunging into the future. He fumbled in his right trousers pocket to make sure that the little wallet with its two hundred dollars was still there.

In the baggage area, he quickly spotted his suitcase. Just prior to his departure, he had secured his case with one of the rope belts his mother had woven for him. Under German occupation, he developed a phobia for the hastily tied packages carted by his family during numerous migrations. While waiting for his suitcase, he tried to hide a sack of provisions under his arm. It contained a present from his mother to Margit, his cousin by marriage: an embroidered tablecloth and a box of Suchard chocolates.

At the immigration desk, he offered his passport opened to the page stamped with the visa. The immigration officer leafed through the pages, stopping at his photo. The face of a bony adolescent, elongated (he hated his pointy chin), burned by two immense dark eyes. The officer stared at him, rekindling habitual apprehension. It was an uncontrollable reflex. Uniforms always had the same effect on him. If he had remained in France, he would be wearing one now somewhere in Algeria. Measuring only 1.63 metres (approximately five feet four inches), he believed he was practically invisible, too small to really exist or, at best, to be taken seriously. Uncomfortable, he shifted the weight of his body now on his left foot, now on his right, as if to better feel his weight and thus verify his existence.

"Paul Fischer?"

"Yes," he replied in an uncertain voice.

"Where are you going to stay?"

He did not understand a thing. In his English classes, no one ever spoke so quickly.

He attempted a reply.

"Ay em ay-teene-y-eeres old."

"Your address in Montreal?" the officer insisted, taking care to articulate every word. Paul caught the words "address" and "Montreal."

"My cooseene. Deux cent trente sept, Villeneuve Streete."

The sound of the stamp exploded like a cannon saluting this linguistic effort, of which he was more than a little proud.

October 9, 1951, the date shone on the page of his passport. The bus heading downtown cost one dollar and fifty cents. Paul, his hand glued to his right pocket, to the one hundred ninety-eight Canadian dollars and fifty Canadian cents left to him, was accelerating toward his new destiny. In front of him, at some distance, he saw a little hill, a tall white tower, and a dome like the Pantheon all encircled by a belt of low-rise dwellings. But, where were the skyscrapers? Where were the Indians hiding? Only the huge, chrome-armoured automobiles resembled the sights in American films and corresponded to the image he had of Canada.

From the bus terminal in Central Station, he hopped into a taxi. For the entire journey, he was afraid that the driver might "take him for a ride," as they did in Paris. Sitting on the edge of the back seat, his eye darting from the meter to the road,

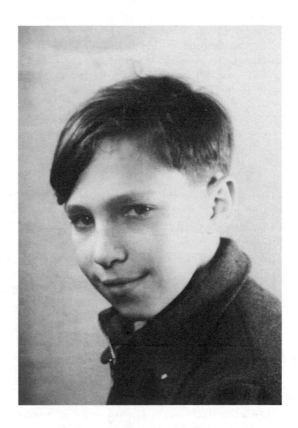

Robert at ten

he couldn't detect any strange detours, even though the route seemed interminable.

The taxi stopped in front of a row of about fifteen identical redbrick two-story houses which vomited, from the second story to the ground, metal staircases seeming to span an invisible danger.

"How ugly!" Paul thought, fascinated in spite of himself by this iterative accumulation of cast iron. Frequently, in the taxi, he noticed these exterior staircases, which appeared to be an architectural particularity of the city. He imagined a miniature sculpture: just a series of staircases leading to nowhere.

[. . .] What good does it do to get excited? to go where? to achieve what? [. . .] Everyone continues to live as though nothing has changed. Is it of any use? The others have already forgotten. [. . .] All his friends were foreigners. He himself was born a foreigner, pristine, without a country. Behind him he felt Agnes, Michel, Louis, Camus, Jean-Paul Sartre, Boris Vian, Ionesco, Adamov, Beckett, the cellars of St-Germain des Prés, the painter Ripolin, and *la Vache qui rit*[1] rapidly disappear into the distance. Tears streamed incessantly down his cheeks. He did not know whether they were provoked by the cold wind whistling across his face, or by the evaporation of the large ball that was formed in his belly, his throat, or in his heart when he left Paris. He understood brutally that he was essential to no one if not to himself.

[. . .] He who has lost everything becomes carefree. He just lost his childhood. He heard himself speak aloud his thoughts at that very instant: "Every child is innocent, why not the adult?"

This is an excerpt from a work in progress. Actually, my first impressions of the Montreal and Quebec of the fifties were quite simply abominable. I was born the first time in Paris in the thirties, the child of Hungarian-Jewish parents. I was born a second time when I landed in the New World at the beginning of the fifties, the child of that dramatic couple, snow and space.

I began, of course, by landing in an inhuman cold which seemed to me—and which still does—unimaginable. More important, *la belle Province* (Quebec) seemed to me eternally petrified in Catholicism, an omnipresent, aberrant, and deadly religion. It wasn't very rich from the cultural point of view either: Sainte-Catherine Street had only four movie theatres; I was very far from Paris . . . At first I perceived only a cold, grey murkiness and poverty, both physical and intellectual. But worst of all was to experience the sensation that nothing will ever move, advance, or progress in the land of Quebec. Of course I was mistaken.

This was the fifties, under the "reign" of Premier Duplessis, which was later characterized as "The Great Darkness." Victor Hugo, Zola, Baudelaire were still forbidden! Even the Bible did not escape censorship, for we were advised to read the expurgated version . . . As for the theatre, the directors of the few theatres that existed remained entirely subjugated to texts from France. No one believed that a French-Canadian (the word "Québecois" was not yet in use) could ever write a theatrical work.

In the meantime, I enrolled at l'École Polytechnique (The School of Engineering at the Universty of Montreal). At that time most of the classes were given in English. I must admit that I did the barest minimum of studies in engineering techniques and the maximum amount of clandestine studies in the good life of Quebec. I also played cards with a passion that remains with me to this day.

I founded le Parti Neutre (the Neutral Party), a party leaning toward Anarchism, whose most important electoral platform was the construction of a pipeline transporting beer from the Sphynx, the tavern on the corner, directly to our rooms at the school. I was so good at this raucous, dissolute life that, not surprisingly, I finished second to last in my graduating year.

Nevertheless, I was immediately offered a job. At that time, the few available engineers were in ferocious demand. Canadian Pacific Railways immediately posted me to its telegraphy sector, overseeing all repeating stations between Newfoundland and Vancouver—another opportunity to go on a spree and travel first-class coast-to-coast. We even phoned ahead to each upcoming station so our colleagues could organize parties for us. The Western provinces with their immense prairies gave me the impression I was acting in an American Western film. I had a wonderful time, even though I felt more and more that there was no place

---

[1] The Laughing Cow, a famous brand of cheese in France with a long-standing widespread advertising campaign. Translator's note.

for me in the English-speaking provinces. So much so that one day I decided *ex abrupto* to resign and return to Montreal.

Upon my return, I immediately found a job as a commercial engineer in heating and ventilation: in other words—as I would do later by writing—I sold air. I joyously pursued my life as an unattached young man. I hung out with the bohemians of the time, painters, architects, artists, and pseudo artists. For the immigrants among them, like myself, America was a new Eldorado. My memories take on the names of the bistros in the western part of the city, the Riviera Café, la Petite Hutte, le Moka and le Pam Pam where we devoured eastern European pastries. I voraciously read everything that fell into my hands. I developed a definite interest for the new novel.

Then I fell in love with Renée, who became my wife and the mother of my two boys. This small, peppery redhead, with sharp eyes and quivering nose, caught my eye. Although I practice no religion, our respective families inflicted two religious weddings upon us, one Jewish and one Catholic.

I was not yet a writer, nor did I feel any need to be one. Renée, on the other hand, was undeniably an artist. Soon she enrolled at the National Theatre School of Canada to study set and costume design, and then took up her career with all the ardour and energy which had so seduced me in the first place.

Although the number of theatres was much fewer than today, there were many festivals and competitions. So Renée and a friend got together to produce a one-act play for l'ACTA (l'Association canadienne du théâtre amateur, The Canadian Association of Amateur Theatre). Renée read excerpts of the play to me. I considered it very bad. I teased her incessantly about it, repeating "Not like that" and "It'll have to be completely restructured." Undaunted, my wife finally challenged me to do it myself if I were so good and if I understood so well how to do it. As a joke, I took up the gauntlet and settled down to the work. Thus I wrote my first play in 1963, the same year as the F.L.Q.[2]

---

[2] *Front de libération du Québec,* Quebec Liberation Front, a clandestine terrorist organization struggling for Quebec independence whose activities culminated in 1970 with the kidnapping of British diplomat James Cross and the kidnapping and murder of Quebec cabinet minister Pierre Laporte. Translator's note.

set off its first bombs. It was called *Le chant du poète* (The Poet's Song), a short play which had no less than fifty-two extras, was full of carnage, and confronted the problems of creation. And, I won first prize.

Nevertheless, writing new plays seemed impossible: theatre directors resisted new works, so much so that when I presented my second play at the Festival d'art dramatique a little later, I was convinced that among the five productions at the festival, mine would be the only new work.

But, surprise! All five productions were by local playwrights, each of whom shared my delusion.

Therefore we decided to create a tool to break down this wall of resistance and created "le Centre d'essai des auteurs dramatiques" (literally The Dramatic Author's Tryout Centre, which would probably be better translated as Playwrights' Workshop. Trans.). The CEAD established the conditions, objectives, and materials necessary to the burgeoning of Quebec dramaturgy. This was the first original, concerted action of its kind, subsequently imitated in Europe, most particularly in France. The meeting places for CEAD moved from one playwright's apartment to another's kitchen, its budget coming from begging and meagre dues. For my own part, I remember investing in Quebec dramaturgy an astronomical sum of coffee and cognac.

Contrary to my first impression, Quebec society did not remain stagnant. In more or less fifteen years, Quebec caught up on almost one hundred years. From being a society with the mission of providing raw materials for American factories and missionaries for the rest of the world, Quebec had entered the twentieth century.

This is how, occasionally, a playwright's career is born: by a blow to the head. Although I was a lethargic, ungrateful, and difficult spectator, I had nonetheless been infected by the demon sting of dramatic writing, never to be cured. To this day, I read a newspaper article, or listen to a conversation, or a detail or trifling incident catches my attention, and it puts down roots, acquiring an immeasurable importance, and I MUST write a play about it. I write because I cannot avoid it. It overpowers me. Situations gush forth, structural links take shape, and I must try to put order into the chaos of the problem. Or, at least, part of it.

Gurik with his wife, Renée, at a rehearsal of Api, *1966*

I work for television and film, but I have always preferred the theatre which has far fewer compromises. I like the raw light that the theatre can throw upon a society, the explosion allowing the multiplication of voices, the brutal efficiency of theatrical concision, and how it can expose to the bright light of day the gear wheels which crush individuals. I was never given to psychology or introspection; my only passions are the mechanisms preventing the individual from being himself. For me, the theatre is the last remaining place for philosophical discussion.

From another point of view, I am astonished, on the one hand, that the majority of productions only use the stage floor and leave its yawning chasm empty, and on the other, I remain fascinated by the fact that scenic action naturally uses ONLY the stage floor. I don't know, perhaps this illustrates my fundamental matter-of-fact nature.

Naturally rebellious, I have always refused to work on commission. When I write, I become irritable over nothing, a distraction makes

me hit the ceiling, and even poker can no longer truly engross me. My nearest and dearest have learned to forgive me this state.

I remained an engineer for quite some time, even while writing play after play. This was because of the absolute need for security I inherited from my childhood during the war. I was named "Man of the Theatre" for 1968, awarded many prizes and honours, but I did not make the jump until 1972.

My image of the theatre is of someone in a closed room, suffocating from lack of oxygen, shattering the windowpanes. The theatre is a breaking of glass. My only quest is to oppose everything that is accepted, everything that is hierarchical, to oppose all structure. From this opposition all my subthemes are born: liberty, happiness . . .

I always work hard to ensure that the audience is never so moved they can no longer think. My theatre is demanding because it provides no answers. Nor does it ever allow us to wash our hands of these questions. The theatre I write asks questions that accompany, follow, and pursue the spectator, because I try to make people understand the necessity of the repudiation of hierarchies, the abolition of classes, the destruction of privileges. I ask people to join with me in the rejection of obstacles.

I do with the theatre what I am incapable of achieving in life. In life, I am incapable of being a political person, of being an orator; in the theatre, however, I express my political point of view. In the theatre I act on politics, while in life—I live.

I continue to fight for our rights, but, like most Quebec authors, I feel isolated. First of all, because there is no milieu for Quebec playwrights—we are deprived of theatres; to be performed in a theatre does not mean that we belong to that theatre—that we have a space at our disposal in which to be performed. Moreover, the very definition of the Quebec author is reexamined with each play: we write one play, then another, and with each one we start over again.

In a broader context, this is above all else a political position. We have entered into the era of the middleman. The closer we are to the blank page, to the moment of creation, the more we are misunderstood and badly paid.

On the other hand, every effort is made to guarantee the middleman the rights of authorship over the work, and the text itself is reduced to the function of a pretext: this is the consequence of the hegemony of monetarism.

I continue to write plays. I teach and am very busy with negotiations defending the rights of authors. What will become of them today in Quebec?

If we judge by productions of recent years, playwrights have not escaped the wave of individualization flooding the western world. In the same vein, the only words in the mouths of the theatre directors, often newly-appointed, are "profitability," "lost income," "net gain": these young wolves do not show their fangs—they show their dentures.

Renée was director and stage-set designer for Api *and eventually designed every stage set and all costumes for her husband's plays*

The collective drive has broken down and plays become "dramatic objects" swarming with deviants, the only possible dissension in this wave of conservatism. The characters of the artist, the criminal, and the homosexual proliferate. The themes of rape, crime, and larceny surface in play after play. All social and political reflection has been banished; it is the triumph of Freudian theatre.

Lacking content, one falls back on form. The object-play, nourished by the development of performance and technique, proliferates. So, in my latest play, as Ben expresses:

"Spectator be surprised
that I present myself before you
like a turd
in a bed of roses
for I know that today
one does not want to hear the creators
but rather the merchant
the expert pollster
the expert page layout designer
the artist's curator
the interpreter's impresario.

It is no longer the winning runner
in the games that is celebrated
but rather the manufacturer of his shoes
or of his thirst-quenching elixir.
Not the discus-thrower
but the vinyl disc distributor.
We have entered the era of profit
of the middleman
of the empty space between the tree and
  its bark.

"So why waste our time
talking about this society in which Liberty's
feet are encased in cement?
Cement is expensive
flesh is cemented.
Why talk about this society
when all cures are spread thin
like a bare wall
too hard or too cured.
Because it is no longer a question of flight
of crying for crying's sake
of laughing just for laughing
for it would be sad to die
sad and stupid to kill yourself.
Because we must try to say

The production of A coeur ouvert, *staged at Le Théâtre de Quatre Sous, Montreal, 1969*

that if there are no absolute solutions
that if they are all wrong
that if all powers are oppressive
then all oppressions are worthless.
Unhappiness is a state
happiness is not.
Finally, happiness does not exist
we must invent it, create it
rationally
knowing that it is an invention
a mirage, a decoy, a creation.
Knowing that we are wrong
and that we are right
that it is not a truth
an obligation
a 'believe or die' situation
a 'believe or kill' situation.

"And, as Aristophanes said:
'For all these reasons,
since as a wise man
he did not thoughtlessly hasten
to speak nonsense,
let us make a great noise
a beating of palm fronds and let's jump
    on board . . .'
the ferryboat to liberty."

My generation wanted to leap on the train no matter what the cost and go together toward a better future.

The following generation wanted to leap off the train.

The new generation is sitting beside the tracks and there is no train in sight.

Let us hope that, after being dispersed on this empty countryside by two useless tracks, the coming generation will put all its energy into the construction of a train.

As for me, I loathe talking about myself. As a subject of literature my own existence, like any strictly individual destiny, is devoid of interest. For the particular is a form of conservatism which obstructs the general, the promise of the future.

—Montreal, December 1995

BOUTS DE FICELLE DE ROBERT GURIK

L'un de mes premiers souvenirs: ma main dans celle de ma mère, nous allons porter des provisions à mon père, artisan lithographe en grève, et qui occupe son imprimerie avec ses collègues. Au travers des grilles, il me glisse quelques chocolats, des chocolats à la liqueur, c'est la première fois de ma vie que j'en mange . . . J'ai quatre ou cinq ans.

Dès lors, peut-être ai-je associé à tout jamais plaisir et lutte des classes? A quoi tient une carrière d'écrivain dramatique? A quoi tient la mienne?

Né en France mais de parents hongrois, j'ai toujours été en recul par rapport aux français, parce qu'en France on reste toujours étranger; je me retrouvais alors dans la position de spectateur, d'observateur, une position idéale pour un écrivain.

A cause de la guerre, ma génération a été vieille jeune. A faire face à la mort on mûrit plus vite sans doute. On m'a souvent demandé, d'ailleurs, pourquoi n'ai-je jamais écrit sur la deuxième guerre, que j'ai vécue comme enfant juif dans Paris occupé. C'est que je répugne au sensationnalisme, au romanesque de la guerre.

J'étais enfant, on pourchassait les Juifs. Mon cousin Georges, à douze ans, que ses parents avaient poussé par la fenêtre du deuxième étage tout juste avant qu'on les emmène, avait traversé tout Paris à pied pour nous rejoindre. Mon cousin Jean, huit ans, a été arraché au camp de Drancy par ma mère. J'ai porté l'étoile jaune et puis, pour d'évidentes raisons, j'ai arrêté de la porter. Mon père se terrait en zone dite libre, et sous la houlette de ma mère, mon frère, mes deux cousins et moi nous nous cachions d'appartement en appartement loués par d'autres. On s'installait pour quelques mois, et une nuit, il nous fallait ramasser nos maigres effets personnels et déguerpir, après avoir enfilé les uns par dessus les autres tous nos vêtements, et avec les bras chargés de sacs et de valises bouclées à la va-vite. Pourtant, à cause de mon jeune âge, rien ne me surprenait, ce n'était pas l'aventure, ni même un jeu: c'était la seule réalité que je connaissais.

Peut-être suis-je resté marqué de la guerre par cet apparent paradoxe: j'ai absolument besoin de sécurité, c'est-à-dire d'un toit et de quoi bouffer, et en même temps je n'attache vraiment aucune importance aux possessions terrestres.

Je n'étais qu'un élève moyen, de ceux auxquels on note "peut mieux faire." Adolescent, comme beaucoup, le foot et les filles me captivaient bien davantage . . . Comme aussi beaucoup d'adolescents d'alors, j'écrivais de la

Gurik before the billboard of his play Les portes, *at
La Comédie Canadienne, 1965*

poésie, du pseudo Prévert. J'avais vaguement
l'intention de devenir journaliste.

Je n'ai jamais eu ni désir d'argent, ni de
biens, ni de pouvoirs. En vérité, tout m'intéressait
en général, et rien en particulier. Mon frère
aîné entreprit des études d'ingénieur. Les premiers troubles en Algérie débutaient. On
recommençait à parler de conscription. Mon
frère partit pour le Canada. Il a été décidé
qu'il valait mieux que je suive ses traces. Comme
le ferait le reste de la famille plus tard. Ou
peut-être, d'origine hongroise donc un peu ro-
manichelle, avais-je de toute façon le nomadisme
inscrit dans les gênes?

C'était l'après-guerre, nous connaissions
toujours diverses pénuries. Tout juste avant
d'émigrer j'ai été pris d'une rage d'opéra et
de théâtre, un coup de fièvre assez curieux
car je n'étais pas, ni ne suis toujours, un aficionado de théâtre. Le théâtre, sauf ces quelques
mois notables, m'a toujours ennuyé. De cette
crise théâtrale d'alors, je fus entre autres
particulièrement frappé par la représentation
du *Diable et le bon Dieu* de Jean-Paul Sartre,
dans une mise en scène de Louis Jouvet, avec
Jean Vilar, Maria Casares et Pierre Brasseur. Je
me souviens encore à ce jour combien je suis
sorti enthousiasmé, soulevé, transporté par cette
pièce. Tant et si bien que j'entamai sur-le-champ
la rédaction d'un texte dramatique philosophico-
social qui atteignait bientôt une trentaine de
pages mal embouchées. Tellement mal em-

bouchées d'ailleurs que ma mère, à court de
"papier cul" comme du reste, découpa et dédia
mes feuillets immortels à ce fort peu reluisant
emploi.

Mes premiers efforts dramatiques littéralement
jetés aux égouts, j'oubliai toute l'affaire aussi
vite dans les préparatifs de mon départ. J'étais
à mille lieux de ce qui m'attendait.

". . . we wish you a happy stay in
Montreal."

Il s'éveilla en sursaut.

"Nous commençons notre descente vers
l'aéroport de Dorval. La température est de
trente-deux degrés Farenheit, le ciel est
couvert. Veuillez redresser le dossier de votre
siège et boucler . . ."

Par le hublot, il vit l'avion piquer dans
les nuages, foncer vers un nouveau pays,
vers une nouvelle ville, s'enfoncer dans
l'avenir. Il palpa la poche droite de son
pantalon pour s'assurer que son petit
portefeuille avec les deux cents dollars était
toujours là.

A la salle des bagages, il repéra rapidement
sa valise. A la dernière minute avant de
partir, il avait substitué une de ses ceintures
à la corde que sa mère avait nouée pour
la consolider. Sous l'occupation allemande
il avait développé une phobie pour les
paquets ficelés à la hâte qu'il transportait
lors des nombreux déménagements de la
famille. En attendant, il essayait de dissimuler
sous son bras un sac de provision. Il contenait
le cadeau de sa mère à Margit, la cousine
par alliance: une nappe brodée et une boîte
de chocolats Suchard.

Dans la pièce de contrôle, il tendit son
passeport ouvert à la page où s'étalait le
tampon du visa. L'officier d'immigration
feuilleta les pages, s'arrêta sur sa photo. Un
visage d'adolescent osseux, allongé (il haïssait
son menton pointu), brûlé par d'immenses
yeux noirs. L'officier le dévisagea, éveillant
en lui l'appréhension habituelle. C'était un
réflexe incontrôlable. Les uniformes lui
faisaient toujours le même effet. S'il était
resté un France, il en aurait endossé un,
quelque part en Algérie. Avec 1 mètre 63,
il avait l'impression d'être quasiment invisible; trop petit pour exister vraiment ou
tout au moins pour être pris au sérieux.
Mal à l'aise, il appuyait alternativement le
poids de son corps sur le pied droit puis
sur le gauche, comme pour le soupeser et
en vérifier ainsi l'existence.

"Paul Fischer?"

"Oui," répondit-il d'une voix mal assurée.

"Where are you going to stay?"

Il n'avait rien compris. En classe d'anglais, on ne parlait pas si vite. Il tenta une réponse.

"I am étine yirs old."

"Your address in Montreal?" insista l'officier, en prenant soin d'articuler. Paul avait attrapé au passage "adresse" et "Montréal."

"My cousine. Deux cent trente-sept, Villeneuve strit."

Un violent coup de tampon vint saluer cet effort linguistique, dont il n'était pas peu fier.

9 octobre 1951, la date scintillait sur la page de son passeport. L'autobus pour le centre-ville coûtait un dollar cinquante. Paul, la main appliquée sur sa poche droite, sur les cent quatre-vingt dix-huit dollars canadiens et cinquante cents qui lui restaient, roulait à toute allure vers son nouveau destin. En avant, au loin, il voyait une petite colline, une grande tour blanche et un dôme comme le Panthéon, ceinturés d'habitations basses. Mais où étaient les gratte-ciel? Où se cachaient les peaux rouges? Seules les voitures, immenses, bardées de chrome, étaient comme dans les films américains et répondaient à l'image qu'il s'était faite du Canada.

Du terminus de l'autobus, à la Gare Centrale, il a sauté dans un taxi. Tout au long du trajet il a eu peur que le chauffeur ne le "promène," comme c'était l'habitude à Paris. Tendu, assis sur le bord du siège, l'oeil allant du compteur à la route, il ne put repérer de détours, bien que le parcours lui parut interminable.

Le taxi s'arrêta en face d'une rangée d'une quinzaine de maisons de deux étages, identiques, en briques rouges. Elles vomissaient jusqu'au sol des escaliers métalliques qui semblaient enjamber un danger invisible.

Quelle laideur se dit Paul. Tout en étant malgré lui fasciné par cette accumulation itérative de fer. A plusieurs reprises, dans le taxi, il avait remarqué ces escaliers extérieurs qui semblaient une particularité architecturale de la ville. Il imagina une sculpture en modèle réduit: juste une série d'escaliers ne menant nulle part.

[. . .] A quoi bon s'agiter? pour aller où? pour atteindre quoi? [. . .] Tout le monde continuait à vivre comme si rien n'avait changé. Il ne servait donc à rien? Les autres l'avaient déjà oublié. [. . .] Tous ses amis et amies étaient des étrangers. Lui-même était né étranger, sans pays, vierge. Derrière lui il sentit s'éloigner à toute vitesse Agnès, Michel, Louis, Camus, Jean-Paul Sartre, Boris Vian, Ionesco, Adamov, Beckett, les caves de St-Germain des Prés, la peinture Ripolin et la Vache qui rit. Des larmes continuaient de couler sur ses joues. Il ne savait pas si elles étaient provoquées par le vent froid qui souffletait son visage, ou par la dissolution de la grosse boule qui s'était formée à son départ de Paris, dans le ventre, la gorge ou . . . dans le coeur. Il comprenait brutalement qu'il n'était essentiel à personne si ce n'est à lui-même.

[. . .] Qui a tout perdu devient léger. Il venait de perdre son enfance. Il s'entendit dire tout haut ce qu'il pensait à cet instant précis: "Tout enfant est innocent, pourquoi pas l'adulte?"

C'est un extrait d'un travail en cours. En réalité, mes premières impressions de Montréal et du Québec des années cinquante furent tout simplement abominables. Je suis donc né une première fois à Paris de parents juifs hongrois dans les années trente, et une deuxième fois lorsque j'ai abordé le Nouveau Monde, au début des années cinquante, enfanté par le couple dramatique de la neige et de l'espace.

J'ai commencé, comme de juste, par débarquer par un froid inhumain, qui m'a semblé, et me semble toujours, inimaginable. Ensuite et surtout la belle Province m'apparut pétrifiée dans la religion catholique à tout jamais, une religion omniprésente, aberrante, mortelle. Du point de vue culturel, ce n'était pas riche non plus: la rue Sainte-Catherine[1] ne comptait que quatre salles de cinéma, j'étais loin de Paris . . . Au début je n'ai donc perçu que froidure, grisaille, pauvreté physique et même intellectuelle. Mais pire que tout c'était d'éprouver cette sensation que rien ne bougerait, n'avancerait, ne progresserait jamais au pays du Québec. Bien entendu je me trompais.

C'était donc les années cinquante, sous le "règne" de Duplessis, le premier ministre de cette époque qui fut qualifiée plus tard de "La grande noirceur." Victor Hugo, Zola, Baudelaire étaient toujours à l'Index! La Bible elle-même n'y échappait pas, car on conseillait de la lire en version expurgée . . . En ce qui concerne le domaine théâtral, les directeurs des rares théâtres étaient encore entièrement inféodés aux textes français de France. On ne croyait pas

---

[1]grande artère commerciale de Montréal, qui la traverse d'ouest en est.

The production of Hamlet, prince du Québec, *staged at Le Théâtre L'Escale, Montreal, 1968*

qu'un canadien-français (on n'employait pas encore le vocable "québécois") puisse jamais écrire une oeuvre théâtrale.

En attendant, je me suis inscrit à l'École Polytechnique. A cette époque la plupart des cours étaient donnés en anglais . . . Je fis, pour ainsi dire, le moins d'études possible en techniques d'ingénierie, et le plus d'études possible en dessous de la vie québécoise. Je jouais aussi aux cartes avec passion, passion qui ne m'a pas quittée.

Je fondai le Parti Neutre, de tendance anarchique, dont l'argument électoral le plus pesant était la construction d'un pipeline de bière à partir du *Sphynx*, la taverne du coin de la rue, qui aurait été relié directement à nos locaux de Poly . . . Je menai tant et si bien cette vie de patachon que je terminai, sans surprise, avant-dernier de ma promotion.

Je fus pourtant tout de suite engagé. Dans ce temps, on se disputait le peu d'ingénieurs disponible. La *Canadian Pacific* n'hésita donc pas à m'affecter à son secteur *Telegraphs* et à la surveillance de toutes ses stations répétitrices de Terre-Neuve à Vancouver. Une occasion de bambocher supplémentaire, et de voyager *Coast to Coast* en première classe. Nous téléphonions même d'avance d'une destination à l'autre, pour que nos collègues nous organisent tous les partys voulus . . . Les provinces de l'ouest, ces plaines immenses, me donnaient l'impression de jouer dans un Far West étatsunien. Je m'amusais bien, pourtant me sentais moins d'appartenance que jamais avec les provinces anglophones. Si bien que je décidai un jour *ex abrupto* de démissionner et de rentrer à Montréal.

J'ai été tout de suite réembauché comme ingénieur commercial en chauffage et ventilation: en somme, comme je le ferais plus tard en écrivant, je vendais de l'air. J'ai poursuivi de plus belle ma vie de jeune homme sans attaches. Je fréquentais la bohème du temps, peintres, architectes, artistes et pseudo-artistes, dont des immigrants comme moi pour qui l'Amérique constituait un nouvel Eldorado. Les souvenirs prennent des noms de bistrots de l'ouest de la ville, le *Riviera Café, La petite hutte, Le Moka*, le *Pam Pam* où l'on dévorait des pâtisseries d'Europe de l'Est. Je lis aussi voracement tout ce qui me tombe sous la main. Je développe un intérêt certain pour le nouveau roman.

Puis je suis tombé amoureux de Renée, qui devint ma femme, et me donnera deux garçons. Cette petite rousse piquante, à l'oeil pointu et au nez frémissant, m'était tombée dans l'oeil. Pour moi qui ne pratique pas, nos familles repectives nous infligèrent deux mariages religieux, un juif et un catholique.

Je n'écrivais toujours pas, et n'en éprouvais toujours pas le besoin. Renée, par contre, était indéniablement une artiste. Elle s'inscrivait bientôt à *L'École nationale de théâtre*, pour devenir créatrice de décors et de costumes, puis entreprenait sa carrière avec toute la fougue et l'énergie qui m'avaient tant séduit.

Si les théâtres étaient alors moins nombreux que maintenant, il existait par contre plusieurs festivals et concours. C'est ainsi que Renée et une copine unirent un jour leurs efforts pour pondre une pièce en un acte pour l'ACTA (*l'Association canadienne du théâtre amateur*). Renée m'en lisait des extraits, que je jugeais fort

mauvais, et je n'arrêtais pas de l'asticoter en lui répétant que *Ce n'est pas comme ça* et qu'*il faudrait tout reconstruire*. De guerre lasse, ma femme finit par me lancer de m'y mettre moi-même, puisque si j'étais si fin et que j'avais tellement l'air de savoir comment m'y prendre. Par jeu j'ai relevé le gant, et m'y suis attelé. J'ai donc écrit ma première pièce en 1963, la même année qu'explosaient les premières bombes du F.L.Q. Cela s'appelait *Le chant du poète*, une courte pièce qui ne comptait pas moins de cinquante-deux figurants, comprenait plein de tueries, et s'attaquait aux problèmes de la création. Et je gagne le premier prix.

La création dramatique semblait néanmoins toujours aussi "impossible," avec des directeurs de théâtre fermés à toute création, si bien que lorsque j'ai présenté ma deuxième pièce au Festival d'art dramatique quelque temps plus tard, je suis persuadé que, parmi les cinq productions du Festival, je serai la seule création.

Or surprise! Les cinq productions en question proviennent d'auteurs indigènes, qui partageaient tous la même conviction que moi.

From Hamlet, prince du Québec, *at Le Théâtre L'Escale*

Nous décidons alors de nous doter d'un outil pour briser ce mur de résistance, et nous créons le *Centre d'essai des auteurs dramatiques*. Le CEAD établit donc les conditions, objectives, et matérielles nécessaires à l'éclosion de la dramaturgie québécoise. C'est une première action concertée, originale, qui sera par la suite copiée en Europe, en France en particulier. Les lieux de réunion du CEAD changent d'appartement d'auteur en cuisine d'auteur, le budget provient de quêtes et de cotisations maigrichonnes. Je me souviens pour ma part d'avoir alors investi dans la dramaturgie québécoise une somme astronomique en café et cognac.

Contrairement à mes premières impressions, la société québécoise n'a pas fait du sur-place. En plus ou moins une quinzaine d'années, le Québec a rattrapé presque cent ans de retard. D'une société dont la mission était de fournir de la matière première brute pour les usines américaines et des missionnaires au monde, le Québec était entré dans le présent.

The production of Le Pendu, *staged at Le Théâtre du XXième in Paris in the early seventies*

Voilà comment peut naître parfois une carrière d'auteur dramatique: sur un coup de tête. Spectateur si peu assidu, ingrat et difficile, j'avais pourtant été piqué, inoculé par le démon de l'écriture dramatique, pour n'en plus guérir. Encore à ce jour, je lis un article de journal, j'entends une conversation, un détail, ou une broutille attire soudain mon attention, pour germer jusqu'à prendre une importance démesurée et il me FAUT alors écrire une pièce de théâtre. J'écris parce que je ne peux pas m'en passer. C'est plus fort que moi. Les situations surgissent, les liens structuraux s'architecturent, j'ai besoin de tenter d'ordonner le chaos d'un problème. Ou, du moins, une partie.

J'ai travaillé pour la télévision et le cinéma, mais j'ai toujours préféré le théâtre, qui représente moins de compromis. J'aime la lumière crue que le théâtre peut jeter sur une société, l'éclatement que permet la multiplication des voix, l'efficacité brutale de la concision théâtrale, et comment il est possible d'y exposer à vif les rouages qui écrasent les individus. Je n'ai jamais versé dans la psychologie ni l'introspection, ne m'ont toujours passionné que les mécanismes qui empêchent l'individu d'être lui-même. Pour moi, le théâtre est le dernier espace de la discussion philosophique.

Sur un autre plan, je suis très étonné d'une part que la majorité des productions n'utilise que le plancher et laisse vide l'ouverture béante de la scène, et d'autre part je demeure fasciné par le fait que la scène n'utilise, justement, QUE le plancher. Je ne sais pas, cela rejoint peut-être mon côté fondamentalement terre-à-terre.

Rebelle à tout pouvoir, j'ai donc aussi toujours refusé de travailler sur commande. Lorsque j'écris, je deviens irritable pour des riens, une distraction me fait sauter au plafond, et même le poker n'arrive plus à m'absorber vraiment. C'est un état que mes proches ont appris à me pardonner.

J'ai conservé très longtemps mon travail d'ingénieur, tout en écrivant pièce sur pièce. C'était mon besoin absolu de sécurité, héritage de mon enfance durant la guerre. J'avais été nommé "homme de théâtre de l'année" en 1968, remporté de nombreux prix et honneurs mais je ne fis le saut qu'en 72.

Mon image du théâtre c'est quelqu'un enfermé dans une chambre, qui étouffe, manque bientôt d'oxygène et qui fracasse les carreaux.

The cast of Le procès de Jean-Baptiste M., *in Paris, 1975*

Le théâtre est un bris de vitres. Ma seule quête aura été de m'opposer à tout ce qui est accepté, à tout ce qui est hiérarchie, à toute structure. De là procèdent tous les autres sous-thèmes: la liberté, le bonheur . . . Je tâche toujours que le public, à aucun moment, ne soit assez ému qu'il n'en puisse plus réfléchir. Mon théâtre est exigeant parce qu'il n'offre pas de réponse. Il ne permet pas non plus de se laver de ses questions. Le théâtre que j'écris pose un questionnement qui doit accompagner, suivre et poursuivre le spectateur. Parce que j'essaie que l'on comprenne la nécessité de la négation des hiérarchies, de l'abolition des classes, de la destruction des privilèges. Je demande en somme aux gens de se joindre à moi pour un rejet d'obstacles.

Je fais au théâtre ce que je suis incapable de réaliser dans la vie. Dans la vie, je suis incapable d'être un homme politique, d'être un orateur, alors qu'au théâtre j'exprime mon point de vue politique. C'est au théâtre que j'agis sur la politique alors que dans la vie . . . je vis.

Je continue de me battre pour nos droits, mais je me sens isolé, comme la plupart des auteurs québécois. Tout d'abord parce qu'il n'existe pas de milieu d'auteurs dramatiques au Québec, puisqu'il n'y pas de lieux; être joué dans un théâtre ne signifie pas du tout que l'on fasse partie de ce théâtre, que nous disposons d'un lieu pour être joué, pas du tout. Ensuite la définition même de l'auteur québécois est remise en question à chacune de ses pièces; on n'est jamais auteur au Québec: on écrit une pièce, puis une autre, et chacune d'entre elles est un recommencement constant.

D'une façon plus large, cela tient surtout d'une prise de position politique. Nous sommes entrés dans l'ère de l'intermédiaire. Plus on est près de la page blanche, du moment de la création, plus on est mal compris et mal rémunéré.

D'autre part, tous les efforts sont faits pour que les intermédiaires obtiennent la paternité de l'oeuvre et que le texte ne devienne que prétexte: c'est la conséquence de l'hégémonie de l'économisme.

Je continue d'écrire des pièces. J'enseigne, et m'occupe beaucoup de négociations et de défense des droits des auteurs. Qu'advient-il d'eux de nos jours au Québec?

Si l'on en juge par la production des dernières années, ceux-ci n'échappent pas à la vague d'individualisation qui submerge le monde occidental. Dans la même veine, les directeurs de théâtre, souvent nouvellement nommés, n'ont plus en bouche que les mots "rentabilité," "manque à gagner," "profit": ces jeunes loups ne montrent pas les crocs mais des dentiers.

Le moteur collectif étant en panne, les pièces deviennent des "objets dramatiques" où foisonnent les déviants, seule contestation possible dans cette vague de fond conservatrice. Les personnages de l'artiste, du criminel, de l'homosexuel, se multiplient. Les thèmes du viol, du crime, de l'arnaque, reviennent pièce après pièce. Toute réflexion sociale ou politique est évacuée, c'est le triomphe du théâtre freudien.

Faute de contenu, l'on se replie sur la forme. La pièce-objet, nourrie par le développement de la performance, des techniques, s'épanouit. Ainsi, dans ma dernière pièce, comme l'exprime Ben:

Gurik as he looks nowadays

"Spectateur soit surpris
que je me présente devant toi
comme un étron
dans un parterre de roses
car je sais qu'aujourd'hui
ce ne sont pas les créateurs qu'on veut
    entendre
mais le metteur en marché
l'expert en sondage
l'expert de la mise en page
le curateur de l'artiste
l'imprésario de l'interprète.
Ce n'est plus le coureur gagnant
des jeux que l'on célèbre
mais le fabricant de ses chaussures
ou de son élixir désaltérant.
Ce n'est pas le discobole
mais le lanceur de disque de vinyle.
Nous sommes entrés dans l'ère du profit
de l'intermédiaire
du vide entre l'arbre et l'écorce.

"Alors pourquoi perdre son temps
parler de cette société où la liberté
a les pieds coulés dans le ciment?
Que le ciment est cher
que la chair est ciment.
Pourquoi parler de cette société

quand toutes les solutions se sont effron-
    drées
comme un pan de mur
trop dure ou trop mûre.
Parce qu'il ne s'agit plus de fuir
de pleurer pour pleurer
de rire juste pour rire
car ce serait triste à mourir
triste et bête à se tuer.
Parce qu'il faut essayer de dire
que s'il n'y a pas de solutions absolues
que si elles sont toutes erronées
que si tous les pouvoirs sont oppressifs
toutes les oppressions ne se valent pas.
Le malheur est un état
le bonheur, non.
A la limite le bonheur n'existe pas
il faut donc l'inventer, le créer
en toute lucidité
sachant que c'est une invention
un mirage, un leurre, une création.
Sachant que l'on se trompe
et que l'on a raison
que ce n'est pas une vérité
une obligation
un croit ou meurt
un croit et tue.

"Et, comme le disait Aristophanes:
'Pour tous ces motifs
puisqu'en homme sage
il n'a pas bondi à l'étourdi
pour dire des balivernes
soulevez un immense bruissement
de paumes battantes et vogue la galère . . .'
ou le ferry-boat vers la liberté."

Ma génération voulait à tout prix sauter dans le train et aller, tous ensemble, vers un avenir meilleur.

La génération suivante voulait sauter du train.

La nouvelle génération est assise au bord des rails mais aucun train ne passe.

Espérons qu'après s'être défoulé sur ce paysage vide rayé par deux rails inutiles, la génération qui monte mettra toute son énergie à construire un train.

Quant à moi, je déteste parler de moi. En tant que sujet d'écriture ma propre existence, comme tout destin strictement individuel, est dénuée d'intérêt. Car le particulier est une forme de conservatisme qui fait obstacle au général, promesse d'avenir.

© Robert Gurik

BIBLIOGRAPHY

Plays in English translation:

Api 2967 (two-act; first produced as "Api or not Api, voilà la question" in Montreal, Quebec, at Théâtre du Gésu, 1966; revised version produced as "Api 2967" in Montreal at Théâtre de l'Egrégore, 1967; produced in English in Regina, Alberta, at Globe Theater, 1974), Factum Inc., 1966, translation by Marc F. Gélinas, Playwrights Cooperative (Toronto), 1973.

Le Pendu (two-act; first produced in Montreal at Théâtre du Gésu, March 24, 1967; produced in English in Kingston, Ontario, at Domino Theater, 1967), Factum Inc., 1967, translation by Philip London published as "The Hanged Man," in *New Drama 4,* New Press, 1972.

Hamlet, prince du Québec (two-act satire; first produced in Montreal at Théâtre de l'Escale, January 17, 1968; produced in English in London, Ontario, at London Little Theatre, 1978), Editions de l'Homme, 1968, translation by Marc F. Gélinas published as *Hamlet, Prince of Quebec,* Playwrights Cooperative, 1981.

Le Procès de Jean-Baptiste M. (two-act; first produced in Montreal at Théâtre du Nouveau Monde, 1972), Leméac, 1972, translation by Allan Van Meer published as *The Trial of Jean-Baptiste M.,* Talonbooks, 1974.

Le Champion (two-act), Leméac, 1977, translation by Allan Van Meer published as *The Champion,* Playwrights Cooperative, 1982.

Translation of *Liberty* (two-act play) by Joel Miller, 1996 (not yet published).

Plays in French:

Le Chant du poète (one-act satire; title means "The Song of the Poet"), first produced in Montreal at Théâtre de la Mangragore, 1963.

Les Portes (one-act; title means "The Doors"), first produced in Montreal at Théâtre de la Place Ville Marie, 1965.

Les Louis d'or (two-act; title means "The Golden Louis"), first produced in Montreal at Théâtre de Saltimbanques, 1966.

A coeur ouvert (two-act; title means "Open Heart"; first produced in Montreal at Théâtre de Quatre Sous, 1969), Leméac, 1969.

(With Jean-Pierre Morin) *Allo, Police!* (one-act; first produced in Montreal at Théâtre du Gésu, 1970), Leméac, 1974.

Les Fourberies de Scapin (adaptation of work by Molière), produced in Ste. Thérèse, Quebec, at College Lionel-Groulx, 1970.

D'un séant à l'autre (one-act; title means "Coast to Coast"; first produced in Montreal at Troupe des Arlequins, 1971), produced and published in *Les Tas de sièges* (also see below), revised edition produced and published as "Un plus un egale zero" in *Sept Courtes Pièces* (also see below).

Les Tas de sièges (three one-act plays; contains "D'un séant à l'autre," "J'écoute" [title means "I Listen"] and "Face à face"; first produced in Ste.-Foy, Quebec, at CEGEP Ste.-Foy, 1972), Leméac, 1971.

Play Ball (one-act; first produced in Montreal at Théâtre Populaire du Québec, 1971), produced and published in *Sept Courtes Pièces* (also see below).

Q (two-act), first produced in Ste. Thérèse at Collège Lionel-Groulx, 1971.

La Palissade (two-act; title means "The Fence"; first produced in St. Jean, Quebec, at Collège Militaire, 1973), Leméac, 1971.

Le Tabernacle à trois étages (two-act; title means "The Three-Story Tabernacle"; first produced in Chicoutimi, Quebec, at Théâtre de la Cite, 1973), Leméac, 1972.

Sept Courtes Pièces (title means "Seven Sketches"; includes "Phèdre," "La Sainte et le truand" [title means "The Saint and the Robber"], "Un plus un égale zéro," "63," "Le Signe du Cancer," "Play Ball," and "Le Trou"; produced in Plessisville, Quebec, at CEGEP Plessisville, 1974), Leméac, 1974.

Lénine (two-act; first produced in Cotonou, Benin, at Théâtre de l'Arc en Ciel, 1978), Leméac, 1975.

Un plus un (one-act), first produced in Plessisville at CEGEP Plessisville, 1975.

Gurik en morceaux (one-act; title means "Gurik in Pieces"), first produced in Montreal at Centre d'Essai des Auteurs Dramatiques, 1976.

La Baie des Jacques (two-act; title means "Jack's Bay"; first produced in Ste. Thérèse at Collège Lionel-Groulx, 1976), Leméac, 1978.

Hocus Pocus (two-act), first produced in Montreal at National Library, 1977.

Also author of unproduced and unpublished plays, including "Echec à la Reine" (two-act; title means "Queen's Gambit") and *Aux pieds de la liberté* (two-act; title means "At the foot of liberty").

Fiction:

Spirales (title means "Spirals"), Holt, 1966.

Jeune Délinquant (title means "Young Delinquents"), Leméac, 1980.

Être ou ne pas être (title means "To be or not to be"), a collection of short stories, XYZ, 1991.

Screenplays:

"Les Vautours" (title means "The Vultures"), Films J. C. Labrecque, 1969.

"Le Toasteur" (title means "The Toaster"), Cinéac, 1975.

"Les Années de Rêves" (title means "The Dream Years"), Ciné Vision 4, 1984.

"La femme de l'hôtel" (title means "The woman from the hotel"), Cinéminaire, 1988.

Other:

Author of scripts for radio and television, including, with Jean-Paul Fugère, "Jeune Délinquant" (five one-hour television series on juvenile delinquency; different from Gurik's novel of the same title), 1980; "La Pépinière" another five one-hour television series; and "Comment acheter son patron (title means "How to buy your boss," four one-hour series), all directed by Jean-Paul Fugère. *Il teatro sociale di Robert Gurik,* was written about Robert Gurik by Marinella Colombo, University of Milano.

Rachel Hadas

1948-

AUTHOR'S NOTE: *My initial problem with the assignment of writing even a brief autobiography was this: a chronological account of my own life seemed doomed to be intolerably boring, lifeless, plodding, and inaccurate—not to mention being something of a duplication of what already exists in the form of a curriculum vitae and an annotated bibliography. How much simpler, I thought, to urge any curious reader simply to read what I've written. Wasn't it because I was a writer in the first place that anyone would look me up? I think it was Apollinaire who said that each of his poems commemorated an event in his life. Motherhood, a friend's death, a winter walk—read what I've written, I want to snap, if you're curious how it felt to me. I've even been tempted to excerpt some of my own essays—after all, they're personal—in lieu of an autobiography.*

Alas, both these expedients are unfair to the reader who, whether or not she has read any of my work, is simply in search of facts about me. So in lieu of an autobiography I offer here an alphabetized list of items. Alphabetical order seems to me a more neutral principle than chronological order. Other ordering principles, like the periodic table of the elements in Primo Levi's wonderful book of that title, were beyond my reach—but let me pay tribute here to the compelling and inventive ways to order their own stories found by Iris Origo in Images and Shadows *and Sharon Olds in* Satan Says.

Unlike section D ("Dramatis Personae") of James Merrill's "The Book of Ephraim," another important source, the following list isn't restricted to characters; it includes entries such as Education and Friendship, one of which normally finds a slot in a c.v. while the other doesn't. The resulting index to my life is undoubtedly incomplete, idiosyncratic, and confusing—but so is any account of a life, not to mention the life itself.

A final note: in order to halfway satisfy my lust to tell potential researchers to read my work, I not only list all my books here but refer to passages in the books that may be relevant to particular items on the list.

Rachel Hadas

Alan Ansen, 1922–

My dear friend, whom, thanks to John Hollander, I met in Athens in 1969: an expatriate, a poet, a wonderfully hospitable and generous, eccentric polymath, who read Dante with me in his apartment in Kolonaki, in a tall old house, now demolished, on Alpekis Street.

I've written about Alan in my afterword to *Contact Highs,* (his *Selected Poems*) and elsewhere. At a time in my life when I was drifting and frightened, Alan always made me feel completely safe and welcome. He had much more to teach me about literature than just about any of the professors I'd had at Harvard, though some of what I learned from him (love for Auden's work, or for that matter for Alan's own rumbustious poems) ripened only later. Giving me a book about Auden's poetry, Alan inscribed it, "A cart before a heavenly horse." Just so: now, teaching myself, chained to the academic routine, I sometimes feel like a nonheavenly horse, but I was shown the heavenly cart before my real work began.

Disorderly Houses, Alan's 1959 volume from Wesleyan, is dedicated in part to Pindar, "whose [houses] never were." Alan's life might be chaotic—the dying flowers in their vases, the boys coming and going. There is surface scuzz and mess, and there is also devotion to the world of art.

ARSON

In the spring of 1973, in the olive oil press my then husband Stavros and I were running on the island of Samos, there were a couple of unexplained fires. We went to America for the summer, and when we came back he and I were separately indicted for arson, the idea apparently being that we had "burned down the factory" (it was still standing) for the insurance money. Eventually we were tried and acquitted, a process both slowed down and probably mellowed by the fact that in the meantime (summer 1974) the Greek junta had fallen and democracy had been restored.

My memories of these nightmarish events are intermittent, comical, and scary. It's much easier to recall what I was wearing for the trial (one long day in March 1975), or that I had my period, or that during lunch on the Vathy waterfront I talked about New York schools with the lawyers, than to grasp the whole episode in all its long drawn-out absurdity and danger. What's clear now is that the trial, and the long, long months leading up to it, gave me a gift. For henceforth what might have seemed challenging situations (defending a Ph.D. thesis, for example) were comparatively benign: I knew people were on my side. And having been under house arrest, that is, forbidden to leave the country until the trial, has given me a greater appreciation of freedom.

ARTISTS' COLONIES

At the MacDowell Colony in Peterborough, New Hampshire, my first night at dinner—it was July 1, 1976—I made the acquaintance of a tall, gaunt composer who could tell by looking at me, he said, that I wasn't a composer and was probably a poet. I'd never met a composer before, though I've met many since, and composing twenty seconds of music a day seemed a very slow pace to me.

With her son, Jonathan, 1985

The tall thin composer was George Edwards; two years later we got married. We've gone off at intervals to artists' colonies ever since, George always to MacDowell (he's there as I write this), I to Virginia, Ragdale, and Yaddo. After ten or twelve days at a colony, I find I want to get back to my home routine, and after about two weeks I'm too restless to work well. But in the first spread of space and time colonies afford, a tremendous amount of work of different kinds gets accomplished. Turning forty at Ragdale, writing prose about the past, I felt as if I were on an island in the middle of my life; I could see with new clarity where I had been, if not where I was going. And at Virginia, the fall after my mother's death, I filled a roomy studio with my grief: papers piled on the floor, grandfather's letters on a side table, me at the desk, writing, weeping, writing.

People who have children especially need the time offered by artists' colonies, but the pull of a child also means, perhaps for women in particular, that one's stay may be short. For those two or three weeks, a colony represents the only form of house arrest (see "Arson") that I can now imagine without shuddering.

Charles Barber, 1956–1992

In his short life an actor, director, dancer, critic, essayist, and poet, Charles was my student in a poetry workshop at Gay Men's Health Crisis from late 1989 until shortly before his death in the summer of 1992. He was also my beloved friend; he had a rare gift for friendship, and I am still basking in the affection we shared even as I continue to mourn his loss. Many, many of my poems in the past six years are in one way or another addressed to Charles; his death, together with that of my mother, is the subject of *The Double Legacy*.

BREAD LOAF

I was a student poet at the Writer's Conference in 1976, but my cherished and formative memories of Bread Loaf date from 1958, 1960, and 1961 (I think these dates are right), when I was a faculty brat, since my father taught at the School of English. I remember croquet, Ping-Pong, milkshakes in the Barn, the peculiar smell of the bathrooms in Maple, the faculty wives shopping for cocktail hors d'oeuvres, plays at the Little Theater. Wylie Sypher, tall, genial, and bald, wearing a seersucker jacket and binoculars around his neck, was a dedicated birdwatcher; Lucy, his wife, a foot shorter, trotted after him with hard-boiled eggs (his midmorning snack) in a basket. Lucy corresponded with me for years, sent me cookies when I was in college, met me for lunch at the Wurst Haus in Cambridge, and—most important of all, I now think—had the imagination and generosity to send me many of those little books about great artists that the Boston Museum of Fine Arts used to publish. "An unbirthday present," she'd write on the flyleaf. The cookies are gone, and the lunches, and Wylie, and Lucy. Even the purple finches that flocked in a certain larch tree one summer are gone. But the little books about Degas and Gauguin, Botticelli and Van Gogh and Goya, are still on my shelves. This

coming Saturday morning my son will start art classes.

CHILDREN

Our son, Jonathan Hadas Edwards, was born on February 4, 1984, and promptly began allowing me, at the age of thirty-five, to relive my childhood—nursery rhymes, a dependence on my mother, the joys of children's books. I've written about some of these matters in *A Son from Sleep* and "The Cradle and the Bookcase" and in my long poem "The Dream Machine." Jonathan as he grows up walks through other poems, notably—on his way to school—"The Red Hat." But he is not a model, a subject, a muse; he's a separate, complicated, sometimes opaque, and quickly changing person, who so far, I hope, defies Proust's gloomy prediction that children inherit the worst qualities of both parents.

The Double Legacy

This little book of prose consists of various essays around the central theme of mourning. "Double"

Rachel and Jonathan, Maine, 1988

refers to two deaths that happened six weeks apart in 1992: first my mother, then Charles Barber.

DREAMS

Dreams and poems are engaged in some of the same tasks and use some of the same tools. Both, in my experience, somehow know and can convey unappealing truths to which the waking person, the person living her daily life in prose, seems to lack access—or is it rather that she lacks courage? I was writing poems foreshadowing the end of my first marriage long before I had admitted to myself that it was ending. A dream informed me of my mother's fatal cancer a week or two before her diagnosis.

Both poetry and dreams make lavish use of images; both often move laterally, erratically, by means of what I think of as lyric leaps. Both can be screamingly clear or hermetically difficult to construe. Both are mysterious in their provenance, seeming to come from deep within the self yet also reaching us as if from outside. Both can be zanily solipsistic yet can also command an impersonal kind of authority.

Unlike poems, of course, dreams often melt away, leaving, as Prospero puts it, not a wrack behind. The medium I use for simultaneously fixing dreams in my memory and trying to make sense of them is poetry. It's hardly surprising, then, that many of the dreams I succeed in remembering touch upon the same themes many of my poems do—people I have loved and lost and continue to love.

A recent dream about the poet James Merrill tugged at me all the next day, though each time I tried to reconstruct it, fewer details were available. I'd seemed to be standing with Jimmy and a few other people at twilight just outside a building, an apartment house, under a canopy. Inside had been a kind of boudoir with a travertine dressing table and a tall, four-paneled mirror. There was the sense of going out on the town for the evening and also of looking out on the passing world, critically but not unkindly, with laughter. There was much more I couldn't recall—the substance of what was said. . . . What made the dream especially poignant was that I was aware in it that Jimmy didn't have long to live. It was such a

strong and pleasurable dream that I hated to wake up.

Not until late afternoon did it dawn on me (hardly the *mot juste* in this connection) that the day's date, August 6, was precisely half a year after the date of Jimmy's death. I felt at once abashed to have been so slow to realize this; grateful for the continued loving intimacy the dream had abundantly conveyed; and mystified at how I had subliminally recalled this six-month mark. "There *are* subconscious connections, Mom," said my son wisely. Indeed there are. The significance of the date finally became clear to me at the moment when, trudging barefoot along a Vermont dirt road that humid, sleepy Sunday afternoon, I was thinking about a passage in Merrill's *Mirabell* I'd recently reread:

> Trials and tremors, David's operation
> Fills him with foreboding. He dreamed last
>   night
> Of Matt and Mary. As he woke they slowly,
> Achingly changed into two piles of clothes.
> What did it mean? Had they come for him?
>   Was he going
> To die in surgery? I have a hunch
> Matt Jackson died a year ago today
> —Which proves correct.

February sixth to August sixth. It finally clicked.

I haven't, or haven't yet, captured the details of my August 6 dream in a poem. Perhaps I never will. But so much buried love, memory, and meaning clustered even in the few vignettes I was able to retrieve that it was as if I'd tapped into a rich vein of subterranean significance. Remembering the dream, I felt desolate but also consoled; bereaved but also lucky. As the late British writer Angela Carter observed, "The dead know something we don't, although they keep it to themselves." Dreams are a triumphant loophole in that law of silence.

During the twenty-six years of my friendship with James Merrill, I dreamed about him many times. Death, while it has changed the tone of these dreams, hasn't broken the continuity of the messages.

It would be pleasant to dream of great poets of the past, as Elizabeth Bishop dreamed of George Herbert. Robert Frost did appear to me once in a dream some years ago, but never Dickinson or Keats, Shakespeare or Sappho. I can hardly complain, though, as long as Merrill continues to be a living presence in my dreams.

EDUCATION

Nursery school: Tompkins Hall, at 21 Claremont Avenue, across the street from Barnard College. Cooperative; the mothers—faculty wives—used to help out. I remember playing on the roof, and having my temperature taken, and eating—or throwing up—a baked apple. I remember quiet-voiced, gray-haired, buck-toothed, besmocked Miss Edith Morton. But 21 Claremont came alive for me again in the fall of 1976, when George, whom I'd met earlier that summer, and who was about to start teaching in the Columbia Music Department, moved into his Columbia Housing–provided apartment on the ground floor of 21 Claremont, right across the hall from where I'd gone to nursery school. Sometimes we'd see lines of small children moving through the lobby, undeterred by obstacles like (one day) George's upright piano being maneuvered around a corner. "Make way for ducklings," George murmured.

Elementary school was much farther away from home (home being 460 Riverside Drive); too far, I now think. I went, as my older sister had, to Hunter College Elementary School, then on Park Avenue and Sixty-eighth Street. In the mornings, if we were early, all the children would have to walk around and around the block until we could go into the lobby. The elevators were big and smelly.

But my imagination out-Orwelled the reality. I remember worrying that kindergarten would be a big dark room with hapless children bent over their desks. (Had I been read Dickens at age five? Where else did such a stern Victorian fantasy come from?) In fact Hunter was benign enough. Reading was easy for me, though the penmanship teacher admonished me to "Write, Rachel, don't draw!" By third or fourth grade I was helping some of the other kids with reading. French started in fourth grade, with Mme. Hopstein pointing down her throat and gargling "La gorrrrge." The art teacher, Marie Boylan, looked like a 1950s (well, this *was* the fifties) poodle: rhinestones, swirling felt skirts, lots of pink and turquoise. Pug-faced, pear-shaped, ancient-seeming Dr. Anna Chandler presided over a Hunter Elementary special called Audio-Visual Enrichment, AVE for

short. We sat in the dark and looked at slides; I'm sure many people often fell asleep, as I did, but we also learned about Winslow Homer and Pollaiuolo, Albert Ryder and Raphael.

For some unexplained reason, I was one of six children "accelerated"—skipped, or rather shot from cannons, from fourth to sixth grade—none of whom succeeded in passing the newly established test to get into Hunter High. So instead of following my sister to Hunter, I was sent to Riverdale for seventh through twelfth grades. A pattern of lopsidedness had already been set: I was good at English and French and Latin, passable at history—forget math and science. I was only ten at the start of seventh grade, "flat as a pancake," as my best friend Barbara Foley put it, but I made up for my youthfulness by the time I was sixteen or so with determined frivolity . . . or was I just in search of boys to write love poems about? My best memories of Riverdale are of the sun on the fields in the morning—I was a terrible hockey player, but it was nice to feel almost in the country—and of the relief, as I experienced it at ages maybe ten to fourteen, of not having boys in the class (Riverdale wasn't coed at that time). Every afternoon the school bus would take us up the hill (a hill so steep it allowed for many precious snow days) from the Girls' School down by the river to the Boys' School, where the boys would join us for the bus ride home to Manhattan. Every afternoon on that bus most of the girls would get out their compacts and apply eyeliner and foundation and lipstick.

At Radcliffe I majored in classics, for several reasons. First, sibling rivalry—my sister was an English major already, and I didn't want to follow in her footsteps any more than I already had. Secondly, majoring in English seemed silly when I could and did read Dickens and Shakespeare, Keats and Jane Austen, and the poems of my father's student, the emerging poet John Hollander, on my own. Finally, I was in some ways a very cautious and conservative young person. Taking courses that involved more of what I knew how to do already—looking up words in lexicons—felt comfortable and safe. Was there parental pressure to study classics? Not any more than there had been to do well in school and go on to college; it was in the air my sister and I breathed. No one made an issue of reminding me that my mother's father had been a classicist, or that my mother had been studying Latin prose composition at Columbia the summer she and my father met. My father did, toward the end of my freshman year, send me a brief letter complimenting me on my grades and adding that I didn't have to major in classics and didn't have to get all A's. I think he meant it, or that he thought he did, but there was little time to discuss my future; he died the August following my freshman year.

The teaching in the Harvard Classics Department wasn't, for the most part, inspiring. I do remember with most fondness two early-morning classes on the third floor of the Fogg Museum: David Mitten's Greek sculpture and Sterling Dow's Greek history. Homer with Gregory Nagy and Aristophanes with Harold Gotoff offered more memorable moments than a dry-as-dust Oedipus with Wendell Clausen, who preferred Alexandrian poets to classical tragedians. My Latin training was stronger than my Greek, and I probably learned the most about poetry (genre, meter, imagery, temperament, tradition) from G. P. Goold on Roman elegy and, above all, J. P. Elder on Lucretius.

However dubious my motives may have been, and however large a percentage of what I learned I have forgotten, I've never regretted majoring in classics. Recently, translating some Seneca and Tibullus—and my next project is a play of Euripides—has taken me back to the days hunched over a lexicon in Whitman Hall, with trimeter and hexameter ringing in my ears. To reenter, however gingerly, the world of classical scholarship is a removal, a renewal, a return to the source. Nor have I ever regretted that the only poetry-writing class I took was with Robert Fitzgerald, a piercingly, almost alarmingly low-key, gentle, and charming man. Robert Lowell's gigantic reputation made me nervous, not that I knew much about his work or indeed about the man himself, but a palpable aura of charismatic damage surrounded him— damage his students, it seemed to me, eagerly imitated and shared.

I was in love a lot at college, sometimes with spectacularly unsuitable people (a heroin addict who dropped out of Harvard soon after I met him and is probably dead by now stands out in my memory), sometimes with young men who are so kind and ardent and interesting in my faded memories that I only wish I could recall them better. There was also a married poet; there was a health food store–running

hippie up in Vermont. After my father's death I was off course for years to come, easily attaching and detaching myself, panicky, dependent. My first husband, the man who said, "I grew you up and then you left me," was not someone I met at Harvard, and neither was George.

I finished college in 1969 and was away from educational institutions and out of the country for the next few years, but in 1976–77 I went to the writing seminars at Johns Hopkins. One could study either poetry or prose, and about half the students were teaching fellows in a freshman course called "Contemporary American Letters," a subject about which I knew very little. The syllabus featured work by writers like Pynchon, Barthelme, and Barth; I learned as much as my students. The poetry workshop was useful chiefly because of some of my fellow poets. Tom Sleigh, Molly Peacock, Lisa Zeidner, and, above all, Phillis Levin had a lot to teach me about poetry and about critiquing others' work sharply but not cruelly. Different styles flew around the room like germs; there was no prevailing aesthetic that I remember.

The year at Hopkins, I was mostly in New York on weekends, visiting George (we had met at MacDowell that summer). On the train rides to and from Baltimore, it was a pleasure to be alone and write! Back at Hopkins, I audited graduate courses in the Romantics with Jerome McGann and the pre-Socratics with Diskin Clay. Library books piled up on the floor: "Beppo," "Julian and Maddalo," Solon's "Hymn to the Muses." I stopped using my married name—I was separated from my first husband—and reverted to Hadas.

It was clear by the middle of my year at Hopkins that an M.A. in poetry (it wasn't called an M.F.A. for some reason) and a token would get me a ride on the subway. I wanted to be back in New York, where George was teaching at Columbia. After dipping a toe into the waters of graduate school at Hopkins, the prospect of going deeper was less frightening. I wanted a program that would make use of my newly acquired modern Greek without letting me turn my back on the classics. The doctoral program in comparative literature at Princeton was, as graduate studies go, painless, even pleasurable. I remember Robert Fagles's seminars on epic and tragedy, Edmund Keeley's tutorials in modern Greek poetry, Theodore Weiss's repair work on my ignorance of American poetry, Clarence Brown's uncanny seminar on Stevens, Ralph Freedman on Rilke and Valéry, William Meredith (who had waltzed with my mother at Bread Loaf in 1960 or thereabouts) giving a guest seminar on Auden—all this was a wonderful corrective to poetry workshops on the one hand and readings of Sophocles that emphasized the aorist tense on the other.

Last spring I had the pleasure of teaching a course at Princeton in the Hellenic Studies Program; I'd gotten older, but everything else had pretty much stayed the same.

So many years spent in classrooms! And this September marks my fifteenth fall at Rutgers. My father once wrote, "I am a teacher. Except for wars and holidays I have never been out of the sound of a school bell." I've been spared the wars.

The Empty Bed

This collection was going to be called *Red House,* the title of a poem in turn named after a Malevich painting. The present title is probably too gloomy; even though much of the book is elegiac. I now see *The Empty Bed* as the middle of a trilogy whose first and last volumes are *Unending Dialogue* and *The Double Legacy.*

FATHER, Moses Hadas, 1900–1966

My father was forty-eight when, the younger of two daughters from his second marriage, I was born; he already had a teenage daughter and son from his first. When he died I was seventeen. Not only did I not have very many years in which to get to know him, but the years we overlapped were the busiest in his busy life. Furthermore, his was not at all a transparent personality. There's an alarming amount about his life that probably no one now living knows (my half-brother David knows more than most people); I'd have to hire an investigative journalist to do the sleuthing if I wanted to find out in any detail about my father's family connections, childhood, education in Atlanta and then New York, life as a rabbi, first marriage. . . . But in a way, what I already know is enough for me. It's not as if even that small stock of memory doesn't constantly change, abetted by a letter unearthed here, an anec-

The author's father, Dr. Moses Hadas

dote shared there, and the fact that I am fast approaching the age my father was when I was born.

To put it another way, love is enough for me—living and dead, absent and present, the love we shared. Rightly or wrongly, I've always thought I probably resemble him in temperament (not looks) more than any of his other three children. I used to feel what I thought of as a pointing finger, admonishing me not to be lazy, not to waste time. Your father, my shrink would say. But in time I came to be able to localize the insistent prodding and found it originated inside me. My father, then, was in a way myself.

Tired at the end of his long days of teaching (he taught classics at Columbia for forty years), tired with a tiredness I understand better every semester, my father would lie down when he got home from work, do the *Times* crossword puzzle, relax. I'd lie down next to him for companionable help with my Latin homework; we read a good deal of Cicero's *De Senectute* together. One afternoon I asked him to transliterate the word "fuck," spelled in Greek ØYK, in a poem of e. e. cummings. I thought I knew what the letters sounded out but wasn't sure. He looked at the word a long time. "I can't read it," he said.

The temperamental match: no matter how many honorary degrees he got, no matter how many accolades from grateful students, my father always needed more praise than seemed forthcoming—from inside as well as outside. (Inside the family? inside himself? where was the pointing finger?) Alas, it was, of course, easier to wow students than the quiet wife and the two recalcitrant teenagers who faced him across the dinner table. Once I remember telling my father to shut up; of course I had to leave the table. But beyond or beneath all this, I understood increasingly as I got to be sixteen or so the need he felt for unconditional praise and love. (Did I share this vulnerability already?) Besides, though he boasted some at dinner, my father was anything but long-winded about his own concerns and doings. He wasn't one of those men who feel the need to tell their families what they've been telling other people at work all day. If anything, often by dinnertime words would have all but deserted him; he'd point to the butter or horseradish in silence. I understand it so well now, the queasy-making roughness in any teacher's life of the alternation of speech and silence.

This is not the place to rehearse my father's long and complicated career as a rabbi, in the Office of Strategic Services, or at Columbia. Virtually no personal papers have been left behind; my half-brother and sister know more than I do, as do various distant cousins who surface from time to time. Of course I can and do read and reread various of my father's books; I welcome hearing anecdotes about him. What matters most to me at this stage is that, dead for almost thirty years, my father has come closer to me than when I was a seventeen-year-old shell-shocked by his death. Lovable, charismatic, mysterious, vulnerable, talkative, silent, contradictory, versatile, exhausted—human.

Love is a leap, an arc, an improvisation, a surprise. An overcommitted forty-eight when I was born, a grandfather by the time I was six or so, my father had no empty place for me in his heart. Love turns out not to work that way; it creates its own resting place, which death is then powerless to abolish.

FATHER-IN-LAW

Was it no more than a remarkable coincidence that both the men I married had, unknown to me, lost their fathers at eighteen or so, the same age I had? Maybe I was drawn to some signal of that shared loss, some enzyme or odor of adolescent bereavement, some gap in the story. The practical result suited me fine: I never had to deal with a father-in-law, only memories. Living or dead, one father was enough for me.

Form, Cycle, Infinity: Landscape Imagery in the Poetry of Robert Frost and George Seferis

My doctoral dissertation at Princeton; also my way of marrying the landscapes of Greece and Vermont, two places where I'd spent a lot of time, under the twin auspices of two fearsome old men.

FRIENDS

One of the great blessings of my life. Friends surface and vanish; if one lives in New York, someone is always passing through town on their way someplace else or for some brief, hectic event. And then it turns out life is like that: we're passing through. Friends are associated with times and places in a life: the benches surrounding a sandbox in Riverside Park, a seminar room, a certain stretch of Broadway, or summers in Vermont or Maine or wherever. Friends can be pried loose from their context and find a new niche: Missy Roberts, my best friend when we were growing up on Riverside Drive (our mothers were best friends too) more or less disappeared from my life about 1960 for the next thirty years, but luckily for me, now she's back. Reeve Lindbergh was on a lofty pedestal, concealed in her white hilltop farmhouse in Peacham, for fifteen years or more, but she's down on my human level now, and I know and love her much better than before.

When I was auditing his course in pastoral at Princeton, Paul Alpers said something to the effect that the impulse to pull away from a group, go sit under a tree, and discuss things with one other person was a pastoral impulse.

If so, I'm one of nature's shepherds. I want to buttonhole my beloved interlocutor and get him or her away from the crowd, face to face— or even not face to face so long as, the way one can on walks in the country, we're looking in the same direction.

Because in my experience many poets are letter writers, the line between friend and colleague or acquaintance can be blurry. Of course, there are hierarchies, pecking orders, disappointments. I've unintentionally gotten close to one or two people whom somewhere along the way I wounded unforgivably. These contretemps made me feel cautious or guilty or angry, as the case may be. And the passage of time always tempts one to draw the line: no more time and space for friends. Luckily, the world doesn't work that way.

If I had the slightest talent for writing fiction, friendship might well be a subject I'd want to explore. Certainly it's among the themes of much great fiction from Jane Austen to Tolstoy and beyond. And yet lyric poetry, with its plethora of pronouns, its incurably personal and imme-diate point of view, its penchant for apostrophe, is just as much the genre of friendship as it is of love. From Sappho's message of longing to Keats's chatty sonnets to Montale's wry meditations, lyric is usually addressed to someone. Maybe I'm so drawn to friendship in theory and practice because I'm an addict of the apostrophic mode. Mark Rudman, Eleanor Cory, Reeve Lindbergh, Lisa Hull, Charlie Barber— among many others, let me lovingly name you here.

GMHC

Gay Men's Health Crisis, one of the first organized responses to AIDS in New York City in the early eighties, is now a formidably large and complex bureaucracy. From early 1988 into 1994, I ran a poetry workshop for clients, most often in a windowless basement room I grew very fond of. I want to name the people who worked with me and some of whose poems can be found in *Unending Dialogue:* Charles Barber,

Leading a poetry workshop at Gay Men's Health Crisis, New York City, 1992

Glenn Besco, Dan Conner, Tony Giordano, Kevin Imbusch, Glenn Philip Kramer, Raul Martinez-Avila, Gustavo Motta, Michael Pelonero, and James Turcotte. Between 1990 and 1995, all of them died.

GRANDPARENTS

My father's father, David Hadas, emigrated from somewhere in the Pale to Atlanta around 1900 and died many years before I was born. My father's mother, Gertrude Draizen Hadas, was, I think, alive for at least some of my childhood, but although she lived in Manhattan, she wasn't interested in meeting this second and incompletely Jewish crop of grandchildren. My father was not in the habit of talking about his early years, and these grandparents are almost completely mysterious to me, though I know (how?) that she was blond, and that he ran a dry goods store, had a horse and cart, was a scholar, and wrote a book. But was it essays or Talmudic studies? And was it in Hebrew or Yiddish?

My mother's father, Lewis Parke Chamberlayne (1879–1917), died when she was only two, perhaps of influenza. A classicist who had gone from the University of Virginia to study for his doctorate at the University of Halle in Germany, he was a gifted poet and translator. A very incomplete but still precious set of his papers came to me when my mother died, including an essay about his boyhood in Petersburg, Virginia, near the site of the Battle of the Crater. His father, who died when my grandfather was small, had been a captain under General Lee; the children playing in the yard found bits of bone.

My mother's mother, Elizabeth Claiborne Mann Chamberlayne, who was born in the 1880s and died around 1956, is the only one of my grandparents I ever saw. She visited us in New York more than once and was staying with us when her arteriosclerosis suddenly worsened and she died. I remember her tall, big-boned, deep-voiced presence; I remember her reading to us; I remember that she was scandalized when the family cat Butterscotch climbed onto the dining-room table and licked butter off the butter plate (no one else seemed to care). I remember walking on Riverside Drive holding her hand and calling her "Grandma" just to hear how the word sounded. I remember peering into the little room halfway down the hall and seeing her lying on the bed, dead.

David Hadas, 1931–

Summers in Vermont during my childhood, this gentle, funny man was halfway between a brother and a father to me and my sister. He had two small children of his own, but he read my sister and me Dickens, taught Beth to drive, was endlessly available and affectionate. A great reader, often lying down to read (it clearly runs in the family), David was legendary for getting through Calvin's *Institutes* one summer. He doesn't publish, but he can and does teach anything from the Book of Job to Stanley Elkin's novels. He currently teaches and has taught for many years at Washington University in St. Louis.

Elizabeth Hadas, 1946–

My sister Beth, two and a half years older than I, in relation to whom I defined myself when we were growing up. I used to beg her to play with me, and often enough she complied; we used to have elaborate games of paper dolls on Sunday mornings when our parents slept late. She went to Hunter, I went to Riverdale; I followed her to Radcliffe but not into an English major. Since 1970 she has lived in Albuquerque, where she is now head of the University of New Mexico Press. Despite temperamental clashes, I have great respect for her judgment and integrity. We don't always like the same books, but we continue to listen to each other's opinions on books. The same things make us laugh, and our laughs sound alike.

Living in Time

A collection of essays with a long poem sandwiched in the middle. I'll always be grateful to Kenneth Arnold, former director of Rutgers University Press, for his leap of faith in publishing this and two subsequent books by me.

MARRIAGE

In November 1970, I was married at City Hall in Manhattan to Stavros Kondilis. We weren't divorced until 1978, but I saw him for the last time (so far) in September 1976, when he put me on the train to Johns Hopkins. I've written about this youthful marriage in "Mornings in Ormos" and other essays, as well as more obliquely in poems. Twenty-five years on, this marriage seems remote and unlikely rather than unpleasant. Stavros kept me company and in his own way took care of me as I mourned for my father and decided, by not deciding, what to do next. When I finally did take several steps, including leaving him, he was sad rather than bitter. My second husband, George Edwards, and I celebrated our seventeenth anniversary last summer. George grew up in Wellesley, studied at Oberlin, did graduate work in composition at Princeton, and taught music theory at New England Conservatory before coming to Columbia in 1976 and moving into the building where I had gone to nursery school. Inconceivably naive after my years abroad, I asked George in the early days why, if he was a composer, he taught music theory and didn't simply compose. "To support my habit," he replied. We've both been supporting our respective habits ever since.

James Merrill, 1926–1995

This catalog-in-lieu-of-a-memoir is being written toward the end of a year colored by the death of this incomparably rare genius—a matchless writer and an equally matchless friend. Soon after his death on February 6, 1994, I wrote the following tribute.

The last poem I wanted to show Jimmy Merrill was a ballad written by Saint-Exupéry at the age of eighteen or so, which had leaped out at me from a less memorable though usually interesting source, Stacy Schiff's recent biography of the aviator/writer. The slightly aggrieved, wistful tone of Saint-Exupéry's lines is perfectly captured in Mary McCarthy's 1986 description of Merrill's voice, both, one gathers, in life and in his work—as "a very light voice . . . no organ tones; rather a boy's voice that has only

In the port town of Ormos, Greece, 1972

just changed and keeps a slight hoarseness."
The speaker is a schoolboy's desk which has
been cruelly confiscated:

> *Les souhaits que je pouvais faire*
> *se bornaient tous au status quo.*
> *La paix ne fut pas que passagère.*
> *Et moi, vieux meuble rococo,*
> *banni de cette quiètude,*
> *je fus éxilé, comme un roi.*
> *Je moisis dans un autre étude,*
> *ô mon vieux maître, loin de toi.*

I prefer not to allegorize the desk and its master.
But I know Jimmy would have enjoyed the rhyme
of "rococo" and "status quo," and I would have
enjoyed hearing him laugh. Besides, as far as
I could remember, *Le Petit Prince* was one book
we'd never talked about.

Last November, I flew to St. Louis to participate in a cluster of events I then thought
and still think of as James Merrill Weekend.
There were to be readings, lectures, a panel
discussion—all to celebrate the fact that Merrill's
papers were lodged (is that the word?) in the
library of Washington University. For some reason,
as the plane climbed into the cold morning
sky, I felt unusually conscious of connections,
of chronology, of the present moment as one
in a series. I tried to make order in my mind,
to isolate various past events like dots that I
would later be able to connect into an intelli-
gible shape—events of which, since I had met
Jimmy in 1969, this weekend would be the latest in a long series. I didn't think at that time
it would be the last.

Nor, in a way, was it. In December there
were chatty phone conversations, though final
exams and houseguests prevented me from getting across town to see Jimmy's tree. On January 12 there was a delicious long phone call
from Tucson; among the things we talked about
were a mutual friend's childhood and Jimmy
and Peter's project of finding a few suitable
lines from Auden's *Thanksgiving for a Habitat*
to be translated into German and hung on
the wall of the *Kirchstetten bierstube* under what
Jimmy said was a wonderful photo of Auden
by Rollie McKenna.

Even after the numbing news of Jimmy's
death, there were other social events in which
he was a presence: the vigil in his apartment
the day before the funeral, and then the fu-

With James Merrill, 1988

neral itself. In all this, the living person had
hardly receded at all. It may well be that very
bad news is slow to sink in; I'm not sure that
by the day of the funeral any of Jimmy's innumerable friends had really understood that he
was gone. On the other hand, his living presence is part of me. To quote from a card he
sent me in 1976 giving news of some back problem, it "will pass & recur, pass & recur, and
finally go away, with me, for good." Not until
every last person who knew Jimmy is gone will
he really go away for good—and even to say
so is monstrously untrue, for it is to ignore
the poems.

As I looked out the plane window that
November morning, images would open out into
events, or at least scenes. December (isn't it?)
1969: the first time I'm at David and Jimmy's
house in Athens. Jimmy, standing at the top
of the stairs to greet guests, is wearing a belt
with a beautiful silver buckle. As if I were
waist-high, the buckle seems to be what I first
focus on.

Sometime in 1973 or '74, sitting at my
kitchen table in Samos, I type a letter to my
mother on my rusty but trusty Olympia portable, quoting for her lines from "Days of 1935"
that make me splutter with laughter each time
I read them. The wealthy child, kidnapped by
his fantasy couple Floyd and Jean, overhears
his captors making love, and they know he
overhears them:

Jean: The kid, he's still awake . . .
Floyd: Time he learned . . . Oh Baby . . .
   God . . .
Their prone tango, for my sake,
Grew intense and proud.

January 1975: Jimmy and I, sitting in the living room, are among the people gathered in Chester Kallman's Athens apartment. Earlier that morning, Chester has been found dead in bed. There are other people around, making phone calls, making coffee in the kitchen. Next to me on the sofa or even in one of Chester's huge, enveloping black leather armchairs, Jimmy puts his hand comfortingly on mine. I liked Chester, but I am not devastated by his loss; probably I'm too young and callous to be in need of consoling. But I love the feeling of Jimmy's hand on mine, and we sit like that for a few moments. After Chester is buried the next day in the Jewish section of an Athenian cemetery, everyone in the car back to Kolanaki is out of sorts. Has Alan Ansen taken exception to Bernie Weinbaum's tears, or are people worried by the fact that Chester died intestate, or is it something else? In the *zacharoplasteion* where we testily repair for drinks and cake, there are problems about who should sit next to whom. "How characteristic of Chester," murmurs Jimmy, "that his funeral should leave everyone in a blind rage." Whereas Jimmy's funeral only left everyone blind with tears.

*   *   *

I was barely twenty-one when Jimmy and I met; I'm older now than he was then. In the years of our friendship, the age gap of twenty-two years shrank, by the end, to almost nothing. Now, fast becoming a *vieux meuble rococo* in my turn, I often find myself irritated by the rawness, the shyness, the inarticulate strengths and troubles and weaknesses of students in their early twenties. The impulse to retreat, to kvetch, to withdraw—I see it daily, in my contemporaries and colleagues as well as myself. And then I remember Jimmy's generosity and patience, his unfailing appetite for the human comedy, his kindness to—among countless other people—a self-absorbed, confused, and fearful young woman still shaken by her father's death a couple of years before.

Not that Jimmy took my father's place exactly. For one thing, I got to know him when I was already (if barely) an adult. For another, we were in constant touch for the next quarter-century. Unlike my father, Jimmy knew both my husbands well. He knew and loved my son; he knew and encouraged me with all my books. I cannot imagine the past years without his friendship. And though it is impossible to disagree with Harry Mathews's words, "Even at the bitter news of his death, I felt, thinking of the marvelous life now ended, an urge to rejoice," it is also impossible not to feel abandoned and bereft. Saint-Exupéry's ballad ends with a plea on the part of the desk's owner:

> *ENVOI*
> *Prince, qui par un geste inique,*
> *êtes devenu son bourreau,*
> *daignez, touché par sa supplique,*
> *me rendre mon petit bureau.*

Its contents remain, but the "discret et pacifique" little desk is no more.

Mirrors of Astonishment

This collection of poems began as a group of sequences, but some shorter pieces made their way into the central section, which is probably now my favorite.

MOTHER, Elizabeth Chamberlayne Hadas, 1915–1992

Quiet and shy in life, at once articulate and withheld, loving and understated, my mother has, according to what's becoming a familiar pattern, become more present to me in the years since her death. That death and its aftermath, in tandem with the parallel last days of my friend Charles Barber, are the subject matter of *The Double Legacy*. But just as in life my mother often faded into the background of even a small gathering, so in death she was in some ways eclipsed by him. He was so young and beautiful, and I'd known him so short a time, I was so greedy for more, that I couldn't bear the fact of Charlie's slipping away—whereas my mother, having been part of me for my whole life, couldn't slip away. Or could she?

I'd rather explore my mother's life than her death. Alas, very few papers survive, though she scrupulously kept the transcripts from her studies in classics at Columbia, where she studied in the summer of 1942 and met my father. My mother was born in Columbia, South Carolina, where her father was teaching classics at the university. After his sudden death, his widow took her two small daughters back to Richmond, Virginia, where my mother grew up (she also spent a good deal of time with her grandparents in Petersburg). She went north to college, Bryn Mawr, taught at St. Timothy's School, and was studying for her M.A. in Latin at Columbia when she met my father. They married in 1945, in Washington, D.C., where he was working for the OSS (he had been overseas earlier) and she worked for the Library of Congress until my sister was born. When they moved to New York in 1947 or 1948, she worked for a while at the New York Public Library; after I was born, she stayed home with us girls until we were in seventh and ninth grade, respectively, and then went to work part-time teaching Latin at the Spence School, where she remained for twenty-five years. When she retired in 1984, it was partly to help me with my son, for whom she was a blessedly present grandparent for the first eight years of his life. I wish it could have been longer. But loving relationships and cherished memories aren't the worst of all possible worlds.

Until the last couple of years of her life, my mother was almost never ill. More than sturdy, she seemed indefatigable, walking, gardening, baby-sitting. Her unemphatic presence, like her intelligence and judgment, was so dependable and undramatic that I was apt to take them all for granted—a mistake I no longer have the luxury of making.

ORMOS

Port town on the Marathokampos, a village on the southwest coast of Samos, in the eastern Aegean. Marathokampos was my husband Stavros's village; we lived in Ormos for almost four years in the early seventies. I visited there briefly ten years later, but another dozen years have passed since I've seen the place.

Ormos was on the edge of the world. I loved the nearness of our tiny house to the ocean; the clarity of its north/south orientation (one looked out the kitchen window south to the sea) reminded me of the grid of Manhattan, where as a child I'd looked out the window west to the Hudson River and the set-

ting sun. Elementally bare yet also lush with bright colors—the green of fig leaves, the sapphire of the Aegean—Ormos was, from my egotistical perspective, a background for the dramas of my belated adolescence or young wifehood (both phrases seem all wrong), as well as for whatever larger domestic or civic or historical dramas played themselves out against what I called in an early poem the blue proscenium of sea.

Other Worlds Than This

Collection of my favorite translations from Latin (Seneca's *Oedipus,* some poems of Tibullus), French (favorite poems of Hugo, Baudelaire, Rimbaud, Valéry, and La Forgue) and modern Greek (Karyotakis).

Pass It On

The first collection of my work I organized on my own, without help or advice from anyone— which solo practice I've adhered to ever since. The thematic strands seemed to braid themselves without much help even from me: the book had something to tell me.

The Princess and the Goblin

George MacDonald's children's story—the first book of any difficulty I ever read to myself— turns up in more than one of my essays. The powerful, magical great-grandmother and the beloved, bearded father no doubt attracted me, but the most crucial thing I took away from the book was the idea of giving someone a present that one can also keep at the same time. Like a name. Like a book. Like teaching. Like writing.

PUMPKIN HILL

Around 1955, my parents bought a tumbledown farmhouse and thirty acres of land in an area called Pumpkin Hill between St. Johnsbury and Danville in northern Vermont. For the last forty years, I've spent most of my summers there, as well as an occasional fall and even, once, winter until March. The house isn't winterized; isn't glamorous; is barely comfortable. Most of

It was a dark apartment, and my father never had his own study, and the fact that we were on the ground floor meant there was less floor space and less privacy and less of a view than if we had been higher up. Still, it was wonderful to look across the street at Riverside Drive and beyond that the park and the river. I felt almost as if I were near the ocean.

RUTGERS

Like many people, I didn't even know that Rutgers had a campus in Newark until, in the spring of 1981, consulting MLA job lists, I compiled a long list of colleges within commuting distance of New York where I hoped I might find a probably part-time teaching job. One thing led to another, and I've been at Rutgers Newark since the fall of 1981. I can be irritated or exhausted or distracted or bored or full of stagefright or unprepared or many of those things at once, but essentially I love teaching and am very fortunate in my Rutgers colleagues and students.

Rachel Hadas and George Edwards,
Sewanee, Tennessee, 1992

Slow Transparency

My first full-length book of poems. Like many such, it was compiled over the course of years and is hence very full and probably somewhat disjunct. It avoids narrative but nevertheless more than touches upon both some of the events of my years in Greece and my marriage to George Edwards.

A Son from Sleep

Many of the poems in this book were written when Jonathan was an infant. No doubt, the resulting work is more generic than I intended or thought at the time. After a reading, a man came up to me and said enthusiastically: "When our baby was little, my wife was writing those poems too."

the people who've spent time there have had things they wanted to do more urgently than to fix the place up—work in the garden, write a poem, translate, compose. As long as the house is standing (and we've fixed the foundation so that it will, we've been told, last our time), and there are still cows across the road; the place is a priceless blessing.

RIVERSIDE DRIVE

One of the points of my inner compass. I grew up in a ground-floor apartment (thunderous sneezes from doormen in the lobby; doorknob trembling while on the other side of the door its brass is being polished) at 460 Riverside Drive, toward the northern end of the long block between 116th and 119th Streets. My parents moved in, in 1947 or 1948, and the apartment was vacated only with my mother's death in 1992. When I walk in the park now I like to look at the lighted window and know another family is living there.

Starting from Troy

My first book, a chapbook in the Godine series. The earliest poems in it were written when I was a senior in high school; others date from college and my early years in and immediately after Greece. James Merrill, who very kindly read the galley proofs in Athens in 1974 and early 1975, said the book was about growing up, losing a father, and transferring my affections to a husband.

TRANSLATIONS

The task of translating combines two kinds of challenges: that of an assignment and that of a puzzle. To translate a poem is a workout; it's also serendipitous and mysterious. Where is the author going, and how to follow him or her down the track? But also, why has this particular text turned up to be translated at this stage of my life? Recently, I was offered the choice of translating either the *Hecuba,* the *Iphigenia among the Taurians,* or the *Helen* of Euripides; I couldn't avoid pondering the emblematic aspect of this choice.

Unending Dialogue: Voices from an AIDS Poetry Workshop

This hybrid book grew out of the poetry workshop that I ran at the Gay Men's Health Crisis. Its heart is forty-five poems by my students there, preceded by an essay of mine and followed by some of my own poems, with commentary.

BIBLIOGRAPHY

Poetry:

Starting from Troy, David Godine, 1975.

Slow Transparency, Wesleyan University Press, 1983.

A Son from Sleep, Wesleyan University Press, 1987.

Pass It On, Princeton University Press, 1989.

(Editor) *Unending Dialogue: Voices from an AIDS Poetry Workshop,* Faber & Faber, 1991.

Mirrors of Astonishment, Rutgers University Press, 1992.

The Empty Bed, Wesleyan University Press, 1995.

Essays:

Living in Time, Rutgers University Press, 1990.

The Double Legacy, Faber & Faber, 1995.

Other:

Form, Cycle, Infinity: Landscape Imagery in the Poetry of Robert Frost and George Seferis, Associated University Presses, 1985.

(Translator) *Other Worlds Than This,* Rutgers University Press, 1994.

Author of translation of Seneca's *Oedipus the King.*

Work represented in anthologies, including *Ardis Anthology of American Poetry.* Contributor of poems, articles, translations, and reviews to magazines, including *Atlantic Monthly, Harper's, National Forum, New Republic, New Yorker,* and *Ploughshares.*

Michael Kammen

1936-

Michael Kammen's paternal great-grandfather Gedaliah (Gedalyahu) Meirson (1850–?), in Ekaterinislav, the Ukraine, 1880s. He was a prominent cantor and sometime operatic performer. He did not come to the United States, but his daughter did in 1903.

Near the beginning of a dramatic drive along Route 12 from Missoula, Montana, to McCall, Idaho, an honest sign says: "Winding Road Next 77 Miles." And so it turns out to be, as it passes through some of the finest forest scenery to be found anywhere in the United States. Having made that spectacular trip, I should advise the reader at the start that my personal road has *not* been a notably winding one. I have been a student and a teacher (hence a perpetual student) for fifty-four years without interruption: no military service; no time off for alternative or experimental employment; no institutionalization for injury, lunacy, criminal behavior, or boredom. I have now been "in school" since the age of five. Nonstop.

Do I have regrets? Only a few so far as my life as a student, teacher, and writer is concerned. I wish that I had been better at all three pursuits—perhaps that adds up to one fairly major regret—yet I resonate with a sentence written in 1948 by R. H. Tawney, a noted British historian. "If a man has important work," he remarked, "and enough leisure and income to enable him to do it properly, he is in possession of as much happiness as is good for any of the children of Adam."[1]

Perhaps one other prefatory observation is in order. I never expected to become a "writer" and did not really consider myself one until well into the 1970s, less than twenty-five years ago. By then I had published a handful of books and won a Pulitzer Prize for history, so I must have become a writer *malgré moi*. But one of my young sons put it well at that time when someone at school asked him what his father did. "My daddy is a studier," he said. It was true then, and that still remains the best answer.

The same designation can be made in fancier ways, of course, though the eyes of a child are so wonderfully clear and uncomplicated. The Fogg Museum of Art at Harvard has an engraving made in Rome by Pietro Testa during the 1640s. It bears the motto: "I have no other delight but learning." Or consider a conversation that occurred at the Collége de France following a lecture by Michel Foucault. When the discussion became heated, someone challenged Foucault: "What is your intellectual authority for these assertions, these interpretations?

---

[1] R. H. Tawney, *The Acquisitive Society* (New York, 1920, 1948), p. 179.

With his sister, Edith, and their maternal grandparents, Ida and Abraham Lazerovitz, in Baltimore, 1938

What are you, anyway? Are you a historian? A philosopher? Or something else? How can you legitimize your conclusions?" Foucault responded quite simply, "I am just a reader."[2] The French "lecteur" does not translate very well, because there are ordinary readers and there are privileged ones. Clearly, Foucault was a particularly privileged and insightful reader. In my own rather different way, I too have been a privileged reader first and a writer second.

Given that prioritization, perhaps it should be acknowledged that I do have a special fondness for reading the biographies and autobiographies of writers. In the former category, for example, I recall with special fondness both Ellmann's *Joyce* (1959) and his *Wilde* (1988), Bate's *Samuel Johnson* (1977), Justin Kaplan's *Mr.*

Clemens and Mark Twain (1966), Stegner's *DeVoto* (1974), and Edmund Morris's *Theodore Roosevelt* (1979). In the latter category I have particular affection for *One Writer's Beginnings* by Eudora Welty (1984), *Half the Way Home: A Memoir of Father and Son* (1986) by Adam Hochschild, *Blackberry Winter: My Earlier Years* (1972) by Margaret Mead, *Ancestors* (1971) by William Maxwell, and two rustic works by former Cornell colleagues, *Crossroads: An Autobiographical Novel* (1968) by James McConkey and *On Being Negro in America* (1951) by J. Saunders Redding.

So I have become a reader and a writer with a curious fascination for the things that writers read as well as the things that readers write. But it was not always so. I became a serious reader relatively late and a self-aware writer later still. Is there no line of continuity, then, that connects my literate adulthood with my preliterate, wayward youth? I think that there is, and I find it in a quality confessed by Nicolas Poussin, the seventeenth-century French painter. "My nature forces me to search for and to love well-ordered things," he declared, "fleeing confusion, which is as contrary and inimical to me as deep darkness is to light."[3] From childhood through adulthood I have had a penchant for well-ordered things.

My grandparents emigrated from the Ukraine, Russia, and Lithuania in the first years of the twentieth century—on my father's side settling in the tenements of the Lower East Side of New York City and on my mother's side briefly in Boston and then permanently in Baltimore. My paternal grandfather, whom I hardly knew, began as a peddler and eventually "moved up" to become a middling but unsuccessful shopkeeper. My maternal grandfather, who died of cancer from lead in paint when I was three, supported his wife and five children as a housepainter. More important, perhaps, I learned later that he had been a fearsome disciplinarian and terrorized the entire menage with his martinet's temper. Whereas they were strict Orthodox Jews, living according to the letter of the law, my father's parents were reasonably observant yet considerably more relaxed.

---

[2]Michel de Certeau told me this story at Cornell in October 1984.

[3]Quoted in Bryan Jay Wolf, *Romantic Re-Vision: Culture and Consciousness in Nineteenth-Century American Painting and Literature* (Chicago, 1982), p. 41.

My great-grandfather on the paternal side had been a prominent cantor and occasional opera singer in Ekaterinislav in the Ukraine. His daughter (my grandmother) inherited a lovely voice and sang Russian lullabies and songs incessantly, with a superabundance of good cheer. Hence my father also loved to sing and did so while driving, gardening, washing the dinner dishes, and sometimes even at the dinner table, a habit that my mother reluctantly tolerated but never became fully accustomed to. She had grown up in a household of semi-silence by intimidation, whereas my father emerged from an ambience of lyrical exuberance.

Their personalities reflected their respective domestic circumstances as children. My father was the gentlest and kindest person I have ever known. I think that he may have reprimanded me a total of three or perhaps four times in my life, and when he did, the provocation had to be immense. Even then, his anger was tempered by a kind of socializing savvy. On one occasion, when I must have been giving my mom some utterly dreadful back talk, he ended the incident with these words: "I don't care how you talk to your mother, but don't you *ever* again speak that way to my wife." He never lost his equanimity or his sense of humor, even under stress. As I remarked in a eulogy at his gravesite in 1988, I envied especially one possession of my father's: his self-possession.

By contrast, my mother lacked his sense of playfulness, never mind his sense of humor. She became, partially by default, the family disciplinarian, although as the eldest of five, perhaps she was figuratively her father's daughter: judgmental and serious. Because she always seemed to be a woman of such virtue, I didn't fear her wrath so much as her moral anguish and disappointment. When I misbehaved in elementary school, which apparently happened with some frequency, it would be my mother who had to attend a conference with my teacher and the school principal because my father was at work.

There is a portrait of my mother done in charcoal around 1936 when she was thirty-two. (She was five days older than my father.) Her long, thick, coal-black hair is pulled back into a single braid, and her appearance reminds me of those young Renaissance beauties painted with austere precision in the fifteenth and sixteenth centuries. Later in life, following minor facial surgery, she developed a slight but quite noticeable involuntary tic on one side of her face. That added to her apparent severity and, unfortunately, compounded the judgmental look that she usually conveyed.

My father was beloved by everyone who met him. Utterly lacking in ambition, he was never in a hurry to get anywhere or do anything. Perhaps his most memorable phrase, reiterated in response to my mother's prodding that they needed to get ready for something, or to get somewhere on time, was "So what's the big rush?"

During the mid-1920s he briefly attended rabbinical school in Cincinnati for one year, rejected that and became a social worker following his education at the City College of New York (class of '26). He then got a job with Jewish social services in Baltimore, where he met and married my mother in 1929 (six weeks after the stock market crashed in October); moved to a similar but better paying job at Rochester, New York, in 1935 (where I was born one year later); and in 1941 moved to Washington, D.C., where he became executive director of the Jewish Social Service Agency and the Jewish Community Council of Greater Washington, which had a sizeable and swiftly growing Jewish population.[4]

Instead of attending college my mother studied classical piano at the Peabody Institute in Baltimore, on scholarship, and she later gave piano lessons to youngsters in order to supplement my father's modest salary. She also devoted considerable time and attention to charitable work as a volunteer and to being the "switchboard" for her extended family in the Baltimore-Washington area. Relatives who did not get along with one another particularly well communicated through her, and our home was invariably the site for all family gatherings—in part because my parents worked very hard at being the connecters and in part because they alone kept a kosher household where my maternal grandmother would eat.

My parents also had a great many friends and entertained people from all walks of life, ranging from the state department to teachers

---

[4]See Hasia R. Diner, *Fifty Years of Jewish Self-Governance: The Jewish Community Council of Greater Washington, 1938–1988* (Washington, D.C., 1989), pp. 34, 36, 41, 43, 49, 59.

to people in commerce (they called it "business"). I have clear memories of sitting at the bottom of the stairs to the second floor listening to their concerned conversations about the war or domestic social issues. Without exception, of course, they were all Roosevelt Democrats, and I vividly remember the anguish and tears on April 12, 1945, when news came that FDR had died. A few days later the four of us (my sister Edith was born in 1932) joined the crowd lining Pennsylvania Avenue to pay our respects as the president's coffin was solemnly carried to the Capitol to lie in state at the rotunda.

My parents had good books and phonograph records in abundance, almost all of which I ignored until my midteens. They faithfully listened to radio broadcasts of the Metropolitan Opera on Saturday afternoons, which struck me as a lot of tedious and incomprehensible screaming. They never bothered to explain to me what was going on and never handed me the kinds of succinct plot summaries that (I subsequently learned) are available in *The Victor Book of the Opera* (1936) and *The Metropolitan Opera Guide* (1939). That problem in turn became part of a pattern, because in Hebrew School (ninety minutes each day following public school), in Sunday school classes, and in the eight- or nine-month preparation for my Bar Mitzvah in 1949, almost everything that I "learned" involved rote memorization of Hebrew liturgy and songs, the actual meaning of which was obscure to me.

The odd thing is that my mother faithfully attended adult education classes in modern Hebrew literature taught at night in a nearby high school. That might have been more meaningful for me—though I suspect I would have considered it a gross imposition at the time. In any case, despite being a "star" pupil in Hebrew school for five years (i.e., I could memorize more and sing better than anyone else), despite being elected president of my Sunday school class, and despite conducting the entire service on the morning of my own Bar Mitzvah, an unprecedented performance in my synagogue (I did everything except give the homily to the Bar Mitzvah boy), I basically "dropped out" the following year and silently resented going to services even on the High Holy days. I completely lost interest and commitment. I have been a nominal "cultural Jew" ever since, mar-

Parents, Blanche Lazerow and Jacob Merson Kammen, Skyline Drive, Virginia, overlooking the Shenandoah Valley, about 1947

ried a Protestant, and our two sons received no religious education except for a year of weekly Bible reading at home—mainly the Old Testament, I think—a kind of perfunctory course in ancient literature that mostly served to assuage parental guilt. The boys endured it with calm resignation.

In 1976, when I was invited to give a sequence of lectures at universities in Iran, Turkey, and Italy under the auspices of the U.S. Information Agency, all four of us had to fill out visa application forms for Iran and Turkey. Where the form asked for religion, I put Jewish, my wife put Christian, but our sons, then fourteen and ten, found themselves in a great quandary. For several days there was absolutely no resolution in sight, but the very challenge seemed more provocative than leaving the space blank, or writing in NA, or putting a dash. We (or at least I) had not fully faced up to the question of religious identity for the children of a nonobservant, mixed marriage.

Finally, the fourteen-year-old came home from school one day with what felt like an inspiration if not a revelation. "I am a rationalist," he announced. "Me too," proclaimed the ten-year-old. So that's what they put down; we sent in the forms, and the Iranian Embassy promptly processed and approved visas for one lapsed Jew, one lapsed Presbyterian, and two ardent rationalists. The rationalists have remained so ever since—diluted a bit, perhaps, because the older one eventually married a believing Methodist who is Nigerian-American, and he joins her at worship, whereas the younger one, now thirty, has wedded himself to Marxism, which does not undermine his rationalism but makes it somewhat more skeptical than, let us say, the rationalism of eighteenth-century deists who tended to be considerably more optimistic about human nature and the future prospects of mankind.

Being fairly nonintellectual as a child—all those classics of world literature on my parents' shelves looked just as tiresome as the

*On Fern Street, Washington, D.C.,
opposite Walter Reed Army Hospital,
about 1945*

Metropolitan Opera sounded—I preferred to play with friends from school (marathon games of monopoly, for instance), collect and trade baseball cards, spend countless hours at the National Zoo, which I loved, and even longer hours across the street using the sports facilities of Walter Reed Army Hospital, where soldiers wounded in World War II were brought for rehabilitation and physical therapy. I played many hours of basketball with veterans, or with my neighborhood friends if the courts were not being used by those who were recovering from injuries, and I watched endless games of fast-pitch softball, astonished at the skills displayed by men with missing fingers, or an arm gone, or wearing a brace on one or another part of their body. Surely, few youngsters have grown up with more complete gymnasium facilities than I had about two hundred yards from my home. Perhaps that is why I have remained a lifelong sports fan.

My public high school class graduated in June 1954, one month after the Warren Court handed down its decision in *Brown v. Board of Education.* Throughout my entire precollegiate education, therefore, I lived in a segregated city and attended segregated schools. The extent of my moral outrage was confined to the world of sports. The white high schools played one another in every sport, and a championship team eventually emerged each season. The same thing happened among the Negro high schools, like Dunbar and Armstrong. It always seemed stupid to me that the two champions did not ultimately play each other to determine the real champion of the city.

My contact with African Americans, therefore, was exceedingly limited. I saw them in custodial positions, I saw them downtown because quite a few worked for the federal government (usually in menial positions), and I saw some in playground basketball competition, where occasionally I would be in the very same "pickup" game with Elgin Baylor, who went to John Carroll, a Catholic high school nearby. Yes, he was an awesome athlete even as a teenager. And as an individual he personified the notion of grace under pressure.

Our "maid," Catherine, traveled a very long distance across town by bus to our home once a week, and her husband, James, would come occasionally on a weekend if there was some sort of "heavy" work to be done around the house. Our relationship somehow managed to be simultaneously cordial and polite yet informal and relaxed. Everyone behaved with great courtesy and dignity, but the deferential hierarchy was so well defined that one scarcely even thought about it. (Perhaps it would be more accurate to say that *we* scarcely thought about it.) I'm not absolutely certain, but I believe that my parents were called Miss Blanche and Mr. Jack. Catherine and James were called Catherine and James.

On the other hand, during the 1960s, when white flight to the Maryland and Virginia suburbs began and when blacks began to buy homes in our neighborhood, my parents were quite actively involved in forming the Shepherd Park Citizens' (Homeowners?) Association, the purpose of which was mutual agreement *not* to sell-and-run, so that the neighborhood and its elementary school would remain racially mixed rather than turn, almost overnight, from white to black—a dominant pattern elsewhere in the city. My parents' commitment to racial integration was so strong that they remained in the comfortable home where I grew up long after my sister and I had left, long after it had become too much for them to manage, and long after my father's arthritis had made gardening impossible for him. They did not move to a Rockville apartment until they were in their seventies—and they eventually went to the suburbs mainly for health-related reasons and because their synagogue had been relocated and they wanted to be within walking distance. They also wanted to serve as volunteers at the Hebrew Home for the Aged, near the synagogue, which made them feel quite youthful!

Given the realities of time and place—Washington really was a southern city during the 1940s, '50s, and even the '60s (several homes in my neighborhood, for example, had on their lawns cast-iron black jockeys with brightly painted livery)—my parents and their friends seemed to me at the time admirable liberals. Although they had not been ardent activists for civil rights prior to 1954, they behaved with integrity and decency thereafter in their commitment not merely to formal racial integration but to friendship and mutual trust. When blacks moved in next door (a school principal and his wife, a teacher) and then across the street (a physician and his wife), my parents welcomed them into our home. Years later, when I came back to visit during the 1960s and early '70s, I was pleased to find my mother giving piano les-

sons to several black youngsters who lived a few houses down the street.

If my public school experience was lily white, as we used to say, at least it was integrated in terms of social class. My junior high, and my high school to an even greater degree, served a diverse array of residential areas that ranged from upper middle class to what might be called upper working class. We may have been color blind by default because we were racially monochromatic, but white, blue, and pink collar all blended together in a benign way, as did Protestant, Catholic, and Jew. In fact, we dated and "went steady" in such ecumenical patterns that many of our parents became genuinely upset at the prospect of a melting pot that seemed to be homogenizing our generation much too fast. More than a few homilies were heard at home, in church, and in synagogues on the subject of "friendship, yes; romance, no. Stick with your own. Do you want your kids to face impossible problems?"

Despite having diverse friends and being reasonably well-liked—I think that I was elected treasurer of my senior high school class—I nonetheless recall spending a fair amount of time by myself between the ages of about fourteen and eighteen. In part that happened because my fascination with the National Zoo made me want to become a veterinarian, so I got a part-time job in an urban practice with two doctors of veterinary medicine. A couple of years of cleaning kennels and pens, cropping puppy ears and docking tails, but above all, assisting in some gruesome surgery situations cured me of that vocational aspiration. In part, also, my isolation happened because I began to explore my parents' library and collection of classical recordings—at first only when they were not at home. At the age of sixteen it seemed inconceivable to give them the satisfaction of learning that I rather liked Beethoven, Brahms, and my father's absolute favorite, Mozart.

Whatever the reasons may have been, I can see in retrospect that I began a pattern of existence that would eventually make me what the French call *un homme seul,* a solitary person or a man apart from others. I find in my journal (which I have never reread until now) that on July 4, 1982, I copied out the following passage about an Oxford don: "what he loved best was privacy. He might have agreed with Pascal that many of the ills of mankind come because men will not stay quietly in a room."[5]

I am intrigued to find several similar statements in my journal, including one that truly seems to connect the self-contained scholar that I have become with the somewhat insecure, puzzled student that I was more than forty years ago. This passage comes from an interview with Garson Kanin, the playwright (also born in Rochester, New York):

> The most important thing is concentration. The two enemies of any kind of creative work are interruption and distraction. Which is why so many writers feel they have to go away somewhere. . . . You have to sit by yourself in a room for four, five, six hours a day. That's something you have to conquer in your own way. I don't find the loneliness oppressive. I find it peaceful and I enjoy writing.[6]

Despite my highly tentative growth of bookish curiosity in high school, I was not a particularly motivated student and earned mostly low A's and B's. At least there was no longer a grade category for deportment, which had been my nemesis (and my mother's humiliation) in earlier years. The extent of my teenage rebellion, however, stopped with turning away from Judaism, dating non-Jewish girls, and occasional sullenness at mealtime—customarily an occasion for animated conversation, singing, and guessing games initiated by my father, which we loved. Those activities could make Sunday dinner, especially, into a ninety-minute "program" with my sister and me as contestants. There were no prizes, no awards, no incentives of any sort. It was pure fun, and looking back I am astonished by the inventiveness of my father's mind and the sheer pleasure that he derived from delighting us by challenging us.

Because the family had such limited resources, I could not go away to college. I never even considered it. Very few of my friends did, actually. I won a partial scholarship at The George Washington University, seven blocks from the Eisenhowers' White House, and I sold men's and women's shoes for Flagg Brothers and Holiday Shoes. We salesmen worked on a commission basis, and the large national chain kept statistics on numbers of shoes sold by individuals as well as gross cash figures. More than once during the summers following my sophomore and junior years in college, I won the weekly distinction (there was no actual prize) of selling more shoes than anyone else in the whole chain. One learned to move fast, talk fast, be able to wait on several customers at the same time (remembering each one's size), but above all, memorize the inventory cold. A trip to the stockroom for an 8B shoe that we did not have meant time wasted. One learned to show what one had and to persuade people that what one did have would look much better on them than what one didn't have (which the customer had walked in to request). Perhaps all those years of mindlessly memorizing Hebrew texts translated into the highly functional (and lucrative) memorization of shoe inventories. In any case, I sold a lot of footwear, held some attractive ankles (an accepted part of the job), and dated some interesting women I would *never* have met under any other circumstances.

I finally became a serious student in my first year of college. In 1954 the Cold War could not have been more intense, and the United States military still had a draft for which anyone, including college students who did not rank academically high in their classes, was eligible. I shall always be grateful that my sister (then finishing college) warned me—I had not given it a thought—that if I did not get serious about my schoolwork I could find myself in the army—a dreadful prospect. (The Korean War was over and U.S. intervention in Vietnam lay a full decade ahead. I worried about regimentation and the horror stories that I had heard about recruits assigned to ridiculous peacetime duties. The most notorious tale involved a math genius assigned by the army to drive trucks in the motor pool.) As a high school senior, when I turned eighteen, I had registered for the draft and then put it out of my mind. Edie's warning came as more than a wake-up call. It was rather like a resounding tocsin.

During the next four years I rarely earned less than an A- and mostly straight A's. The secret did not lie in being smart, which I am not, at least not especially so. The secret lay

---

[5]Isaiah Berlin, "John Petrov Plamenatz," *Personal Impressions* (New York, 1981), p. 121.

[6]Garson Kanin, "Self-Expression," *Backstory 2: Interviews with Screenwriters of the 1940s and 1950s,* edited by Pat McGilligan (Berkeley, 1991), pp. 102, 110.

in being determined, well-organized, and orderly. When Brissot de Warville visited the United States from France following the American Revolution, he remarked upon "the orderliness, which the [Quakers] are taught from childhood to observe in their work, their thoughts, and in every moment of their existence. They apply this principle of order to every aspect of their life; it teaches good behavior and it saves time, effort, and money."[7] If not a birthright Quaker, I did develop their daily habits and have never abandoned them. All that I needed was a rationale that would alter the basis for my work ethic from fear to love, and that too came within a few years. It has grown steadily over the past three decades.

Neither my parents nor anyone else had *ever* proposed or even suggested any specific course of study in college, never mind a particular vocational pursuit. Not once. I never had a conversation with a guidance counsellor. Not once. (After I stopped being willfully naughty [elementary school] and sometimes antisocial [junior high school], the counsellors had other fish to fry. As a reasonably reputable citizen, I could be ignored.) But I did enjoy my precollegiate history courses—I really have no clear idea why—so I majored in history at The George Washington University and had some conscientious, lively lecturers who made learning about the past engaging. I had absolutely no notion where the choice of such a major might lead. Not a clue. My professors seemed so incredibly learned that I couldn't imagine becoming what they were and doing what they did. Since most of them published very little, the thought of *writing* history was even more remote. So at that stage I selected history for a reason that I did not see in print until more than twenty years later: "Self-indulgence."[8]

I concentrated on the history of international relations from the later eighteenth cen-

tury until World War II, where all respectable courses in modern history stopped at that time. Only political scientists and journalists ventured much beyond 1939. No distance, no detachment, insufficient sources, and no perspective. As a senior in college I took two graduate-level research seminars in the history of U.S. diplomacy, and for each of them, being in Washington was an immense advantage because I was able to do primary research at the National Archives and at the Library of Congress. Those two seminars didn't exactly teach me how to *think* like a historian, but I did learn how to use primary sources and how to organize materials into a narrative with an explanation if not a cogent argument. That turned out to be a highly valuable apprenticeship.

So then I was a twenty-one-year-old senior. I still had to stay in school to avoid being drafted. I learned from a fellow history major (she married me three years later) who worked for the chairman of the department that a senior professor earned about nine thousand dollars a year. I could do better than that with Flagg Brothers and Holiday Shoes. Perhaps if I could memorize enough inventories and clone myself into several salesmen, I might earn scads of money and gently squeeze enough pretty ankles to satisfy me for a lifetime. But running to and from the stockroom turned out not to be as interesting as studying the past. So I decided to apply to graduate school to pursue a Ph.D. in history even though I still could not envision myself in a classroom, could not imagine writing anything for publication, and the only aptitude test that I had ever taken showed *conclusively* that I was ideally suited for a career in business!

I applied for a Woodrow Wilson Fellowship (a national competition organized by geographical regions), and for reasons that I cannot comprehend in retrospect I applied to only one graduate program—at Harvard. I got the fellowship, was admitted at Harvard, and worked very, very hard there because it seemed as though everyone in my cohort, indeed, everyone that I met, was so much better prepared than I. Scared to death of failure—and then the army or possibly selling shoes again if I should be so lucky as to flunk the military physical—I read and took notes, went to lectures and took notes, went to where the rare books and manuscripts were kept and took notes. Ever the crypto-Quaker, I was orderly and organized in con-

---

[7]J. P. Brissot de Warville, *New Travels in the United States of America, 1788,* edited by Durand Echeverria (Cambridge, Massachusetts, 1964), p. 307. See also p. 200.

[8]See the preface to William Stanton's engaging book, *The Great United States Exploring Expedition of 1838–1842* (Berkeley, 1975), ix. In 1969 Arnold Toynbee wrote the following sentiments, which I happen to share. "When I am asked, as I sometimes am asked, why I have spent my life on studying history, my answer is 'for fun'. I find this an adequate answer, and it is certainly a sincere one." *Experiences* (New York, 1969), p. 89.

fronting my tasks at graduate school. I worked exceedingly hard, but I did so far more from fear of failure than fondness.

Well, not yet love of history, at least. I had, however, met my future wife when I was a senior and she a junior. We very much wanted to get married, ideally just as soon as I had passed my Ph.D. general exams, which ordinarily occurred in the third year, usually after five semesters of course work. Her parents—and mine—were unenthusiastic about our relationship, so we needed to demonstrate to them that at some future time I might actually be able to earn nine thousand dollars per year. So my generals were scheduled for January 1961 and our wedding for February.

Before moving forward any faster in time, however, I need to pause long enough to explain two pieces of "baggage" that I took with me from Washington to Cambridge plus a critical decision that I made soon after arriving at Harvard. During the summer after my graduation from college, as well as the following summer, I worked in Washington for the federal government at the Office of Naval History. I was supposed to collaborate with a young engineer on a history of flying boat operations (huge seaplanes used mainly for air-sea rescue situations) during World War II. The engineer apparently got a better-paying job at the eleventh hour, so the entire project fell to me. Fortunately my supervisor had been trained as an engineer before turning to the history of naval aviation, so he got me oriented and helped me out. During those two summers I learned a great deal about archival research, explored government documents that had remained classified for almost twenty-five years, and wrote my first two monographs—which no one has ever heard of, never mind read.[9] Be that as it may, they advanced my apprenticeship in several respects. I was a published author—sort of.

The second piece of baggage took much longer to become meaningful; in fact, for nearly two decades it was more like lost luggage. It did eventually turn up, however, and has made

a considerable difference in my orientation and work as a historian. Washington, D.C., is truly a treasure trove of art museums. There are many more now than there were forty years ago. But while I was an undergraduate I often slipped off on Friday afternoons to the National Gallery of Art, or to the Freer, or else to the Phillips (a privately endowed collection located near DuPont Circle), looked at paintings, and then tried to read about them, the artists who produced them, and even the political and social circumstances under which (or sometimes despite which) they were produced. Subsequently I even began to read authorities like Gombrich and Panofsky in order to understand what iconography and iconology were all about. But these seedlings would only bear fruit later when I began, almost twenty years ago, to use visual evidence as source material and tried to connect artistic with literary "texts" in studying American cultural production.[10] Those projects had their unintended genesis in my unfocused, capricious, purely curious decision to look at the pictures that Washington displays in such abundance.

Then there was the critical (in fact, fateful) decision that I made soon after arriving at Harvard. The Ph.D. program required a knowledge of four fields of history, and one of them had to be ancient or medieval. If one specialized in American history, one dealt with it as two distinct fields: the period of colonization plus the revolutionary era prior to 1789, and then the so-called national period since 1789. I didn't know *anything* prior to 1776 and really not very much prior to 1789. Moreover, the young instructor in colonial history who succeeded Samuel Eliot Morison and had just recently become a tenured associate professor, Bernard Bailyn, was reputedly brilliant but very tough. Clearly, I needed remedial work, and a lot of it; so in my first semester of graduate study I took Bailyn's lecture course concerning

---

[9]See *Operational History of the Flying Boat: Open Sea and Seadrome Aspects, Selected Pacific Campaigns, World War II* (Washington, D.C.: Navy Department, 1959), and *Operational History of the Flying Boat: Open Sea and Seadrome Aspects, Atlantic Theatre, World War II* (Washington, D.C.: Navy Department, 1960).

[10]See "From Liberty to Prosperity: Reflections Upon the Role of Revolutionary Iconography in National Tradition," *Proceedings* of the American Antiquarian Society, 86 (1977), pp. 237–72; "Changing Perceptions of the Life Cycle in American Thought and Culture," in *Proceedings* of the Massachusetts Historical Society, 91 (1980), pp. 35–66; *Meadows of Memory; Images of Time and Tradition in American Art and Culture* (Austin, Texas, 1992), the Anne Burnett Tandy Lectures in American Civilization presented at the Amon Carter Museum in Fort Worth.

early American history as well as his graduate research seminar. He turned out to be a charismatic lecturer, the most engaging I had ever heard, and a truly cerebral, stimulating seminar leader who taught, Socratically *and* by example, what the historian's craft was all about.[11]

I was hooked, and well before that first seminar ended I decided to scrap the history of U.S. diplomacy as well as my pro forma (i.e., poorly informed) proposal to the Woodrow Wilson Foundation concerning the Enlightenment. I would specialize instead on political aspects of seventeenth- and eighteenth-century Anglo-American history.[12] As it happens, although serendipity explains more than either design or self-conscious desire here, my Ph.D. dissertation (which became my first substantial book and led me to do yet another related one two years later) also made a small contribution to our understanding of the disintegration of the British empire in the twenty years prior to 1776. In doing so it may well have been my final fling in diplomatic history.[13]

After doing archival research on that dissertation in England during the summer of 1961 and also in many American repositories in 1961–62, I learned in April 1962 that Harvard had awarded me an unusual fellowship for the coming academic year. Rationalized by a bequest based on the assumption that travel is highly educational, the only condition attached to this fellowship was the requirement that I live anywhere outside of the United States. Because I now had a wife and a newborn son, we needed a place where three of us could live on a stipend (three thousand dollars) that had been intended for one person. I had done

my "early" field in the history of ancient Greece, so we were delighted to learn that a Harvard-trained Ph.D. in early American history was married to a Greek woman whose mother owned a cottage on Hydra, an island in the Saronic Gulf several hours by boat from Athens. The cottage was available from November 1962 to May 1963 and it was cheap. So was the cost of living in Greece. We packed our trunks with clothes, special food supplies for our highly allergic son (the island had no physician; the mayor doubled as amateur doctor and professional undertaker), and some 3,500 five-by-eight-inch research notes for writing my dissertation as well as several cartons of books. We couldn't travel light.

Late in October, at the very peak of the Cuban missile crisis, we sailed from Brooklyn on a Greek freighter, and nineteen days later we landed in Piraeus. The long but tranquil voyage gave us a chance to see the Straits of Gibraltar and of Messina, Sicilian cities and hill towns, schools of graceful Mediterranean dolphins, and above all, gave us time to become acquainted with demotic Greek—assisted by a grammar book, a small dictionary, and many conversations with the crew.

We happened to dock at Piraeus at about 8:30 on a Saturday evening, and I needed to cash a traveller's check in order to pay for our lodging that night and for the boat heading out to Hydra at eight o'clock the next morning. Banks in Piraeus were closed, of course, so I left Carol and little Daniel in what we assumed was a taverna and set out to find some kind of night club or tourist bar that might be willing to cash a fifty-dollar check. It took me almost forty-five minutes to accomplish that mission, and when I made my way back to rejoin Carol and the baby I discovered that the taverna where I had left them was actually a brothel. Fortunately, the U.S. Sixth Fleet was at sea that weekend practicing maneuvers of a different sort, so the kind women at this whorehouse/taverna had nothing better to do than sing and dance for Daniel's amusement, warm his bottle of powdered soybean juice (a milk substitute because of his allergies—we had hauled along a nine-month supply), and then sing some more. Never on Sunday, perhaps, but exuberantly on Saturday night.

As we prepared to leave after having a soft drink, one heavyset woman, perhaps a madam—what did we know?—turned to Carol and said,

---

[11]I have written about this educational experience with Stanley N. Katz in James A. Henretta, Kammen, and Katz, editors, *The Transformation of Early American History: Society, Authority, and Ideology* (New York, 1991), pp. 3–15.

[12]See Kammen, "The Causes of the Maryland Revolution of 1689," *Maryland Historical Magazine,* 55 (December 1960), pp. 293–333; Michael G. Hall, et al, editors, *The Glorious Revolution in America: Documents on the Colonial Crisis of 1689* (Chapel Hill, 1964); "Virginia at the Close of the Seventeenth Century: An Appraisal by James Blair and John Locke," *Virginia Magazine of History and Biography,* 74 (April 1966), pp. 141–69.

[13]See Kammen, *A Rope of Sand: The Colonial Agents, British Politics, and the American Revolution* (Ithaca, 1968); *Empire and Interest: The American Colonies and the Politics of Mercantilism* (Philadelphia, 1970).

Michael and Carol Kammen with their one-year-old son, Daniel, and two Scandinavian friends on the terrace of their cottage on the island of Hydra, Greece, early 1963

"Honey, I am no whore, but you never know about the rest of these girls; so when you get your baby to the hotel, be sure to wash him very carefully!" We proceeded to find a nearby hotel that was clean and quite satisfactory even though it didn't have a private bath. I will always remember the neatly printed sign next to the paper towel dispenser in the toilet room on our floor: PLEASE DO NOT PUT YOUR TOWELS IN THE BOWEL.

The island of Hydra is basically a dramatic rock that rises from the sea with a pinnacle surmounted by a monastery. According to local lore the island had 365 churches and chapels, but we came to believe that that count had to include some very small sites with a crucifix that did not qualify by our standards as a chapel even though a person certainly could pray there if he or she wanted to. In any case, the island community's *raison d'être* included the Greek naval academy (rather modest), a small but quite cosmopolitan artists' colony (the island could not have been more picturesque;

in recent years several films had been made there, including Alan Ladd in *Boy on a Dolphin* and another one starring Sophia Loren), and commercial fishing done by locals from fairly flimsy boats.

When the fishermen brought in their catch of the day at midmorning, they ordinarily took it to the fishmongers' setup on the quay. But if they happened to catch some genuine delicacy or rarity of real value to a local restaurant, they would take such fish to be weighed precisely and honestly on the venerable brass postal scales. The fishermen simply did not trust the fishmongers' scales. One day, when I had completed a chapter of my dissertation and wanted to mail it to my mentor at Harvard, I arrived at the post office and found two fishermen in line ahead of me. Each one slapped his prize fish on the brass scales, and when my turn came, my nine-by-twelve envelope went right where the fish had been only seconds before. About a month later I received a letter from Professor Bailyn. "It reads OK," he began, "but it stinks!"

Kammen upon receiving his Ph.D. in history, standing with his father at Lowell House, Harvard, June 1964

When I finished a draft of the dissertation late in April, we moved from Hydra to Athens and used the ancient city as a base for exploring historical sites all over Greece. Travel on public transportation with a baby (just before back-strap carriers were developed), a porta-crib, our supply of powdered Soyamel, cloth diapers (disposable ones did not yet exist), and two suitcases somehow boggles my mind even after thirty-three years. I have no idea how we did it, but I know that it wasn't easy. Nevertheless, we saw much of Greece and also made a two-week trip to Israel, unexpectedly shortened to ten days because we absolutely ran out of money. Flat broke. The inexpensive nature of life in Greece had spoiled us for economic reality in more "advanced" countries where inflation is inescapable.

We returned to Harvard by freighter later that summer, and fortunately we had been invited to live in Lowell House, a residential unit for almost four hundred undergraduate males, where I had been affiliated as a nonresident tutor (teaching fellow) in 1961–62. This meant that we had a five-room suite rent-free, and I was also entitled to free lunches (and even some dinners if I wished) with the undergraduates in the house dining hall. Eventually, the housemaster decided to open a fire door that connected our apartment to what had been a student suite, thereby giving us a guest bedroom, a second bathroom, and a study for doing my work and seeing students. This was truly an elegant and luxurious setup. I don't know many young academics who left graduate school for their first job with savings rather than being in debt.

My principal responsibility at Lowell House beyond teaching and the maintenance of decorum ("parietal hours" meant that women were only allowed on the premises during carefully restricted times each day) involved making arrangements for distinguished guests to visit Lowell House for several days, meet with students informally, and give some sort of public presentation open to the entire university community. I had a modest but adequate budget that enabled me to host such diverse guests as Benjamin Spock, Elizabeth Gurley Flynn (former head of the U.S. Communist party), Allen Ginsberg, Gunther Schuller, William L. Shirer, Dwight Macdonald, Alfred Knopf, and, most memorably, Jack Kerouac, who managed to drink himself into oblivion for much of the visit but sobered up long enough to read poems by Emily Dickinson with great feeling.

The Lowell House Senior Common Room brought together a blend (sometimes lively but sometimes rather stuffy) of very senior and very junior scholars from all the academic disciplines. Interaction with these men (in those days the senior common rooms were all-male preserves) provided my first exposure to casual conversation with people following very diverse academic pursuits, an experience that has recurred for me on numerous occasions over the years ever since: as a fellow at the Humanities Center at The Johns Hopkins University in 1968–69; as a fellow at the Center for Advanced Study in the Behavioral Sciences in Stanford in 1976–77; as director of the Society for the Humanities at Cornell, 1977–80; as a visiting professor at the École des Hautes Études en Sciences Sociales in Paris in 1980–81; as a Regents Fellow at the Smithsonian Institution in Washington, D.C., in 1990; and at the Villa Serbelloni, the Rockefeller Foundation Study and Conference Center in Bellagio, Italy, overlooking Lake Como, where I am writing these words in July 1995.

Harvard could not have been more generous to me throughout my time there. After receiving my Ph.D. in 1964 I became an instructor in history, which provided me with time to begin converting my dissertation into a book, time to initiate new research projects, time to gain some basic teaching experience under nonintimidating circumstances, and time to enjoy the luxury of patiently waiting for an ideal teaching position to come along. Several attractive offers occurred in 1964–65, but each time my wife said "not yet." Early in May of 1965, when Cornell invited me to come to Ithaca as an assistant professor of history, everything about that opportunity seemed exactly right: a reasonable teaching load; a structurally new and outstanding research library, especially in the field of history; a rustic and safe setting ideal for raising a family (Carol was five months pregnant with our second child when we moved in July); bright and highly motivated students; and a starting salary of ten thousand dollars. I was beginning at just about the level of pay where my undergraduate teachers were closing their careers.

Except for an occasional sabbatical year spent away, or an extended lecture tour, I have remained at Cornell ever since and have no regrets whatever. Sooner or later almost everyone interesting, or musically entertaining, visits Cornell; and the long winter, often lasting into early April, makes it much easier to keep our students focused on their academic work. I am convinced that faculty as well as students are more serious and productive in less benign climates, though I must admit that I have colleagues at Berkeley, Stanford, UCLA, and Duke who provide significant exceptions to my "rule."

Travel at home and abroad has been one of the great delights of my life, and I am persuaded that the pleasure I derive from travel closely parallels the pleasure that I derive from studying the past. In Macaulay's essay "History," written in 1828, he remarked that "the effect of historical reading is analogous, in many respects, to that produced by foreign travel. The student, like the tourist, is transported into a new state of society. He sees new fashions. He hears new modes of expression. His mind is enlarged by contemplating the wide diversities of laws, of morals, and of manners."[14]

With his son, Daniel, at Lowell House, Harvard, June 1988, when Daniel received his Ph.D. in physics. Daniel wears the same robe that Michael wore in 1964. Michael and Daniel were both members of the Lowell House Senior Common Room, almost twenty-five years apart.

Thanks to the U.S. Information Agency, I have made trips during the past two decades to attend conferences and give lectures in Europe, the Near East, East Asia, and parts of Latin America. An invitation to give the Paley Lectures in American Culture and Civilization at the Hebrew University in Jerusalem provided an opportunity to spend several weeks in that fascinating city early in 1983. Another invitation a year later supplied a stunning experience in China, from Beijing to Guelin, over a five-week span. Still other conferences took me to Spain and Portugal; to Japan, Taiwan, and Hong Kong; to the Netherlands, Germany, Austria, Italy, the spectacular Dalmatian coast of what in 1987 was still Yugoslavia, and to Scotland.

The most unforgettable travel of all, however, had nothing whatever to do with being a historian or a scholar. In January 1992 my older son—the one entertained by whores in Piraeus when he was nine months old—married a wonderful Nigerian-American woman in her father's ancestral village of Ifaki-Ekiti north of Ibadan. The wedding ceremony lasted for most of two-

---

[14]Macaulay, "History" (May 1828), *The Works of Lord Macaulay: Essays* ([London], 1900), I, p. 232.

and-a-half days: the first day (7:00 A.M. until almost 11:00 P.M.) taken up by "traditional" Yoruba marriage customs, some of them actually transcending tradition because no Yoruba person present had ever seen or participated in so many rites (though many wished that they had); the second day taken up by a very long ceremony (in Yoruba and English) in the Methodist cathedral at which no fewer than eleven clergymen participated, including the absolutely marvelous Methodist bishop of that area, a man of great warmth, humanity, and wisdom; and the morning of the third day devoted to a Service of Thanksgiving at which the spirit of local fund-raising prevailed over other spiritual concerns. The elders and leaders of that congregation were determined to avail themselves of the presence of so many guests to rejuvenate their cathedral and perhaps put away a supply of cash for the next restoration several decades hence. Charity may begin at home, but we foreigners got "hit up" pretty good during that long and wonderful weekend.

When it was all over we had acquired about one thousand new Nigerian relations; our kids went off to honeymoon in Senegal, where the food is French-African and therefore heavenly; and we devoted ten days to tourism in Nigeria, where the food is English-African and therefore more earthly than heavenly. Nigerians specialize in a dozen different ways to prepare yams, which are not a culinary delight under optimal circumstances.

Because Nigeria has a military dictatorship and is run like a police state, because the roads are extremely hazardous (improvements and surface repairs are many years overdue), because inflation is racing out of control and the populace is suffering woefully as a result, because one encounters corruption at every turn along with the prospect of serious mugging in places like Lagos, I found new meaning in Wallace Stegner's observation that "the writer has only the obligation to be open to experience, even to personally and socially destructive experience."[15] We learned after we left Ifaki-Ekiti that the Celiat Motel and Paint Company, where we all stayed, was actually a tax-evasion "front" for Nigerians involved in international

drug traffic! We had been baffled that it functioned so poorly as a motel!

Stegner goes on to say that a writer must be responsible "to his personal vision of truth and social justice, to his gift." We saw little in the way of social justice in Nigeria, however, despite the saintly bishop of Ifaki-Ekiti, despite the powerful presence of evangelical Christianity in southern Nigeria (the north is predominantly Moslem), despite the authentic kindness of so many among our new Nigerian relations. It is an unattractive and deeply troubled country in which some supremely lovely people lead lives of anxious desperation. That is why Chinua Achebe, from the Ibo tribe in south-central Nigeria, writes books with titles like *Things Fall Apart* (1958) and *The Trouble with Nigeria* (1983).

Getting into Nigeria for the wedding involved an endless series of headaches for my brother-in-law because he arrived alone, whereas we arrived as a party of eleven from the states including Nigerian Americans savvy enough to avoid trouble upon entering. Johnny, my wife's brother who works as a dentist in a women's prison in Pennsylvania, was essentially kidnapped at the Lagos international airport, swindled out of his U.S. passport by treacherous military officers, relieved of several hundred dollars in cash, and dumped in a downtown hotel without a clue as to where he was or how to contact us several hundred miles to the northeast where the Yoruba part of the wedding had already begun. (A driver who awaited Johnny's flight in order to drive him to Ifaki-Ekiti never saw Johnny emerge from the customs control area because he had been spirited away by corrupt "authorities" several stages before customs and hustled off to a private office where they started to "perform" their shake-down.)

Getting Johnny out of Nigeria two weeks later was almost as difficult as getting him in. Because he had a newly minted replacement passport just issued by the U.S. Embassy, it lacked a Nigerian visa and a stamped date of entry. Therefore officials at the departure process—which we called the Stations of the Cross because someone tortured us with a bribe request every step of the way—could insist that he must have entered the country illegally. Actually, he *did* enter illegally because of his Nigerian-army welcoming committee. So Johnny and I were taken to a series of small rooms and shaken

---

[15]Stegner, "The Writer and the Concept of Adulthood," *Daedalus*, 105 (fall 1976), p. 40.

Son, Douglas Anton Kammen, at Borobudur,
a ninth-century Buddhist temple in central Java,
Indonesia, about 1986

down by assorted petty officers who wanted one hundred dollars in U.S. currency before they would legitimize Johnny's passport and allow him to board our flight from Lagos to New York. I finally outbluffed the corrupt officers by telling them that my new daughter-in-law's uncle, a three-star general, and his brother, a cabinet minister, would soon be coming through to join us for our flight and would be exceedingly angry to learn of this mistreatment of foreign guests. The general and the minister were figments of my imagination, but the two petty officers, one male and one female, promptly settled for twenty dollars (U.S.) and let us go. I have never in my life felt so relieved as when that 747 took off at 1:30 A.M.

By way of compensation we have also enjoyed the considerable pleasures of vicarious travel—without running the risks of malaria, dengue fever, cobras, mambas, and Komodo dragons—because our sons have travelled extensively in parts of the world where we have not—notably in sub-Saharan Africa and in Southeast Asia. Douglas first went to Indonesia at the age of seventeen, has made countless trips to the region since then, and has now become a professional Indonesianist. He has brought back beautiful batik for Carol, charming works of sculpture from Kalimantan (Borneo), and beautiful, big shadow puppets that decorate our walls.

We have listened to Douglas's stories about life in Surakarta, Jogjakarta, Djakarta, Palembang, Malang, Manado, Kuching, and Kota Kinabalu (in Sarawak) with such rapt fascination that we can tell his tales almost as though they are our own. Douglas served as the interpreter when both "boys" went together to Flores and Komodo islands in the Lesser Sundas (eastern Indonesia), and we often recall our high anxiety during the summer of 1987 when Douglas and Daniel crossed the dense jungle of Kalimantan on foot, bearing very heavy packs on their backs (and wearing condoms to keep the river flukes [leeches] from entering their systems through the urethra). On the heart of their detailed maps of Borneo was a large blank region with the words: "this area unknown." They made it across, accompanied by three Dayaks. Only a few non-natives accomplish that feat each year. Douglas and Daniel published an account of their daring trek in *Harvard Magazine.* Daniel just barely avoided a cobra. Douglas came home with a mean case of scurvy.

Crossing the United States by car, coast to coast, which we have done twice in each direction (going to Stanford in 1976–77 and Pasadena in 1993–94) was quite literally an uneventful breeze by comparison with two weeks in Nigeria. Just the American place-names alone make it wonderfully worthwhile: the Mad River and then Chagrin Boulevard in Beechwood, Ohio; Cretin Avenue in Minneapolis; South Scalp Creek in South Dakota; Tongue River and Hideout Creek in Wyoming; Papoose Creek and Squaw Creek in Idaho; Remote, Oregon; Difficult Run, Virginia; Cheat River, West Virginia; and a sign on Route 50, beyond Romney, West Virginia, for "Order of the Owls, Nest 406" ahead.

Then there are the marvelous signs on and in various establishments. Take just one eastern example, an eatery called the Dory specializing in egg dishes, located on India Street in Nantucket. It has three terrific notices behind the counter:

This zoo is open from 6 A.M. till the
    Chicken Croaks!!

People Who Believe That the Dead Never
    Come
Back to Life Should Be Here at Quitting
    Time!

Enjoy the Island—They're Not Making Any
    More!

In the Nantucket harbor there was a moored yacht called My Psychiatrist. Its dinghy was called Little Shrink. Driving from Nashville south into the Cumberland Mountains (en route to an ecumenical Christian chautauqua called the Monteagle Sunday School Assembly) I found myself following a car hauling a big power boat on a trailer. The name of the boat? Wet Dream.

I might add that I was on my way to Monteagle in the summer of 1988 to give a public lecture occasioned by the bicentennial of the U.S. Constitution. Oliver Wendell Holmes, Sr., the physician and autocratic poet, once (1857) called anyone who went on the lecture circuit a "literary strumpet." Be that as it may, my life has been immensely enriched and diversified thanks to lecture invitations from all sorts of wonderful places and also from *places* that were not so wonderful but where the people were.

Moreover, just getting "there" as well as the process of returning can be awesome: flying west from Teheran to Istanbul and watching a sensational sunrise over Mount Ararat. Flying in the evening from Buenos Aires to Rio de Janeiro and watching the sun set over the southern Andes. Flying overnight from New York to Athens and seeing the morning sun make the Alps a shimmering, silvery-white jagged mass. And flying west to Salt Lake City or to San Francisco and following the sun as a brilliant fireball descending behind the Rockies. Those are imperishable memories.

Last, though hardly least, are the delights of familiar music in unfamiliar places: hearing Mstislav Rostropovich play Dvořák's cello concerto at the Royal Festival Hall in London; a dazzling performance of *The Mikado* at the Glimmerglass Opera House in Cooperstown, New York; an early music concert by Aston Magna, conducted by John Hsu, at St. James' Episco-

Michael Kammen about to address a Phi Beta Kappa convocation at California State University, Long Beach, May 1977

pal Church in Great Barrington, Massachusetts; and then the incredible array of concerts at the acoustically awesome Ambassador Auditorium in Pasadena, California, ranging from Leontyne Price to the New England Ragtime Ensemble. But also coming back to Cornell's Bailey Hall to hear Rudolph Serkin perform a flawless concert of Beethoven sonatas with elegance so sublime it seemed as though the audience of two thousand held its collective breath throughout.

A bit earlier I quoted Wallace Stegner's statement about the writer's obligation to be open to experience. That supplies a useful segue here because I need to say something about the writer—or at least, about *this* writer—being open to stylistic experiences (or influences) and to intellectual experiences (or influences), but also the imperative at certain times *not* to be open, but rather to cocoon oneself, in a way, for emotional or cerebral protection, or sometimes simply in order to "get on with it"—to bring some task or objective to completion. One pays a price for cocooning, to be sure, but one also purchases something precious for that price. Charles Burchfield, the amazing water-colorist and one of my favorite American artists, once observed in his journal that "all the great works of art . . . have been created by artists, for themselves in solitude (spiritual solitude if not physical)."[16]

I can deal most easily, in my own case, with being open to stylistic experience. Late in the 1960s, when I began *People of Paradox: An Inquiry Concerning the Origins of American Civilization,* which may be, in stylistic terms, my most exuberant book, I wanted to write, in some sense, like Perry Miller. I enjoyed reading him because the sheer intricacy of his prose and his use of words I did not even know seemed like a splendid challenge to the reader. His eloquent complexity sometimes verged upon baroque loquaciousness, but I didn't quite see that at the time. I was only beginning to think of myself as a writer and lacked a distinctive voice. Besides, I had been present in the fall of 1963 when Miller gave a reading at the Signet Society in Cambridge at which he offered passages from Ahab's soliloquies in *Moby Dick.* Three weeks later he was dead of alcoholism, and those of us who had been moved to tears that evening at the Signet now understood just how much this man, like Ahab, was literally driven by self-destructive demons.

A few years later, however, after my father had dutifully read *People of Paradox,* probably in the summer of 1973, after it won the Pulitzer Prize, he said some complimentary things but then asked me, "Why didn't you write it in English?" By then I had just finished editing the correspondence of Carl Becker, perhaps the most gifted prose stylist among the entire pantheon of America historians in the twentieth century, and my editorial work had required me to read virtually everything that Becker had ever written. All of a sudden, simplicity seemed the key to clarity—and therefore to effective communication with a wider audience. So I aspired to simple, lucid prose that was not quite my natural "register" but was, I think, a dis-

tinct improvement, for me at least, over Perry Miller's lush opaqueness.

Then, a little later in the seventies, after I got to know Wally Stegner at Stanford, I developed an abiding admiration for his ability to join style and substance in just the right way: in his fiction, in his essays, and in his delightful biography of Bernard DeVoto, a wonderful author himself but one whose prose seemed a bit too flamboyant and contrived for my taste, an upscale version of what the *Saturday Evening Post* had wanted in DeVoto's heyday. Stegner's *Angle of Repose* (1971) struck me as the greatest American historical novel. I was, and I remain, in awe of Stegner's achievement in that book. And on through *The Big Rock Candy Mountain* (1943) and his wonderful biography of John Wesley Powell, *Beyond the Hundredth Meridian* (1954), and *The Gathering of Zion: The Story of the Mormon Trail* (1964) and *Recapitulation* (1979) and *Crossing to Safety* (1987).

By the later 1970s I was sensible enough not to try to imitate Stegner. I am not even sure that I could have because his authorial voice is less distinctive than either Miller's or Becker's. But Stegner made writing seem effortless rather than contrived, and in the process he made reading his work seem equally effortless. If I could somehow do *that,* and find a style suited to the substance of each project that I undertook, I would be OK. After Stegner, I stopped looking for stylistic models.

As for this writer's "obligation" to remain open to intellectual influence, there have been at least four seminal sources for me, each one from a different discipline and influential in a different way. The first was Bernard Bailyn, my Ph.D. mentor, who demonstrated, mostly by example but also in one brief essay, that excellence in the historian's craft is all about asking the right questions and noticing the kinds of anomalies that lead us to address important problems concerning human experience. He taught me that good historical writing should be taut, it *must* have focus, the extraneous stuff stripped away—a lesson, alas, that I have not always kept as clearly in view as I should. From the outset, in 1958–59, Bailyn made me realize, in a way that no previous teacher had, that the epicenter of the target is marked "how" and "why." In his phrase, the historian seeks "explanatory power." And then, almost thirty years later, he reminded me, and others, that

---

[16]Burchfield's journal for October 23, 1938, is quoted in John I. H. Baur, *The Inlander: Life and Work of Charles Burchfield, 1893–1967* (Newark, Delaware, 1981), p. 188.

history is also about storytelling. Inscribe your explanation in a narrative and more people will read and want to understand it.[17]

My second seminal influence was the psychoanalyst and psychobiographer Erik H. Erikson. Most of all I found his essays in *Childhood and Society* (1950, 1963) clarifying and comforting, especially chapter eight, "Reflections on the American Identity," where he discusses the unavoidable presence of contradictory tendencies in any culture, but especially in the United States. I read and reread that chapter during the later 1960s when I was struggling to make sense of all the ambiguities and dualisms that I seemed to find in the first half of American history. Erikson rather obviously helped me to bring *People of Paradox* into focus.[18]

What I now realize, however, after reading through my journal for the first time, is that long after I ceased to believe that *People of Paradox* was a very satisfactory explanation of American origins, after I had become disenchanted with key aspects of Erikson's universalization of his model of the psychosocial life cycle, and even after I had stopped quoting or citing Erikson's work, I continued to resonate with his emphasis upon personal as well as cultural ambivalence.[19] In my journal for April 1978 I noticed that Lionel Trilling was haunted by the problem of "reciprocal truth," that is, for every perspective on one side of an issue there was a perspective with at least *some* validity on the other side. Five months later I commented that Johan Huizinga, the great Dutch medievalist and historian of early modern Europe, delighted me because, as Karl J. Weintraub put it, Huizinga was "deeply convinced that human thinking vacillates between antinomies, that is, that man is constantly forced to admit the validity of seemingly opposite points of view."

Six years later, when Richard Rovere's last book was published posthumously, it intrigued me to note that he described himself as being "conservative by temperament, radical by conviction, liberal by compromise." He then added: "I have no particular philosophy of history. I tend to believe that, in the final analysis, there is no final analysis."[20]

The third significant influence upon my work involved a combination of the (then) symbolic anthropologist Victor Turner and the earlier Belgian ethnographer Arnold Van Gennep, each of whom, in very different ways, described and theorized about rites of passage from youth to adulthood as ceremonies that were not merely individual and personal but could also be perceived in subsequent generations as collective, cultural, and even political. Turner, especially, provided me in the mid-1970s with a theoretical and comparative basis for considering *rites de passage* as a metaphorical way of understanding the meaning of a rebellion or a collective action with such complicated transformational consequences as the American Revolution.[21]

The fourth significant source of influence on my work was the social theorist Edward Shils, whose impact occurred at two very different times in my career and in totally different ways. The first, and perhaps less important, provided a useful insight when I was writing *People of Paradox,* namely, the presence of an antinomian strain in American society revealing that our basic respect for institutions and the rights of others has been interrupted by periods of intense disrespect for law and irreverence toward figures of authority.[22]

The second, and considerably more significant, arose from Shils's enduring theoretical interest in the social, cultural, and political role of tradition at different stages in a nation's

[17]See Bailyn, "The Problems of the Working Historian: A Comment," in Sidney Hook, editor, *Philosophy and History: A Symposium* (New York, 1963), pp. 92–101; Bailyn, "The Challenge of Modern Historiography," *American Historical Review*, 87 (February 1982), pp. 23–24.

[18]See Erikson, *Childhood and Society* (2nd edition: New York, 1963), chapter 8; Kammen, *People of Paradox: An Inquiry Concerning the Origins of American Civilization* (New York, 1972), especially chapter 4 and p. 274.

[19]See Kammen, "Changing Perceptions of the Life Cycle in American Thought and Culture," reprinted in Kammen, *Selvages & Biases: The Fabric of History in American Culture* (Ithaca, 1987), pp. 181, 182, 187, 197, 207, 209–17.

[20]Weintraub, *Visions of Culture: Voltaire, Guizot, Burckhardt, Lamprecht, Huizinga, Ortega Y Gasset* (Chicago, 1966), p. 210; Rovere, *Final Reports: Personal Reflections on Politics and History in Our Time* (Garden City, N.Y., 1984), reviewed by Anatole Broyard in the *New York Times*, Feb. 4, 1984, p. 15.

[21]See Kammen, *A Season of Youth: The American Revolution and the Historical Imagination* (New York, 1978), especially chapter 6; Nicole Belmont, *Arnold Van Gennep: The Creator of French Ethnography* (Chicago, 1979), chapter 4.

[22]Kammen, *People of Paradox,* p. 107; Shils, *The Torment of Secrecy: The Background and Consequences of American Security Policies* (Glencoe, Illinois, 1956).

development, a subject that preoccupied him intermittently for more than a dozen years and aided me tremendously in conceptualizing the most ambitious project of research and writing that I have undertaken, one that required more than thirteen years of work and resulted in *Mystic Chords of Memory: The Transformation of Tradition in American Culture* in 1991. As Shils observed in 1971: "Traditions are beliefs with a particular social structure; they are a consensus through time. . . . They are beliefs which are believed by a succession of persons who might have been in interaction with each other in succession or at least in a unilateral . . . chain of communication. This structural property of traditional belief is distinct from the substantive properties of the beliefs, i.e., the extent to which the beliefs themselves refer to the past and to which their legitimation refers to the past."[23]

For many years Edward Shils was generally perceived as being ideologically conservative. Because I have not been sympathetic to people of that persuasion—or perhaps I should simply say that I have never been empathetic to the persuasion itself—I had a very tough time at first feeling sanguine about my long-term enterprise involving the history of tradition, patriotism, and memory in American life. Surely those were topics tailor-made for a conservative historian. Imagine my fascination (and bemusement), then, when I found this long entry in my journal, dated July 4, 1980, more than a decade before I finished *Mystic Chords of Memory:*

> For several years I have felt a certain guilt or anxiety about my growing interest in the role of Tradition in American culture. Wasn't it really an old-fashioned, elitist topic that would almost inevitably require me to concentrate upon the mainstream, the consensual, the highly literate, the Nativists and chauvinists, etc.? Was I going entirely against the grain? Was my 15-year project a naive "defiance" of the major trends in U.S. his-

torical scholarship over the *past* 15 years? During the last few weeks, especially, my reading has persuaded me that my topic can be as populist or as elitist as the investigator chooses to make it: e.g., that one can explore Carter Woodson and the work he did in 1915 as well as preservation-oriented activities of the D.A.R. But that's only part of the reason for my new "comfort" with my project.

> Reading Robert J. Smith and V. S. Naipaul these past few days on popular perceptions of national history in Japan and Argentina has made me strongly aware of what is really at stake in my project: how and why does one nation feel about itself as it does? What has been distorted in the national consciousness? What has been repressed? How does our "record" of distortion and repression compare, say, with that in England or in France? What can we learn from the differences and similarities? . . .

> These issues go to the very heart of a nation's identity and existence. They also affect international understanding and hence international relations. They pertain to the lives and consciousness of ordinary people as well as elites. . . . And, of course, no social stratum has a monopoly upon historical self-deception. The elite does it as well as the workers. The elite *ought* to know better, however, and the elite often distorts history in order to maintain its hegemony, whereas the "folk" may warp the past in order to make their subordination more bearable, or more comprehensible, or in order to find some glimmer of hope for the future.

Rediscovering that I once had such ruminations and revelations, if I can call them that, more than fifteen years ago, helps me to realize just how deeply engaged I had become with the *problématique* of this big project. In fact, it seems clear in retrospect that ever since the mid-1970s my writing had ceased to be "work" in any customary sense of that word and had become instead a compelling labor of love. In July 1978 I transcribed into my journal a sentence written in 1864 by William Dean Howells from Venice to his sister: "I delight in the work, and consequently though I work pretty hard, it doesn't fatigue me much."[24]

---

[23]Shils, "Tradition," *Comparative Studies in Society and History,* 13 (April 1971), p. 126; Shils, *Tradition* (Chicago, 1981). See also Shils, *The Calling of Sociology and Other Essays on the Pursuit of Learning* (Chicago, 1980), pp. 134–256; T. S. Eliot, "Tradition," in *Points of View* (London, 1941), pp. 21–34 [written in 1917]; Joseph Epstein, "My Friend Edward," *American Scholar*, 64 (summer 1995), pp. 371–94, especially pp. 372, 376.

[24]Quoted in Kenneth S. Lynn, *William Dean Howells: An American Life* (New York, 1971), p. 119.

Leafing back through my journal has also helped me to recognize that a cluster of connected changes occurred in my life at the end of the 1970s, and that I emerged from that time of transition as a more self-aware, perhaps less anxious and better integrated person than I had been. I began to understand, as I never had before, what it really means for a person to have a past, a present, and hopefully a future, and that disruptive changes so evident in one's life are nonetheless balanced by continuities that are less obvious. Perhaps three very different kinds of entries that I made in successive years will illustrate this with regard to writing, teaching, and family relations.

The first of these entries, made right after Cornell's commencement late in May 1978, relates to my initial "discovery" of intellectual continuities in my life:

> What intrigues me is the way an author may self-inscribe without even meaning to. One can examine the earliest writings of some figures—done before their authorial voice had been established—and find clear premonitions of the persona to come. I have reread things I wrote ten years ago and am shocked to find a certain characteristic mode of expression, or the anticipation of an idea, or an interest which may be quite important to me now but which I would not have expected to find in my vocabulary of thought ten years ago. So we inscribe ourselves self-consciously, but also without even intending to!

Comparable entries recur during the seventeen years that followed, most commonly when I completed one project and turned my attention to a new one, a time of transition that involves taking stock, going over preparatory notes that I began gathering years earlier, before I really understood what the thrust or shape or texture of the new project would be.

The next entry appears in September 1979, a few weeks into the new academic year, and this one involves reflections on teaching, more specifically, changes in my intellectual relationships with students, and more particularly, a strong sense of generational differentiation. My students were now not much older than my two sons.

> Something very odd seems to have begun a year or two ago, and seems to have intensified this term. Students have become less and less predictable in their responses to the books I assign. Once upon a time, I would assign an intelligent, well-written book and expect that students in my courses would find the book pleasurable and admirable. Not beyond criticism, but nonetheless acceptable, its very real merits indisputable. No longer. Cash's *Mind of the South?* "I think the author must be a racist." Hexter's *Doing History?* "The author can't write."[!] Parkman's *The Oregon Trail?* "He must have been an imperialist."

At that point I had been teaching for fifteen years, and the realization suddenly hit home that I belonged to a very different generation, intellectually and culturally, than my students. I was not quite forty-three at the time. An even greater shock occurred about six years later when I assigned David Potter's *People of Plenty: Economic Abundance and the American Character* (1954) to a graduate seminar. Although the book is not above criticism, especially in the wake of thirty years of swift social change, I have always viewed it as a magnificent example, not merely of the historian at his innovative best, but of man thinking. It had long been a formative and an exemplary book for me. My graduate students (one each from Japan, Korea, Brazil, France, and two each from the People's Republic of China and the United States) found it uninteresting, wrongheaded, and perhaps even a little perverse! I was shocked and deeply disappointed. I have not assigned it again since then.

The third entry, from June 1980, after the close of that academic year, indicates a troubled time of personal transition in my family life that coincided with a genuine caesura in my professional career. In retrospect it may very well have been the most stressful convergence of that kind in my experience:

> Last week, with Dan about to go to England [to work as a junior astronomer following his graduation from high school], I fell apart emotionally. Too many transitions, major transitions, are going on at once. Dan leaves the roost. I leave the Society [for the Humanities] after three years [as director] and return to History. All professional projects and obligations are fulfilled; and for the first time in 22 years I have few immediate, compelling pressures. I don't owe a book manuscript or an article to anyone. So the question arises: what direction to take with my future work? What path or

paths to explore? There are many options. Freedom brings the anxiety of choice, of decision-making, and also the realization that one made some wrong decisions in years past. Plus planning to go to France [to teach in Paris for a year at the invitation of the Ministry of Education]: living there and not living here. Renting our home and trying to lease (if not purchase) a foreign language. So many decisions about the future make one very self-conscious about the past: errors of judgment, the price one pays for success, sins of omission and commission. It's a bit much. . . .

A little more than two years before that moment I had carefully copied out a sentence written by Henry F. May of Berkeley, a scholar whose temperament feels very different from my own, but whose sensibilities are strikingly similar in certain crucial ways. May commented that his "sympathies are with those who are not sure that they understand themselves and the universe rather than with those who make hard things easy."[25]

Clearly, I passed through an important phase of growth, self-awareness, and change at the end of the '70s. Yet it was neither abrupt nor traumatic. I am intrigued by an observation that Clifford Geertz makes in his very recent retrospective book:

> Historicizing yourself, dividing your past into periods, is an uncomfortable sort of thing to do. It is uncomfortable not just for the obvious reason that the further you move from the beginning the closer you come to the end, but because there are so many ways to do it; any particular one seems arbitrary, rooted in very little else but narrative convenience. If you are concerned merely to relate what you've seen and been through that doesn't matter so much. Nobody's under oath in autobiography, whose purpose is normally to keep an illusion in place. But if you are concerned with tracing the movement of a discipline by packaging your experiences into emblematical units it is rather more troubling.[26]

I am aware that my challenge here is considerably less vexing than his for several reasons: first, being ten years younger than Geertz, I presumably am not quite so close to the end, though one never knows; second, dividing my past into multiple phases seems less arbitrary to me than it does to him, perhaps because my past has been far less notable and has had many fewer institutional and geographical settings; and third, because it would never occur to me to "package" my own trajectory with that of my discipline. They simply do not make such a good match.

One way that I *know* the match isn't especially good arises from the varied response to my books. The ones that I am now less fond of were basically well received and remained in print for a very long time: *A Rope of Sand* (1968), *People of Paradox* (1972), *Colonial New York* (1975), and *A Machine That Would Go of Itself: The Constitution in American Culture* (1986). My two strong favorites, on the other hand, have been *A Season of Youth* (1978), not as well received, and *Mystic Chords of Memory* (1991), which got wonderful reviews yet did not sell and languishes on the verge of expiration as I write this.

One does learn after a while that writing, editing, publishing, reviewing, and the whole reward structure are all highly capricious matters. Especially reviewing. The most widely used book that I ever produced was a collection of essays that I commissioned and edited for the American Historical Association by means of a grant it received from the National Endowment for the Humanities. Titled *The Past before Us: Contemporary Historical Writing in the United States,* its genesis was prompted by the Fifteenth International Congress of Historical Sciences held at Bucharest, Romania, in August 1980. All of the contributors were very experienced and distinguished historians, yet some of them turned in copy that required a *lot* of editing—a deeply disillusioning experience for me. According to one reviewer, *The Past before Us* examined "the vast enterprise of professional historians who write history according to scholarly cannons."[27] I'm really not sure whether I want that to be a typographical error or not!

The title of that volume, by the way, brings to mind the name of a pleasant old bookstore

---

[25]May, *The Enlightenment in America* (New York, 1976), p. xvii.

[26]Geertz, *After the Fact: Two Countries, Four Decades, One Anthropologist* (Cambridge, Massachusetts, 1995), p. 109.

---

[27]Gerald A. Danzer in *The Annals of Iowa,* 46 (winter 1982), p. 232.

Accepting the Henry Adams Prize for A Machine That Would Go of Itself *at the National Portrait Gallery in Washington, D.C., April 24, 1987. In 1990 Michael returned to the Portrait Gallery as a Regents Fellow of the Smithsonian Institution.*

that I once found on a side street in Concord, Massachusetts: Books with a Past. That's a delicious double entendre, especially for someone who writes history books.

I have very rarely responded to critical, unfair, or inaccurate reviews of my work. It simply isn't worth it. For one thing, when we come to blows in academe, perhaps there ought to be a genuine battle of the books. In 1744 Dr. Johnson (having been called a liar) knocked a man down using an immense sixteenth-century Greek Bible as his weapon! And for another thing, it is probably true that it is better to be controversial than to be ignored. Dr. Johnson saw the advantages in being attacked as well as praised. "Fame is a shuttlecock," he said. "If it be struck only at one end of the room, it will soon fall to the ground. To keep it up, it must be struck at both ends."[28]

And besides, by the time reviews appear I am, invariably, deeply involved in a new and very different project. I have not entirely lost interest in the previous one, but I am no longer emotionally engaged by it. The academic writer is finished with writing a book almost a full year before it actually appears, and it takes yet another year before the serious reviews emerge. After two years I cannot remember many of the things that I said, and some of the prose does not even sound like my own.

This tendency to be intellectually restless, however, moving relentlessly from the seventeenth century to the eighteenth, from political to cultural history, from the nineteenth century into the twentieth now, from historiography to constitutional history, then to art history, back to cultural history once again, and most recently on to the history of cultural criticism, has resulted in the unfortunate "dynamic" that I seem to be perpetually out of sync professionally. I am always being asked to review

---

[28]Walter Jackson Bate, *Samuel Johnson* (New York, 1977), pp. 225, 469.

books or give papers at conferences on subjects that I have left behind because they no longer interest me. I would like to be asked to review books or participate in symposia devoted to issues that I am presently working on. Unhappily, most book review editors and conference organizers have no idea what currently interests me. So more often than not I am obliged to decline invitations because they are sent to the writer that I used to be. If it is true that there is a collective past before us, it is equally true that there is a personal past behind us. My inclination has been to leave it there.

All of this restlessness on my part, this moving on to new endeavors, can be explained in various ways—each one of them revealing only one portion of the underlying reality. I guess I would call attention to a trio of factors: the opportunity for growth, ambition, and the idiosyncratic nature of personal temperament. The common denominator for all three, I think, involves a coming to terms with my solitary ways and recognizing that certain kinds of satisfactions transcend the loneliness that is required for serious commitment as a productive scholar. Ultimately I am in sympathy with a comment that Justice Holmes made to the Federal Bar Association in 1932: "At times the ambitious ends of life have made it seem to me lonely, but it has not been."[29]

Being a university professor is an enormous privilege because it offers a degree of autonomy that I cannot begin to imagine in any other walk of life. No one tells me what courses to teach, or how to teach them, or when. No one tells me what projects to undertake, or how, or when. The very nature of my vocation *requires* me to make my own decisions—all within the framework of Cornell's wonderful tradition that Carl Becker first defined as freedom and responsibility. He subsequently expanded that framework from being descriptive of Cornell's distinctiveness to being prescriptive for American distinctiveness in general.[30]

Given that expansive formula of freedom and responsibility, I have regarded my life as a mandarin as the ideal opportunity for intel-

lectual and personal growth. To accomplish those ends, however, an academic is obliged to do something for which the Victorians had a euphemism: "sporting the oak," i.e., closing the door. People wondered how Elliott Coues was able to write so much on ornithology in particular and on natural history in general during his association with Ferdinand V. Hayden's U.S. Geological Survey of the western territories during the 1870s. David Starr Jordan, a Cornell-trained naturalist (who later became Stanford's first president), recalled seeing a large placard with bold lettering on the wall of Coues's den: "I dread interruption more than the devil."[31] My only regret in this regard is that I am not very adept at *disguising* the fact that at certain times I dread interruption.

I can relate with congenial feeling to an entry that Charles Burchfield, a singular artist in more ways than one, made in his journal late in 1931 when he was only thirty-eight. "The realization of my utter loneliness," he wrote, "and its uncompromising necessity swept over me, almost crushing me with despair. That is gone now and I sit surrounded by all the ideas I love, freed by the realization that crowds and companionship are not for me."[32] He cherished the companionship of his wife, Bertha, and went off to Manhattan once each year to see his dealer and to fulfill his responsibility as a juror in art competitions. But the companionship that Burchfield really craved he found in nature and in his instinctive responses to nature.

The physical places where writers work have always intrigued me—almost as much as how they work and how they feel about the ways in which they do their work. Nathaniel Hawthorne, for example, worked in the Boston Custom House from 1839 to 1841 and subsequently became surveyor of the Port of Salem (1846–49). Although he lost that job because of a change in political administrations, in 1850 he published *The Scarlet Letter* with its notable and long introduction titled "The Custom-House."

---

[29]Max Lerner, editor, *The Mind and Faith of Justice Holmes* (Boston, 1943), p. 451.

[30]Becker, *Cornell University: Founders and the Founding* (Ithaca, 1943), pp. 193–204; Becker, *Freedom and Responsibility in the American Way of Life* (New York, 1945).

[31]Paul Russell Cutright and Michael J. Brodhead, *Elliott Coues: Naturalist and Frontier Historian* (Urbana, Illinois, 1981), p. 199; and for "sporting the oak" see Kammen, "Moses Coit Tyler: The First Professor of American History in the United States," in Kammen, *Selvages & Biases*, p. 234.

[32]Quoted in Baur, *The Inlander*, p. 188; and see J. Benjamin Townsend, editor, *Charles Burchfield's Journals: The Poetry of Place* (Albany, 1993), passim.

In 1374 Geoffrey Chaucer was awarded a free, lifetime lease on a house above Aldgate, most likely so that he could be close to his new work as customs controller, a job just awarded to him. In June of that year Chaucer was also appointed controller of customs and subsidies of wools, hides, and woolfells for the port of London. Soon after that he became controller of petty customs of wines for the port of London as well. But these positions were not a writer's sinecure. He had to attend to the work in person, and he wrote out the rolls in his own hand.[33]

In 1819 James Mill was appointed to a place in the East India House (assistant to the examiner of India correspondence), something of a sinecure that he held for a decade. Albert Einstein worked in the Swiss Patent Office as a patent examiner from 1902 until 1909, a period of astonishing intellectual creativity for him. By contrast, Herman Melville held a minor appointment in New York City as an outdoor customs inspector from 1866 until 1885, but these were his years of bleak obscurity rather than bountiful creativity. For Melville, the custom house must have been a rather sad kind of ashram, whereas Hawthorne, Chaucer, Mill, and Einstein seem to have flourished in theirs.

When my sons were younger and living at home, the university supplied my meditative ashram—a silent faculty study in a newly erected research library where virtually every book and journal that I needed was nearly at my fingertips. Unlike the work that Hawthorne, Chaucer, Melville, and Einstein did in their civil service posts, however, which sustained them but did not contribute very much to their writing, my role as a university teacher of graduate students and undergraduates has always had a genuinely symbiotic relationship to my work as a writer. I assign and discuss many books with my students because I need to come to terms with those publications and I am eager to hear their views concerning them, pro and con.

The most apposite illustration possible is *People of Paradox,* perhaps my best-known book but one that I never actually "set out" to compose as a book. When I started teaching early American history at Cornell in 1965–66, I wanted

to develop a schematic course that would be highly interpretive, a creative synthesis of all the innovative scholarship then appearing on every aspect of the colonial and revolutionary eras. After about three years it dawned on me that I had worked out a way of looking at the first half of American history, along with its implications for the remainder, that could not be found anywhere in print. During my first study leave from Cornell in 1968–69, I began to transpose that material from a format suitable for undergraduate lectures to a book-length interpretive essay. Most of the critics liked it (by no means all), it won a Pulitzer, and then the U.S. Information Agency initiated translations into languages ranging from Korean and Japanese to French and Spanish to Indonesian and Burmese. The important point: that book had its genesis in the classroom, in every sense of the word.

After our sons had grown up and left "the nest," the comfortable home in which we raised them began to seem too large, too costly to heat, the taxes too high, and the grounds too much to maintain. My wife and I were ready for a different ashram, smaller, less formal, requiring much less maintenance, and enjoying more of a relationship with the marvelous natural beauty in the environs of Ithaca. So my wife located a superb site overlooking Cayuga Lake, less than six miles from Cornell; we hired an innovative architect who was enchanted (and challenged) by the beauty of the site and who was willing to design a contemporary home that could nonetheless accommodate our traditional furnishings, antiques, and highly miscellaneous collection of art.

We signed on with the architect in April 1984, plans were completed by the later part of June, assorted subcontractors were fully lined up in July, work began early in August, and we moved in six days before Christmas, exactly on schedule. For about six weeks after Christmas we had workmen finishing up interior touches, completing the big deck that is cantilevered over a cliff to maximize our view of the lake, and building a winding set of outside stairs leading up to that deck. We were blessed by ten days of utterly clear and balmy weather during late December and early January. The workmen finished "Il Nido" (The Nest) in shirtsleeves, working mainly out of doors. No one could believe that it was the dead of winter. We truly were lucky.

---

[33]John Gardner, *The Life & Times of Chaucer* (New York, 1977), pp. 156, 206.

"Il Nido" (from the east), the home that Carol and Michael Kammen built in 1984 when their sons had left the "old nest." Michael's study overlooking Cayuga Lake is at the upper right, a crow's nest atop the rest of the house.

Having the holidays in a brand-new but not quite finished home prompted wonderfully creative yet highly unconventional Christmas presents. Our younger son, Douglas, gave Carol a Collins axe-eye maul for splitting firewood. It weighed almost nine pounds and looked absolutely lethal. Carol gave me a "dry chemical fire extinguisher (#300)" made by a subsidiary of American La France with the splendid early American name of Badger-Powhatan. Our home is entirely of wood construction: pine framing, white oak trim and red oak stairs, Idaho cedar siding. Douglas gave me a Black & Decker double insulated three-eighths-inch variable speed reversing drill. Daniel came home from his first semester of graduate study at Stanford with a big box of adult fortune cookies from San Francisco. "Fu Ling Yu Says: Bachelor is one who is foot-loose and fiancée free." My mother-in-law sent us a firewood carrier and a Federal-period brass door knocker with KAMMEN engraved on it. This surely was the most enchanted Christmas ever.

A few weeks later, purely by chance, I stumbled across a book written by Vida Scudder, a woman who had taught English literature at Wellesley for many years. "It was the right time to move," she wrote. "And what sense of escape we had."

> If there is any happier game than building a house, I have failed to play it. . . . My house tempts me to garrulity. . . . [Referring to her top floor study.] Here I find my solitude. . . . Released from the constant impact of city sights and sounds, I found the pure activities of thought enhanced. Energy was focused less in action, more in gaining a farther and more detached perspective on many matters which had agitated me.[34]

Because our home is located in Lansing, New York, a township just north of Ithaca, I

[34]Vida Dutton Scudder, *On Journey* (New York, 1937), pp. 272–75.

promptly began reading the few booklets that had ever been published about the area, initially known as Teetertown after the first white settlers arrived in 1791. Once a post office had been established in 1830, the name was changed to Lansingville. Much of the land in this area had actually been part of the Military Tract—land used to compensate men who had fought in the War for Independence. According to local lore, however, the land had been purchased from an Albany land speculator with the memorable name of Jealous Yates. Andrew Myers, Jr., a son of the first white man to live at Myers Point (now the site of the town park), married Mandana Mack. Benejah Strong settled nearby on Salmon Creek, the population center of this bustling "town," and Zenas Tucker lived closer to our new homesite in South Lansing. A woman by the name of Wealthy White graced the community after she married Mervin Bower. Subsequently, Andrew Myers, Jr., and Mandana Mack had a son named Bengo who later became a spiritualist. Our part of upstate New York would eventually become notorious for spawning spiritualists, inauthentic and otherwise.

During the five-month stretch of summer and fall when Il Nido was under construction, Carol and I lived directly below it in a charming two-level lakeshore cottage. Carol served at the time as director of the Tompkins County Arts Council, so she went downtown to her office each day. I was writing *A Machine That Would Go of Itself* (the start of a sabbatical leave in 1984–85 supported by a Constitutional Fellowship from the National Endowment for the Humanities) and worked at the cottage every day, always available to pay urgent bills and answer questions from our architect or his staff, from the framing crew, the electrical, plumbing, and septic crews, or, during the later part of autumn, from the people doing cabinetry, masonry, woodwork, building stairs, installing windows, and so forth. Not that I had one iota of expertise, but there were occasional choices to be made: where should television hookups be placed? electrical sockets for lamps? the essential height for shelves in my wine-cellar? . . . Things like that.

Every afternoon at around three o'clock I would climb the winding hill three-tenths of a mile, accompanied by Sandy, our Orange Belton English setter, and carrying either six-packs of beer or else apples from the Cornell orchards for the work crew. The interesting thing was that most members of the crew were college-educated or else college dropouts. They were "sixties people" who had rejected conventional professional career paths because they wanted to work with their hands, build things, be skilled artisans, and not lead the kinds of "regimented" lives that their parents had led. They were highly intelligent, honest, very skillful, and great fun to be with.

From time to time the contrast between their daily way of life and my own seemed very striking. They did manual labor and I did not—though sometimes writing by hand for a whole day certainly seems, quite literally, like *manual* labor. Be that as it may, I thought back almost seven years to the time we visited the beautiful Salarjung Museum in Hyderabad, India. In the section devoted to textiles a sign explained that "Kalamkari" meant textile-designing work. *Kalam* means "pen" in Telugu and *kar* means "work." Literally: work done with pen in hand. "Kalamkaris" are textiles so done. I liked the phrase because it also describes the manual labor that historians do (or at least used to do before the PC) and that I *still* do: work with pen in hand. For a while I privately called my books *kalamkaris*. (The idiom is actually derived from Sanskrit and has been adapted into Telugu, the language of southcentral India.)

There is a story told about Justice Oliver Wendell Holmes that that self-assured Brahmin suffered from only one anxiety: namely, that come Judgment Day God would ask him to report on those books which he ought to have read but hadn't. Perhaps that is the ultimate anxiety of the Calvinist scholar. I am not the most voracious reader, but come the Day of Judgment I suspect that I will have to answer for more serious lapses than books not read.

Perhaps I might move toward closure by indicating those books (not by historians and not previously mentioned) that have meant the most to me. There are fewer than twenty, and they really fall into three remaining categories because I have already enumerated biographies and autobiographies. The least important category, perhaps, includes collected essays. Joan Didion's *The White Album* (1979) offers fascinating reportage and perspectives on life in America, mostly California and Hawaii in the late '60s and early '70s. Her special gift is the "story without a narrative." Isaiah Berlin's *Personal Impressions* (1981) has superb essays on Sir Lewis Namier (the fastidious historian), Felix Frankfurter at Oxford, Richard Pares, Sir Maurice Bowra, Aldous Huxley, Chaim Weizmann, Albert Einstein, and Israel.

In the category of nonfiction for sheer fun I would list Maurice Rheims's *The Glorious Obsession* (1980, first published in 1975 as *Haute Curiosité*), the memoirs of an auctioneer and dealer in pictures, the decorative arts, and antiques who was a wonderful raconteur with an abundance of rich and whacky clients. Then I commend Paul Fussell's *Abroad: British Literary Traveling between the Wars* (1980), an arch and opinionated book that is equally engaging. And finally (in this category) two books that explain why we get the bulk of our mail, i.e., catalogues and solicitations, plus a whole lot of unwanted telephone queries. I have in mind M. R. Montgomery's *In Search of L. L. Bean* (1984) and Erik Larson's *The Naked Consumer: How Our Private Lives Become Public Commodities* (1992). Richly informative and amusing (in a rather depressing way).

My biggest category is fiction, and I have to repeat that Stegner's *Angle of Repose* tops the list. The next best among historical novels are John Barth's *The Sot-Weed Factor* (1960), a brilliant and bawdy tour de force of Chesapeake Maryland late in the seventeenth century, and T. Coraghessan Boyle's *World's End* (1987), an equally bawdy but somewhat less philosophical meditation on possession and dispossession that manages to weave back and forth between the seventeenth century and the twentieth along the lower Hudson River Valley. Then there is E. L. Doctorow's *Ragtime* (1975), a wry and clever evocation of historical characters in New York City between 1906 and 1914. When you have J. P. Morgan and Emma Goldman in the same book . . . well, don't forget to keep one eye on the closet.

Three momentous novels about the meaning of the African-American past for people once colored, then Negro, and later black—but also for white Americans as well—are Toni Morrison's *Song of Solomon* (1977), wherein Milkman Dead makes a journey of discovery into his family's past, Morrison's *Beloved* (1987), which I deeply admire but found more difficult to follow, and Ralph Ellison's *Invisible Man* (1952), long since canonized as a classic, and deservedly so.

That leaves four non-American novels—as different as they could possibly be: L. P. Hartley's *The Go-Between* (1953), set in the summer of 1900, evokes England's golden age and has those unforgettable lines, "The past is a foreign country: they do things differently there" (page 3) and "the past kept pricking at me" (page 16).

Thomas Flanagan's *The Tenants of Time* (1988) is actually the equal of *Angle of Repose* in terms of narrative power, suspense, and poignancy. It may even surpass Stegner's masterpiece in historical significance. Flanagan looks back at the futility of Fenian nationalism in late nineteenth-century Ireland from the perspectives of a historian and a retired schoolmaster who feel despair in the face of a buried past that they cannot reconstruct. Flanagan shows as well as anyone ever has how the realities of local history get distorted into romantic legends in less than a generation. Recorded history, moreover, fails to capture the complexity and the ambiguity of human motivation, nonrationality, and self-defeating impulses.

The Tenants of Time is a powerful page-turner composed in moving prose that will make you weep: "It is not, I am persuaded, that memory is random, brutally indifferent, but rather that it has its own strict hierarchies, which are hidden from us." (page 382) And

> . . . youth falls away from us, crumbles and vanishes, and we do not know that; we believe ourselves to be in the thick of it, until one day, of a sudden, something will remind us that it is over, done with, swallowed up in Time's maw. We are all the tenants of Time, and whatever it is that reminds us, that thing we will convict as a murderer, like the messenger bringing bad tidings. (page 428)

One does not need a special love of Irish history to be overwhelmed by the lyrical lamentation of Flanagan's message and his prose.

Then there are two allegorical novels that I greatly admire. One reads Russell Hoban's *The Lion of Boaz-Jachin and Jachin-Boaz* (1973) to learn things about oneself and because it will make one's life a little different ever after. One reads Milan Kundera's *The Book of Laughter and Forgetting* (1980) to laugh at the absurd situations he creates, the fantasies, the sheer playfulness, and the underlying commentary on what used to be called the "human condition" until that became a hollow cliché.

Michael Kammen, Carol, and her brother John in the Cathedral of Ifaki-Ekiti, Nigeria, for the second full day of marriage ceremonies between Daniel and Bamidele Fayemi, January 3, 1992. Their Yoruba robes were specially made for the occasion in Lagos. They are singing an old Methodist hymn in the Yoruba language.

Finally, I have to commend two lectures that were promptly published as ephemera. The first is Gershom Scholem's *Walter Benjamin* (1965), the Leo Baeck Memorial Lecture number eight, in which Scholem called attention to the last paragraph in Benjamin's work that can be chronologically placed, part of a quasi-Marxian text on historical time that also reads like an apotheosis of Judaism:

> To the soothsayers time—time whom they asked to yield the secrets of her womb—surely was neither homogeneous nor void. Bearing this in mind we may possibly appreciate how time past is perceived in remembrance: namely, as neither homogeneous nor void. The Jews, we know, were forbidden to explore the future, whereas the Torah and prayer teach them remembrance, and remembrance strips the future of the magic spell that binds those who seek the soothsayer's advice. Nonetheless the future did not become a homogeneous and void space of time to the Jews. For each single second in it was the small door through which the Messiah might enter. (page 24)[35]

The second lecture, titled "The Discourse on Language," was Michel Foucault's inaugural lecture at the Collége de France, given on December 2, 1970, and first published in English four months later.[36] All of it is exceedingly thoughtful and provocative; much of it is now, after twenty-five years, fairly familiar, ei-

---

[35]See also Gershom Scholem, *From Berlin to Jerusalem: Memories of My Youth* (New York, 1980); and Gershom Scholem, editor, *The Correspondence of Walter Benjamin and Gershom Scholem, 1932–1940* (New York, 1989).

[36]"The Discourse on Language," in *Social Science Information*, April 1971, pp. 7–30; reprinted as an appendix to Foucault, *The Archaeology of Knowledge* (New York, 1972), pp. 215–37, the quotation at pp. 216, 220.

ther at firsthand from reading Foucault, or else disseminated by his many disciples, or simply extracted or redacted at thirdhand. I want to quote two passages that are especially germane for those of us who deal with discourse in its cultural context, and with historical discourse more particularly. Foucault's stance is that of a radical critic, of course, and by now it has lost a little of its belligerent edge. Try to imagine, however, what it might have meant to read this in October 1972, when Vietnam was still being hotly contested in the United States, when the presidential campaign between Richard Nixon and George McGovern had one month yet to go, and when the limits of dissidence at my own university, Cornell, continued to be intensely divisive.

It also helps to recognize that something is lost in translation. It sounds more stilted and formulaic in English than it does in the original:

> I am supposing that in every society the production of discourse is at once controlled, selected, organised and redistributed according to a certain number of procedures, whose role is to avert its powers and its dangers, to cope with chance events, to evade its ponderous, awesome materiality. . . . Similarly, historians have constantly impressed upon us that speech is no mere verbalisation of conflicts and systems of domination, but that it is the very object of man's conflict. . . .
>
> There is barely a society without its major narratives, told, retold, and varied; formulae, texts, ritualised texts to be spoken in well-defined circumstances; things said once, and conserved because people suspect some hidden secret or wealth lies buried within. . . . We know them in our own cultural system: religious or juridical texts, as well as some curious texts, from the point of view of their status, which we term "literary"; to a certain extent, scientific texts also.

As I gaze retrospectively and reflect on some of those texts, fiction as well as nonfiction, that have moved or stimulated me during the past thirty years or so, I am aware that as an academic historian *what* I say has largely taken priority over *how* I say it. Saul Bellow once remarked that "writers don't have tasks, they have inspiration." That's engagingly aphoristic, but it really isn't true for scholars. Even if we

love what we do, as I do, we most certainly do have tasks. Nonetheless, I would never scorn inspiration. I welcome it. Yet with the passage of time I am ever more aware that the shelf life of historians is short. We only endure if we are readable, like Francis Parkman and Henry Adams, Edward Eggleston or Carl Becker, Richard Hofstadter and C. Vann Woodward. "Readable" requires inspiration or genius, and preferably both.

If 99 percent of us do, in fact, have a short shelf life, if our work and our reputations are, indeed, ephemeral, then why bother? I see a satisfactory answer in a critical essay that Mary Douglas once wrote about James Frazer—a situation in which a fourth-generation anthropologist, as it were, was embalming a founder of the discipline. "Within each new dimension of understanding," Douglas asserted, "the process of passing judgment on another generation's work seems necessary."

> The judgments partake initially in what Lawrence Gowing calls "the apparent arbitrariness of a continued and unending process of redefinition, on the basis of a past which is itself in a perpetual state of rediscovery and revaluation." But if later judgments upon one-time achievement are not themselves to be devalued and arbitrarily dismissed, we should seek laboriously means for reconstructing the old dimension of understanding.[37]

That seems fair enough, especially to this historian whose job it is to mediate between the past and the present, and who is obliged to take special care not to discard texts concerning the past until we know with assurance that they are wrong or else have been genuinely supplanted by qualitatively better narratives and more persuasive explanations. Ultimately, I suppose, I would eagerly welcome some of Mr. Bellow's inspiration, but my top priority has to remain explanation rather than inspiration. Perhaps that's even at the very core of my creed as a historian.

Once when Charlie Parker, the inspired saxophonist, was asked by an interviewer about

---

[37]Douglas, "Judgments on James Frazer," *Daedalus* 107 (fall 1978), pp. 152–53. Cf. Marc Manganaro, *Myth, Rhetoric, and the Voice of Authority: A Critique of Frazer, Eliot, Frye & Campbell* (New Haven, 1992), pp. 38–39.

his religious affiliation, he replied with five words: "I am a devout musician."[38] More and more, as time goes by, I have come to realize that I am a devout historian. It is like an incurable addiction; it's a way of comprehending the world; it's a way of life. I can think of worse ways to live, but not very many that would be better.

BIBLIOGRAPHY

Nonfiction:

Operational History of the Flying Boat, Open Sea and Seadrome Aspects: Selected Pacific Campaigns, World War II, U.S. Navy Department, 1959.

Operational History of the Flying Boat, Open Sea and Seadrome Aspects: Atlantic Theatre, World War II, U.S. Navy Department, 1960.

A Rope of Sand: The Colonial Agents, British Politics, and the American Revolution, Cornell University Press, 1968.

Deputyes and Libertyes: The Origins of Representative Government in Colonial America, Knopf, 1969.

Empire and Interest: The American Colonies and the Politics of Mercantilism, Lippincott, 1970.

(Contributor) *Essays on Anglo-American Political Relations, 1675–1775,* Rutgers University Press, 1970.

People of Paradox: An Inquiry Concerning the Origins of American Civilization, Knopf, 1972.

Colonial New York: A History, Scribner, 1975, Oxford University Press, 1996.

(With J. P. Greene and R. L. Bushman) *Society, Freedom, and Conscience: The Coming of the Revolution in Virginia, Massachusetts, and New York,* Norton, 1976.

(With Kenneth E. Boulding and Seymour Martin Lipset) *From Abundance to Scarcity: Implications for the American Tradition,* Ohio State University Press, 1978.

---

[38]Ross Russell, *Bird Lives: The High Life and Hard Times of Charlie (Yardbird) Parker!* (New York, 1973), p. 270.

A Season of Youth: The American Revolution and the Historical Imagination, Knopf, 1978.

A Machine That Would Go of Itself: The Constitution in American Culture, Knopf, 1986.

Spheres of Liberty: Changing Perceptions of Liberty in American Culture, University of Wisconsin Press, 1986.

Selvages & Biases: The Fabric of History in American Culture, Cornell University Press, 1987.

Sovereignty and Liberty: Constitutional Discourse in American Culture, University of Wisconsin Press, 1989.

Mystic Chords of Memory: The Transformation of Tradition in American Culture, Knopf, 1991.

Meadows of Memory: Images of Time and Tradition in American Art and Culture, University of Texas Press, 1992.

Contested Values: Democracy and Diversity in American Culture, St. Martin's, 1994.

The Lively Arts: Gilbert Seldes and the Transformation of Cultural Criticism in the United States, Oxford University Press, 1996.

Editor:

(Co-editor) *The Glorious Revolution in America: Documents on the Colonial Crisis of 1689,* Institute of Early American History and Culture, 1964, revised, 1972.

Politics and Society in Colonial America: Democracy or Deference?, Holt, 1967, second edition, Krieger, 1973.

The Contrapuntal Civilization: Essays toward a New Understanding of the American Experience, Crowell, 1971.

The History of the Province of New York, 2 vols., Harvard University Press, 1972.

"What Is the Good of History?" Selected Letters of Carl L. Becker, 1940–1945, Cornell University Press, 1973.

The Past before Us: Contemporary Historical Writing in the United States, Cornell University Press, 1980.

The Origins of the American Constitution: A Documentary History, Viking, 1986.

(Co-editor) *The Transformation of Early American History: Society, Authority, and Ideology,* Knopf, 1991.

Contributor to *Studies Presented to the International Commission for the History of Representative and Parliamentary Institutions,* 1970, and to numerous periodicals and journals.

Norman Levine

1924-

Norman Levine, on his return to Canada after thirty-one years in England, 1980

and King Edward. Streetcars ran on tracks along St. Patrick, Rideau, and Dalhousie. There were also cars and trucks. And wagons pulled by horses. In winter the horses pulled sleighs.

My father and mother came to Ottawa because my mother's uncle invited them. He was the banana wholesaler for Ottawa. (He showed me the railway spur, just outside Ottawa, where freight cars brought him green bananas from Guatemala. And the warehouse where stalks of bananas were hanging from the ceiling.) Not only did he supply the Ottawa stores but the fruit and vegetable peddlers who came early to the market to buy their produce. Load them onto their trucks and wagons. Then go through the wealthier streets to sell them to their customers.

In Ottawa my father was a fruit peddler. In Warsaw he lived a different life. He, and his partner, had a shoe store on Marshalkovska. Years later, in London, I went to a reception for a visiting theatre company from Poland. And asked an actor if he had heard of a street in Warsaw called Marshalkovska.

"Eet ees like your Piccadilly," he said.

In Ottawa, in a drawer, I came across a studio photograph, taken in Warsaw, of my father. I didn't recognize him. He is well-dressed. He has a large moustache, thick wavy hair.

I grew up in Ottawa in the Lower Town of the late nineteen twenties, thirties, and early forties. The centre of Lower Town was the market with the Parliament buildings, rising on the slope, beside it. At the far end was the Rideau River with the Minto bridges over the river and a separate bridge where only freight trains went by. And scattered were the Catholic churches, the Separate schools. Most of the inhabitants of Lower Town were French Canadian.

The finest street was King Edward with its central boulevard of elms. My parents rented a large tall house on the corner of Guigues

French boy in Lower Town, Ottawa Market, 1918

Father, in Warsaw, about 1920

The person I knew was clean-shaven and bald. And knew a few words of English and French. And less about horses. At the back of the house, across the yard, we had a wooden stable.

My father never talked about his earlier life. And never used the dark brown stick, with its silver-topped handle, that he brought with him. It was my mother who told me of their European past.

"We had a lovely house and we owned it. We had a servant. When I was coming to Canada she begged me to take her with me."

On days I didn't have to go to school, and in the summer holidays, I helped my father. The white horse pulling the high red wagon through the Ottawa streets. Monday, Wednesday, Friday, we went to certain streets. Tuesday, Thursday, Saturday, we went to others.

When I could leave school, at sixteen, I did. And started to work in the government. In the Department of National Defense. It was an old building by the Rideau Canal. I answered the phone, looked after the blueprints and the specifications. (Those who worked there were civilian architects and engineers, and architects and engineers who were in the army.) After a year, I was allowed to do a linen tracing (for a blueprint) of the ground plan for a prisoner-of-war camp to be built in Canada for people interned because of the Second World War.

In 1942, at eighteen, I joined the Royal Canadian Air Force. And remained in Ottawa, living at home, along with quite a few others. We had to do a three-month course to bring our education (mostly mathematics) high enough for us to go to Souris, Manitoba, for a further two months before we could start the necessary training.

I did all mine in Western Canada: in Saskatchewan, Alberta, Manitoba. On graduation, at the end of 1943, I received a commission as a pilot officer. And went overseas, to England, in the spring of 1944. And more training there, on several other aircraft, before going to 429 Squadron, a Lancaster squadron, at Leeming, Yorkshire.

I was on the squadron for the last three months of the war in Europe. Took part in a few night raids, dropping bombs on Germany. And one daylight: the railway marshalling yards on the outskirts of Leipzig.

The war determined the texture of our existence. But at the time I didn't know it. It wasn't the flying but what I was discovering away from the flying station. Going to London, meeting people mostly in uniform around my age from all over, seeing paintings, hearing concerts, reading new books and *New Writing*. And, especially, seeing how the English lived and behaved in wartime.

While on the squadron, every two weeks, we had to take a weekend leave. Usually we went to London. From station gossip we knew there was a receptionist, Irene, in the Cumberland Hotel at Marble Arch. And that she had a weakness for Canadian air force officers. We would arrive and always get a room.

After breakfast, Sunday morning, I would cross the road to go and hear the soapbox orators at Speakers' Corner in Hyde Park. The war was coming to an end. There was talk and speculation, in the papers, on the BBC, of what peace would be like.

Most of the speakers had heavy European accents. But spoke with eloquent gestures. Their arms punctuating their words.

I was walking towards a speaker who had the largest audience. I could hear laughter from the crowd. And astonishment from the speaker at this reaction to what he was saying.

He was finishing another short passionate speech. When, triumphantly, he ended with:

"Vat the pipple vant . . . und vat the pipple get . . . ist piss."

He brought the house down.

And he could not understand why.

I like to think this was the first time I became aware of the possibilities of language.

The war in Europe was over and while still on the squadron, the education officer asked. What would I like to do back in Canada?

"Go to university."

He arranged for me to go to Trinity College, Cambridge, for several weeks.

I ate at the High Table. Once, sitting next, was a tall distinguished figure, Sir John Frankenstein, the former British ambassador to Austria. He told me what Austria was like before the war. And I told him how long it took to fly to bomb Germany near Austria. And that the doctor on the station gave us pills to take for the return flight so we wouldn't fall asleep.

Another time, I sat beside an American movie mogul. We were eating wartime food and rations on expensive-looking dishes. "If you come from the English aristocracy," he whispered loudly. "And you go here. You don't take exams. Your parents just give a set of these gold-plated dishes and you get your degree."

I went punting on the Cam. I was invited to tea. Met several people who had published books. Met Maurice Dobb and, from him, had confirmation of the political change taking place in the country. I also met R. C. Trevelyan. He looked very English in his plus fours, brown brogues, and walking stick. And someone gave me a thin book, *A Selection of Poems by Ezra Pound,* published by Faber in the Sesame Series.

At the first postwar election in England I won money from the other members of the crew. They were sure Churchill was going to get in. From what I had seen, read, and heard, I knew it would be Labour.

I returned to Ottawa in the late summer of 1945, received my release from the air force at Rockliffe, and was told about the Veteran's Act. The government paid your fees and gave you sixty dollars a month to live on while you went to university. I went to McGill. And it was there that I began to write.

Professor Harold G. Files, a soft-spoken Bostonian in the English department, began an informal course for anyone who wanted to write. You went to see him, in his office, once every two weeks. His window overlooked the campus, the ginkgo tree, to Sherbrooke Street. And he read and corrected what you had written (usually grammar). I started a novel that way. And when I finished a version of it, Jack McClelland, who was then working for his father (McClelland and Stewart), was going across the country, to the various English departments, to see if anyone was writing a novel.

After he read it, he said, "It's a good novel." (Which it wasn't.) "Now you have to find a New York publisher or a London publisher. If you find one, we will take copies from them for Canada."

When I heard that I knew I would head for London.

This was made possible because two fellowships were being given, to two ex-servicemen,

Mother, in Vilna, about 1920

for two years, to do postgraduate work at a British university. The fellowships were established from the profits made during the war (in the canteens where Canadian soldiers, sailors, airmen visited). The money, frozen by the first postwar Labour government, had to be used in England. One fellowship went to a French-speaking Canadian. The other to an English-speaking. I had the English one. And, on a bright June day in 1949, sailed from Montreal for England on a freighter to go to King's College, London in September.

But before going there, I spent the summer in St. Ives, Cornwall.

My first reaction—I hadn't seen anything like this. The colours of the sea, the sky, the clouds, the far shore fields. Godrevy Lighthouse in the bay (I found out was Virginia Woolf's *Lighthouse* even though she placed it in Scotland). The fine yellow sand beaches. Empty. The cobblestone streets with the narrow sidewalks, the passages between cottages. The front doors, of the cottages, cut in two like horse stables. The black nets, spread out by the fish-ermen, on the grass of the Island to dry. The walk along the quay. And the smallness of the place. It was made for the human scale.

And when I wanted to go out with the fishermen, I had to be vetted, in the cottage, by the elderly father and mother—as well as their working sons. For they all had shares in the boat.

Then watching, in the harbour, after the boats had come back and began to unload their catch. A short, elderly man standing up in a high cart with large wooden wheels, holding the horse's reins. (A blind dog was always between the wheels.) And the horse would pull the cart across the sand of the harbour to the quay where the boats were tied. And the fishermen, with hooks, would throw the fish (usually flat fish) from the boat to the high wooden cart.

When it was full, the horse and cart would go, slowly, across the wet sand to the slipway (the blind dog between the wheels). Then up from the slipway, near the Sloop Inn, to a large flat metal scale set in the cement, to weigh the fish.

St. Ives, Cornwall

After they were weighed the small man in the empty cart (the dog underneath) would start to go back across the sand to the beached boats for the next load. But the wooden wheels of the cart had gone through the slime from the dumped fish on the scale. And as the cart went across the harbour the wind blew through the spokes, making from the slime, strange balloon shapes.

There was Jacob the town crier. (When he wasn't doing that he swept the streets.) There was the Salvation Army singing in the streets. And at Christmas singing carols at night, flashlights under their chins so that their faces were lit. There were the funeral cards in the windows: of the fishmongers, the fruit and vegetables, the bakers. And tacked on the black sides of the fishermen's shelters, already pockmarked by the cards that had been tacked up in the years before. And there were all the different places of worship, especially Methodist.

Into this community came sophisticated people who were mainly painters. The railway had not long started. But in 1949, St. Ives was still off the beaten track. Though painters had been coming to St. Ives for quite a while. Mostly academic, they would put up their easels outside, often on the sand of the harbour or in the Back Roads, and paint what they could see. As did similar painters in art colonies, by the sea, in France.

When I arrived the older generation was Bernard Leach, Barbara Hepworth, and Ben Nicholson. They had come to St. Ives because of the war. And the next generation, nearer my age, would become my friends. Most had taken part in the war: Peter Lanyon, Terry Frost, Patrick Heron, Roger Hilton, Alan Lowndes, Bryan Wynter . . . the list could go on. There was still some postwar idealism about. And English class differences were still blurred although they hardened soon enough.

Within ten years, other painters arrived because of those who were here. Notably, Francis Bacon in the autumn of 1959.

What I got from the painters, at the start, was the conviction that painting and writing were worthwhile occupations. They encouraged me to write simply by saying, "I just finished a painting. I'd like you to see it." Afterwards, I would want to go away and write. And when I had something published I would show it to them.

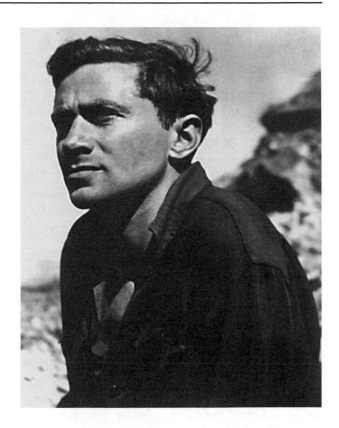

The author, St. Ives, 1952

There was also a sense of continuity.

The girl in the newsagents told me her father was taught French by D. H. Lawrence when he lived with Frieda in Zennor. I saw the cottage with the bell tower, near where the Lawrences lived, where Katherine Mansfield stayed. And, in a secondhand bookshop in St. Ives, I bought for twenty-five pence a selection of Chekhov's stories (inscribed by Katherine Mansfield: to Mary MacKenzie for Christmas 1918) which I still have. I was shown where W. H. Hudson walked on the moors and read what he wrote of this area.

And there was Guido Morris, a printer, who did everything by hand on his Latin Press. I had not heard of him. But was told that he did the posters for the Victoria and Albert Museum. And saw the posters he did for the exhibitions of the younger generation in St. Ives as they began to show their work. Guido's work was simple, clear, and direct. And the first book he printed (at the end of 1950) was a selection of poems I had written mainly about the physical presence of St. Ives. I called it

The Tightrope Walker. It was published in a limited edition and sold by subscription.

Although my friends were the younger painters, the painter who made me write my first short story was Alfred Wallis. He had died in the Madron workhouse in 1942. I saw his grave above Porthmeor Beach, in the cemetery, with tiles made by Bernard Leach covering it.

I had seen paintings by primitive or naive painters. But not any like Wallis painted. His instinct with colour, the way he placed things (usually on ordinary cardboard) was sophisticated.

Then I met people who knew him. And found out that, in his youth, he had gone fishing in the boats that went to Newfoundland. Then became a rag and bone man in St. Ives. And took to painting, in old age, after his wife died. He also heard voices coming down the chimney.

Mr. Veal, a retired carpenter, told me, "If you think I'm daft, you should have seen Wallis."

What may have suggested the form of the story was seeing Ben Nicholson go out with a sketchbook and sketch the boats lying on their side, at low tide, in the harbour. That made me go out with a notepad, early in the morning, and describe what I could see.

And this led to the writing of "A Sabbath Walk." It describes Alfred Wallis (I call him Alfred Adams) walking through St. Ives before it becomes awake.

"A Sabbath Walk" was published in Rome in *Botteghe Oscure.* Edited by Marguerite Caetani, an American living in Italy. It was then the best international literary magazine. All the writers were published in their own language.

In the autumn I went up to London to go to King's College. I liked King's because it was in the Strand and there was a pub, Mooneys, by its entrance. One day at noon, after a lecture, I went to the bar at Mooneys with a just-bought new book of poems by Louis MacNeice. And there, at the bar, was a tall man with curly (beginning to go grey) hair also with the same book by MacNeice. It was Norman Cameron, whose poems of the Second World War I can still remember. ("They say that women in a bombing raid. . ." "It happened a long time ago, the first pressure on the trigger. . . .") He was also a translator from the French and Spanish. I especially liked his version of Lorca. At that time he was working in an advertising

agency near the Strand. When I mentioned I might be going to Austria for Christmas, he brought out his address book and gave me names and addresses of people he knew. Apparently he was there, in intelligence, just after the war.

And going to see the Boat Race, near Hammersmith Bridge, in another pub, I was introduced to George Barker. His first words:

"Sorry chum, nothing personal. But coming from Canada, you haven't got a chance."

And I met Stevie Smith who was then secretary to the editor (Evans) of a popular weekly, *John O'London's Weekly,* where I had some early verse published. Short, bright, black hair in a fringe, slightly mischievous looking, didn't say much. But gave my first novel, *The Angled Road,* its most perceptive review.

But while meeting writers I had heard of was a novelty and getting to know postwar London which despite (or because of) the rationing, the bomb-damage, the seediness, was exciting, I didn't take to writers as I did to painters. I was stimulated by the painters. They seemed to be more open, extrovert, enthusiastic. And, in conversation, they didn't keep their defences up, as most of the writers did. We talked freely.

I also knew that my interest was not in the academic. After a year, I wrote to the fellowship committee. Instead of continuing with postgraduate work could I spend my time revising the first novel?

They agreed.

The novel, *The Angled Road,* was accepted about the same time I met Margaret Payne in 1951. Born in Blackheath, London. And evacuated to Cornwall during the war, to a farm near Truro. She was going to a teacher training college near London. We were married at the start of 1952. And we had three daughters.

After *The Angled Road* was published, towards the end of 1952, I remember thinking: I've had three thin books published, none of which I thought much of. There must be more to writing than this. And noticed that, though I was living in England, I was thinking of Canada.

In 1954, I decided to make my first visit back: to Ottawa, Montreal, and Toronto.

While in Montreal, I saw Professor Files. He took me to the McGill Faculty Club for lunch where I met John Steegman, the director of the Museum of Modern Art in Montreal, on nearby Sherbrooke Street.

I told him I was living in England, in St. Ives. That there were some good young painters there. He asked who they were. I told him: "Peter Lanyon, Terry Frost, Patrick Heron, Bryan Wynter, David Haughton. . . . Why don't you show them in Canada?"

"Why are you doing this?"

"Because they are my friends."

He waited about five seconds.

"All right."

He would arrange for them to go across the country, for the next two years, to all the leading provincial galleries. He told me about Bourlet in London. "They will collect, pack, and insure the paintings." He asked me to do the catalogue. I called it: *6 Painters from Cornwall.*

The only painter, of the six, who was then in St. Ives was Peter Lanyon. The others were up-country on fellowships or teaching at art schools or working in London.

When it came to listing the prices of these large oils for the catalogue, I said to Peter, "Fifty dollars is too low. People will laugh."

"What do you suggest?"

"A hundred dollars."

(Some of these paintings are now in leading permanent collections.)

But for most of this visit I stayed in Ottawa. And walked, reacting to the physical changes, especially in Lower Town. And I knew that the next book would have to be about this.

When I returned to St. Ives, I realized that because I was living in England my experience in Canada had stopped. And I had, in front of me, on the wall of the room where I worked, an imaginary map. It was divided into the different areas that I knew: Lower Town Ottawa, Wawa, McGill, Ile Aux Noix, Quebec City. And whenever I wanted to write a new story I would project this map and see what area to consider.

This way of writing started in 1955 when I wrote "A Small Piece of Blue," about the summer I worked in northern Ontario at Helen Mine, Wawa, while going to McGill.

I sent the story to John Pudney. He edited, for Putnam, "Pick of Today's Short Stories." He was also one of the directors of Putnam. I asked him if Putnam would be interested in my doing a travel book about Canada. They said they would.

The author's wife, Margaret, and their children: (from left) Kate, Rachael, and Cassie, 1957

Peter Lanyon, 1961

I had to accept that Canadian publishing was closed to my work. It was only Robert Weaver, through his CBC radio series, "Anthology" (1954–1984), which broadcast and commissioned my stories, that kept me going.

So I walked to the small St. Ives library on Gabriel Street and looked through *The Writers and Artists Year Book* for a possible literary agent. Picked Ruth Liepman in Zurich. Sent her a copy of *Canada Made Me.* She replied that she was only halfway through the book but wouldn't have any trouble getting a German publisher. And she did. Claassen published it. And a clause in the contract said that a book of short stories would follow.

When the translation of the stories came in Ruth (who was born in Hamburg) didn't like it. And sent the stories, and the translation, to Heinrich Böll. He wrote back that he would take care of it.

He called the collection *Ein kleines Stückchen Blau* ("A Small Piece of Blue"). And he and his wife, Annemarie, did the translation.

I went to London to see him. And, from the conversation, realized we had different books in mind.

"Don't date it," he said.

And I knew, even then, that all books are dated. It is only if they are any good that they begin to float through time.

Putnam gave me a modest advance, as did Jack McClelland. It was to be a co-publication between Putnam and McClelland and Stewart. But when Jack McClelland saw the manuscript he didn't like it. Putnam, mainly because Roger Lubbock, the chairman, liked the book, said they would publish it on their own. So Jack McClelland said he would take five hundred copies for Canada, but he didn't want his name on it.

Canada Made Me was published by Putnam in November 1958. A long review by Paul West in the Christmas issue of the *New Statesman & Nation* was read by Honor Balfour of the London office of *Time.* She interviewed me. When her piece appeared, the five hundred copies that McClelland had went quickly. He wouldn't take any more. Nor would any other Canadian publisher.

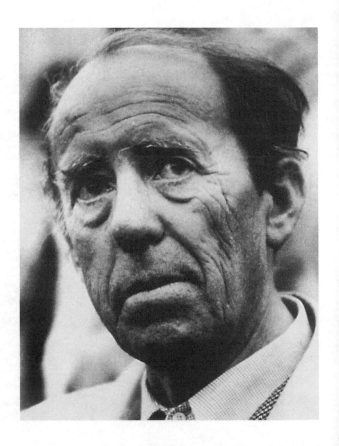

Heinrich Böll, 1980s

It was because of Böll that the East German publisher, Reclam in Leipzig, soon brought out two large editions of the stories. Afterwards other European and Scandinavian countries followed.

I first read a Böll short story, in translation, in *Encounter*. After that I looked out for his work. Of his novels, I prefer *The Clown*. But it is his short stories that matter to me. He trapped the way the Germans lived in immediate postwar Germany, on all levels, with humour, irony, and especially poignancy. They have stayed with me. As has an entry in his journal of himself, a German soldier, a Catholic, in a troop train going to the Russian front. And as the train goes through the little towns of Poland he prays for the Jews who live in these little towns.

I never met Böll. Nor did we correspond. But we would talk through my Zurich agent.

After my last collection, *Django, Karfunkelstein & Rosen,* was published by Claassen, I was invited to Cologne where Böll was born. (There is a Heinrich Böll Platz near the cathedral and by the art gallery. And over thirty schools in Germany have been named after him.)

I was a guest of the main city library. There were three microphones. I was sitting up there with the translator of my last book of stories and this young German writer. He began to read the last story in the book, "Because of the War." And there is a line in the story that says: "Kill Jews." Before he got there his reading became slower and slower and slower. I was following, in English, what he was reading. And when he came to that part, he stopped. He couldn't go on. So I picked it up in English and went on. And I wasn't touched or moved by what I was reading.

Of the painters in St. Ives, Peter Lanyon and I got on because we were both in the air force. And because we both had a growing family of young children. And when he saw I was interested in other parts of Cornwall he drove me, all over, to show how a particular place resulted in a particular painting.

I also got to know him because, near the start, he was the only one down in St. Ives. The others were teaching at different art schools. Or, like Terry Frost, at Leeds University with his family, on a painting fellowship.

Terry Frost is my oldest friend of the painters. We go back to the summer of 1949. And

when the children were small he let me put my typewriter on the large windowsill of his studio and write, and look out on Porthmeor Beach and the Atlantic, while behind me he was busy painting.

A generous, witty, and extrovert person. He laughs easily. And writes delightful letters while travelling on the early morning train from Penzance to Paddington because he has to be in London. He is a constant encourager telling me to keep on working. And he is well-read. Has done a fine suite of prints to go with Lorca's poems.

Like some of the people mentioned in this essay they sometimes appear as "characters" in a short story or a novel. And I particularly like it when Terry appears. Here he is as "Henry," in a Portuguese seafood restaurant in Toronto:

> After the meal we went into the other room, stood at the bar, drank with the proprietor and his wife. Neither could speak much English. She was telling me that her husband played football for Portugal when

Terry Frost, 1962

a slight man, in a light-grey summer suit, joined us. He must have had his meal somewhere in the large room. But we didn't notice. He said he was an American. After a while he said he worked for the CIA. Still later, Henry and the CIA man began to dance. I danced with the proprietor's wife. Then we all put our arms over the shoulder of the person on either side. The proprietor joined us. And we moved around the empty restaurant as a chorus line. Henry singing, "Life is just a bowl of cherries."

Out in the street we asked the CIA man where he was staying. The Windsor Arms. So we walked to the nearest main road and waited for a taxi to drive by. The grey light of early morning. It was cold and shabby. A gusty wind. Loose newspapers. And no cars. The CIA man began to take out dollar bills from his jacket pocket and threw them up into the air. The wind blew them away. Henry and I went after the loose bills . . . on the road . . . the sidewalk . . . across the street . . . and stuffed them back into the man's pockets. Then he took them out again and threw them in the air. And again we went after them . . . Until a taxi finally came along.

Since then Henry has called that night magical. A word I never use.

(From the story "Soap Opera" in *Something Happened Here*)

From all the painters, the only writer in Cornwall I have known from those early years is Charles Causley in Launceston. When I first knew him he was a schoolmaster and had not long started to publish his poems.

From the beginning, Charles's notion of being a friend was to encourage you to be a writer. And he worked at this friendship. He sent people to see me. He reviewed a new book when it appeared. He arranged for radio and TV programmes to happen.

Then I began to see him in Launceston. He would show me the sights (and how they connected with the past) and show me the places that appeared in his work.

But what impressed me most was the way he was saying Hello, right and left, as we walked through the streets. Everyone seemed to know him . . . young men and women, girls and boys . . . people he had taught as a schoolmaster . . . their parents. I envied him this. He belonged to the place where he lived. In St. Ives most of the artists I knew (apart from Peter Lanyon) had come from somewhere else.

In September 1959, Peter and I had gone on a two-week gliding course at a small disused wartime airfield by the cliffs at Perranporth. On the weekend we returned to St. Ives to be with our families. And arranged to meet in The Golden Lion, by the parish church, for a Saturday noon drink. When we came out of the pub we saw Francis Bacon, and a young man, coming down the same narrow sidewalk.

He told us he had come down to Penzance, to get away from London, in order to paint for his first show at the Malborough Gallery. But he didn't like Penzance. He thought he would come over to St. Ives. Peter knew of a vacant studio in the Back Road. And we took him to see Boots Redgrave who would know what cottages were available. She suggested St. Brigid's, a cottage on the front that Francis rented.

We were then in Teetotal Street (in Wilhelmina Barns-Graham's cottage) before moving, in November, to the house in Bedford Road. And Francis would come for dinner and talk.

And it was his talk and his presence that stimulated us. He was the best-read of all the painters I knew. (Perhaps because he didn't have any formal education.) When I first knew him, Proust was the writer he liked. Then it was T. S. Eliot, the Greek plays. And, towards the end of his life, Shakespeare.

He also said things in conversation which I could connect with my work.

I told him I was in London, in Paddington, waiting for the midnight train to take me, overnight, to St. Ives. I went into the bar at the station to have a drink. The only other person was a woman in her mid-forties. She was sitting on a stool by the bar also having a drink. It was winter, she had on a fur coat. I went over and started to talk.

Then she said quietly, "I know what you want."

And Francis replied, "That's a very sophisticated statement."

In three months he finished the paintings for his new show and went back to London. And he began to send me books. The first one: *The Letters of Van Gogh*.

Soon after he would phone from London. Could I get him a room in a hotel as he would like to come down for a few days.

And we would have a small party for him. Inviting the other painters and their wives. There was always a sense of excitement when Francis came down.

And he continued to tell me things.

Once, in St. Ives, we were waiting for a bus to take us, across the moors, to Penzance. When he said: "The whole person is in the physical appearance if you know how to read it."

Over lunch I said, "You're giving me all this. What can I give you?"

"Send me a copy of a new book as it comes out. Someday you'll tell it to somebody else. Which is how it works."

But after a while, when Francis would arrive on a visit, I would say, "I'll phone Peter and tell him you're down. And we'll get together."

"Must I?"

"He's my best friend here. If he knew you were down and didn't see him—it wouldn't be good for me."

I soon realized that Francis, for some reason, didn't like Peter. Perhaps because sexually they were so opposite. Francis would say to me, "He's such a romantic———."

And when I told Peter that Francis phoned to say he was coming down, Peter said with a smile, "We'll have to find some young man for him."

Or was it something else? Something that George Dyer—(who Francis came down with and later sent down so he could get on with some work in London).

I asked George if he saw Christopher Isherwood when he was in London? I read in a paper that Isherwood had been to England.

George Dyer didn't know who Isherwood was.

I started to explain.

"Him," George Dyer shouted. *"He hates him."*

(Except George, like the French, did not pronounce the *h*'s.)

For George went on. "He must be good. Francis butters up painters if they are not much good. But if anyone *is* good———."

Or perhaps, it was Margaret who saw Francis more clearly than any of us.

Years later, I came across a notebook where she wrote things. About Francis. How he could ensnare you with his talk, his warmth, his presence. "I was coming down the stairs and at the bottom of the stairs, he holds my hand to say goodbye and I can look down into his eyes. His wicked eyes, grey like stones. And the smile is there, and I wonder if there's a fine contempt behind it."

When I would go up to London to see a publisher or an editor, or to have a break from St. Ives, I would phone Francis to let him know I was taking the overnight train.

He would leave the front door ajar—and come down when I knocked. After asking about Margaret and the children he would, without any preliminaries, talk about the work he was doing. What was difficult.

"As soon as you introduce a second figure on the canvas you halve the immediacy—instantly."

I thought: Is that why he paints triptychs?

And said, "The most difficult thing I found was to describe someone going to the toilet. I ended a bad first novel with that."

For about ten seconds he was quiet. And looked down. Then looked up and said in his flat voice, "That would make a good picture."

Next time I came up, for his new show at the Malborough with Henry Moore, there was

Francis Bacon, 1963

a new triptych. The left-hand panel had the figure of a man in the nude, his back to you, sitting on a toilet. And a white pipe came away from the toilet towards the edge of the painting.

In 1964, Peter Lanyon died as a result of a gliding accident. He was on a high performance glider in Somerset. And when he came to land he came in too high. He reacted as a racing driver (which he told me he wanted to be) by putting on the brakes. On a glider the effect of this is to stall the glider.

Peter was forty-six.

A few weeks after the funeral—Francis phoned. He would like to come down. Could I get him a room in a hotel?

I arranged for a number of people to come the next day to the house. Mostly painters and their wives.

We were all in the large front room, the tall dormer window, the small garden in front with the mimosa. Francis was sitting in the comfortable chair that he liked, looking at everyone. Who, in turn, were looking at him. When he said, "Is everyone glad that Peter is dead?"

In 1965 I went back to Canada, to the University of New Brunswick in Fredericton as their first resident writer. I stayed three months in the autumn and early winter. And three months from January to the early spring of 1966.

The people at the university couldn't have been nicer. But I didn't like Fredericton. I felt cut off. And couldn't wait to get back to St. Ives and the family.

Yet, when I returned to St. Ives, I wrote two stories, "By a Frozen River" and "Thin Ice," because of living in Fredericton. And, twenty years later, when I was living in Toronto, writing the stories for the collection *Something Happened Here*, I wrote "A Maritime Story" that went back to that time.

I also started the novel *From a Seaside Town* in Fredericton. And continued to write it, for the next four years, in St. Ives.

Perhaps the isolation I felt in Fredericton connected with what I felt in St. Ives. I wanted to write about a family, on their own, and the friends they had.

When Francis came down on a visit, I said, "I'm thinking of putting you in a novel that I'm writing."

"Make me the way I am. Make me a queer."

"I intend to."

When I finished the novel, I took the family for a holiday in London. Francis came to dinner. Gave Margaret French perfume, the children £5 notes, and in a plain brown paper bag gave me two bottles of Chateau Haut Brion. "Open them on publication."

From a Seaside Town was published in July of 1970 by Macmillan of London and Macmillan in Canada. It was Philip Oakes's essay in *The Sunday Times* which sold out the UK edition.

Heinrich Böll also liked it. He and his wife, Annemarie, did the first translation. The last was done in 1991 by my Dutch translator Pleuke Boyce, for Van Gennep, Amsterdam.

In 1974, when she was forty-four, Margaret was told that she had cancer.

A few days later, not knowing what to do, I went to the large attic room and wrote "A Writer's Story" about our early years together.

She died in the front room of the house—where I brought down a bed. The large dormer window looking out to the small garden and the mimosa tree. The fireplace with the nice tiles. The two deep alcoves on either side for which Peter Lanyon said he would paint pictures for us. And the piano which she used to play.

She was perceptive about people and made it possible for me to write in circumstances that other wives would not have accepted. But she was also independent and tough.

The BBC was making a film not long after *From a Seaside Town* was published. The last day's shooting was finished, and the producer and the cameraman would be returning to Plymouth. The producer took us out to dinner at The Ship Inn in Mousehole. The cameraman had too much to drink. And it was his powerful car we were in to return to St. Ives. On a dark night he began to drive too fast for the narrow winding roads of the North Coast. When Margaret said loudly, her hand on the door handle, "If you don't slow down *right now*, I'm opening the door and jumping out."

He slowed down immediately.

Afterwards, she said, "I was thinking of the three children."

In 1977, while Margaret could still walk slowly in the house, with a stick, I had a telephone call from Canada, from Ottawa. It was Denis

Deneau. He told me he had not long started as a publisher. He would like to commission me to write a sequel to *Canada Made Me.* "Show how it is today."

I thanked him. But said I was not interested.

"You don't have a Canadian publisher," Deneau said.

"That's right."

"Can I publish your next book?"

"It will be a book of short stories, *Thin Ice.*"

"Fine."

"You can have the stories, if you publish *Canada Made Me* first."

"I would be delighted."

And that is how the first Canadian publication of *Canada Made Me* came about in the spring of 1979, twenty-one years after it was published by Putnam.

In the autumn of 1979 Deneau published *Thin Ice.* (All of the fifteen stories in it were broadcast on Robert Weaver's "Anthology.") Deneau arranged a promotion tour for both books starting in Vancouver and ending in Halifax. A new generation had grown up since the 1958 Putnam edition of *Canada Made Me.* And there was a different reaction. Deneau published a second edition in 1982. And the book is still in print in Canada.

When Margaret died I stopped writing. I didn't see any point in writing. And then, when I wanted to write, I kept asking my painter friends. Has it gone? And they said, Oh no, it'll come back. But I wasn't very happy.

On an invitation, I went to East Germany because my publisher, Reclam in Leipzig, was bringing out a second and larger selection from my stories. I stayed in Jena, was shown around Leipzig, Dresden, Weimar, Meissen. But East Germany did not make me start to write again.

With *Canada Made Me* and *Thin Ice* recently published in Canada I decided, early in 1980, to go to Toronto (a city I had never lived in before). Paule Deneau got me an apartment in Yorkville near Yonge and Bloor. I wrote every day but things were not connecting.

I only had a few weeks left in Toronto (before returning to St. Ives) when the Book Page editor of the *Toronto Star,* Peter Sypnowich, and his wife, Marcia, invited me to a dinner party. They had other people, but it was for Anne Boyd (née Sarginson) and me to meet. She lived across the road.

After the dinner party, late at night, we walked through the little park opposite—I remember the fog. And postponed my flight back to St. Ives. When I did go I came back quickly. We were married in August 1983 in Toronto City Hall.

Anne was a teacher of French in public schools in Toronto. She was born in England, in the Lake District, went as a companion-governess to a family with six children in Notre-Dame-de Grevanchon, thirty minutes from Le Havre. Then to a teacher training college (Goldsmiths) in London. And after teaching in London she went to Paris where she lived in the 1960s before coming to Canada.

The first story I wrote, after we met, was "Because of the War." (It was the first story I had written in five or six years.) Set in Toronto, it would become the opening story of the new collection, *Something Happened Here.* It was commissioned by Robert Weaver for CBC "Anthology." It was the final story in the new German selection by Claassen. It was the title story of my first book with my Dutch publisher, Van Gennep. It was published in *Encounter.* (As were most of the stories in the new collection.) And it was the first story translated (more than once) into Chinese and published in Beijing.

I enjoyed living in Toronto because of Anne. Her house, right opposite the park, was also close to a ravine where we would walk the dog. And where Sarah, our young cat, would come up the little park to meet us. There were good bookstores, good libraries, close by. And a vast cemetery laid out like a botanical garden.

Deneau had put five of my books in print. And Penguin had brought out a generous selection from the stories.

Once a month I went to the Bookmen's Lunch Club where members took turns to host. Most of the members were publishers and some literary journalists, a few writers. But the talk was often lively. And it usually went on for several hours. Hosts also invited guests. One time, sitting opposite, was the present prime minister of Canada, Jean Chrétien. (At that time he was in Opposition.) He was a guest of his publisher, Anna Porter. A book had come out, his autobiography. And it was selling well. I thought he had written it. (Later, I was told someone else did.) I asked him: Did he think of writing a novel? He looked slightly startled. He didn't know that politicians wrote novels.

Names began to be mentioned, starting with Disraeli. It was a lively lunch.

Toronto in the 1980s was a new Toronto I was getting to know. It had a lot of vitality. Often at a dinner every person there came from a different country.

For the next eight years I wrote the rest of the stories for *Something Happened Here*. Writers, writing about these stories, have said: "This collection is markedly different from the rest. There seems to be a deepening. Or, there's another layer that's being added to the story."

Technically, the stories are different from those before. But it was because of Anne that I was able to write them. Not only did she make it possible for me to concentrate on the work, by looking after the practical things. But she brought so much that was new to me and to the way we were living. And especially her love for France.

In 1981, on our first holiday, she said, "I want to show you why I love France so much."

She showed me first the Paris she knew. All the places, the restaurants, I had only read about. Then to the Auvergne, near Le Puy, where we stayed with her friends, Georges and Jeannine Moiselet. She met them when she was an English teacher at the Berlitz school in Paris in the early 1960s. And they were her pupils. Then we went back to Paris. And before the end of the holiday I suggested we go to Dieppe.

This came together in the next story, "Something Happened Here." The character "Georges" in Dieppe is based on Georges Moiselet in Le Puy.

But these first two stories, "Because of the War" and "Something Happened Here," had one thing in common. I couldn't get an ending to them.

I wrote "Because of the War." And it didn't work. No matter what I tried nothing seemed to work. There were a number of scenes. But they didn't hold together. After six or seven months, I decided to introduce a new character, a Mrs. Kronick. She appears in only three short scenes scattered throughout the story. But they have the effect of stitching the story together. I wrote the first one, then the second. And wondered how to end the story. And remembered Francis Bacon. The last time he came to the house, after Margaret came back from hospital—he wanted to see how she looked. And said, "She looks better than I have ever seen her."

Sitting around the table having lunch. Francis said, "When I leave a person I don't care if I never see them again." And Margaret said, "What about those you love?" And he said, "Of course, with those you love there's always regret." And I remembered that. And put it at the end of "Because of the War." And I knew I had the end of the story.

The same thing happened with "Something Happened Here." After Anne and I were three days in Dieppe, we took the ferry to Newhaven. (We were to fly back to Toronto from London.) I said to Anne on the ferry (I still rented the place in St. Ives) that I'd like to go there and do a rough draft of a story. I saw Anne off, went to St. Ives, wrote the story. But I couldn't get an ending to it.

I would work in the morning then go out at noon for a walk. Up the slope of the steep hill, to the other side where Porthmeor Beach is with the cemetery above it. And walk towards the Bronze Age fields, with the stone fences, by the cliffs. Then come back the same way. This went on for almost two weeks. Then once, on my way back, I saw the cemetery above Porthmeor Beach (I must have seen it, over the years, thousands of times) and noticed that all the gravestones were facing the other way. What I was seeing were blank gravestones. And I knew I had the ending of the story.

Then an unexpected connection was made between St. Ives and Canada. Anne went for a holiday to Cuba with her daughter, Pippa. They were on a beach when she noticed a man was reading *Pride and Prejudice*. She began to talk to him. He was the Canadian painter Ron Bolt. He was on holiday with his wife Judy and daughter Kelly. After they came back we went to their place in the country in southern Ontario. And they came to see us in Toronto.

I began to tell Ron Bolt about St. Ives and the painters I had known. He read my books, went over to St. Ives, and said he would like to do a fine art book, entirely about St. Ives, using (for text) writing from my work.

The result was *The Beat & The Still*.

The title I took from the opening line of a poem that I wrote in St. Ives not long after I arrived. It describes the way the bird flew. It also made me realize that the leaner the language the more ambiguous it becomes and the more suggestive.

*Norman Levine with his wife Anne,
near Le Puy, France, 1984*

Ron Bolt made a second visit to St. Ives. Took a lot of photographs. (He works from photographs.) And there are some haunting images in the book.

It is a splendid book. Its strong point is the way Ron Bolt designed it. He did original work for it: lithographs, etchings, serigraphs. And a suite of prints to go with it. He also painted a number of large paintings that are reproduced in the book. And he supervised its production, in Toronto, by European craftsmen.

For text he has the early poems. The early story, "A Sabbath Walk," about Alfred Wallis. A generous section about St. Ives from *Canada Made Me*. And from the last story that I wrote for *Something Happened Here,* "Gwen John."

Towards the end of the 1980s, Anne's health could not take another Canadian winter. She decided to move to France. She went over, found this villa by the Bassin d'Arcachon. "As soon as I came to the Bassin I knew I wanted to live here."

On Boxing Day in 1990, she came over with her mother, Evelyn, and our two cats and the dog. I came later after the publication of *Something Happened Here.*

Anne has made a splendid garden around the villa. There are a lot of trees. Passersby stop to look and I hear them call it "The English garden." And she is a very popular English teacher. Has over a hundred pupils, of all ages. They come from different parts of this area.

And we have explored it on bicycles. The place is flat but you wouldn't know it because of the vegetation. Pine forests are all around. Oaks, catalpas, mimosa, plane, and plum trees are in the boulevards, the streets, and the gardens. Where the train used to run the tracks have been paved over to make a bicycle path. And we go around the Bassin on this bicycle path.

Or we go on other bicycle paths. These go through forests to the Atlantic. The local historian told me: these paths through the forests to the Atlantic were built by slave labour during the war. For the German soldiers to get to the coast if there was an invasion. Now, the beach is almost deserted.

And, an hour's drive inland, east and north from here, is Bordeaux.

In the long final story, "Soap Opera," in *Something Happened Here,* I have towards the end:

It had rained during the night. Then it froze. On the train back to Toronto the smaller trees were bent over. Some were broken by the weight of the ice. But it all looked pretty. Mile after mile. I thought of a friend, a professor of mathematics at the University of Toronto. He has devoted his life to mathematics and to logic. I asked him, what did he make of it all.

He said. "Nothing lasts. Everything changes." Was this why we keep making connections? Why do I connect Gino's sculpture to that tall brick chimney to those saplings with Joseph Podobitko to Mr Thomas Sachs on the door of the hospital room to those little Jewish cemeteries on Roselawn?

But then, whenever I go to a new place and walk around to get to know it, I inevitably end up in a cemetery.

I like to leave a trace of a person, in a particular place, at a particular time, or in a certain situation. And that, usually, is the impulse to write a story.

But once I start writing, I now expect the story to change.

I started to write "Django, Karfunkelstein & Roses" as a tribute to my literary agent in Zurich, Ruth Liepman. As I was writing it began to change to become about memory. And how it works.

Or it can be a visual connection, as in "Something Happened Here." Seeing blank gravestones in a St. Ives cemetery and connecting with what I was writing about Dieppe.

And while writing this essay, I realize why this autobiographical material becomes more interesting as a short story or a novel. Because only in fiction can I make connections. Between the personal and (something that wasn't there) something larger.

BIBLIOGRAPHY

Poetry:

Myssium, Ryerson, 1948.

The Tightrope Walker, Totem Press, 1950.

I Walk by the Harbour, Fiddlehead Poetry Books, 1976.

Short-story collections:

One Way Ticket, Secker & Warburg, 1961.

I Don't Want to Know Anyone Too Well, Macmillan (London and Toronto), 1971, Deneau, 1981.

Selected Stories, Oberon, 1975.

Thin Ice, Deneau, 1979, Wildwood, 1980.

Why Do You Live So Far Away?, Deneau, 1984.

Champagne Barn, Penguin (Canada and United Kingdom), 1984, Penguin USA, 1985.

Something Happened Here, Viking (Canada and United Kingdom), 1991, Penguin (Canada and United Kingdom), 1992.

Novels:

The Angled Road, Werner Laurie, 1952, McClelland & Stewart, 1953.

From a Seaside Town, Macmillan (Canada and United Kingdom), 1970, Deneau, 1980, Porcupine's Quill, 1993.

Travel memoir:

Canada Made Me, Putnam, 1958, Deneau, 1979, Porcupine's Quill, 1993.

Other:

(Editor) *Canadian Winter's Tales,* Macmillan (Canada and United Kingdom), 1968.

The Beat & The Still, images and design by Ron Bolt, North Editions/Ron Bolt, 1990.

Larry Levis

1946-

First Impression

It isn't dramatic or fashionable to begin with being born, but for me it was an important event. According to the diary of my grandmother, in which little is noted except a half century or more of weather, I was born at 3 A.M. in a rainstorm on the last day of September 1946. When I was twelve, driving a tractor, furrowing out a vineyard of muscats for my father one day, I was for some reason immediately impressed by how lucky I was to have been born at all, especially to be born as a human being rather than, as I wrote later in a poem, "a horse, or a gnat." I was easily impressed, I guess, but the moment was full of wonder.

First Confession

My mother, whose maiden name was Carol Clement Mayo, was Irish. I was raised as a Catholic, which is to say, raised to believe that such terms as "mystery," "spirit," and the "Holy Ghost" were real presences rather than abstractions. To be raised as a Catholic is to grow up feeling guilty for something but not to know quite what it is. At seven, like other children, I went to my First Confession so that I could receive, afterward, my First Communion. Like other children, I had to make up sins on the way to my First Confession, mostly venial sins, like lying or having "bad thoughts." I had made up about ten little sins, but I felt I ought to confess to at least one big Mortal Sin, just to get it down somehow, from the start. A mortal sin was serious business. If you didn't confess, do penance, and gain absolution by Communion, you would go straight to hell in the next life without a lawyer made of air at your side, without even an arraignment or hearing. I looked at the list of the ten mortal sins and realized right away that I didn't qualify as a transgressor for nine of them. The only

one left was a word I didn't understand, and so I thought that must be the sin that I had committed, the one that applied to me. And so, at the age of seven, after confessing my little, imaginary venial sins, I confessed to adultery. I did it in a casual, offhand way, "And uh . . . I committed adultery," I said. The priest stopped mumbling to himself in Latin. There was, in the shadowy, screened, small space of the confessional where I knelt, a silence, a pause. I could tell I'd made some sort of impression. He asked, "How many times, my son?" "Just once," I replied. And then he asked, "How *old* are you?" "I'm seven, Father," I answered. And so he then explained what adultery was. And after he had finished, I said, "Oh no. I haven't done *that!*" And so it must have been something else that I had done that I wished to atone for, though I didn't know what it was. I still don't. But Catholicism works its shrewd miracle in the seven-year-old psyche, or soul, before the mind can question it.

You feel guilty for something or other you've done or just thought about doing, and you can't remember what it was or know what it was, and it keeps you in line, for a while at least, off the streets and out of trouble. Sometimes it works for ages. What else could have coerced peasants to lug huge stones up a hill for a cathedral except a hope to atone for the only sin they had all committed, the sin of being mortal, of being born and knowing they were flesh, and flesh must die. They didn't do it out of *altruism*. It doesn't exist. I was eight or nine when I realized this. I was loitering around by my father's abandoned chicken shed, a long, low building that still smelled vaguely of chicken dung. I was trying to pray without any self-interest. I couldn't do it. St. Augustine knew this long before I did.

Besides, it was a world with a chicken shed in it. My father once had a going egg business. He hated it. He hated chickens, and he finally grew to despise even their eggs. "What was the happiest day of your life?" I once asked him. "The day I got out of the chicken business," he answered; there was more to the world than belief, or disbelief.

I wasn't religious and never have been. The Mass was in Latin, and the incomprehensible sound of it had a beauty, but going to Mass always bored me. It seemed like a complete waste of time. And catechism classes were worse. The nuns longed for any opportunity to punish us. They watched as if we were a group of suspects the police had rounded up. They knew we were guilty of *something*.

The Catholic church understood Freud's concept of the superego centuries before he articulated it in 1940. The cathedral on a hill is its palpable and visible representation, or, in Freud's simile, the superego is "like a garrison above a captured town." In the case of the church, it is a garrison so effective that it doesn't even need soldiers. Its windows are beautiful. Its frescoes and painting and sculptures, depicting absence in enormous detail, are priceless. It enabled Dante to imagine hell, and it was at least the stepmother to a ninety-year period of Italian art, a period of corruption, betrayal, incest, assassination, intrigue, and unsurpassable art. The church knew beauty and evil were sleeping together, and gave both allowances to do it. Two thousand years of stolid, industrious virtue and Swiss peace perfected the cuckoo clock and the dairy cow. I suspect the Swiss dairyman had a good deal of placid self-esteem. Michelangelo hated himself. And a later figure, Caravaggio, was mean-tempered, an inadvertent murderer whose self-portrait, as Goliath, is full of self-contempt and despair.

In the Age of Therapy, First Confessions could be seen as a ritualized form of child abuse, psychological in method, permanent in effect. But you can't take the Vatican to court. The painting on the chapel's ceiling doesn't respond to a summons and is tricky evidence.

In my case, I would lie awake as a child, full of vague yearnings which were sexual, which I did not know were entirely normal. I was never abused nor molested nor violated as a child. I simply felt that I *was* a violation of some kind, that my being alive was a violation, that I was guilty of being alive.

But if it was a violation, it was a pleasure. Besides, how guilty can anyone feel, at seven or eight? I was a boy like other boys. I didn't rebel against guilt, I forgot about it.

Before I was born, a priest drowned in our swimming pool. He had a weak heart and dove into cold, fresh water. My mother came out with a tray of glasses and ice tea and saw him bobbing there. She felt terrible about it. I always thought it was amazing. Priests were full of a mysterious divinity. They had a little bit of God in them. They weren't supposed to die like other people. This one was a young priest from Kingsburg. His lungs were full of water. His body was heavy. My mother pulled him out and tried to revive him with artificial respiration, but of course it didn't work. I always imagined him floating face down in a robe and vestments, dressed for saying the Mass, and asked my mother about it once when I was still a child. "No, silly," she said, "he had on bathing trunks." God died in his bathing trunks, I thought then, for priests were the form He took on earth. Did He really die, I wondered, or did He just do it to show that he could do it too, flick *It* into the pool water like a Fourth of July sparkler burning too close to the hand? He did a lot of things just for effect, I thought: Yosemite National Park, for example.

Thinking about God made me tired. I had trouble believing in everlasting life. What did it look like? It seemed more likely that one just died in the end, and that was that, I had begun to think. If the spirit rose off you like a mist, so what? I'd hunted quail in thick ground fog that broke up and parted like mist when the sun burned it off. I hunted without a dog and entirely by intuition and always found quail. My senses grew alive and sharp when I hunted. The quail would burst up around me. I had a twenty-gauge shotgun and would usually bring down four or five by the time I'd finished. It felt real. It was pointless to think about God. Heaven made me feel tired, baffled, resigned, sad as when someone tells you a lie, and you know it's a lie, and wonder why he had to do so. When I cleaned the quail they were still warm inside. Their feathers gave off a pungent, wild smell that was like nothing else. I neglected to cut their feet off; it didn't seem important. My mother hated cooking them. I'd have to break the thin gray sticks of their legs off before she was willing to.

People now confess to all kinds of things, in public, on television. I have a feeling they too make up the things they confess to, just as we did, at seven. But they enjoy it, they like confessing to things. If they've done something that can still shock an audience, they even get paid for it, or make money later by confessing it in a book. They are absolved of their sins by the show's ratings and by book sales. We were supposed to feel embarrassment, shame, and contrition over what we had done. We were just kids. But we tried. We'd shut our eyes and concentrate and try to feel each one of those things. We couldn't, and we would feel sorry when we couldn't. They should have paid us money for it.

"But God comes to see without a bell."

The Ranch

Everyone who lived there or worked there always referred to it as, simply, "the ranch." My mother, who is eighty-four now, still lives in the old white brick-and-frame two-story house attached to a weathered, frame windmill tower where there hasn't been a windmill for years. A long gravel driveway lined with orange and olive and tangerine and cypress and palm trees leads up to it, and the gravel looks almost white in the moonlight. A family of owls nests in the spreading—and I was almost about to say "ancient"—limbs of some kind of pine above the roof, and anyone sleeping upstairs can be awakened by their shrieks and screeching at night as they hunt or come back with some drained field mouse to feed to their young. Except for that it is so quiet at night you hear only the quiet if you've been away and lived in a city and come back. In the morning now I am awakened by the sound of a rake over gravel because Johnny Dominguez, who is retired from work on the ranch, still rakes leaves and pine needles from the gravel each morning, either out of habit or because he promised my father he would do so after my father died whether there were leaves or anything to rake there or not. When there are no leaves, he rakes the gravel.

I was born in 1946 in a place that seemed to exist, the fields and vineyards and even the sky over it all, in some motionless and unchanging moment. From the upstairs bedroom window, the rows of vineyards run on to a horizon of foothills, and it has the quiet and proportion of a landscape van Gogh painted once, nothing at all like *The Starry Night,* which changed painting forever perhaps, but the ordered fields he clung to as he painted as if he was clinging to sanity itself before him. My California, the vineyards and orchards on the east side of the San Joaquin Valley, have remained unviolated, for the most part, by developers and suburbs. The land looks as if nothing has changed there. But that isn't so.

The land was settled, and then it was unsettled. My father and other small farmers, in order to keep up economically with a market that demanded earlier and earlier varieties of fruit, especially peaches and plums, tore out old orchards of Reynosa and late Elberta peaches and orchards of late plums and supplanted them with new varieties developed by University of California, Davis that they could harvest in late May and early June and send on refrigerated boxcars to markets in the East. The new varieties, especially peaches with unsigned, authorless, corporate names like Early May Golds or whatever, were attractive to shoppers in supermarkets: they had size, texture, and lots of color, and they were in the markets by late spring. The new varieties of peaches had no flavor and no sweetness. Their flesh was tough instead of ripe and tender. They were the products of modern farming, which had become a product of modern business. And small farmers as well, as Wendell Berry has pointed out in *The Unsettling of America,* a brilliant and too often ignored book, were encouraged to think of themselves as businessmen, as participants in agribusiness as completely as large corporate farmers participated in it. The orchards and vineyards dozed on in their blankets of chemicals, everything from sulphur and malathion to DDT and parathion. As an example of what happened to the land in the midtwentieth century, parathion is interesting: after parathion was sprayed on an orchard, signs were posted along its borders, warning everyone to stay out of it for a week because, theoretically at least, the chemical on unprotected skin could affect the nerve endings and, in dosages large enough, could even paralyze someone who happened to take an innocent stroll through the trees.

The trouble with all this is that small farmers were not corporate business managers. They were small farmers. They took pride in what they did. Agribusiness and modern marketing had little to do with them, but they had to survive and go along with what was called "progress" in those days even when they knew it was someone's idea of a slick hustle.

Laughing in Spanish

That land! It was a kind of paradise preserved, held intact, by the toxic perfume of malathion and sulphur, insecticide sprays, fertilizers, and by the people who worked on it, who were Mexican if they were older, Chicano if younger, who spoke Spanish mostly, and who were underpaid. Many of them lived in poverty and the intermittent misery of unemployment. It's wrong to characterize a people, but in an interview, late in his life, Cesar Chavez gestured toward a family of farm workers sitting under a tree after lunch and said to the journalist next to him, "You see? They are so . . . innocent." I knew exactly what he meant.

"They" were not a "they" to me. They were men I worked with in orchards and vineyards. Their names, which deserve to be mentioned and which won't be unless I do it, were Angel and John Dominguez, Tea, Ignacio Calderon, Ediesto and Jaime Huerta, Coronado, Fermín, and the older man who had beautiful manners and who rarely spoke and who ate his lunch alone, apart from the others, whom they called Senor Solo.

I worked with them regularly, season after season on the ranch, and they teased me endlessly and with great affection. They called me by their chosen nickname for me, Cowboy, the accent falling on the last instead of the first syllable, Cow*boy.* I felt honored to work beside them because I *was* only a boy, and an Anglo boy at that, and the son of the *patron,* my father. They would have found the term "Hispanic" imprecise and puzzling and amusing, and the new word, Chicano, had a political hue to it and referred to the young. As far as they were concerned, they were Mexicans. Toward women and children they were gallant and infinitely considerate. They talked and sang in a Spanish that seemed to me full of mysterious grace and almost courtly manners which they blended with put-downs in slang to hilarious effect: "Con su permiso, Jaime, su cafe no vale tres chingaderas. Pero muchisima gracias, sin embargo." Which is to say: "With your permission, Jimmy, your coffee is not worth three motherfuckers. But I thank you for it with an infinite gratitude nevertheless." To which Jaime, holding his thermos of coffee, might reply, though I translate it: "Though I have so far refrained from mentioning it because it was a task requiring no courage and performed as an act of simple decency and out of sanitary considerations, it has occurred to me that I did, however inadvertently, save your life the other day. I killed a shit eating dog." And they would go on: "Spoken thanks, in that case, would be a form of dishonor. And therefore my gratitude shall take the material form of five million frozen turds paid to you in installments the day after each Christmas for as long as I live, Don Pínche."

Fermín made it into an art, almost. He had been well educated somewhere, and was articulate in Spanish and English, but had got into trouble of some kind either here or in Mexico, and so slipped into the anonymity and oblivion of migrant labor camps. Once, pretending to be a kind of deposed *grandee,* he began his elaborate put-down in this manner: "Most of us working patiently alongside you today, *Querido Flaco,* though we did not enjoy it nor do we expect any payment for laboring overtime, did try, last night, out of our kind consideration for your happiness, to instruct your *novia* in the art of love. I will say she began to respond with more and more enthusiasm, but with only a slight improvement in skill. She is, however, an eager student whose attention and stamina never wavered even after she had exhausted her teachers, who remain—even if one of them said, later, that 'it was like trying to teach a stick to fly'—your loyal and generous friends. I think, *Kamikajisimo,* I should mention that at one point in the night, brushing out her *pendeja,* she compared your *falo,* you know, your *pleaser,* to a communion wafer in church, and said that the wafer, the host, stayed harder longer as it melted in her mouth in a matter of seconds than your *pene* ever has, wherever she has found it. But as for what she might confess next time before she takes Communion, I wouldn't worry too much. One must feel some contrition for one's sins in order to confess them, and what she feels is far from even the remotest forms of regret. As Father Cabrón explained it to me when I asked about it, her sensual anticipation of further instruction as well as her almost continual state of expectant sexual arousal these days are in reality not feelings at all, but sensations. In such a condition, he said, clear thinking is impossible for her, just as it always has been."

Apparently it mattered little to Fermín that Kijima was almost sixty, had emigrated from Okinawa, spoke nothing but Japanese, and had never had a girlfriend or even a friend, as far as anyone knew, except for a half-blind mottled dog that slept in the shade under someone's car or pickup most of the afternoon.

Everyone had laughed, of course. And Kijima smiled with pleasure and complete incomprehension. But then the oldest men there, at first Angel Dominguez, and then Tea, told Fermín that the joke was unkind, that it amounted to no more than the pointless humiliation of an old man, even if that man did not understand a word of it, and that he, Fermín, should feel ashamed and should apologize to Kijima even if he could not understand the apology either. We worked on, picking peaches, in silence after this, for most of us had laughed. No one had ever contradicted the judgement of Angel or Tea, and no one did so now. Finally, after about an hour, Fermín went up to Kijima and apologized for telling the joke. Kijima bowed and smiled, not understanding a word. And then, slowly, one by one, everyone working in the trees would come down from his ladder and go up to Kijima where he was working and apologize, in Spanish, mostly. In my case, in English. Kijima had no idea what we were saying to him, but he bowed to each of us and smiled anyway.

"You see? They are so innocent," said Chavez. They had dignity as well. The slow ritual under the trees by which each of us gave back to Kijima the dignity we had swiped from him by laughing was part of the innocence of that world. It is not extinct, that innocence, even now. It exists on the outskirts of small towns like Parlier and Del Rey, places where "executives would never want to tamper." It would make it easier for us to live, I guess, if it were extinct, because then there would be nothing to remind us of how much of it had disappeared, nothing to disgrace us by the sudden austere appearance of dignity in the voices of two old men laboring in the trees, working in a slow but unwavering rhythm, as if there was in it a pride to maintain, in each numberless and quiet twist of their wrists something that can no longer be understood, some *dignidad*, something completely unmarketable in the world.

I idealize them, of course. They would be puzzled by my praise of them. And tease me about it. One day after work Ignacio said, "Hey, Cowboy, it's payday. You wanna come with me to Parlier? I know this place where they have *putas*. I like the big ones myself, the ones with

real long legs, but they got some little tiny ones too, if you want. Come with me." I was maybe twelve at the time. "I can't," I said, "My mom won't let me." But after a few seconds had passed, I asked, "How much are the little tiny ones?" And they all howled with laughter. I'm sure I idealize them. But oblivion has no right to claim them without my respect, without their names written down, here and elsewhere.

My Parents and One Good Line I Wrote at Sixteen

Their morals were Victorian and their politics were conservative. They were children of the Depression and wary of most social change. They were also children of the Cold War and its successful propaganda, which made them fear communism and the labor union Chavez organized. They belonged to the Skeleton Club and would go dancing there in a large hall with other farm families, but they remained suspicious of the Grange, which they thought leaned toward socialism.

Once, while I was working with Tea in a vineyard of muscats, I made some complaint about my father. Tea felt I was wrong and hastened to correct me. "No," he said, "Su padre tiene dignidad." I asked him what things made up *dignidad*. "Corazón," he replied, and then smiled, "Corazón y cojónes." Heart and balls. Courage, in other words. My father certainly had that. Once, as I was riding with him in his pickup along a two-lane country road surrounded by vineyards, we came upon a small group of men in the middle of the road, a circle with two men inside it. They were young men, farm laborers, Mexicans, and one held a grape-cutting knife with a sharpened blade in his hand, his fore and index finger on either side of the curved point so that it could slash like a razor. The other may have had a knife as well, but all I saw was a coat rolled around one arm to ward off the other's blade. My father abruptly stopped the truck, told me to stay in it, got out and walked without any hesitation right into the middle of the circle, between the two men, shoving each one roughly back and away from the other, and then demanded that the one holding it give him the knife. The man did so, an expression of surprise or consternation on his face. My father got back in the truck but didn't say anything about it. We drove on and had coffee in a little lunch counter in Parlier where other farmers usually gathered in the late morning to kid each other and to complain about poor prices, poor crops. My father didn't mention the fight even then, when someone asked him what he'd done that morning. I didn't either. They were ranchers, farmers, and they looked like it in their rumpled work clothes and hats with soiled brims and stained hat bands. I didn't say anything there unless one of them asked me a question.

When we got back to the house, my father did what he always did. He ate a light lunch, went into the living room to rest for a half hour or so before going back to work, and listened to classical music or opera while he lay on the couch. He was neither articulate nor talkative. Like Robert Lowell's portrait of Colonel Shaw, my father seemed "to wince at pleasure / and suffocate for privacy." I asked him once if he believed in God. He said he did. I asked him if that guaranteed everyone some kind of eternal life. He said he didn't see how it could and that such a thing seemed impossible whenever he had thought about it.

He was reserved, but not dour. He could always make my mother laugh with some joke or other, and did so almost daily. By the time I was in high school, my sisters and my brother were off in college, and I was the only child still living with my parents. It was clear to me, especially as they grew older, that the two of them really loved each other, even delighted each other. They were an example of something, especially to me. I've been married three times and divorced three times. But I did at least once witness a marriage that was happy, one that lasted. In my case, I could say, with Yeats, that one must make a choice between one's art and one's life. Once or twice, I have done that, I suppose. But it seems to me I had to choose between one kind of life or another kind of life. Yeats makes the choice sound rather grand and heroic and heartbreaking. I'd say, in retrospect, that it's heartbreaking enough, for everyone involved. But to actually split up with someone because you believe it is a sacrifice for Art is, it seems to me, a kind of semiprecious delusion, as Yeats suggests as he concludes his poem.

In his whole life, my father wrote only two letters to me. Both began "How's tricks?" My father felt about as comfortable with writing as someone might who holds a poisonous snake on the end of a stick, or, on these occasions, at the end of a pencil. But my father was full of contradictions, as most people are. If he wasn't terribly talkative, the things he did say mattered. And I might as well continue with the aforementioned snake. My family had a cabin in the Sierras at Shaver Lake, and, one afternoon, hiking with my brother and my sisters, all of them far older than I, I saw, or at least I thought I saw, a rattlesnake resting under a manzanita bush, and I shouted and screamed. We all raced back to the shore of the lake where our boat was tied and where my father and mother were preparing a picnic. My brother and my sisters, by the time we got there, had ceased to believe that I had seen a snake at all, and, I confess, I was beginning to disbelieve it myself. It might have been the way the sun was shining on the manzanita limbs and the ground beneath them. But they kept teasing me, until I felt humiliated and began crying. I was maybe seven or so at the time and kept insisting to my father that there really was a snake at the top of the path above us. I was simply afraid of rattlesnakes, and I was a child, and at that moment I suspected that I had imagined seeing one when there was nothing there. My father turned and went up the path and then, a few minutes later, came back. They were still teasing me and I was still crying and still angry at them and at myself, and, by then, I was certain I had only imagined the snake. My brother looked at my father and said, sarcastically, "Well, what about it? Was there a snake up there?" I waited for my father to confirm everyone's suspicion that I was lying about the whole thing. A summer of endless teasing and humiliation stretched before me. And then my father said the most marvelous thing, which I was sure, even then, was a lie. He said, "Yeah, there was a snake up there. I saw it." My father lied for me! He could see I was miserable, and he lied for me. I knew it and he knew it. If the snake had existed, how would he have known where to look for it? Why would it still be there if he had known?

Years later, I would still remember the incident. I do not know whether my father had an imagination or not. He did not allow it to show, if he did. But he certainly defended the imagination, or my imagination, by lying for me that day. And he saved it from ridicule.

As a child I drew all the time, and by the age of twelve I was drawing nudes in school when I was bored. One day my mother found a kind of obscene anatomical sketch of a naked woman in my pants pocket and showed it to my father later in the day. My father was outraged. "Did you draw this?" he asked me. I couldn't answer, but my face told him all he needed to know. "I'm disgusted with you," he said.

Love and shame. Imagination had its consequences. His remark had expelled me from the paradise of his affection. I no longer thought of myself or was capable of thinking of myself as categorically *good*. As in "a good boy." Of course my father forgave me and meant nothing final by what he had said. But it had changed things. It had changed my relationship to him and changed the way I saw myself. My sketch mocked the woman in it, who was fat, naked, with huge breasts and thighs and flourishing pubic hair. And my father had only contempt for the kind of disrespect in it. The drawing meant nothing much to me. I was twelve. I was interested in sex. And afraid of sex. I had to imagine a naked body I could not have in the flesh. But the sketch changed things. I wasn't a good boy after that. I did not have to try to be a good boy, especially, because I wasn't one. My father had as much as said so.

My father couldn't have prepared me better for my life as a poet if he had tried, if he had read Homer to me every night, for in two years I would take up smoking, out of a sort of rebellion, and at the age of fifteen I was the only kid for miles around who owned an album by Bob Dylan, and I was certainly the only kid in my high school who read poetry, who loved T. S. Eliot mostly, who read Frost and then Stevens. Four years later, when I was sixteen, I decided, one night, to try to write a poem. When I was finished I turned out the light. I told myself that if the poem had one good line in it I would try to be a poet. And then I thought, no, you can't say "try." You will either be a poet, and become a better and better one, or you will not be a poet. The next morning I woke and looked at what I'd written. It was awful. I knew it was awful. But it had one good line. One. All the important decisions in my life were made in that moment.

My father died at seventy-eight of a combination of Parkinson's, a series of small strokes,

and old age. After the largely unconvincing Catholic service, my family went back to the ranch, and I held the box with his "ashes" in it. It was heavier than the term "ashes" implies. His remains were bits of whitened bone mostly, and, with my family around me, I strewed them into a furrow in an orchard of Elberta peaches he was proud of. No one mentioned God or Heaven or anything like that. It would have been tasteless somehow. No one said anything except my mother, who said "He's home." We all walked back to the house.

My mother's hair is snow-white. It has been for years. She never moved from the ranch after my father died, and she is still strong and plucky. She needs a knee operation which she has no interest in getting. She will sometimes tell me that certain things in my poems didn't happen the way I said they did, that I had made up things and made them sound like facts. I remembered them, or remembered them told to me, as I wrote them. But perhaps she's right. Anecdotes don't reveal her. She has always been more a presence in my life, someone forgiving, sympathetic beyond what I sometimes deserved, loving, irreplaceable. When I go to the ranch now to see her, she holds my arm as we go up the steps. This step. Then the next.

Blame and accusation fill the best-selling memoirs of our time. The parents are usually indicted for just about every kind of neglect, abuse, and failure. I couldn't blame mine for anything, not even my father's remark, which was mild enough as things go with parents and children. If I took it seriously enough for it to liberate me in some way, I guess I can only blame my shrewd, calculating unconscious for that. For my father and mother, I feel only gratitude. They always helped me. They didn't see how I'd ever make a living as a poet, and they worried, and they always helped me.

High School

I was reading Yeats. I had my own copy passed down by my sister Sheila, who has always encouraged me. I was glad to have my own book because our high school librarian had taken Yeats's poems out of the stacks. One day he had surprised two girls laughing over "Leda and the Swan," which their teacher had recommended they read. I don't know why he removed it except that the high school was in the country, in a farming community. Sex with swans is not funny in a farming community, I guess. Sex with animals period is not funny, I suppose our librarian believed. Yeats was banned. Yeats was obscene. That was that.

One of the girls (they *were* girls, then) said, "She did it with a *swan?* She was pregnant and told everyone a *swan* knocked her up? Yeah right." The girl's name was Liz. I had an unspoken crush on her for four years. I had acne. I was shy around girls, though I desired them. I wasn't much good at football and only mediocre as a swimmer. I had the world's slowest car, a 1957 four-door Plymouth Plaza with a push-button transmission and a flathead six engine. I had been on horses that were faster, both in acceleration and top-end speed. I tried to mask my insecurity by seeming worldly and indifferent, a cynical, adolescent clown. I didn't "get laid," as they put it then, though I wanted to. Sex in high school was less common in the midsixties than it became later, although some couples who were "going together" had achieved that important, decently human pleasure. In my senior year, I took Liz home from some class party or other. She kissed me goodnight, sweetly but seriously. If she had merely intended it as therapy, it worked far better than weeks of counseling. When I saw her twenty years later at a reunion, she had become a vice president of some corporation in Oregon and a marathon runner. She was still beautiful. They had all grown up, Liz, Cathy, Sharon, but they were all still beautiful, I thought, and they were now far more interesting. Cathy asked me about a book by the poet Sharon Olds because I'd written something for the jacket copy. I was amazed. I thought she lived in the untroubled waters of the Beautiful and had no need of poetry. My innocence was mostly ignorance, I thought then, after we had spoken.

Jeff Riehl was my best friend in those years, and Frank Anderson and Wayne Ota were close friends. I was lucky to know them. No one could have had better company than theirs. They were intelligent and funny. We could talk about anything together, no matter how foolish it was. They knew I was interested in poetry, and they didn't ridicule me for it, or ask what I'd do with it in the future, or how I would make a living. No time in my life was as emotionally awkward and difficult as adolescence and high school. I felt ridiculous for a

year and a half before meeting them and becoming friends. There's nothing corny or sentimental about remembering them and how they interrupted my useless loneliness and useless self-pity, both of which are ways vanity disguises itself.

By 1965, some of the boys in my high school would go off to Vietnam, some would die there. The young woman who did it with a swan created tragedy. The swan went back to being just a swan, after he did it with her, and no one could find him among the innumerable others. The librarian also taught Latin. I don't know what became of him or if he's still alive. But he looked ageless, fifty or more with the face of a boy. Easily embarrassed. So much of the world seemed obscene to him then, when it was not, especially.

Hearts and Minds

As the years went on, it was the Vietnam War that became obscene. My friend Ed Zamora died in Vietnam. He was Hispanic or Chicano or simply of Mexican origin, however you prefer to say it, and he had dropped out of Reedley Junior College because he couldn't afford college and had to go to work, and the draft picked him up. He died and I'm alive. I don't understand it. The injustice of it, the random, unpatternable thing life was, and is, feels like guilt at first, and then matures (though the verb is obscene in the context) into sorrow. I lived, he didn't. Helen is brushing her hair. Troy is burning. Robert McNamara wept last night on television. It took him thirty years, but he did it, finally. The swan is squabbling over a crust of bread thrown by a child. The rented paddle boats make a splashy sound on the pond. The swan is just a swan.

Nineteen years after his death, I found my friend's name on the wall of the Vietnam Veterans Memorial in Washington, D.C. I touched the carved letters of it with my fingers, then my face was wet with tears before I had any warning. Usually there is a second or two in which I have always been able to stop myself from crying. Those occasions are so infrequent. Our country teaches us not to weep. Not to grieve. It's almost a part of some curriculum of indifference, as if a new car could console us. I begin by thinking those years are part of my past, and the time swarms around me with its presences. Troy is a few acres of blurry grass, scattered stones, wind. The students I teach feel about as much for the Vietnam era as they do for the fall of Carthage, and they have a right to. But for most of my generation, that time lives on like an incurable affliction, like a tremor in the hand. I remember President Clinton at a news conference on television. He paused, listening to a difficult question. He listened but was thinking of something else, the famous "thousand yard stare" on his face, I thought, the trait, the ineradicable if intermittently appearing, unasked-for tattoo of a generation.

A Misdiagnosis

I wasn't brave about it. At seventeen I simply knew that I did not want to go to Vietnam. I was afraid. I didn't want to die there. I didn't especially want to kill anyone, either. And I knew that if I didn't want to shoot a soldier in the Viet Cong, I probably would not. Being a Communist did not seem a sufficient reason for killing someone. But he might have had several good reasons for killing me.

There were ways to avoid the draft, and the most expedient was to stay in college. I heard of one young man who showed up at the induction center in Oakland with his father's deer rifle, a 30.06, I think it was. He told the officials there that he wanted to go, he wanted badly to go to Vietnam, but, he said, "I just wanna kill 'em with my own gun, OK? Is that so hard to unnerstan', hunh?" They didn't take him.

It seemed only a matter of time before the war escalated enough so that they would draft students anyway. If the critics of Dan Quayle are correct, I wasn't brave either. I did what he did. I signed up for the California Air National Guard. My brother was in it, and somehow they found a place for me. I didn't last long. I may have the shortest military career on record: four days.

My balls kept me out of Vietnam. Not anything "ballsy" or rebellious that I did. No, I thank my balls, my testicles, for keeping me out of the Vietnam War. Let me explain: The year before I entered high school, my testicles, especially the right one, began to grow in size. I was scared and too embarrassed and ashamed to tell anyone about this. But after a few weeks,

my scrotal sack was the size of a large grapefruit. Because of my Catholic upbringing, I thought it was my fault, that I had caused this to happen, that it was my punishment for the arousals and hard-ons of adolescence which happened with the frequency of thirst, punishment for the ways I fantasized about women, all women, younger, older, real, completely imagined, thin as pages in magazines or bosomy in the school desk beside mine. Our family doctor, Campbell Covington, also a Catholic, a man with a rich Carolina accent, said, "Wow, that thing's as big as a softball!" But it was only a hydrocele, a water sac around the right scrotal sac. It required a simple operation. When I asked him if it was because of something I'd done, he knew immediately what I was thinking and feeling. "No way," he said, "You haven't done anything. What's happened to your right nut, that's congenital, that was in the cards years ago. Now give me all that guilt you've been walking around with. Yeah, give it up. Leave it right here in the office." Portnoy knew what he was doing. I didn't, exactly. But after Dr. Covington talked to me, a vast weight lifted off my naive, provincial shoulders. I knew so little. I may as well have been raised by wolves in comparison to kids who had grown up in the town.

And so, six years later, at nineteen, I failed to pass the medical exam for induction into the California Air National Guard. I didn't know what I was doing there anyway. I had arrived late on my second day at base, wearing my new, very dark green fatigues, and was told to race to the parade grounds. I couldn't find my "unit" there. I didn't even know who they were, and so I "fell out" with guys who looked like me, guys dressed in fatigues, and therefore formed the only one-person line in the formation, standing at the back. When the sergeant shouted, "About Face!" everyone turned around, and I found myself leading them, a company of airplane mechanics. That was why they were dressed in fatigues. I was an Admin. Spec. 4.; I could type. If I was ordered to go with the mechanics and work with them in the hangar, I could foresee the fiery wreckage of a jet. All because of me. I wandered back to the building and there was nothing for me to do, of course, and so I was told to get coffee for everyone, six cups of coffee. I was walking back when I spilled one of them, and my fatigues had a yard-long dark stain through the rest of the day. I felt as ridiculous as I looked. There was again nothing to do, so I was given a manual to read. One chapter was about what to do with top secret information in the event of imminent capture by the enemy. There was only one correct answer: "Refer to your commanding officer."

Two days later they told me I was discharged from the guard. It was a medical discharge, and so, I guess, an honorable one. They said I would have to have exploratory surgery done because I had a tumor, maybe benign, maybe malignant, on my right ball. It had always been larger than a normal right ball, I thought then; even after the water sac operation. God was punishing me slowly and gradually, I thought, by giving me cancer of the right nut! I had tried to avoid dying in Vietnam by joining the jet jockeys local, only to find out I was dying anyway! And even if I wasn't, even if the tumor was found to be benign, I would then be transferred, according to military procedures, not back to the air national guard, but to the army and, probably, to Vietnam. Driving home that day, thinking I probably had cancer, I looked at the leaves on the passing trees, the sunlight on them. If leaves could sing, they were singing "I'm glad I'm not Larry."

But I didn't have a tumor. Dr. Covington said, "Those fools! That's just how I had to sew up the membrane after the operation. There's nothing there. No tumor. No cancer."

No Vietnam, either. I registered late for my sophomore year and felt deliriously happy to be in school again. It was what I had longed to do. Not because I was an especially good student, but because I had already taken Philip Levine's workshop in my freshman year. He liked my work. I was a poet; I was going to become a much better one with any luck and a lot of work, and I had the great good fortune to have found a poet and genius for a teacher, one who has become a close and dear friend. I have written about Philip Levine elsewhere, but I feel certain that I would not have become a poet without being his student. He was simply amazing. His classes were better than any stand-up comedy act around, but his humor was serious. So was his passion for poetry. And he taught passionately. In many ways, he made my life and my poetry possible.

There were other poets at Fresno who were brilliant as well: Peter Everwine, Robert Mezey, Charles Hanzlicek. I absorbed all I could from

them and learned as well from Jacque Ries, who taught comparative literature, and from Mort Bennett, who then owned the Cafe Midi, where I hung out and, for a brief time, worked, washing dishes.

If my right testicle kept me from being sent to the regular army and on to Vietnam, it's true that no one really escaped that war. In college I would join others and protest it. We would occupy buildings and block off streets. In a way, no one stayed out of Vietnam, because Vietnam grew immense enough to include us all. Protesting the war did not make most of us feel brave. Sometimes it at first seemed a kind of lark, closing off a street, sitting and joining arms there in it. When the buses pulled up and the riot police unspooled out of them in helmets and marched in formation toward us, what I felt was fear. I was scared. I think most of us were. The police had clubs. We didn't. They kept coming toward us to break us up or arrest us if we didn't leave. In those days, no one went peacefully. No one knew how to yet. It was something one had to learn. The current media caricatures of such protests make the demonstrators appear to be spoiled children at a naughty picnic. It wasn't so. The picnic turned bloody. It wasn't a joke. And it wasn't entertainment, either.

"Entertainment Is America's Passion," read a slogan on the back of a passing bus the other day. It was an ad for something or other. But for a few seconds, I thought it was a brilliant indictment of what the country had become. Fin de siècle America seems at times to be a nation of voyeurs. I'm not above it all by any means. I too watch television, though I don't own one anymore. I hadn't bothered to buy another one, for some reason. And I haven't had cable for years. Except for sports, news, public television, and a few movies, network TV shows are about as exciting as Novocaine to relieve the pain of the sponsors' ads. I read late into the night, I read in bed, I read just about anything that interests me.

Demonstrations against the Vietnam War were confrontational. After the war, the country seemed to pass into history. It existed somewhere, but in a haze. You can't confront a haze. You can't block off a street all by yourself. When Noam Chomsky makes sense, there is a critic quick to characterize him as paranoid and include him with the paranoia of the right wing, as if all thought came to the same result. It doesn't. Power is hidden now. It views most of my students as a market and nothing more, and the media seems less independent than it did thirty years ago.

In such a world, I was lucky. I became a poet because of a misdiagnosis. My balls did not want to go to war, it seems. I was in complete agreement with them.

An Ear

After Fresno, I went to Syracuse University for graduate study because the poet Donald Justice taught there. Justice had an *ear,* as we say in poetry. An ear doesn't sound like much in a world going deaf, but it may be as important in poetry as it is in music. Justice was a master not only of the music in poetry but persuaded you that a certain kind of uncompromised intelligence, not just imagination, was called for if you wanted to try to make a thing that might last. When I later went to Iowa for a Ph.D., where he taught for years, I continued to learn from him. One night I was working late in my office, and he was too. I saw him going home in the corridor, dressed in a black overcoat. He was not especially well then. He had undergone bone or some sort of bone marrow surgery a few times for lingering if not chronic osteomyelitis. He was warning me about something or other—working too hard or staying up too late—I forget what it was exactly. In his black overcoat he seemed like César Vallejo, like a "presence" somehow, and as a poet I think he is at least as important as Vallejo, though completely different: for Justice, Reason itself was the mystery, an affliction which nothing could cure. It had a perverse beauty. Both poets, one a Peruvian Indian, the other the child of Georgia "crackers" who struggled against poverty, were acquainted with pain. At times, it kept intimate, inscrutable company with them. Vallejo's life was shorter, more tragic, but both poets had acquired a kind of bitterness, maybe the bitterness of the unacknowledged. The black overcoat is not insignificant in my portrait of him here. Justice once told me he had left Harvard in the winter of his freshman year because he couldn't afford an overcoat. The price of a coat does not seem like something that might determine one's fate, but this is so only if you have the money for one and the coat remains only a coat and doesn't stand for larger and more bewildering things you can do nothing about.

"Never forget what it meant to be truly poor," Pasolini once wrote. My teachers Philip Levine and Donald Justice did not forget what it meant. But they approached it far differently. I think of Levine, getting off the night shift at Chevy Gear and Axle at eighteen or nineteen, furious at how his life and the lives of those he loved was wasted by factory work, how his memory of it will become the great frankness and the vision of his poetry: "They feed they lion, and he comes," and, after he did come, the city that did not listen became an unlistening cinder; and of Justice, a child sitting on the rotting front porch of some general store in Florida, eating crackers and cheese, some phrase of Mozart running through his mind, becoming, in a key impossibly transposed— out of a changeling's childhood in which he must have just *assumed* he was the lost dauphin—the poetry he would write later: "The artist will have had his revenge for being made to wait, / A revenge not only necessary but right and clever— / Simply to leave him out of the scene, forever."

My respect for them never lessened or diminished. I became a teacher. Their example showed me that it was a serious thing to do. It is difficult to do it well, and worth it. There are poets I've met who disparage teaching, who do it only as a sort of chore, who think they're too good to teach. I don't know. I've worked in warehouses and packing sheds; I've driven trucks twelve hours a day and worked in fields and vineyards. I was not "too good" for that kind of work. But when I teach, I touch the past, the present, and the future, all in the same moment. Who is too good to do *that*? A poet who feels above such work might try to explain why to the guy coming off the swing shift in the grinding shed at Crucible Steel. He's had to inhale iron filings all evening because he can't make his quota while wearing the mask with the filter on it they give him. He can't even breathe if he wears that.

Luck

My first book of poems won the U.S. award of the International Poetry Forum and was published by University of Pittsburgh Press in 1972. My second, *The Afterlife,* was published in an edition of two hundred or so copies, beautifully printed by Kim Merker at the Windhover Press, but, as it won the Lamont Prize that year, the University of Iowa Press brought out a much larger edition. My third collection, *The Dollmaker's Ghost,* won the Open Competition of the National Poetry Series and was published by E. P. Dutton. My fourth and fifth collections, *Winter Stars* and *The Widening Spell of the Leaves,* were both published by University of Pittsburgh Press. I also wrote a book of prose, or stories as they may be, called *Black Freckles.* It was published by Peregrine Smith and sank like a stone in terms of sales or commentary. It freed me from any illusion that I might "try fiction."

I was awarded three NEA fellowships, a Guggenheim, and a Fulbright. I've taught at California State University, Los Angeles, Missouri, Iowa, Utah, and presently at Virginia Commonwealth University in Richmond.

I worked hard to write poetry. But I've had, I think, an enormous amount of luck as well.

Loves

I was married to the poet Marcia Southwick for almost ten years. We have a child, Nicholas, who is now seventeen. I was also married, at the age of twenty-two, to Barbara Campbell, and divorced four years later. In 1989, I married Mary Jane Hale, but we divorced a year later.

But the story of my love for them, and for other women, is part of my poetry and belongs there, not here.

And that is where it shall stay. After all, they are not memories.

Working Notes

I've mostly accounted here for my childhood, adolescence, and youth, perhaps because I can see it more clearly from this distance in time than I can see or remember in telling detail my adult life. But it seems to me that those early years were what determined everything, and what made me a poet. What kept me going as a poet were and are a lot of late nights, working until I get something, and then until I have it right, until the gray light of morning comes and I feel surprised that I've been working for so long. It never seems like work to me. It feels like pleasure. And even though I know it's toil, I keep that knowledge secret from some part of myself.

BIBLIOGRAPHY

Poetry:

Wrecking Crew, University of Pittsburgh Press, 1972.

The Rain's Witness (pamphlet), Southwick Press, 1975.

The Afterlife, University of Iowa Press, 1977.

The Dollmaker's Ghost, Dutton, 1981.

Winter Stars, University of Pittsburgh Press, 1985.

The Widening Spell of the Leaves, University of Pittsburgh Press, 1991.

Stories:

Black Freckles, Peregrine Smith, 1992.

The poet reads eight of his poems and comments on his work in a sound recording broadcast October 1977 on the radio program "New Letters on the Air," Kansas City, Missouri. Larry Levis and Thylias Moss read their poems in a sound recording made February 14, 1991, in the Montpelier Room at the Library of Congress, Washington, D.C.

Naomi Long Madgett

1923-

Naomi Long Madgett, Detroit, Michigan, 1993

a choice. The mouth opens intuitively and music comes out unbidden.

Another question students frequently ask is how much money one can earn as a poet. Their faces fall when I answer. What good is poetry, then, if it offers few monetary benefits? I attempted to answer that question in my acceptance statement for the Michigan Artist Award in 1993 when I said, in part:

> Poetry, perhaps the least recognized of the arts and certainly the least lucrative, holds a place of distinction in the souls of people everywhere, even when we are not aware that this is so. Many who claim they don't like or understand it are nevertheless deeply moved at times by music, little realizing that the song that holds great meaning for them could not have been sung without the words composed by an often uncredited poet. Poetry reaches to the depth and breadth of human experience, expressing our loftiest aspirations, our most profound emotional needs, our most crucial disappointments. It sustains us through our most overwhelming griefs.
>
> When President John F. Kennedy was assassinated, the *New York Times* reported receiving hundreds of original poems, many from people who had never written a poem before, indicating the natural appeal of this art form as a means of creative expression. Torn from the shores of Africa, how could the slaves have survived their dehumanization in an alien land except through the noble poetry of their Negro spirituals? And who of us today has not turned to the poetry of the Psalms for comfort in our hours of need, or been sustained at times by the words of some more modern David?

In one form or another, poetry has been the center of my life for as long as I can remember.

BIRTH AND CHILDHOOD

Students in schools I visit often ask what made me decide to be a poet, and I can only answer that I never did decide. Poetry was a part of my earliest consciousness. I doubt if anyone can *learn* to be a poet who does not have the tendency lying dormant in his or her being, although one can learn to become a *better* poet. If the tendency is there, sooner or later, I believe, it will manifest itself. And I must emphasize that this manifestation may often come later. My own awareness might be compared to that of a child with a natural singing voice. He or she does not consider singing as

I was born Naomi Cornelia Long in Norfolk, Virginia, on July 5, 1923, the third child and only daughter of the Reverend Clarence Marcellus Long, pastor of Bank Street Baptist Church, and the former Maude Selena Hilton, a homemaker and former teacher. Prior to my second birthday the family moved to East Orange, New Jersey, where my father had been elected pastor of Calvary Baptist Church.

I was a lonely and introverted child who felt isolated and different. The only girl in my neighborhood, I was frequently teased by my brothers and their friends who excluded me from their play in spite of my being a quite capable tomboy.[1] For years I thought the family portrait on my mother's dresser, taken before I was born, did not include me because nobody wanted me in it.[2] I contented myself with toys stored in a corner of the kitchen which I considered mine while my mother went about her endless chores. It was there at about the age of four or five that I made up my first meaningless rhyme. For many years after that, one memory lingered with me and became symbolic—myself in a blue straw hat with a streamer down the back, locked outside on the porch one cold fall day to play when there was nobody to play with, my pleas to be let in unanswered. Years later when I tried to articulate my feelings, I was misunderstood; thereafter, I kept them to myself, expressing them only in poems such as "Silence." ("I have learned to be silent. / My life's oppression, / Suppression, / Have made me so.")[3]

My loneliness and sense of alienation were reinforced at school where I became the only black child in my classes through the eighth grade, most African Americans and Italians being relegated to the lowest division of each grade. The school system in East Orange refused to hire African Americans in any capacity, and it was not uncommon for teachers at Ashland Grammar School to engage in discriminatory practices or to permit racial jokes in the classroom. The city's only theater and the ice cream parlor next door, along with a number of other businesses, denied equal rights to their black customers in spite of state law to the contrary. Nevertheless, many of my early poems appeared in the mimeographed school paper.

Naomi Cornelia Long, East Orange, New Jersey, about 1927

When I was in third grade my cousin Helen and her mother came to live with us, bringing me welcome companionship, but when they moved to Richmond, Virginia, two years later, I was devastated. My natural reaction was to write a poem. When my father went to Europe in 1934, my anxiety about his safety crossing the ocean prompted me to write again. When I was twelve, one of my poems, "My Choice," was published on the youth page of the *Orange Daily Courier* on October 30, 1935.

Early Reading and Writing

Sensing my loneliness, my father always made me welcome in his book-lined study, offering me material which I could understand. I wore thin the covers of *Æsop's Fables* and a large, handsomely bound volume, *Pearls from Many Seas*, in which I rushed to the poems before reading anything else. Sitting cross-legged on the floor, I discovered rhythmical poems by Tennyson and Longfellow, as well as *Bulfinch's Mythology*,

---

[1]See "Sunny" and "Album: Photo 2" in *Exits and Entrances*.

[2]See "Family Portrait" in *Exits and Entrances*.

[3]*Songs to a Phantom Nightingale,* ca. 1940.

which later proved helpful when I began to struggle with a few poems by Keats. I also cherished my mother's old "elocution" textbook from normal school, committing some of the poems to memory.

I was fascinated by the typewriter which was usually open on my father's desk. When he was not using it, I would practice typing with one finger as I had seen him do, composing my own "newspaper" which included, among other articles, a badly misspelled account of the kidnapping of the Lindbergh baby. My brothers never let me live it down.

Blank sheets of paper were a challenge and a delight. Covered with my poems they became "books," folded and held together with safety pins. Although I filled several notebooks purchased at the five-and-ten-cents store with fragments of thought, as well as lists of imaginary students, lesson plans, and tests, they seemed marred by the commercial printing on the cover. My brief life of crime began when I stole from the cupboard of my classroom one of the plain-covered, blank notebooks which the school provided. Writing was the only way I could cope with the frustrations of my childhood. By the time I was twelve, I had composed one hundred poems. After that I stopped counting.

One of those first hundred, "Welfare Days,"[4] reflected my concern about the Depression, although my knowledge was related more to dinner table discussions and the complaints of church members who sometimes brought their problems to the parsonage than to personal inconvenience. I was aware of strange men who occasionally came to the back door begging for food or money,[5] but I had no personal sense of being poor. While I wore hand-me-down clothing, including my brother's outgrown coats, and was subjected to the embarrassment of long underwear tucked inside cotton-rib stockings while my white classmates wore short socks and stylish snow suits, we were never hungry and were frequently reminded how well off we were by comparison to other families we knew. From just a cupful of leftovers my mother could make enough hash to feed an army, and the "pocketbook" in Dad's chiffonier always seemed to have

money in it whenever we needed something. During the time that he voluntarily reduced his already low salary, he earned two graduate degrees and traveled a great deal, paying his expenses with speaking engagements along the way. After attending the World Baptist Alliance in Berlin, he spent the rest of that summer touring other parts of Europe, Egypt, and the Holy Land, later lecturing on his travels using the motion pictures he had taken. How proud I was when he gave me permission to show the reel on Egypt to my sixth-grade class in ancient history! And every summer we spent a few days on the "colored" beach in Long Branch and another week or two visiting my maternal relatives in Richmond.[6] While my mother was constantly busy with household chores, she found enough time to study arts and crafts with the doctor's wife across the street[7] and was able to stay at home and rear her children in an atmosphere of love and security.

Because of the reading to which I was most often exposed, my poetry was inevitably locked into the traditional patterns of diction, rhyme, and meter. I was impressed with my father's ability to read the New Testament in Greek, and the classical curriculum I selected in high school, which included the reading of *The Iliad*, *The Odyssey*, and Tennyson's *Idylls of the King*, helped to validate these formal styles.

Racial Consciousness

Nothing in the school curriculum presented positive images of African Americans or acknowledged their contributions to literature and history, but I was fortunate in the resources available at home. One of the books we had was Robert Kerlin's anthology, *Negro Poets and Their Poems*, published the year I was born. There I discovered a very young Langston Hughes along with Paul Laurence Dunbar, Anne Spencer, James Weldon Johnson, Georgia Douglas Johnson, and others. Later, when my father taught adult evening classes funded by the Depression-era Works Progress Administration of New Jersey, I had access to the mimeographed textbook *An Anthology of Negro Poetry*, compiled with the assistance of Langston Hughes, Countee Cullen,

---

[4]ca. 1935.

[5]See "He Lives in Me" in *Adam of Ifé: Black Women in Praise of Black Men*.

[6]See "Fifth Street Exit, Richmond" in *Exits and Entrances*.

[7]"My Mother's Roses," 1993.

The poet with her brothers, Clarence (left) and Wilbur, 1937

and Sterling Brown. I still cherish the family's plaster-of-paris copy of the bust of Dunbar sculpted by Isaac Hathaway in 1915.

I was about five when we were visited by a Philadelphia clergyman, aged but tall and still erect, who I was told had composed the words and music to many of the hymns we sang in church. Meeting this remarkable turn-of-the-century hymnist, the Reverend Charles A. Tindley, made a tremendous impression on me. Because the church was the focal point of our family life, I was deeply immersed not only in the poetry of the Bible and the words of other hymns but also the plaintive lyricism of the old slave spirituals and the traditional gospel songs of Thomas A. Dorsey and Lucie Campbell. My father was not a "bushwhacking" preacher, but visiting evangelists conducting revivals at our church sometimes introduced me to the old-time, down-home variety of black sermon in which much racial culture is rooted. During prayer meetings and Communion services, the "testifying" and praying of the saints demonstrated another form of folk poetry. All of this

was later reinforced for me in James Weldon Johnson's marvelous collection, *God's Trombones.* It was much later, however, that these cultural influences were reflected in my own work, as in "Soon I Will Be Done" and "'The Sun Do Move.'"[8] The latter is based on the most famous sermon of the Reverend John Jasper (1812–1893 or 1901), a former slave who was a self-taught student of the Bible and accepted every detail as accurate. So thorough was his research and so dramatic and convincing his oratory that he could "prove" the flatness of the earth and the mobility of the sun with Scripture. Whenever he preached "The Sun Do Move and the Earth Am Square" at his church in Richmond, Virginia, or to the attendants at an all-day country camp meeting, he was so convincing that one of his contemporaries, a white minister, wrote that, after listening, he was thoroughly convinced for a moment that what he said was true.

---

[8]Both in *Octavia and Other Poems.*

Who wouldn't believe,
who wouldn't,
who wouldn't believe?

Camp meeting outside
the city limits.
Corn-high, the yellow wave
of faith, gushing
on his word.

    And God said. . . .
       Preach it, brotha!
    The Good Book reads. . . .
       Yes, it do, Lawd, it do!
Day climbing over the southeast
corner of the earth,
grasping for the truth.
       Tell it, John Jasper,
       Hallelujah!
All day long, all Sunday afternoon
the fields outside of Richmond rocking.

Sun melting down like lard
on the griddle of the world,
the hungry square of earth swallowing
it up again.
       Come, Jesus!

Who wouldn't believe,
who wouldn't, who
wouldn't believe!

At the dinner table we were kept informed of news and attitudes affecting black people through the Norfolk *Journal and Guide* to which my parents subscribed, and my father's every prayer contained a reference to "the Scottsboro boys."[9] He frequently involved himself in situations where some black person was victimized by racism. In a recent poem, "He Lives in Me," I describe him as "the blackest man I knew," in spite of his near-white complexion.[10]

The prejudice I experienced both firsthand and vicariously turned me into a fourth-grade rebel who became somewhat confrontational in the classroom and refused to salute the flag or repeat the Pledge of Allegiance. The victories of Joe Louis, whose camp at Pompton Lake we had visited several times, once coming face to face with Jack Johnson, gave me cause to

exult and taught me that triumph over adversity can take many forms. Eventually my rage subsided as I began to realize that it was more destructive to me than to those responsible for it and that "building in salt is no better than building in sand."[11] I learned that I could not change attitudes through hatred and found more productive ways of dealing with racial problems. While some of my mature poems have become more overtly racial in content, few have been as direct as "On Democracy," written when I was a high school freshman, in which I bitterly contrast the bugles, flags, and songs of patriots with a southern lynching.[12]

ADOLESCENCE

Eventually my poetry became the vehicle for expressing the romantic yearnings I began to feel for boys my brothers brought home from school and others I knew at church. I guarded these compositions, along with the first of many journals, as best I could from prying eyes. Throughout this period my poems, whether about love or not, were highly imaginative and melancholy in tone and, though based on honest emotions, were often not noticeably related to the source of their inspiration. One might assume by reading them that I was prematurely worldly and subjected to much hardship and denial while I was, in fact, among the most sheltered and innocent of youngsters, even for my time.

My brothers and I all graduated in June 1937, I from grammar and they from high school. Up to that point I had always excelled in English and managed to remain in the "A" division of my grade but, except for my writing, had not been otherwise outstanding. My teachers had often told my mother that I was not working up to my capacity. That was probably true since I had experienced several incidents of being denied honors which I had admittedly earned.[13] Three months after entering East Orange High School, which had closed its pool

---

[9] An infamous case involving several black youth in Alabama framed for the rape of a young white woman. Even after she admitted that she had lied, they continued to be held in prison for years without trial.

[10] In *Adam of Ifé: Black Women in Praise of Black Men.*

[11] "Salt and Sand" in *Pink Ladies in the Afternoon.*

[12] *Phantom Nightingale: Juvenilia.*

[13] In "Reluctant Light," 1993, I recall my mother "tapping your umbrella against my fifth grade teacher's desk / to punctuate your firm demand for justice" in one such incident.

to avoid integrating the required swimming classes, we moved to St. Louis, Missouri, due to my father's acceptance of the pastorate of historic Central Baptist Church. That move was the turning point of my life.

Sumner High School

I entered Charles Sumner High School, founded in 1875, in January 1938. Legally segregated, it had a black faculty and student body and was located in an all-black, middle-class community complete with restaurants, a theater, and numerous black-owned businesses. Unlike many inner-city schools of today's urban north, Sumner was superior in every way. Its alumni remain the most loyal of any I have known, and its long list of outstanding former students attests to its emphasis on excellence. A few that come to mind are operatic singer Grace Bumbry, cartoonist E. Simms Campbell, attorney Margaret Bush Wilson, tennis champion Arthur Ashe, comedian-activist Dick Gregory, and prizefighter Henry Armstrong. From the choral music room facing the front door of the school, students could occasionally catch a glimpse of some famous graduate coming back to visit.

On my third day there, a National Honor Society induction ceremony took place in the auditorium, the most impressive event I had ever witnessed. After that the principal, George D. Brantley, took the stage and introduced an unimpressive-looking boy who sang a solo in a baritone voice such as I had never heard before. Looking down from one of the two facing balconies, I knew immediately that I had come to a place where I could be anything I was good enough to be and that no one would deny me what I had earned. Years later when I read an article announcing a musical "first" in the *Detroit Free Press* bearing the caption, "Negro Makes Met," I knew before reading it that it was Robert McFerrin. I soon joined Robert in the exceptional a cappella choir directed by Wirt D. Walton and gave him his middle name which he later legalized and passed on to his now famous son "Bobby."

Partly because of the opportunities offered by nearby Stowe Teachers College, the majority of the students were college-bound. It was popular to be smart. The quality of teaching was excellent, and the personal interest taken in students was unusual. After meeting the rigid requirements of Honor Society membership, I turned my efforts toward graduating with an average above 90 percent.

My new life was fuel for my poetry, much of which was regularly published in the yearbooks and other school publications. My writing flowed with comparative ease reflecting the heights and depths of my adolescent emotions. I developed the usual desire for independence from parental control and fell in love with new boys with amazing frequency, imagining on the page situations that never occurred. My sense of isolation did not lessen but became more intense. In spite of the recognition I received, I felt inferior to many of the students who possessed more self-assurance than I in social settings which were new to me. I had many individual friends but did not feel comfortable in the groups to which they belonged.

In 1940 my brother Clarence, who had transferred from Stowe to Lincoln University in Jefferson City, discussed my writing with Sterling Brown and encouraged me to write to him. In my letter I mentioned my enjoyment of solitude. Professor Brown's reply advised me that if I wanted to be a good poet, I would have to become more involved with people. It was not until about my junior year in college, however, that I was able to recognize and begin to deal with what I conceived of as my invisibility and to become more comfortable in groups.

I discovered the poetry of Robert Browning, who became one of my lifelong favorites. My escape from the formality of traditional European poetry was still several years away, evident in the embarrassing archaic diction of "To a Man with Wings,"[14] written in 1943 when my brother Wilbur became a fighter pilot with the now-famous Tuskegee Airmen.

Recognition

In about 1944 a fellow student at Sumner and I were among the only five high school students in the entire city to win national recognition for our entries in the *Scholastic* magazine contest, he for his visual art and I for poetry. In addition, I won several local and regional writing competitions, one of which was judged by a cousin of Sara Teasdale, herself a poet. She took an interest in my work and

---

[14]*Phantom Nightingale: Juvenilia.*

At Virginia State College, Petersburg, Virginia, 1942

submitted a poem to the *Missouri School Journal* which was published.

The community, too, was extremely supportive of the arts and the efforts of young persons. Robert McFerrin and I were frequently invited to sing and read on public programs. I was about fifteen when I read some of my poems on the radio. At about the same age I met Langston Hughes for the first time when he spoke for a ladies' literary club. He encouraged my writing and gave me an autographed copy of *A New Song* which had been published recently.

First Book

In 1939 my father signed a contract with the Pegasus Publishing Company in New York to have a small collection of my work published. During the next two years while the accepted manuscript languished, the company went through a change of ownership. It was not until June 1941, several days after my graduation, that *Songs to a Phantom Nightingale* was published by Fortuny's Publishers. With about three excep-

tions, this volume did not include any of the poems written during the two-year delay.

When my book came out I was the same age as Phillis Wheatley was when in 1770 her first poem was published, to be followed by her book three years later. Margaret Walker, some years older than I, was probably looking forward to the publication of her first collection, *For My People,* in 1942. Gwendolyn Brooks, also my senior, was perhaps working on *A Street in Bronzeville,* which would appear in 1945. While my small collection did not possess the maturity of those that followed and attracted little attention, the very fact of its existence has come to be of some value to literary historians. Although Lucy Terry's crude rhyme "Bars Fight" (1746) would win no laurels as literary art, it is still recognized as the historical beginning of recorded African American poetry.

The significance of *Nightingale,* published under my complete maiden name, did not fully occur to me until 1980 when Dexter Fisher, in her introduction to *The Third Woman: Minority Women Writers in the United States,* cited it as the beginning of a thirty-year period of contemporary poetry by African American women. Subsequently—and because the first book represented only a small sampling of my early work—*Phantom Nightingale: Juvenilia* was published in 1981 in order to put on record a number of additional poems written before, during, and for two years after the period covered by the first publication.

Although my work has naturally matured and improved considerably over the years, I feel that this early publication was justified by its intrinsic value. It is certainly not typical of what I have observed in student writing, and the publisher evidently agreed. One would not assume that "When I Was Young,"[15] for example, was written by a sixteen-year-old.

> When I was young and loved life's laughter,
> I climbed tall hills and touched the sun.
> I did not know till long years after
> That ecstasy and pain are one.
>
> But now that I have ceased pursuing,
> My laughter has been hushed by time
> For pain is all left for pursuing.
> There are no more tall hills to climb.

---

[15] *Songs to a Phantom Nightingale.* It had appeared about a year earlier in the *St. Louis Argus* or the *St. Louis Call.*

In spite of the publisher's bankruptcy not too long after publication of *Nightingale*, my book enjoyed fairly good sales. Priced at one dollar, it was purchased by numerous members of my father's network of black clergy across the nation and easily satisfied the number of guaranteed sales required by the contract. In addition to public libraries, an occasional copy still turns up now and then in a used bookstore or university library.

Defined as "a small, Old World migratory bird noted for its melodious nocturnal song," my imaginary nightingale was a symbol of my quest for elusive happiness and my other-worldly flights into youthful fantasy as expressed in my 1945 poem, "Quest":[16]

> I will track you down the years,
>   Down the night,
> Till my anguish falls away,
>   Star by star,
> And my heart spreads flaming wings
>   Where you are.
>
> I will find you, never fear—
>   Make you mine.
> Think that you have bound me fast
>   To the earth?
> I will rise to sing you yet,
>   Song of mirth.
>
> I will let you think you won,
>   Perfect dream,
> Till I creep from dark and toil
>   To your side,
> Hold you to my heart and sleep,
>   Satisfied.
>
> I will track you down the sky,
>   Down the blue,
> Till my song becomes the sun
>   Of the years
> And the golden April rains
>   Are my tears.

College and War

The summer after graduation I got my first job singing with a choir sponsored by the National Youth Administration under the direction of Kenneth Billups. I later incorporated one of his choral arrangements of a biblical

passage in my poem "Grand Circus Park."[17] That September I entered Virginia State College for Negroes (now Virginia State University), my mother's alma mater, class of 1902, when it was a normal school.

Soon after that, World War II was declared. But in spite of the related inconveniences, there was much for which to be grateful. I was fortunate to be offered courses in Negro literature and Negro history, the latter taught by Dr. Luther Porter Jackson, Sr., author and foremost authority on the free Negro in Virginia. I also had Professor Felicia D. Anderson, whose literature classes were especially rich and exciting and whose philosophy concerning unresponsive students, expressed to me privately, later supported me through twenty-eight years of my own teaching.

It was my intention to leave "State" after two years to study journalism at Kansas State University, but I became a member of Alpha Kappa Alpha Sorority in my sophomore year, gaining a lifetime local and nationwide sisterhood. Life then was so fulfilling that I could not bear to leave.

On March 11, 1942, Langston Hughes came to the campus for an evening reading. Meeting with him that afternoon with other members of a literary club, I timidly asked him to look at one or two of my poems neatly typed in a looseleaf notebook. He agreed to do so, promising to return them after the reading. That night he surprised me by interrupting his own poems to read several of mine, saying some words of praise which left me dizzy. I later discovered that he had gone through all the poems, making penciled notes on some of the pages.

Then in the library I found Countee Cullen's address in Tuckahoe, New York, not far from the city where we then lived. I wrote him and asked if I might meet with him during the summer. He replied with his telephone number and an invitation to call him when I got home. On the agreed date, my father drove me to his home where we were greeted at the door by his wife, Ida, and a kitten whom he identified as a grandson of Christopher Cat, nominal author of *My Lives and How I Lost Them*. While my father and Cullen's father, both ministers, chatted in the living room, we went into his study to talk. Reading several of my

---

[16]In *American Literature by Negro Authors*, edited by Herman Dreer (Macmillan, 1950); collected in *One and the Many*.

[17]In *Pink Ladies in the Afternoon*.

The Long family: (back row, from left) the Reverend Clarence M. Long, father, and brothers, Lieutenant Wilbur F. Long and Clarence M. Long, Jr.; (front) Maude S. Long, mother, and Naomi Cornelia Long, New Rochelle, New York, 1943

poems, he looked up and said, "Well, you're a poet." As a great admirer of his work, I considered that a supreme compliment. He cautioned me against becoming discouraged by rejection slips, showing me a short poem which he said he had never been able to get published in spite of his fame. His wife sent me an announcement of his death about a year later. Such was the encouragement which I received as a young poet.

In college I discovered many other literary voices but was influenced most by Emily Dickinson and Walt Whitman. Many of my poems appeared in the college paper. The *Virginia Statesman* earned a high rating by the Associated Collegiate Press All-American Newspaper Critical Service, which included special mention of my poetry as "far superior to the usual run of college verse."[18] "Midnight Magnolias"[19]

was one of several reactions to the segregated South.

When my brother's plane was shot down over Hungary and he was reported missing, I wrote "White Cross,"[20] fusing him with my cousin Helen's boyfriend, also a fighter pilot, who had been killed in action. The family later learned that Wil was a prisoner of war in Germany. He returned to the states the day I graduated from college. The class of 1945 had the distinction of being the only one in the college's history whose years of attendance coincided with a war. We were also the last class to have the hated phrase "for Negroes" printed on our diplomas.

A PERIOD OF CHANGE

In February of my freshman year, my parents had moved to New Rochelle, New York, a

---

[18]*Richmond Times-Dispatch*, Saturday, May 12, 1945.
[19]In *Phantom Nightingale: Juvenilia*.

[20]In *One and the Many*.

city in which I have never spent a full year. My father was pastor of Bethesda Baptist Church and became the first African American to serve on a board of education in the state of New York, a post which he held for ten years. I had not been enthusiastic about leaving St. Louis and, except for one brief visit a year later, could not bear to go back for fear of finding the reality of the city less glowing than my memory.[21] When I did return twenty-three years later, I was not disappointed.

After some months in New Rochelle, during which time I began graduate studies at New York University, I married Julian Fields Witherspoon, whom I had met briefly at Sumner High and then again when he was stationed at Camp Lee, Virginia. We moved immediately to Detroit, Michigan, where he had lived before going into service. For several months in 1946 I worked part-time as a writer and copyreader for the *Michigan Chronicle*. Many of my poems appeared there under my new name. One day the editor, Louis Martin, called me to his office to compliment me on my poetry, giving me his personal copies of Robert Hayden's *Heart-Shape in the Dust* and *A Street in Bronzeville* by Gwendolyn Brooks. I had never heard of either poet and had no idea how much I would come to admire both of them as artists and friends.

I left the *Chronicle* before the birth of my daughter in April 1947. The following year the marriage, plagued with deception and financial irresponsibility, came to an end, and a job became a necessity. Boarding my toddler with friends during the week and borrowing money for carfare, I began work as a service representative in the only public office of Michigan Bell Telephone Company, located in "Black Bottom," which hired Negroes. My beginning salary was only thirty-seven dollars a week, but I had no rent to pay as my parents had purchased the little house we lived in. From that point on I was determined to support myself and my daughter as best I could without further parental favors. When I recall the rigors of those six years, I wonder how I survived. No doubt my parents' values and example of "making do" with little helped to sustain me, and I grew stronger for the challenges I had to meet. The nature of the work and even

disposition and unobtrusive guidance of the manager, Ramon S. Scruggs, taught me a great deal about interacting with people and handling frustration and anger productively. The camaraderie of my coworkers helped to keep the turmoil of my personal life confined to my poetry.

Even though I knew I could not take the necessary time off to earn a teaching certificate or complete a master's degree, I enrolled in several courses at Wayne University (now Wayne State University) and continued with my writing. In 1949 one of my poems, "Refugee,"[22] appeared under the name Naomi Long Witherspoon in *The Poetry of the Negro, 1746–1949*, edited by Langston Hughes and Arna Bontemps, and a group of my poems was included in *American Literature by Negro Authors*, edited by Herman Dreer, in 1950. I was occasionally asked to read publicly. I also spoke at several functions which included two lectures on Robert Browning for the Detroit Study Club, a group of African American women who had organized as the Browning Study Club at the turn of the century. Such engagements provided more self-confidence and ease among groups. I began to think about the possibility of another book.

A New Career

For most of my life I had resisted the idea of teaching, but motherhood had gradually convinced me that I would do well in this profession. My marriage to William Harold Madgett in 1954, through which I acquired two sons, Harold, Jr., and Gerald, permitted me to leave the telephone company and attend college full-time. In one year I earned a teaching certificate and completed a master's degree at what is now Wayne State University.

I began a twelve-year career as a secondary English teacher in September 1955. Most of that time was spent at Northwestern High School, a somewhat typical inner-city school with an almost all-black student body. Aside from the fact that most of the teachers were white, this school bore no resemblance to Sumner, yet it had much to offer, and my happiest and most fulfilling days in education were spent there. I felt that I understood the needs of many of

---

[21]See "Sarah Street" in *One and the Many*.

[22]ca. 1941, in *One and the Many*.

my students with whom I developed rapport, stretching them to high academic standards. Most of the faculty were dedicated, but some doomed their students to failure through stereotypical images and low expectations. One such youngster, whose demeanor was misunderstood, became the fictional Sylvester whose "easy lie . . . swaggering gait . . . darting eye [and] stormy frown" led to his failure. Several other poems including "Culturally Deprived," "Teacher," and "Black: A Chant for Children," grew out of my high school teaching.[23]

Bringing in my own materials, I introduced my American literature classes to black poetry, almost none of which was included in their textbook, and led the fight for textbook reform for fairer representation of the contributions of African American authors. During the summer of 1965 a special grant allowed me to teach an experimental class in Afro-American literature which was visited by poet Melvin B. Tolson. The following year the course became a part of the high school curriculum citywide. I also introduced the first accredited creative writing course which had as one of its students poet and playwright Pearl Cleage.

I was once named Distinguished English Teacher of the Year by the Metropolitan Detroit English Club, and in 1965 I won a statewide competition for the first Mott Fellowship in English. I spent that school year as research associate at Oakland University, developing integrated American literature materials and testing them in inner-city schools nationwide. I returned to Northwestern High School for the next two years. In 1967 I traveled through Europe and the Middle East, our cruise ship being the first to land in Haifa following the Six-Day War.

A FELLOWSHIP OF POETS

Under my present name my second book, *One and the Many,* was published in 1956, a very dry period nationally, with few collections of poetry by black authors being published. At the time I did not know of any other African American poets in Detroit. My book created such a stir locally that all the black newspapers, the *Michigan Chronicle,* the *Pittsburgh*

With her daughter, Jill Annette Witherspoon, at the time of publication of One and the Many, *Detroit, 1954.*

Courier (Detroit edition), and the short-lived *Detroit Metro,* carried feature stories. I was interviewed on the Dick Harris Show, carried by station WJR in Detroit, and was invited to read for a literary club in Grand Rapids. A glowing review by scholar and critic J. Saunders Redding appeared nationally in the *Afro-American Newspapers,* and I made my first commercial flight to Philadelphia to read there. In the meantime my poems continued to be published in little magazines.

I eventually met Oliver LaGrone, a poet and sculptor. He had published a chapbook and received some national attention in *Saturday Review.* It was good to make contact with a kindred spirit. On several occasions we engaged in dialog or read our poems together on radio.

Rosey E. Pool

On the night before Thanksgiving in 1959, I was visited by Dr. Rosey E. Pool, a Dutch scholar then living in London. In Detroit doing research at Wayne State University, she had been

---

[23]"Sylvester Expelled" and others mentioned in *Pink Ladies in the Afternoon.*

told of my work. During our conversation I learned that she had become interested in African American poetry in 1925 with the discovery of Countee Cullen's first book in the University of Amsterdam library. Time spent in a concentration camp during World War II led to a more personal identification with it. She later began to correspond with several of the authors. She also lectured on British radio, eventually editing a series of anthologies published in England and the Netherlands. She gave me a copy of one of them, *Ik Zag Hoe Zwart Ik Was* (*I Saw How Black I Was*), published in 1960, and I reciprocated with a copy of *One and the Many*. Several weeks later she began the practice of ending her lectures with the first stanza of one of my poems, "Not I Alone."

Her presence in Detroit, interrupted by a brief visit to Mexico, was the catalyst for a significant period of literary activity. Her series of lectures and readings on educational television, entitled "Black and Unknown Bards," drew

together other local, black poets who had not known each other before. Her next anthology of African American poetry, *Beyond the Blues*, published by the Hand and Flower Press in Kent, England, in 1962, as well as *Ik Ben de Nieuwe Neger* (*I Am the New Negro*), a bilingual volume published in the Netherlands in 1965, included the work of several of the Detroit poets. She visited Detroit again in 1963 before leaving to lecture at black colleges throughout the South. During her first visit I had written "Midway" (December 1959), and it was she who was responsible for its publication in the fall 1961 issue of *Freedomways*. "Alabama Centennial"[24] was an outgrowth of a discussion during her second visit in May 1963. (The reference to Selma was later appended.)

During this fertile period a number of things happened. A verse choir publicly performed

---

[24]"Midway" and "Alabama Centennial" both in *Star by Star*.

Reading at Boone House while Edward Simpkins holds the microphone; Harold Lawrence sits at left, Detroit, 1963

poems by black authors, and dance teacher Vera Embree directed a video performance which featured local black artists in various genres along with a dance which she had choreographed. A small group of black poets began to meet in each other's homes for informal discussions and workshops. In addition to LaGrone and me, they were Dudley Randall, who had returned to Detroit in 1956 from Morgan State College; James W. Thompson; Harold Lawrence, a teacher whose primary interest was African history; one of his colleagues, Edward Simpkins; Alma Parks; Betty Ford; and a talented high school student, Gloria Davis.

Boone House

Soon after Margaret Danner left Chicago and came to Detroit in 1961 as poet-in-residence at Wayne State University, she received permission from the Reverend Theodore S. Boone, pastor of King Solomon Baptist Church on Fourteenth Street, to live in an unoccupied house next door to the church and use it for her own writing and as a community art center. Her occupancy in what came to be known as Boone House lasted from 1962 to 1964 during which time she and Dudley Randall worked on the poems for a small cooperative collection. We poets met there each month on a Sunday evening and took turns reading our work to each other and to a handful of people who rarely numbered more than five or six. The most regular attendants were Arthur and Carolyn Reese, teachers and civil rights activists. While Danner and I were the only members of the group who had published full-length collections of our work, we all met as equals who shared the spotlight and were qualified to be mutually helpful in our critiques. No one individual stood out as a leader or star.

To my knowledge, these readings represented the most visible activity of the house. Other than a few children's drawings I once saw on display, I do not remember any other significant community arts activities. While Randall himself, in a 1971 interview by A. X. Nicholas,[25] mentioned jazz sessions and creative writing classes for children, he does not now recall any such activities.[26] If they took place, they were evidently very private affairs. The old house was beautiful in its details but in poor repair. It lacked central heat, some of the lights did not work, and the toilet lacked a seat, but we were glad to have this meeting place and to huddle together good-naturedly in front of the fireplace in cold weather. Except for Rosey Pool's lecture and reading there on May 10, 1963, celebrating the publication of *Beyond the Blues,* and Langston Hughes's brief visit in February 1964, I know of no connection that any other poets such as Robert Hayden, who was not living in Detroit, or Owen Dodson had with Boone House with the possible exception, like editor Hoyt Fuller, of a personal visit to see Margaret Danner.[27]

Ed Simpkins edited the October 1962 issue of *The Negro History Bulletin,* which focused on Detroit writers. Featured were Lawrence, Parks, Ford, Thompson, Simpkins, Randall, LaGrone, and myself, all members of our group, as well as the elderly poet James Edward McCall, now inactive, with whom Dr. Pool had corresponded for many years, and two less known poets who were not a part of our circle. Several other writers and playwrights were represented including Woodie King and Powell Lindsay.

On March 22, 1963, our group presented to a large and enthusiastic audience at Hartford Avenue Baptist Church a joint performance of our work entitled Poetry Unlimited, reported by the *Michigan Chronicle* as "An Expose in Talent." Two months later, Dr. Pool, LaGrone, and Danner were among several guests at my home, along with arts supporter Irma Wertz and Tamunoemi David-West, a Nigerian student who was the subject of one of Danner's poems and later one of mine. Danner brought in a photographer to record the occasion. Her new collection, *To Flower,* came out in October of that year.

Early in 1964, the group began to disperse. Margaret Danner suddenly dropped out of sight, James Thompson moved to New York, and Harold Lawrence changed his focus to history

---

[25]"A Conversation with Dudley Randall" in *Black World,* December 1971. Reprinted in *Homage to Hoyt Fuller,* edited by Dudley Randall (Detroit: Broadside, 1984).

[26]Randall was also mistaken in that interview about the name of the church which owned the house, which he reported as New Bethel Baptist Church.

[27]This information on Boone House corrects several poorly researched, published reports which are in error.

With the scholar and critic Dr. J. Saunders Redding, University of Iowa summer institute, 1972

and his name to Kofi Wangara and went to Africa.

When the mood changed in the early seventies, the role that Rosey Pool had played during her two extended visits to this country was conveniently forgotten because of her race, and her intentions viewed in the media with suspicion. In "Poets beyond the Blues,"[28] dedicated to her memory, I write "Someday we will remember how it was before you came," continuing:

> We were like particles of metal dust floating
>   on stagnant air,
> visible only in our separateness, until you
>   rose among us
> with a solar clarity that magnetized us
> with your sharing of our pain. . . .

Those of us who remained in Detroit continued to thrive individually. Hughes's anthology, *New Negro Poets: U.S.A.,* included some of our work in 1964. In 1965 LaGrone and I be-

gan our participation in Detroit Adventure, forerunner of the Michigan Council for the Arts and its Creative-Writers-in-the-Schools program. My poems continued to appear in anthologies, journals, and magazines such as *Negro Digest,* later named *Black World.* That year my third book, *Star by Star,* was published by Harlo Press, to be followed in 1972 with a second edition published by Evenill, Inc., and Dudley Randall founded Broadside Press with the publication of his poem "Ballad of Birmingham." In 1966 his first little chapbook, *Poem Counterpoem,* with Margaret Danner was published.

Second Group

Eventually a second informal workshop group was formed to include from the original one LaGrone, Randall, Gloria Davis, and me, in addition to Joyce Whitsitt and a few other newcomers. We were joined by several white poets, Juliana Geran, a brilliant and talented young Romanian Jew, Professor Louis J. Cantoni of Wayne State University, Ethel Gray Seese, and Robert Honigman, a young lawyer. From

---

[28]*Exits and Entrances.*

our association came the anthology *Ten: Anthology of Detroit Poets,* published in 1968 by South and West.

Such workshops provided wonderful companionship and support to buffer the loneliness of our profession. We had moved a long way forward from the dry period in which *One and the Many* was born.

COLLEGE TEACHING

In September 1968 I began a sixteen-year tenure on the English faculty at Eastern Michigan University, entering as an associate professor and later being promoted to full professor. While there I introduced the first course in Afro-American literature, an undergraduate survey course, as well as a graduate course called the Harlem Renaissance and Beyond. I also taught creative writing, eventually completing a textbook for the course.[29] One of my former students, Loren Estleman, is now the successful author of more than thirty novels. In 1970 I also taught a course in Afro-American literature at the University of Michigan in Ann Arbor. The following year I spent five weeks in west and central Africa. "Phillis,"[30] recreating the slave voyage of Phillis Wheatley from Senegal, and the three short poems comprising "Glimpses of Africa" were reactions to that visit.[31] Toward the end of my tenure I completed my dissertation, the final requirement for a nontraditional Ph.D. earned at the International Institute for Advanced Studies (now a part of Greenwich University) whose credits included studies and seminars taken at various traditional universities.

BECOMING A PUBLISHER

Lotus Press came into being in 1972, shortly after my third marriage to Leonard Patton Andrews, my second marriage having ended in divorce in 1960. I had been seeking a publisher for a new manuscript unsuccessfully. The ever-present problem of rejection by white publishers, who often branded the work of black

authors as either "not black enough" or "too black" (expressed as "not universal") was accentuated by the mood of the Black Arts Movement. The market had been deluged by books which either waved red flags of rage, titillated the reader with lurid details of ghetto life, crime, and broken families, or touted the glories of Africa and black identity while playing on the collective conscience of Whitey by flagellation and insult. My quiet, reflective poetry, dealing with blackness in more subtle ways but also transcending race, stood little chance of acceptance. By now the small press movement was under way and several independent black companies had been established, but the response I got from their editors was hardly better than from their fairer-skinned peers. The racial divisiveness of that period is the subject of "Newblack"[32] which discusses

> them kneegrow poets that aint black enuf
> that jes wont lissen when we tell m
> whut they oughta be n do
> that wont be Blackwashed by th talk we talk
> they a strange breed n due to meet they end
> wid all them uther toms. . . .

One of these editors told me years later that he selected manuscripts on the basis of their ability to make a profit, and mine was not directly political or relevant enough to qualify.

During a casual conversation with three friends one day, I expressed my frustration over the future of this manuscript. One, who had always been supportive of my work, mentioned the possibility of publishing the work as an independent project. The others were receptive to the idea but felt that they lacked the necessary experience for such a task. Some weeks and several conversations later, it was decided that they would contribute the funds if I would do the groundwork. Since publication of my earlier books had taught me something about promotion, I agreed. In thinking of a name, I ran across some information about the lotus plant in north Africa, so late that year *Pink Ladies in the Afternoon* was published by Lotus Press, "Flower of a New Nile."

During its first two years *Pink Ladies* did reasonably well because of my readings. I felt that it should have gotten stronger promotion,

---

[29]*A Student's Guide to Creative Writing.*
[30]Written for and first read at the Phillis Wheatley Poetry Festival at Jackson State University, Jackson, Mississippi, in 1973.
[31]*Pink Ladies in the Afternoon.*

[32]*Pink Ladies in the Afternoon.*

but my benefactors evidently felt that they had fulfilled their obligation and became involved with other interests. They agreed to let my husband and me take over the name and the existing stock for a minimal sum which did not begin to reimburse them for their investment. We parted company on friendly terms. By their request they have remained anonymous.

I had no intention of publishing additional books, but one of my students, Pamela Cobb (now Baraka Sele), occasionally brought her poems to my office for my comments. After working with her for some time, I thought that, since I owned a duplicator, I could encourage her by producing a small collection of her poems. I typed *Inside the Devil's Mouth* on a typewriter with proportional fonts and, after discarding the first batch of printed pages, badly misnumbered, put together this chapbook by hand, binding it with a used saddle stapler.

Another early project was a collection of "poster-poems" by twenty living black authors, entitled *Deep Rivers*, intended for use in secondary schools as a means of demonstrating the rich variety in African American poetry at a time when one white teacher told me, "If you've read one, you've read them all." I included in this packet a teacher's guide which offered discussion questions on each poem, related writing activities, and suggestions for introducing a unit of poetry. The National Council of Teachers of English purchased several hundred copies of this portfolio for distribution.

Later I met veteran playwright-poet May Miller at Southern University in Baton Rouge where both of us participated in the Melvin Butler Poetry Festival. I liked the style and mature vision of her poems and offered to publish her next book, *I Never Scream*.

It went on from there to the first publication by a young woman I had met in one of my poetry workshops. After several nit-picking sessions with her, *Love Poem to a Black Junkie* by Paulette Childress White was published.

Up to this point all the poets had been black. The first of several manuscripts by Caucasian poets was *Sunspots* by Louie Crew, whose writing preceded the formation of support networks for gay writers. I was particularly interested in material of literary merit which did not necessarily follow current trends and was therefore not likely to be published. Always aware that sales would not cover expenses, I never-

theless felt strongly about the importance of my commitment. A publisher told me once that he had stopped accepting poetry because it just didn't pay. My reply was, "But *some*body has to do it anyhow."

I was determined not to get into debt and was careful to pay for services as they were performed. I did not wish to taint the integrity of the press by requiring authors to pay, so for the first few years I spent between three thousand dollars and five thousand dollars of my own money to support it.

Except for an occasional volunteer or intern, I worked alone handling all the details of typing, layout, cover design, promotion, invoicing, bookkeeping, packaging and shipping, along with reading manuscripts, making editing suggestions, conducting occasional workshops, and corresponding with aspiring poets. None of this activity was supported by grants. All this time I continued to commute almost forty miles each way three days a week to the campus in Ypsilanti. An instructor at a local university once assigned his students reports on publishing, and two of them came to interview me. Their reports received an unsatisfactory grade with the comment, "No one person could possibly be doing all those things." When the students called me back, I invited them to go through a miniversion of the process with me in my basement office. "Go back and tell your instructor," I said, "that one person is indeed doing it all."

In 1976 Lotus joined a group of local independents who combined to form the Associated Black Publishers of Detroit, Inc. I served as treasurer of that group which included Agascha Productions, Pamoja Press, and Black Graphics.[33] We usually met at each other's homes and exchanged information and techniques. It was through one of the members that I learned an alternative to saddle stitching which resembled perfect binding and could be done by hand; *The Persistence of the Flesh* by Herbert Woodward Martin was the last book bound by that method. We occasionally sent representatives to book exhibits in other cities and, in June of 1977, rented space at the Alexander Crummel Center located in the basement of a black church to put on a successful poetry festival.

---

[33]Broadside Press was possibly inactive at that time due to Randall's illness.

With baritone Robert McFerrin, more than fifty years after first meeting, St. Louis, Missouri, 1993

Although I was now having the books printed from typed masters and bound commercially, Toi Derricotte's book, *The Empress of the Death House,* was the first to be typeset.

In 1980 Lotus Press became a nonprofit corporation and the following year received tax-exempt status as a 501(c)(3) organization. My financial burden was somewhat lightened, but I continued to work without remuneration. Several generous donations permitted the purchase of our first computer system which eventually included a laser printer. I later employed the services of a storage and fulfillment company but still had to prepare invoices and shipping labels. With two brief exceptions, my occasional helpers donated their services. The 1981, cloth-covered limited, numbered edition *Phantom Nightingale: Juvenilia* was published in an effort to raise funds for the press.

In 1984, feeling overwhelmed by my effort to juggle teaching and publishing, I retired from Eastern Michigan University as professor emerita.

The independence of the individual artist has been important in my selection of manuscripts. The seventy-six titles published therefore represent great variety in subject matter and style, the one criterion for selection being literary excellence. Many of these books have received excellent reviews in prestigious journals, and some of the authors' careers have

flourished as a direct result of their having been published by Lotus. It is rewarding to see how many of the subjects in *The Dictionary of Literary Biography,* Vol. 41, are Lotus Press authors. The highly acclaimed twentieth-anniversary anthology, *Adam of Ifé: Black Women in Praise of Black Men,* represents a timely breakthrough in the way the African American male is viewed, especially by African American women.

Realizing that my work as publisher was severely limiting my own writing, I decided to restrict future publications to poster-poems and to investigate the possibility of having distribution taken over by another company. As a result, Michigan State University Press became our distributor in June 1993, at the same time establishing the Lotus Poetry Series and naming me its senior editor. These arrangements freed me from invoicing and other paperwork while permitting me to continue to select manuscripts for publication and work with authors. My eighth book, *Remembrances of Spring: Collected Early Poems,* introduced that series. This cloth-covered collection includes a new preface, *Songs to a Phantom Nightingale* and *One and the Many* in their entirety, and the majority of poems from *Juvenilia.*

The Before Columbus Foundation recognized my contributions as a publisher and editor by selecting me for a 1993 American Book Award presented in Miami Beach at the American Booksellers Association Convention.

Also in 1993 the Hilton–Long Poetry Foundation established an annual Naomi Long Madgett Poetry Award for an outstanding manuscript by an African American poet. Each of the winners receives five hundred dollars in cash and publication by Michigan State University Press.

RECREATING OCTAVIA

My most challenging and personally satisfying collection is *Octavia and Other Poems,* published by Third World Press in 1988. It began with old family letters, photographs, and documents which my parents had brought when they came to Detroit to spend their last years with me. While my brothers and I had always been close to my mother's family, we did not have the same exposure to my father's side. My paternal grandmother and my father's beloved sister Octavia had died before I was born, and my grandfather died in 1928 without my knowing him. Aunt Ethel, mother of our only paternal cousins, lived on the campus of Wilberforce University, and my only contact with them had come through several brief visits. Uncle Robert, living some distance away, had also visited only once or twice.

The family letters, rediscovered after my parents' deaths, revealed a great deal about personalities and family history. As I became more fascinated with them, I found myself concentrating on Octavia, whose physical and temperamental resemblance I bore. As a child I had been so often compared to her that I sometimes felt like her reincarnation. The prologue of the title poem begins:

> When as a child I wore your face, Octavia
> (three years returned to earth), and christened
>   with your name,[34]
> set forth on my own odyssey,

---

[34] I was given Octavia's middle name because her first name was considered to be too painful a reminder of my father's grief.

I had no clothing of my own, only depressive hand-me-downs, frayed remnants of someone else's outgrown legacy.

My father dressed me in your skin, and such a garment, woven of his fabrication of a second chance, was not to be discarded easily.

In time I visited Guthrie, Oklahoma, the family's last home before the children began dispersing for marriage, seminary, and career, in an effort to flesh out details and get a sense of place in order to recreate Octavia's life in poetry. I was able to locate two of the four family homes and examine records in the Oklahoma Territorial Museum. I also met several aged ladies who had been my aunt's high school English students. The visit was an experience of mystical proportions as was the composition of the poem.

After the personal prologue of the book the entire family moves through the consciousness of an impartial observer with Octavia, the central figure, being addressed directly. The scene

Sitting by the hundred-year-old piano, part of my family history recorded in Octavia and Other Poems

is set in "Oklahoma Territory" in 1902 before statehood:

> A wilderness:
> A barren place
> a place of chalky skies
> of autumn wind and furies
> red dust blowing
> across the open plains
> of discontent.

Cottonwood Creek rises and the family flees the flood, drying out the oak piano on their return. Octavia graduates from Kansas State University, trudges "hatless . . . through alabaster days" to her fifth-grade class, brings reproach from her mother for "her tongue and temper, her hasty / and unkind words" in contrast with her sister, "pristine as a lily . . . always gentle and kind." After a brief marriage in Washington, D.C., she returns to teach at the first black high school in the city, eliciting her absent father's advice "to avoid involvement in the affairs / of others. Do not let your tongue speak / before your brain considers." Ill with tuberculosis, she goes to live with her brother Robert, whose wife banishes her to a barn.

> The isolation of a leper plagues you
> like flies buzzing around an open wound.
> You long for a tin cup of water
> to cool the fever of long Missouri midnights.
> You welcome the company of bats,
> study with awe the symmetry of spiders' silk.

After Octavia's 1920 death at age thirty-four in Charlottesville, Virginia, where her brother (Clarence) Marcellus now lives with his young, growing family, the poet-observer reenters the poem to comment on her visit to Guthrie, ending at Octavia's grave in Richmond, Virginia, where she finally claims a sense of her own identity, declaring,

> . . . I exorcise you
> from my spirit, old skeleton
> rattling around all these years
> in my skin. . . .

I was pleased at the reception of the book and the number of people who identified with it. The College Language Association selected it as the co-winner of its Creative Achievement Award in 1988, and the Detroit Public Schools made it required reading for high school jun-

iors, providing each school with a complete set. This was the first book of poetry to receive such a distinction. One of the appeals of the account, I think, is its presentation of an African American family like many others who, though poor and struggling, nevertheless lived by high standards and made significant contributions to their community. Like strong, positive examples of black manhood, such families are often absent from published literature.

I have continued with my family research, now concentrating on my grandfather, Frank Cornelius Long, who was the first male graduate of Leland University in New Orleans in 1881, the first black instructor at Bishop College in Marshall, Texas, the following school year, the long-time principal of Langston High School in Hot Springs, Arkansas, and holder of a degree in theology from Union Theological Seminary. In 1994 I located his grave and had a new stone erected bearing the words, "Pioneer Educator."

RECENT WORK

In addition to many poems of a general nature I have branched out in several new directions. I recently collaborated with Carl Owens on three of his fine art prints in a circular format. Each of the poems, "Sisters of the Sun," "First Man," and "Children of Eden,"[35] forms a border for the ten heads grouped on the corresponding print and gives the work its title. I have also completed seven poems suggested by Protestant hymns, spirituals, and gospel songs, including compositions by Charles A. Tindley and Thomas A. Dorsey, under the general title, "Hymns Are My Prayers." Printed individually as posters, they represent contemporary situations interpreted through the urban black experience.

Pilgrim Journey, a collection of autobiographical essays, is near completion.

PERSONAL NOTE

I feel quite comfortable in my present role as an elder and mentor to the young. I look

---

[35]From "Images of the African Diaspora," 1992 and 1993.

forward to completing unfinished work and beginning new projects. I have no plan to retire from writing. I enjoy travel and visits with my daughter, Jill Witherspoon Boyer, also a poet, and granddaughter, Liliana Malaika Boyer, a college student, in southern California, and I value the love of my extended family. I am happy in my marriage, although my husband's health is now a major concern. (Having already published under three different names, I decided at the time of this marriage to retain the name under which I was best known.)

COMMENTS ON MY WORK

My poems have been recognized nationally and internationally by inclusion in numerous magazines and journals and about 160 anthologies (including a number of textbooks). A few have been translated into European languages and three set to music and publicly performed. I have received honorary degrees from Siena Heights College, Loyola University–Chicago, and Michigan State University and have recorded at the Library of Congress for the National Archives. My papers are in the process of being deposited in the Special Collections Library at Fisk University in Nashville, Tennessee. On the state level I have received major awards sponsored by Wayne State University, Your Heritage House Writers Series, Michigan Council for the Arts and its successor, Arts Foundation of Michigan, and Concerned Citizens for the Arts in Michigan. I have been given several official testimonials each from the city and state. On January 1, 1975, I read my inaugural poem on the steps of the state capitol.

Still my work has received little critical attention, and my reputation is limited. This is due in part to my not following popular trends and in part to the years I spent promoting the careers of others at the expense of my own. Another consideration is the way most work is selected for reprint in anthologies; many editors merely select material from other anthologies already in print rather than taking the trouble to research newer work. For this reason, the same poems, many of them more than thirty years old, keep getting reprinted while more recent ones go unnoticed. Perhaps some critics assume that there is nothing more recent because they have not seen it or that a career

Naomi Long Madgett with her granddaughter, Malaika Boyer (far left), daughter, Jill Witherspoon Boyer, and husband Leonard P. Andrews, Christmas, 1988

that spans as many decades as mine is not likely to reveal any new directions. At any rate, it is disturbing that I may be represented by what I consider less than my best work.

"Midway," for example, is my most popular poem, but I see it as technically flawed. I understand its appeal; it is direct and rhythmically strong and may be unsurpassed in expressing the determined mood of the Civil Rights Movement, beginning with the opening line, "I've come this far to freedom and I won't turn back." It has lived a life of its own which includes being circulated and quoted from during the Mississippi Freedom Summer, being recited by a Miss America contestant, being set to music and publicly performed, and causing a public demonstration that canceled the major fund-raising activity at a high school in New York state.[36] But I agree with J. Saunders Redding

---

[36]Bob Wacker, "A Poem and Pride Split High School." Selden, New York: *Newsday*, May 9, 1973.

who, in a review of *New Negro Poets: U.S.A.*, found it hard to believe that "Midway" could have been written by the same poet who wrote "Mortality,"[37] which he judged to be superior. Nevertheless, many readers are drawn to my work by this poem alone, and I am happy that it has meaning for them. I only hope that those who may assess my work in the future will read enough of it to form a balanced opinion of a larger body of my work than just the few poems which are most frequently reprinted.

Like Countee Cullen I have struggled with the duality of being bade to sing both through and in spite of race. Recognizing "the black experience" shared by all African Americans, yet equally aware of the variety of individual black experiences, I have tried to be an honest poet and to interpret human experience—real, vicarious, and imagined—as I know it in the best way of which I am capable, hoping that, in doing so, even my most personal poems may in some way enlighten or broaden the path of those who read them.

When I was in high school or college I discovered in an essay by Thomas Carlyle a passage which reads, as nearly as I recall: "'Know thyself'?—Long enough hath that poor self eluded thee. . . . Know thy work and do it. That is thy greater task." Guided by that advice, I have found my greatest fulfillment in my work, first and foremost in my writing, but inextricably intertwined with that and reinforcing it, my teaching, editing, and publishing.

BIBLIOGRAPHY

Poetry:

(Under name Naomi Cornelia Long) *Songs to a Phantom Nightingale*, Fortuny's (New York), 1941.

---

[37]Both in *Star by Star.*

One and the Many, Exposition, 1956.

Star by Star, Harlo (Detroit), 1965, Evenill, 1970.

Pink Ladies in the Afternoon, Lotus Press (Detroit), 1972, 1990.

Exits and Entrances, Lotus Press, 1978.

Phantom Nightingale: Juvenilia, Lotus Press, 1981.

Octavia and Other Poems, Third World Press (Chicago), 1988.

Remembrances of Spring: Collected Early Poems, Michigan State University Press, 1993.

Hymns Are My Prayers (poster-poems; includes "Even Me" [published in *Witness*], "Make Thy Way Plain," "Stand by Me," "To Have a Home," "Pilot Me," "Great Is Thy Faithfulness," and "At the River I Stand"), Lotus Press, 1994.

Editor:

Deep Rivers, a Portfolio: Twenty Contemporary Black American Poets (with teacher's guide), Lotus Press, 1978.

A Milestone Sampler: 15th Anniversary Anthology, Lotus Press, 1988.

Adam of Ifé: Black Women in Praise of Black Men, Lotus Press, 1992.

Textbooks:

(With Ethel Tincher and Henry B. Maloney) *Success in Language and Literature/B*, Follett, 1967.

A Student's Guide to Creative Writing, Penway Books (Detroit), 1980.

Other:

Pilgrim Journey: Autobiographical Essays, forthcoming.

Sandra McPherson

1943-

1

First things

I was born the year of the gray pennies.

("1943," *The Year of Our Birth*)

The adoption had been arranged by Dr. Lenore Campbell of San José Hospital in California. On August 2, 1943, my adoptive father, navy Lt. jg Walter McPherson, and his wife, my mother-to-be, Frances Gibson McPherson, were in Corpus Christi, Texas, when they got the phone call telling them I'd been born. My birth father, John Todd, was also in uniform and about to be sent to the South Pacific. My birth mother, Joyce Turney Todd, was nineteen or twenty, a mathematics student at San José State College, the alma mater of all four parents. My adoptive grandmother, Pearl Karsten Gibson, went to the hospital when I was two days old and mothered me until Frances could reach California. In this way for a short time in infancy I became the child of five people.

I carried one heritage within me, and grew up with an extended adoptive family that frequently gathered together for social and religious occasions. Grandparents, cousins, aunts, and uncles all lived close by in San José and also owned cabins in the Santa Cruz mountains. My parents conceived a child of their own eventually, my brother, Bill, born when I was seven. I was nurtured by this family and by the natural world—ocean, creeks, trails among redwoods—up through my college years. I call my adoptive family Mother, Father, Grandma, and so on, as I shall in this essay.

In my earliest years we shared a couple of houses with Grandma Gibson. One had a small fish pond and irises. The second house boasted a giant old fig tree and oleanders poisonous and beautiful. I enjoyed reminding myself not to eat them. Next door was a screened aviary; I remember it with birds and without birds. That house stood a block away from the college.

"At opening night, exhibit of improvisational African-American quilts, California State University, Sacramento. The quilts figure significantly in The God of Indeterminacy *and also somewhat in* Edge Effect," February 1992.

My father was the basketball coach at San José State during all my formative years. He also coached golf and taught badminton. I spent many leisure hours using the college gym facilities. I walked miles of green golf courses with him and learned about winning and losing from hundreds of basketball and football games I attended or listened to on the radio. I felt every loss as harm come to my dad. Winning supplied the numerous trophies around the house. Tall young men visited our home now and then. My parents are tall. I am 5' 2". My position was guard—I tried to be "scrappy," a quality I understood to be admired in guards— whenever a PE class demanded basketball of us unpracticed girls. My father likes to tell true funny stories. All kinds of people have always enjoyed his company. I like to think that some of my sense of humor and a fair amount of my timing come from listening to him tell stories. The *truth* of them may have eclipsed any attraction to my thinking in fictional terms. I don't write fiction but I like to tell true stories in conversation.

My own mind, when it needs to create, engages itself more with places and impressions than with narratives. Even before I could read, my father's campus was a place, a distinct world, that fed my imagination. I counted time by its carillon. As I grew older, I walked through its palm-tree islands or under its Spanish arches or had the trampoline, climbing rope, and parallel bars to myself in the echoing high-ceilinged gymnasium room. I swam almost alone in the men's pool, checked out the shadows of a concert hall, joined adults on a summer night to square dance in the brightly lit yellow-wooded gymnasium. These atmospheres and architectures still figure almost nightly in my dreams.

Walt and Frances knew each other virtually from birth. I have a photo of them standing next to each other in their second-grade class picture. My mother, like my dad and my birth parents, graduated from San José State, with an elementary school teaching credential. *Her* mother taught elementary school for decades after the untimely death of her young husband, a farmer, during the 1918–19 flu epidemic. My mother liked to read to me, and began doing so when I was still an infant too young to know the words. She taught me many nursery rhymes. My mother and grandmother made sure I could sing and play the piano. I could sing, but after my first solo to a church audience (was I wearing a costume of blue silk Chinese pajamas?) I refused ever again to sing in public. I liked, however, to improvise harmonies and sang parts with my mother and grandmother when very young. I also liked to attend symphonies, to listen to symphonic records, and

At two years and three months, with her adoptive parents, Walt and Frances McPherson, San José, California

to play conductor. At age six I led the rhythm band at Junior Church and recall feeling real zest over it, a love of music overcoming the shyness I would usually feel in public on up through my college years.

The piano in my parents' home was a Kimball spinet; when I was around fourteen, they added a Hammond organ. I took about eight years of classical piano lessons. Because my main teacher was our church pianist, I also learned to play hymns with variations suitable as recital fare. On the stage I once followed a 6' 7" student of Miss Penner's and did not think to pull the piano bench back in toward the pedals and keyboard. I was mortified, but the audience seemed to find my solo of stretched-out arms and legs appealing.

When I was in high school and college, I played for our church youth group services, for "sings," and for Young Life evangelical services in people's homes. I could play easily by ear, transposed easily, and experimented with playing "What a Friend We Have in Jesus" in 5/4 time after immersing myself in a Dave Brubeck album. I would occasionally tease my mother by practicing a hymn for next Sunday's offertory and playing all but the last chord. Or I would resolve the hymn suddenly with a jazzy dissonance. I wanted to play jazz, but lacked training in improvisation. Besides, my favorite keys were D-flat, E-flat, A-flat, and B-flat; I couldn't play well in the "simpler," more universal keys of C, F, and G.

About the time I entered college I applied for a summer job at the Bible conference ground where my family had a cabin. I was turned down because on one "Staff Night," when the staff entertained the public with music and comedy skits, I had accompanied on piano a Mount Hermon employee who played "Tenderly" on his saxophone. The bluesy cocktail strains filling the huge hall in the redwoods horrified the staff director. "Don't you know where the saxophone was first played?" he reproved me later. "In a brothel!"

As a girl, I also enjoyed handwork, and that pursuit has so far not led me into any similar trouble. From my mother and grandmothers I learned how to knit, embroider, and sew. Some of my clothes were homemade; I remember standing on Grandma Gibson's dining-room table while she pinned up a hem on a taffeta Sunday dress, a seersucker pinafore, or a corduroy jumper. I turned around slowly while she measured with a yardstick to make sure the hem was even all around. She knitted almost all my sweaters as well as snow suits and even swim suits. Grandma McPherson tatted and crocheted. I knitted in bed when I stayed home sick from school and added rows of loops down by the confluence of Zayante and Bean creeks on summer afternoons. But I can't remember completing anything. I just liked the math of it, the clacking sound of it, and the woolliness of it. It probably led to my buying a loom when I was a young mother—enjoyment of textures, webs, weaves, and fibers as part of the natural world. Later, my collecting of pieced quilts probably owed a great deal to this early tactile experience. And to the memory of a fan quilt and some crazy quilts I slept under while listening to crickets and raccoons from my bed on the screened porch in the redwoods.

In my young years, I read fairy tales, popular children's mystery books, haiku, *Hiawatha*, dictionaries, encyclopedias, books of maps, *National Geographic*, the Bible, Shakespeare, Dickens, Poe, and James Russell Lowell. We didn't have a lot of books around my parents' house, but all these good ones made literature seem like a world desirable to visit. Somehow, as I perceived it, the written word was inextricable from pictures. Literature was visual. A couple of generations back a cousin had married into a branch of *the* Lowell family—they raised walnuts in Modesto. So I felt a remote connection to James Russell, and later to Amy, from the public library. On the other hand, I didn't know a single relative who wanted her or his child to grow up to be a poet. Grandma Gibson studied at San José State around 1910 with Henry Meade Bland, so she probably thought a poet was someone who had boundless feeling that he kept in check by wearing a skullcap. As far as I knew, my kin saw poetry as rhymed innocence, just a hobby. I don't know how or when I perceived that it was more important than that to me. I do know that in high school I set out to write one hundred poems. And I did write that many. When the trauma of social dancing in the high school gym was the antithesis of poetry to me, I would go home, lock myself in the bedroom, and supply poetry out of privacy, pain, secret joy, and language. A few friends and Lucile Eastman, my senior English teacher, wanted the poems, said the poems meant a lot to them, and called me "Poet Laureate of T-101."

Perhaps I begin with all these extracurricular pleasures because school's official academic pressures were something I rose to but did not enjoy. I was a straight-*A* student, as are many I teach now, afraid that anything less meant I was worth less. I was obedient. But now, admiration for my teachers has replaced the need to meet expectations. Expectancy is a better daily light than meeting expectations.

2

Spiritual history

That which was most inspiriting to me in childhood I often experienced in solitude, or with sympathetic company. On my grandmother's dining-room table I painted watercolors of Yellowstone Park, copying intensely hued photographs of the Morning Glory Pool, yel-

*The author, a few weeks short of six years,
San José, California*

low mud pots, or emerald trees. I painted bouquets, floated them on washes, out of my own imagining. On family picnics I gathered wildflowers from both mountain ranges, the coastal and the interior, surrounding the Santa Clara Valley. I pressed them in volumes of an outdated *World Book*, eventually to mount and label. I found every excuse to keep scrapbooks and to illustrate them—Blue Bird and Campfire Girl notebooks, school term projects on into college, and journals of summer travels my dad loved to take us on, across America to scenic and historic places, to Mexico and Canada. Some of my favorite books classified assortments of things: farm implements, dogs, birds, fish, trees, Japanese clothing, tints and shades of colors. And words: my grandmother's heavy marble-edged dictionary displayed, in comparative panels, alphabets of many languages and eras. I built, out of shoe boxes, ranch homes with recessed entry porches, rooms I designed interiors for, and paper furniture. I amassed a company of dolls, for whom I sewed, but my

instinct for them was not maternal but creatorly. (In this I was not unlike my daughter, who told a vocational rehabilitation doctor that she was more interested in Barbie's bicycle than in Barbie.) I dug landscapes out of the tops of redwood stumps, moving moss around to be forests and pouring water through my wooden canyons. I believe these activities were not mere "crafts projects" but spiritual pursuits, enlarging the vision of how natural and man-made things grow to be made, grow to exist.

In Mount Hermon, a Bible conference ground where my grandmother owned a cabin, I learned to love trails. I would go barefoot down the prickly leaved Tan Oak Trail and hike back in redwood canyons until the trails ran out—but ambiguously, unclearly, as if they drifted off to sleep or didn't want to end or limit themselves. Fern glades were different in spirit from sulphur springs. Every summer I took all this in, the scent of bay trees, squirrels leaping, the waterfall and the story that a horse and rider once went over it, the creek threatening the next step with crayfish, and the high swaying suspension bridges—the one-railed or no-railed across the creeks, one creek stony and the other sandy. I appreciated the fuzzy hazel bushes, the different sizes and colors of ants.

I was neatened up for as many as six church services a week. The Presbyterian church was the center of my adoptive family's life. Somewhere there's an old Bible with the date of my conversion. Though I cannot locate it, I recall a little knot of nearly concurrent events: I think I was four, trying on my mother's pasty pink elastic girdle (which swallowed a toddler up), being asked, "Do you want to invite Jesus into your heart?" and listening afterwards to Edgar Bergen and Charlie McCarthy in the car on the way to church. I suppose laughter, metaphysics, and being female converged for me early on. On my own I generated lots of private fervent praying and made attempts to get Jesus or John or Saint Peter to appear in my room. I was very devout and studious of the Bible, "reading the Gospel of John / in a little red pocket version" on long bus trips ("Open Casket," *The Year of Our Birth*).

> To pray was like living on the road
> that goes on to someone else's house
> even when it is too far to walk.
>
> ("Studies in the Imaginary,"
> *The Year of Our Birth*)

I memorized hundreds of verses from the King James Bible. In Vacation Bible School I liked making models of houses Jesus might have visited in the Holy Land, flat roofs, stairs unfolding as they ascended an outside wall, sand glued down to cardboard to serve as a yard. On the screened porch of Grandma Gibson's cabin I made a scroll map of crucial spiritual sites in *Pilgrim's Progress.*

I was let out of public school once a week for "religious education." There, our leaders' favorite creative projects seemed to be painting word-pictures of hell. Though I loved believing I was a "child of God," I was also instructed in all my denomination's fears. Childish sexual curiosity was branded dirty; I was sent to my room and told to pray about sins I committed as a curious five- or six-year-old. When I was a teenager I was told that for a boy to peel a girl's commonplace California sunburn was naughty, lewd. My chemises and muumuus made one relative feel faint and have to lie down. For a year and a half after high school, I attended a Christian college, Westmont, in the chaparral hills behind Santa Barbara. There, a teacher said to me—as I played what I wished were jazz—that he could feel Satan at a Brubeck concert; jazz vibrated with evil. Though I can't remember what prompted it, I received a letter there from a relative saying, "The only way to be happy is to conform." When I ceased my affiliation with the organized church in favor of spiritual uplift from the natural world, the arts, and theologians not sanctioned by our church, I was told, "We'll have to pick you up out of the gutter."

Creation of art has, I think, always been for me a counterpoint to destructive dogma. "Secular" creation and "sacred" creation do not feel like two separate things, as I participate in them, but a single urge toward rightness and beauty and truth. In fact, even becoming a woman is a creative act, a metaphysical duty. Even the silliness and seriousness of sexuality are better thought of as earnest processes of becoming, not (as I was taught) original sin.

Eventually I wrote of a paternal dark landscape whose horizon felt "submerged like the breath of their god":

> On that dark rim
> they said the children looked
> as brown as quail.

*The author's daughter, Phoebe Carlile,
at age nine, Portland, Oregon*

> But we were really
> blue inside
> like the small triangle of ocean
> having its own sunset
>
> after theirs.

("Childish Landscape,"
The Year of Our Birth)

I love quail, but it is any misrepresentation of a person's soul that I frequently use poetry to correct. We were all said to have immoral earthly hearts that only our denomination of the organized church could correct. Even today, as I write this past my mid-century mark, family members tell others, "I wish they'd go to church. Any church."

Better than I could say it, this affirmation by a Hopi potter demonstrating her art at the Lowie Museum of Anthropology at the University of California at Berkeley in 1981 illustrates how I've come to feel: when I asked Helen Naha, Featherwoman, "Which part of potting do you like the best?" she replied, "Well, there are three dirty parts and two clean parts. The dirty part is molding, sanding, and slipping. The clean part is painting and firing. I guess I like them all." The crafting of things parallels the right care of the spirit. But even if the "crafting" is experimental and focused on the self, Featherwoman's statement is wise. Hers is the kind of wisdom useful to a young person in the process of formation—reading books, seeing great paintings, things that integrate the scrupulous and the messy into a living whole.

Any poem of mine is likely to contain biblical references. This is a microscopic description of the sticky yellow Sand Verbena:

> Like David it picks up stones of sand,
>   quartz rubble,
> whitish, a rare orange, more populous grays
> (each grain with several infinitesimal grains
> of sand on *it*), until the glandular leaves
> and stems grow all too heavy to fling
> one pebble at Goliath.

> ("Yellow Sand Verbena," *Streamers*)

Of a feather that fell from a heron passing over our beach beside a narrow creek, I wrote:

> I accept its descent, a trace
> of a good soul taken in the Rapture,
> its barbs zipped
> like the slacks of men at church.

> ("The Feather," *Streamers*)

Occasionally I attempt what I call a Bible rewrite but have recently learned resembles a Jewish tradition, Midrash. Since Adam got to name the animals, in "Eve" (*Streamers*) I create an order from God to Eve to name clothing, a central concern of God after making Eve ashamed of her nakedness, her good first woman's body. When, in 1979, my daughter nailed her stuffed sock monkey to a cross and stuck it in the vegetable garden, I protested:

> Christ, your abstinence
> denied us neighbors more divine,
> dilute descendants of the Truth and Life.
> We too could have been in your bloodline.

> ("Easter 1979," *The God of Indeterminacy*)

During an early spring teaching residency at Provincetown Fine Arts Center I took an informal survey of writers there, asking them what they found "most spiritual" about the place. The poem concludes:

> For me most spiritual is when I walk out
>   to the edge of town,
> beside the melt-rim of the snow,
> white grass rebounding in the sun,
> and listen to the snakes.

> ("From My Notebook, Cape Cod," *Streamers*)

The young snakes were just beginning to move in the thaw. That, to me, was spiritual revival.

More recently I took some quilts to an African-American reverend for his comment and got in return a sermon to my liking:

> The minister said, "Hell is for angels . . .
> Sin is unhealthy . . . Blues are my colors . . .
> Women sewed banners who couldn't afford pictures . . ."
> And faith—I think he said—is mathematical.
> He said anyone's mother is his mama,
> he doesn't scare with damnation
> those who need joy, said daughters and nieces
> leaving home were saved in patchwork pieces.
> Said he was the worst of us. In the turquoise-
> carpeted sanctuary claimed he'd done
> things he'd never tell. Leaves a door open
> when he counsels women. Always guards a corpse.
> Said so standing beside a sack of Ajax and Chore Boys:
> Saturdays he cleans the church of all the evil he absorbs.

> ("Two Private Sermons from the Reverend Dr. Small . . . ,"
> *The God of Indeterminacy*)

I collect the art now of various spiritual traditions, including Mexican ex-votos, Haitian vodoun spirit flags, African-American visionary spirit-writing, Anglo-American ministers who suddenly start painting with no art training. And I admire Eshu, the Yoruba god of indeterminacy, odd numbers, asymmetry, and one-time events.

> If you spread all your beliefs
> crossways to your disbeliefs
> the square where they intersect
> is holy ground.
>
> Though it is struck from all sides,
> it is your hearth, your patch, your
>   junction of amends.

("Ode for the God of Indeterminacy,"
The God of Indeterminacy)

3

College years

I went to three colleges: Westmont for a year and a half, San José State for two and a half years, and the University of Washington for two quarters of graduate work. At Westmont I learned a great deal from Dr. Jan Kingma, a literature and art history professor who threw his whole body into demonstrating—by becoming—a splayed arch. He ran across the lecture stage, waving his arms roundly over his head. He conveyed passion for whatever he lectured on. Decades later I learned he was gay and, while discreetly helping gay students to feel well about themselves in a hostile environment, felt great pain at religious suppression of his identity. All kinds of mundane enthusiasms were officially quashed there: every student at Westmont had to sign a pledge we would not go to movies, drink, smoke, gamble, or dance. But Dr. Kingma taught *passion* for art, embodied in a *dance* for art, in these circumstances and changed my life.

Westmont performed psychological testing on freshmen. The school psychologist called me in for a private conference because, he said, after calculating my test profile, he had to see what I looked like. He was surprised such a person could exist, or could bear existence. He said, "You have 99 percent energy, 98 percent restraint, and 5 percent social inclination." I

said I did experience a lot of tension but that his tests did not measure the artistic outlets that I enjoyed—music, painting, writing poetry. In the gardens beside streams on campus, I would read Rilke and Pasternak, Basho and Buson, and study small volumes on Klee and Modigliani. This poetry and painting gave me new eyes. My "social inclination" was to seek out these artists' company.

At San José State Dr. Roberta Holloway, teacher of poetry workshops and of modern poets, also affected the course of my life. A single woman whose bodily roundness was equaled by her beauty, she taught poetic modernity as somehow inseparable from her own good humor and glowing humaneness. Like Dr. Kingma, she was someone I wanted to be like. I served as a reader for one of her classes; after graduation I corresponded with her until her death.

Although I can almost completely avoid giving mistaken romance any representation in these paragraphs, one such misadventure did lead to a two-week visit to Manhattan in the summer of 1964 and thus to a scene important to my future. I was engaged for one week to a loose diamond for which no setting could be found. When, the second week, I was abandoned in favor of a young Norwegian woman, I tried to fall into a stupor by taking eight aspirin. I couldn't even fall asleep—did they put caffeine in aspirin, I wondered then?—and ended up turning the radio dial around and around. I heard more polkas than I believed a huge metropolis could dance to. Eventually my would-have-been mother-in-law, an Italian-American who clerked part time in a nuns' and priests' clothing store, found me, laid her hand on my hair, and said, "You're lucky: I married the wrong man."

In 1965 I went to the University of Washington to study with Theodore Roethke's ghost. He was indeed everywhere. His mysticism was part of the weather report. His descents into terror knocked on many a young poet's door in the middle of the night. His one-time students told stories of his exuberant phases—throwing all his pocket change at "Greeks" under a flagpole, yelling, "This is all you want," watching them scoop it up, then going off to commit himself. I met Carolyn Kizer in the offices of *Poetry Northwest* when she accepted the second, third, and fourth poems of mine to be published. My eyes widened to see her six-foot-tall glamor in a robin's-egg-blue paisley dress and matching busy blue paisley stockings. I loved how she gossiped, knew everyone in literature and everything about everyone. I loved her energy. I took a workshop from David Wagoner my first quarter in graduate school; Dave's expansive aesthetic let the genie of my poetry out of its constricting bottle. My small poems turned into long segmented descents with ecstatic or chilling realizations at their outcomes. I went home for Christmas with a sense of real growth.

During that holiday season the course of my life swerved again. A friend in whom I had confided told my parents that my man friend in Seattle was not of their race. I was disinherited and sent to a psychiatrist. Support for my graduate studies was terminated, so I used my savings to fund a second and last quarter at UW. Lucky I did: the poet holding the Roethke Chair was Elizabeth Bishop. My man friend's mother had once been married to a Seattle painter who was now married to a young pregnant woman who would later leave the painter for Elizabeth. The young woman told

me that Bishop was afraid of madness; in class we saw Elizabeth's contempt for the way she felt Roethke's madness manifested itself in his poetry. I admired both poets' brilliant work as well as Bishop's understated manner and humor. From both Roethke and Bishop I learned the art of observation and the different ways it could sound in lines—mystical or homey, for example.

When the interracial relationship came to an end from natural causes, my family reinherited me. But my schooling would be all self-teaching from then on.

4

One marriage

In the winter quarter of 1966 Henry Carlile and I were students in the first poetry workshop Elizabeth Bishop ever taught, at the University of Washington. I used to wear a California-orange raincoat that Henry said you could see for blocks in the Seattle rain. A veteran of Roethke's poetry workshops, he was older than me by nine years. He was born Henry Prieto of a Cuban Spanish-speaking father and an English-speaking American Anglo-French mother. When I dropped out of graduate school and took a job as a technical writer for Honeywell, we began dating. Henry continued to take Bishop's spring quarter course while working in a shipyard.

I became pregnant. Though no magazine ever wanted to publish "Pregnancy" (*Elegies for the Hot Season*), it is probably my most reprinted poem:

Who started this?
An axis, a quake, a perimeter,

I have no decisions to master
That could change my frame

Or honor.
Immaculate. Or if it was not, perfect.

One day after work I chose an inexpensive loose pink dress to get married in. At St. Mark's Episcopal Cathedral we found a priest who would marry us on short notice. I remember that in the prenuptial interview he asked us three reasons why we were marrying. We didn't mention the most pressing reason. We thought of two oth-

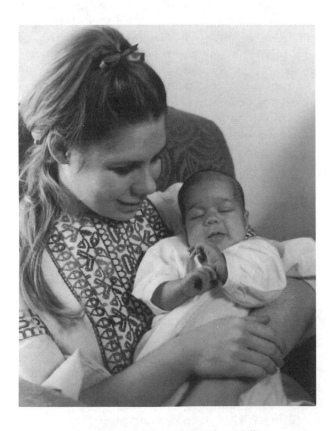

Sandy and Phoebe, Seattle, 1967

"The photo that appeared on the cover of my first book, Elegies for the Hot Season. *The hat was subsequently stolen from me in the Pendleton, Oregon, airport."*

ers but couldn't think of a third. The priest's answer was, to perpetuate social order. I am not sure how well we fulfilled that goal.

My cousin Bruce Robertson gave me away; his wife, Aldene, was maid-of-honor; the best man was a Marquis de Sade libertine and poet, Henry's friend John Pym. The only people in the audience were total strangers—friends of a friend of ours, who wanted their children to see what a wedding was like. While we were reciting vows in a small chapel, someone was practicing the pipe organ in the main sanctuary, thus inadvertently supplying the ceremony with music. Afterwards we caught a ferry and spent our first night in the motel that many years later served, in *An Officer and a Gentleman,* as the scene of a young serviceman's suicide. Do I remember correctly that his girlfriend had lied to him that she was pregnant?

I enjoyed being pregnant. Since I don't drive, I walked miles up and down the slopes of Se-

attle streets, between home and the University Hospital, or to and from the grocery with a wire pull cart. I wore a conical fir-green wool coat, which I completely filled. Once, under an overpass, a strange man confronted and propositioned me. "I can give you a good time," he said. "I've already had a good time," I said back and pointed: "Can't you see?"

At Honeywell, male bosses disparaged my maternity clothes, had me stand through meetings when a room was short on chairs, and made me push my office contents from one end of the building to the other. When my first obstetrician said I was too fat and prescribed a diet drug—some kind of speed—for me, it made my Honeywell work a bit more exciting than usual. But after a week one of my women colleagues said I definitely should not be using that drug or it could harm my foetus. I stopped it, but perhaps damage was done. I changed doctors. A Honeywell engineer, who didn't like to see a pregnant woman walking steep blocks in the rain to the bus before and after work, offered me rides; our boss soon forbade him to do so—because "it didn't look good"—or face being fired. When the gentleman gave his two weeks' notice, he immediately reoffered his services.

My daughter, Phoebe, was born after twenty hours of labor, on the evening of February 24, 1967, in the University Hospital. During the long labor, Henry read to me from Anthony Hecht's *The Hard Hours*—wonderful chilling poetry. I was given a caudal and eventually saw my new daughter, held up next to my face. I thought she was gorgeous, dark, and rosebud lipped. She was the first blood relative I had ever seen.

5

A mother, a housewife

Gooseflesh plaster walls
We live between . . .

("All You Need,"
Elegies for the Hot Season)

In autumn after Phoebe's birth, Henry moved us to Portland, Oregon, where he had been hired to teach in Portland State College's English Department. My joy in creating a home for my own family—in redefining home in my own quirky form—alternated with tensions from income so limited I'd reuse tea bags and make a single pork chop feed two adults for two nights. When a visiting poet came to read at Portland State, we often couldn't afford a babysitter. I missed meeting a few poets in those early years, but occasionally one, such as James Tate, would be brought home for dinner before his reading or to stay overnight afterwards. I felt isolated, and too dependent on my husband's contacts with the "outside world." My Plath-influenced poems from this period show an attempt to praise and affirm, set up against images of suffocation and even assault:

> The house is brimful.
> Eden, pure Eden is chasing us.
> The baby is pounding her bars
> To get out.
>
> ("Keeping House,"
> *Elegies for the Hot Season*)

I drafted poems with Phoebe on the bed beside me or while washing dishes. For pleasure I would wheel or walk Phoebe along the edges of gardens or the skirts of woods whenever it wasn't raining. I tried making things I was less skilled at than writing: I did some weaving with a backstrap loom improvised from string, a couple of dowels, a pencil, and a scarf. A few years later I bought a four-harness loom. I loved wool and linen fiber and studied up on textiles of ancient civilizations. But my domestic life was much smaller than it is now.

Outside the walls life escalated. We took camping trips where Henry fished and I observed nature with binoculars, a notebook, and field guides. During our macrobiotic phase, in a campground textured with lava, Phoebe off-rhymed, "Organic brown rice and organic brown rocks." We spent many weeks beside Oregon fly-fishing-only lakes or the Strait of Juan de Fuca, Puget Sound, Minnesota waters, Montana rivers. I might carry Jean-Henri Fabre along to read about watching insects' lives, or bring Bishop to spur me to write clearly and charmingly about what captured my senses, including the sense of humor. If my results sounded like practicing scales, they were groundwork for what I would attempt twenty years later—to describe, under Gary Snyder's encouragement, specific "places on earth."

I spent plenty of time reading to Phoebe, talking and playing with her, surrounding her with music, art supplies, building blocks, dolls (which she never took to), and toy vehicles (which she loved—her first word was "Machine!"). *The Spaces Between Birds: Mother/Daughter Poems, 1967–1995* draws together her story insofar as I came to poetry with it, but there is, of course, more: late speech, echolalia, confusion of pronouns, obsessive drawings of lawn mowers, pianos, and bicycles—getting the mechanical parts just right—dismantling anything and everything, and getting kicked out of two kindergartens, a third kindergarten wanting to drug her. She had little social understanding outside the home. A pleasant but telling example is when we spent nearly a week on a camping trip from Oregon to the Midwest and took along a student of Henry's who was moving to Iowa City to attend the Writers Workshop. We introduced him to Phoebe, saying, "His name is Reed." For the rest of the trip she addressed Reed as "The Name."

While I thought Phoebe was just a natural poets' kid—vibraphones sounded "like pineapple" to her, yodeling "like noodles"—the schools found her behavior beyond the pale. That is her story to tell, and now that she is reading up on Asperger's Syndrome autism, her finally accurate diagnosis, she is proud of the details of her individuality. Phoebe and I have always been very close. At twenty-eight she has caught up with adulthood at last and is a helpful and patient aid to her less self-knowing disabled friends. (She uses her mechanical skills to fix their wheelchairs.) But during her school years, motherhood was terribly difficult for me: she could only be instructed to do one thing at a time, and that instruction had to be reiterated over and over again; she reacted inversely to praise and encouragement, desisting much accomplishment she was on the verge of. Other children were emotionally brutal toward her, throwing her schoolbooks off a highway overpass, yelling out insults when her name was called at high school graduation. She and I were lucky, though, to be easily able to show our love for each other. She liked to practice being born, to act out her birth with me as late as eight years after the fact.

In 1970 I was—"how unlikely," Bishop would say—a member of the Forum on Individuality for the White House Conference on Children and Youth. When I recommended acceptance and understanding of oddity and eccentricity, I was only at the beginning of Phoebe's and my odd and eccentric odyssey together. Maybe *The Spaces Between Birds,* and Phoebe herself, whose poems are included in the book, will supply needed testimony. Phoebe ends one of her early poems:

> The giant salesman bought the world
> They put the world in a clown's body
> And they put the clown in a joker's body

She had a more profound sense of absurdity as a child than many adults ever achieve. Once she said that going to the same church all of your life is "like eating all your meals at Bob's Big Boy." She did not rate the diversity of the dishes there very high. She also enriched our lives with her perfect pitch. She made a xylophone out of broken glass, which I talk about in one poem, adding, "The only perfect pitch I have / Is seeing numbers in color. / Even counting seconds after the lightning / I cannot escape a blue four / Or a yellow two" ("Ode Near the Aspen Music School," *Patron*

Happiness). I am still unclear on how unusual abilities and disabilities balance or interrelate, but Phoebe and I have tried to enjoy each gift as best we can.

6

Early friendships and associations in poetry

Through Henry, in Seattle, I met Joan Swift, who had also studied with Roethke. Through David Wagoner I met Gwen Head, whose first poems Dave published. He read each of them aloud to me before *Poetry Northwest* printed them. It was for me a pivotal lesson in how to write a vibrant poem. Gwen and Joan and I have been close friends ever since. We have shown each other our work for comment, compared stories of love and motherhood, shared observations of the natural world, and made each other laugh for thirty years now. If I were to say I belonged to a school of poetry, it would

Sandra McPherson (middle) with friends Joan Swift (left) and Gwen Head, at Ballard Locks, Seattle, Washington, early 1980s

quite likely be the school of the many things we have in common. Only many years later would I find the friendship of the other women poets who widen this "society."

Our first apartment after our move to Portland was within walking distance of William Stafford's house. He and Dorothy were kind and welcoming to us. Bill liked to take both good *and* bad photographs of fellow poets. Somewhere exist a few precious, sensitive portraits and a good number of negatives worth burning. Over the next few years we met and tended to many poets who came through on the Northwest Poetry Circuit: Anthony Hecht, David Young, Shirley Kaufman, Charles Simic, Paul Zimmer, John Logan, Edward Field, Robert Huff, George Hitchcock, Mark Strand, Dick Hugo, and many others. We socialized with poets who taught or lived in Portland at that time—Jon Anderson, Michael Harper, Primus St. John, Vern Rutsala. I am leaving out many names, I'm sure, but not many names of women.

David Wagoner was kind enough to offer to send my first book manuscript to Indiana University Press, his publisher. Sometime later he called to announce that Indiana had accepted it. *Elegies for the Hot Season* came out in 1970 with a hot cerise-orange cover. It was a book about my childhood, about making a home, becoming a mother, and experiencing domestic tensions. It echoed Plath and Wagoner in its energies and structures; I hoped it had some of Neruda's virtues, too, and Hardy's and Bishop's and James Dickey's. And something of my own— a voice louder than I dared to raise during my upbringing or the early years of my marriage.

In 1972 we moved within Portland to a home we purchased in a neighborhood of big old maples, elms, rhododendrons, and azaleas, near Reed College. In 1974, after the publication of my second collection, *Radiation*, I was asked to teach at the University of Iowa. I had actually inquired about getting an MFA there, when, to my surprise, Marvin Bell and Donald Justice proposed a visiting lectureship. Having never taught anything longer than a week's workshop, I threw myself into rereading literature I loved, primarily Thoreau, since I wanted students to excel in detailed observation of the natural world. This approach was naive, I learned, since half the students in my first seminar didn't care where on earth they were or what lived out-

With Stanley Kunitz,
San Francisco, California, 1986

side their apartment door. However, their distinct intelligences were dazzling, and many of these writers (not much younger than I was) are now beloved friends and accomplished authors. From 1974 to 1976 I enjoyed identifying Midwest wildlife that was new to me—I'll name birds, perhaps, instead of poets: thrushes, thrashers, nighthawks, flickers, woodpeckers, nuthatches, cardinals, owls. One prolonged snowy winter, seventeen squirrels fed simultaneously from our feeder. I lived above a little zoo in the city park. Braying donkeys, Moulin sheep, bison, prairie dogs, a raccoon family—I would regularly visit these. Lightning would split the oaks in front of the house; clans would hold pig roasts across the street; fireflies would crop up and blink out; I gathered hundreds of shaggy manes there one season. A woodchuck drunk on fermented apples toppled over, rolled around, and scavenged desperately for another alcohol-laced apple from a tree in the yard.

My mother's mother had grown up in Homestead bordering the Amana colonies, and other relatives lived in Kolona. Though I didn't visit with family, I felt quite at home in the rural settings. Sometimes we'd get whole raw milk still warm from a cow on the edge of town. (In San José, my parents were for a time financial partners with the family that owned the land and the cows and the one or two bulls of Evergreen Dairy. I occasionally rode on the milk delivery truck with my father.) At some point Carolyn Kizer and I gave a joint reading at Maharishi University in another Iowa town. Our audience sat meditatively with their eyes closed despite Carolyn's bawdiest, wittiest efforts.

From 1978 to 1980, I taught again at the Writers' Workshop. My third collection, *The Year of Our Birth,* was nominated for the National Book Award. I attended the Carter-Mondale White House reception for poets and shook as I shook the President's hand. I hugged Richard Hugo there for the last time.

7

Finding my way

On returning to the West in the summer of 1980, I took Phoebe with me and taught a workshop at Squaw Valley in the Sierra Nevada. Alone, I took the tram up to High Camp and became quite transported with the elevation and the view. I looked long at alpine wildflowers I'd never seen before. I hitched a ride on a truck down to Shirley Lake. It was hot and dusty and I went for a good cold swim. I stepped on the lake bottom and it dispersed under my foot. I swam further from shore until I was good and cold. Swam back, dressed, and began to take what I thought was the path to the valley a couple of thousand feet below. At some point the path disappeared and the lake disappeared and I realized I was lost. The stream I was following went down into an unreachable, muffling canyon. Later I picked up its sound again and followed it to a cliff, where it split into two distinct courses. I looked down at a hawk. I had to leave the stream again to search for a route to descend. This search and the solitude merged dismay and beauty in a way that occurs in my best states of composition, too.

In 1981 I served as Roberta Holloway Lecturer for four weeks at the University of California at Berkeley. Remembering that the McPhersons had told me, when a teenager, my birth parents' last name, I used the Bancroft Library of books on California history to track down Todds who might be my family. Using Polk city directories (not telephone books) I made lists of all the people with that surname whose occupations sounded "professional" or "artistic" or "mathematical" or "musical," terms

the McPhersons used to describe my ancestral background. They suggested the Todds might have been "lawyers, teachers, engineers."

Up until then, I would only occasionally look in the mirror and try to age my face into what I thought my birth father might look like. I scanned my body and tried to imagine my birth mother's figure. Now I had pages and pages of Todds from my part of the Bay Area, addresses, who lived in what house and what they did for a living. I had always liked the notion that I "came out of nowhere." I felt as if I had grown out of the ground or been dropped from a cloud. Having no blood ties, I felt a sense of imaginative freedom and individuality conducive to an aspiring artist. Perhaps this is the reason several poets have told me that as children they pretended they were adopted. I was never resentful of my biological family; instead, I tended to identify with them, imagining them to be too interested in intellectual and artistic aspects of life to want to spend their adulthood on a child. I looked for my birth parents not to find out "who I was," as they say, but to see if there were others who thought like me. Because I was no longer a child, I was not looking for an extra set of parents but for adults like myself.

One evening I broke the news to my mother and father that I was proceeding with this investigation. Mother lay down on the couch as if she were going to faint, but out of this trance she recalled the first names of my birth parents. I looked over my lengthy list of Todds, and there they were, along with a daughter. Then *I* felt lightheaded. I had found them and I had a sister.

My mother also told me at that time that on the legal papers I had another name: Helen Todd. Donald Justice mused on this for me with a little light verse:

> Ancient mysteries of the womb—
> When you sought a *nom de plume*
> Would it not have seemed quite odd
> Had you chosen Helen Todd?

Although Don added, "You will write all this up— in *prose,* of course," I could only use poetry. I ended a poem for the Helen I would have been: "I was not born. Only you were." ("Helen Todd: My Birthname," *Patron Happiness*).

When I first contacted my birth parents— by mail—they each wrote back their own letter full of warmth and concern. Because the attorney had not been careful to cover the names of the adopting parents and because the Todds had once been shown a newspaper photo of me as a child, they knew my adopted name. Because we were graduates of the same university, they found out from the alumni newspaper that I had published books. Long before I contacted them, they searched for and bought all of my books. When they read, in one, a reference to "the adoption I knew nothing of" ("On Coming Out of Nowhere," *The Year of Our Birth*), they felt they should do something but held back partly because of their other daughter, who had not been told. Now they prepared to tell her. They set up photographs of me around the room and asked Ellayn if they looked like anyone she knew. My birth mother wrote, "All at once there will be two happy sisters!" My sister said, "Well, they look a little bit like *me*," and cried with happiness to find out she was not an only child.

Upon meeting my birth parents, I felt an immediate bond with them and identified with their personalities and quirks. Their house, for instance: it is nestled among wildflowers and wild mushrooms; the trees are full of birds they know all the names of—it seems one can be by heredity a birder; the house is crammed with books on every subject; paintings, pottery, and baskets fill niches in the walls; a Steinway grand takes up half the tiny living room. I saw that all four of us were short with green eyes. My father was a violinist, my mother a pianist, my sister a flautist. My mother, father, and one grandmother were mathematicians; math was my best subject, even if I wasn't attracted to it. My sister got her college degree in art. My birth father was at one time a Spanish teacher and his father a German professor; I believe some of the language skill a writer needs was passed on to me from them, to be combined with the environment of regular reading the McPhersons provided. My birth parents were passionate naturalists and environmentalists, to the point of mysticism. My birth father liked to compose limericks and witty epigrams; his grandfather wrote a forty-page autobiography; his mother loved to write verse and published some in the *Christian Science Monitor* and a seniors' publication. My birth father called himself a philosopher, a monistic pantheist. He would periodically immerse himself in Chinese or Egyptian grammar. Phoebe's gift for electronics and

mechanics found an explanation: her birth grandfather owned a radio repair shop briefly and was an engineer for many years. My birth mother and I had both been valedictorian of our high school class.

The first thing John and Joyce showed me when we met, before I even entered their house, was a "walking" mushroom, called an earthstar, a geaster.

> Geasters. She bent down
> At the dappled base of the tree,
> And among the brown leaves
> Geasters stood up.
>
> Oranges peel like these,
> She said. Rinds bent back.
> When it rains, their legs swell up
> And walk.
>
> > Stranger feet
> > Than mine
> > All these years
> > Outside your door.
>
> ("Geasters, Birthparents' House,"
> *Patron Happiness*)

My birth father used to take stereo photographs of mushrooms. On this first day united, we went for a walk in the baylands and identified dozens of birds and plants. My birth sister, I discovered, walks along a trail the same way I do—stopping to identify snakes and lizards and wildflowers and shrubs. About the cosmos around us, my birth father wrote, "The universe needs your sympathy." Whatever that meant, it seemed to be both a reasonable and ecstatic spiritual principle by which to live. My birth mother said she felt like sending out birth announcements.

8

Happy decade

Henry and I separated in the fall of 1984 and were divorced a year later. Phoebe stayed with me. Hired to fill a vacancy for a poet at the University of California at Davis, I moved there in 1985 with Phoebe and my partner, the poet Walter Pavlich, whom I had met in Portland. A former student of Richard Hugo's, Walter had a forthcoming book of poems, *Ongoing Portraits*, a passion for blues, and a devo-

*"The first meeting with my birth family: me, Ellayn Evans (birth sister),
John and Joyce Todd, at the Palo Alto salt marshes," California, 1981*

tion to old movie comedians, such as Laurel
and Hardy. Once a forest service firefighter,
he now taught poetry in public schools and
prisons. He seemed to me then, as he does
today, to be kind down to his very core, full
of caring, feeling, and wit. He loved his parents and siblings and was religious about making everyone laugh.

Though I was returning to my native California, most everything ahead would be a new
experience for me—my home state became a
new state of being, our residence a new
homeplace to build from scratch. Walter and I
were not immediately enamored of the hot flat
farm land, although we feel great affection for
it now, and I had a teaching and service load
much different from the all-writer faculty, all-
graduate-level duties at the University of Iowa.
But I have a favorite memory from this initia-
tion period. In the first year I tended to wear
gaudy, drapey, conspicuous clothes. At a faculty meeting on the day in question, I was
sporting an unearthly green sweater and skirt

with a seven-foot scarf of green, orange, and
purple stripes, and sitting in the back next to
a sixty-some professor I was fond of, Robert
Wiggins, who also wrote fiction in his youth.
Bob wore his own shade of green golf shirt,
stretched in the stomach and stained, almost
every day. The faculty were discussing whether
to appoint a German academic to a theory
position in our department. An eighteenth-cen-
tury-scholar-turned-mystery-writer protested, "All
his work is in German, on German writers. He
just doesn't *look* like an English professor." Bob
Wiggins turned to me and said, "*You* and *I*
don't look like English professors."

Phoebe moved out to live on her own on
Mother's Day in 1986. Walter and I moved into
a newly built two-story house with the main
floor on the second story—an eccentric floor
plan that always raises spirits. We planted a
lawnless garden of seven different kinds of fruit
or nut trees, grapevines, strawberries, herbs, and
annual tomatoes and peppers. Roses and pines
and multitudes of gazanias. Guava and wisteria

Research on Blues Artists

Sandra McPherson with Little Milton,
Sacramento, California, late 1980s

With Hip Linkchain in a West
side Chicago blues bar. "A
number of the poems in The
God of Indeterminacy *are
about him,"* 1988.

With Buddy Guy and Junior Wells,
Davis, California, 1987

and native ceanothus, toyon, and zauschneria. We got an SPCA cat who looked us in the eye and yelled, "Get me out of here," from his cage in the shopping mall. We named him Doctor Jesus after a Black gospel song.

This has been a decade of fortunate adventures, daily domestic pleasures and goodwill, aesthetic broadening, poetic experimentation, and, of course, teaching, teaching, teaching. More than once my professorial duties have meant saving a student from her violent "lover." Eventually I built a course around the poetry of love and desire. It is a subject close to the hearts of all students, and discussions are lively. The course includes male and female self-portraits, portraits of the beloved, interracial love, eroticism and spirituality, and representation in depth of all orientations. I believe poetry is a source of "information" every bit as much as prose is. In teaching poetry as literature I try to show how poetry conveys usable truths, practical and fresh ways of thinking one's way through life.

With a happy home life, I am able to pursue aesthetic questions that go beyond autobiography. Walter and I have taken two trips to Chicago to see bluesmen perform in their home venues. I'm not precisely sure what my questions were about them, but some that evolved from my state of wonder surely had to do with how some sounds are strictly blues sounds and form a blues language, how gestures do the same. How does poverty contribute to creation of great art? What is the relation of daily life to blues genius? What is blues metaphysics that no other musical form could describe? We chatted at the Checkerboard Lounge with Junior Wells, who went behind the bar and fixed us drinks. Later he gave Walter two harmonicas. We bantered with Jimmy Johnson at another club. We met Hip Linkchain in his van in the parking lot of the Delta Fish Market. He introduced us to Johnny Littlejohn. I visited Hip's mother in her apartment. The friendship with Hip lasted through many phone calls and his visit to California until he was disabled by cancer and died in Chicago less than a year later. I had promised to record an album of his, and he said he'd make it lying down. We were going to call the label "Millionaire Records."

In the voices of bluesmen I heard a language that could not be bettered. No voice could be more complex, more individual, than a blues voice. Notes were nothing. The voices I admired went way beyond notes.

And here he's going home,
who sang not notes

but wide cries, floodings, fishtailings,
and swipes. The found song sounds like that,
  his home voice, field voice,
echoing off the mansions.

("Millionaire Records,"
The God of Indeterminacy)

I felt as if I'd been given new ears. We attended the Sacramento Blues Festival and met Little Milton, went to Oakland to get backstage with Lowell Fulson, heard and conversed with as many bluesmen as we could in order to hear how they viewed life and how they created. The blues—and not ironically—were the catalyst for my first almost entirely joyful book, *The God of Indeterminacy*.

On the trips to Chicago two other passions were ignited: one for improvisational African-American quilts, which shocked me with their powerful asymmetry and flexible patterning, and the other for the work of self-taught/"outsider"/folk/visionary—the terminology is always in dispute—painters and sculptors. A dealer took me to William Dawson's sawdust-strewn apartment studio before I really knew what I was seeing. I have tried to make up for that in recent years by collecting small works by Minnie Evans, J. B. Murry, Victor Joseph Gatto, Justin McCarthy, Lawrence Lebduska, Nellie Mae Rowe, Juanita Rogers, Mose Tolliver, Sybil Gibson, Max Romain, and others, as well as local low-income and homeless people in an "arts empowerment" program, and the odd one-of-a-kind pastel or ink drawing to be found in an antiques-store back room. Wordless pictures and the act of making have filled me with astonishment since early childhood. I revere the urge to create wherever it is found and search out contact with that spark in the often isolated artists whose work lives on my walls.

I eventually secured and documented enough quilts to curate a show on campus. I especially like examples of a quilter's pressuring the "center" of her quilt out of the middle ground and up into a corner—or down, depending on how you turn the quilt. The quilts have been lent to other shows across the country, and I have made liberal use of them in teaching form and free verse.

Walter and I have had other adventures. We spent five days at the convention of the

"Walter Pavlich and I getting our marriage license and waiting for the Civil Marriage Commissioner, Yolo County Courthouse," Woodland, California, January 3, 1995

Laurel and Hardy Appreciation Society in Las Vegas, where people took the art of comedy very earnestly. Walter had a small role in the film *River's Edge;* he is the policeman who opens the squad car door for Keanu Reeves. I was featured on a segment of Bill Moyers's "The Language of Life," on national television. We frequent the numerous events commemorating local crops—the Pear Fair, as well as eggplant, prune, asparagus, and rice festivals—that bring denizens of this valley together in celebration. We attend small gospel performances, where we are known affectionately as "the Caucasians who always sit in the back." We also explore the natural history of the California, Oregon, and Washington coasts. Walter's *Running Near the End of the World* has brought him national attention. We have taught the last four years at the Art of the Wild writers conference in the Sierra Nevada.

We married in Woodland, California, between the light rain showers of January 3, 1995,

under some big evergreens behind the Yolo County courthouse. The civil marriage commissioner, Ana Morales, read our vows with great moment. I wept. We brought a music box that played "Always." Our friend, poet and artist Susan Kelly-DeWitt, was our witness, our steadier, bouquet and champagne buyer, only audience, and chauffeur, driving us back to our home where a rainbow materialized. A couple of weeks later Walter and I drove north to a wetland where I saw my first bittern, after thirty years of looking for one. Walter pointed it out.

My birth father passed away, but the McPhersons met my birth mother and sister, and now they communicate frequently.

Many years ago, knowing I was adopted, musing on my psychological test profile, I came to think of myself as an "experimental human being," some Creator's research. When I see a person working, I often hope that person is doing exactly what he or she hoped, as a child, to grow up to do. Hip had been a musician for forty-four years when he was only fifty-one. He believed it was "born in him." Walter wanted to write books as early as the third grade. Though I don't know exactly what's born, picked up, or taught, I know that nothing *else* was born in some of us who became poets, certainly not a gift for politics, say, or business. As I sat in the huge corporation of Honeywell working as a technical writer in 1966, I kept saying to myself, "But as a child I never longed to be a technical writer. I wanted to paint, play music, write poetry." About that same time, something I had no knowledge of was occurring: my birth father was, at a rather young age, resigning his job as an engineer for an electronics firm so he could devote his days to what he really wanted to do. We are doing now what we were made for.

A few years ago a friend said to me, "You talk funny." When I finally located my birth parents, they could talk funny, too: "The universe needs your sympathy." Walter's written lines talk funny. And my own daughter, at age six or seven had said, "Every single thing except the core of the earth gets touched by something." Talking funny is talking poetry. Or poetry talks *for* us when it is sometimes hard to talk out loud. If I am inarticulate at the start of a poem, by its end the *poem* is articulate. If I am ignorant at the start of a poem, at its completion that poem really knows something.

In "Phlox Diffusa: A Poem for My Fiftieth Birthday" *(Edge Effect),* I view a tiny timberline wildflower autobiographically, as a correlative:

Is it calm after midnight on its rocky
    slope,
exactly fitted to its nice little rubble?
Easy to think it's a bedtime slipper of a
    flower, owning no boots.
It lies flat on its back and looks at stars.
. . . .
"The tiny crammed leaves live in a pocket
    of calm partly
of their own making, and there they trap
windblown particles
that slowly become a nourishing soil."

Taproots eight to fifteen feet.
A throw pillow bolted to granite.
Easy to think it's only three inches tall,
    until you think of that, think of that root.

BIBLIOGRAPHY

Poetry:

Elegies for the Hot Season, Indiana University Press, 1970, reprinted by Ecco Press, 1982.

Radiation, Ecco Press, 1973.

The Year of Our Birth, Ecco Press, 1978.

Sensing (chapbook), Meadow Press, 1980.

Patron Happiness, Ecco Press, 1983.

Floralia (chapbook), illustrated by Claire Van Vliet, Trace Editions/Janus Press, 1985.

Pheasant Flower (chapbook), Owl Creek, 1985.

Responsibility for Blue (chapbook), Trilobite, 1985.

At the Grave of Hazel Hall (chapbook), Ives Street, 1988.

Streamers, Ecco Press, 1988.

The God of Indeterminacy, University of Illinois Press, 1993.

The Spaces Between Birds: Mother/Daughter Poems 1967–1995, Wesleyan University Press, 1996.

Edge Effect: Trails and Portrayals, Wesleyan University Press, 1996.

Other:

(Editor) *Journey from Essex: Poems for John Clare* (chapbook), Graywolf, 1981.

(Co-editor with Bill Henderson and Laura Jensen) *The Pushcart Prize XIV: Best of the Small Presses, 1989–1990,* The Pushcart Press, 1989.

Made a sound recording with James Welch, introduced by William Meredith (includes "For Elizabeth Bishop," "His Body," and "The Jet Engine"), November 20, 1979, Coolidge Auditorium at the Library of Congress, Washington, D.C. Featured with Linda McCarriston, in "The Field of Time," a segment of the television special, *The Language of Life with Bill Moyers,* which aired on June 30, 1995, on WNET.

McPherson's work is represented in numerous anthologies, including *The Pushcart Prize: Best of the Small Presses,* The Pushcart Press, 1980, 1981, 1987, 1995; *The Faber Book of 20th Century Women's Poetry,* Faber and Faber Limited, 1987; *The Best of Crazyhorse: Thirty Years of Poetry and Fiction,* University of Arkansas Press, 1990; *The Vintage Book of Contemporary American Poetry,* Vintage, 1990; *The Forgotten Language: Contemporary Poets and Nature,* Peregrine Smith Books, 1991; *A Song for Occupations,* Wayland Press, 1991; *The Best American Poetry,* Scribners, 1992, 1993, 1996; *Book of Birth: An Anthology of Poems on Pregnancy, Childbirth, Miscarriage and Abortion,* Virago Press, 1993; *No More Masks!* (new edition), Harper-Collins, 1993; *Oregon Literature Series,* Oregon State University Press, 1993.

Articulation: The Body and Illness in Poetry (revised edition), University of Iowa Press, 1994; *The Language of Life: A Festival of Poets: Bill Moyers,* Doubleday, 1995; *Models of the Universe,* Oberlin College Press, 1995; *Mother Songs: Poems for, by, and about Mothers,* W. W. Norton, 1995; *100 Great Poems by Women,* edited by Carolyn Kizer, Ecco Press, 1995; *What Will Suffice: Contemporary American Poets on the Art of Poetry,* Gibbs Smith, 1995; *Words and Quilts: A Selection of Quilt Poems,* Quilt Digest Press, 1995; *The Poetry Dictionary: Definitions and Model Poems,* Story Press, 1995; *The Second Set,* Indiana University Press, 1996; *I've Always Meant to Tell You: Letters to Our Mothers, An Anthology of Women Writers,* Pocket Books, 1997.

Contributor of poetry to various periodicals, including *American Poetry Review, American Voice, Antaeus, Field, Grand Street, Harper's, Harvard Review, Iowa Review, Ironwood, Kenyon Review, Nation, New Republic, New Yorker, Paris Review, Poetry, Poetry Northwest, Southern Review,* and *Yale Review.*

Stanley Middleton

1919-

MY CHILDHOOD IN BULWELL

Stanley Middleton, on holiday with his parents, Thomas and Elizabeth Ann, about 1926

When I was invited to write an essay for this series, I was very doubtful for I've always refused offers from publishers to write an autobiography, on the grounds that it might bring to the surface things better left buried for use in my novels. Furthermore, I'm no sort of historian and have deliberately kept clear of books while I was preparing this. Thus rather than "Bulwell in my Childhood," an accurate title for my piece would be "My Childhood in Bulwell." On the whole, apart from a few *obiter dicta,* things said by the way, I shall talk about Bulwell and Bulwell people in the first ten years of my life and I know only too well how fallible memory can be. You'll understand by the time I've finished that I've tended to recall matters that were later to interest me, or be important to me, as an adult. I can claim to have known Bulwell now during some parts of nine decades, but, then, there's no fool like an old fool. Moreover, a year or two ago I took my watch to a shop in Bulwell to have its battery replaced. While I stood at the counter explaining to the lady what I wanted, the man at her side, perhaps her husband, listened with some interest, and then said in a very friendly way, "Well, I don't know where you come from, but I can hear it in't Bulwell." So perhaps my qualifications aren't as sound as my sponsors think. But enough of these disclaimers.

I'll start by boasting.

I've very little memory of Bulwell or of anything else in the first five years of my life. It's said that at the age of twelve months I was carried into Prince's shop at the top of Minerva Street, where I then lived, and that I looked round the walls and from my father's arms pointed to and read "OXO," to the astonishment of the proprietor. I think I can remember this, but I guess that the tale has been told so often by my elders that I only imagine I can recall it. Incidentally, I read the poet Roy Fuller's account of exactly the same story. It's very likely that a good many children who were regularly parked on their parents' knees to be read to (and I had a brother and sister nearly old enough to be second parents to me) managed to carry out this simple feat.

My reading made very little progress in the next four years, for on my first day in class at the National School, Bulwell Trust, now St. Mary's, I was presented with a shallow, tin tray of fine sand. The girl next to me informed me confidently that we had to trace our names in the sand with our fingers. My brother and sister had impressed on me that if you failed to carry out explicit instructions at school you would be strapped. (There was certainly a fair amount of corporal punishment in the schools of that day, and also in the games of "school" which children played outside, though surely not, common sense suggests, in the bottom class of the infants on the first day.) I recall sitting there in dread, and yet with some stoicism, for I could not write my name, expecting this was where my first punishment would begin. It appeared in due course that the teacher had presented us with the sand to play with, though even now, I'm puzzled as to what I could do with a trayful of sand, except make a mess.

I can't remember learning to read but by the beginning of the third class (Mrs. Revill's) I could do so fluently. My first teachers, Dolly Pearson and Cissy Jones, whose tragic death took place not long ago, must have done the trick for me without too much trouble. And that brings me to think about my teachers, first at the Trust School, infant and junior, and for one year at Highbury School, Albert

"This is the street where I was born. The actual house has been pulled down but was in the second gap on the right." Minerva Street, Bulwell, Nottingham, England.

Street, before I went by tram and later trolley-bus to what was then called a "secondary" school (grammar school after the 1944 Act) where we wore beautifully striped red, green, and yellow caps with the letters HP above the peak. A year or two after I arrived, the authorities changed this to something more sober. (My old friend, teacher, and colleague, Keith Train, was responsible for the heraldry of the badge, though not, I hope, for the dull brown of cap and blazer.) But back to Bulwell. My considered opinion is that in these Bulwell schools I received some of the best instruction I've ever had, or gave for that matter, in my life. And yet these teachers are not in any way commemorated in, for example, buildings or street names. Bulwell's historical society might well look into (perhaps they have already done so) this matter of street names. Who was responsible for Ragdale, Minerva, Merchant, Hazel, Filey, Linby, Jennison (a good old Bulwell name), Montague, Ravensworth, Duke? Shipstone's Yard? Holborn Place? Was it left to the builders to choose, or had they to seek permission for their fancies from some central authority? I feel it a shame that the headmaster of the Trust School, Alfred Russell Clarke, or headmistress Miss Crippen (she must have had a Christian name) are not recalled today. I met Mr. Clarke later in the law courts where I was sitting on a jury and he was still contemplating human folly and wickedness from the public gallery and lamenting his retirement. He used to offer schoolboy delinquents the choice between Uncle Arthur and Uncle Jim, the cane and the strap, but what I remember best was his reading to us each week, his eyeglasses sparkling, about "the great, grey-green, greasy Limpopo River, all set about with fever-trees" from Kipling's "The Elephant's Child." This happened on Thursday mornings, following a period of drawing and colouring maps, of which I was very fond, and after that we were marched up St. Alban's Road to the playing fields, still there, extended even, for football or cricket. It impressed me so much that I realized for the first time that we were working to a timetable. Before that I presumably had thought that what we learnt depended on the whim of the teacher, provided we had obeyed the 11th Commandment and spruced up our brains first thing with mental arithmetic and our religious understanding occasionally with the catechism. There was only a flimsy curtain between the top class of boys and that of the girls so we had the benefit of two lots of teaching at once. But we learnt amongst other things to do as we were told. In this school I had my first day-school prize from Mrs. Hopkins, and still have it. *Vixere fortes ante Agamemnona/ Multi*—Many brave men lived before Agamemnon—the poet Horace reminds us, Greek accusative and all, but are forgotten—*carent quia vate sacro*—because they lack a sacred poet (to write or sing about them). Who remembers Emma Crane? Nancy Thompson? Or from the Albert Street end: William Leaning, "Johnny" Burton, T. S. Fielding, "Bulldog" Hartley, Horace "Jimmy" Sadler (who opened the innings for Cinderhill and was said by opponents to be the hardest man to bowl out in the Border League. "You were lucky to get it past his bat, never mind into his wicket," one disgruntled Derbyshire trundler complained once)? Or my first form master there, a man called Baker, who said that if the weather was too bad for the buses he had thought nothing of walking as a child from Hucknall to the boys' high school? Each morning as he marked the register, he made the class recite the 19th Psalm quietly together:

> The heavens declare the glory of God;
> and the firmament sheweth his handiwork.
> Day unto day uttereth speech, and night
> unto night sheweth knowledge.

Every time I hear those words, I can smell the heavy meat-soup reek of the tannery next door to the school.

Quite recently I was delighted to read letters in the local papers affectionately recalling the teaching staff of Quarry Road School. To my chagrin I knew nothing about these good people, not even their names, and the only thing I can recall about the place was that they sometimes held a "play-centre" there, which I was never allowed to attend. And then at the far end of the main street, beyond the narrowing of the road, stood the Coventry Road Schools, about which I knew nothing at all except that the headmaster, a Mr. Jones, used to wish me good morning, as we passed, walking on our respective ways to our schools.

Of course these official educational establishments were not the only places of learning. We acquired information in the churches and chapels, the cinemas, the theatre, in our homes, in the streets. I remember a boy showing me a "gadder," a catapult, he had made. It was quite beautiful and strong enough to kill a man. It was soon confiscated. We whispered in the corners of the schoolyard, and received amorous messages from time to time from the girls; they were usually oral, and fairly brief and blunt. "Our Betty loves you" or with local litotes more often "likes *you.*" I can't remember any written messages, but the stories brought back by "chikers" (that is boys who went "up Park"—the very expression, or, on t'Fog—on the Forest to spy on courting couples) were the nearest we got to sex instruction in those innocent days. We constantly spoke in this period about the First World War, and often played English and Germans as well as Cowboys and Indians in the streets as well as in the "trenches" on the far side of Little Stinker Wood. Those whose fathers had served in France were listened to with special respect. From what they told us I guess their fathers were pretty tight-lipped and said little of their experiences to their sons. This was a tragic period for survivors of that war; not only was there a bad recession on the way, with widespread unemployment and short time, their "war to end wars" was followed within twenty years by another. And yet I don't remember this as an unhappy time. I was lucky that my father worked on the railway and so was never unemployed. I recall the soup boiled up in the kitchen coppers at the National School and issued to the children of colliers (or such as had remembered to bring intact jugs and to present their tickets) during the Miners' Strike. I have no idea who organized this relief, but I recall my envy of those with their steaming jugs of broth to take home at midday.

Not that I was ever short of food at home, but again I was lucky. People in the schoolyard commonly used to beg "Gi'e us your coggin" (that is "core") if one was eating an apple. My mother baked twice a week, and I came home from school on those days to a "batch," a small loaf about the size of my fist, still warm, and thick with butter. On Sundays at lunch time (dinner was what we called it; "lunch" was what you took to school to eat at playtime) we always had a joint and a suet pudding. My favourites were apple and blackberry or treacle, and at teatime on the Sabbath before we set off for chapel we had a tin of salmon and a tin of fruit. These, like the tea we drank, were served in and on matching china taken on this one day a week only from the china cabinet in the front room. This particular room was rarely used; you never knocked at the front door of a house you were visiting; you always used the back way in. In the front room, some began to call it more pretentiously the parlour, Christmas parties were held or special visitors received, and if a member of the family died the blinds were drawn and the corpse would lie there in an open coffin until the funeral service, in an overpowering scent of eucalyptus.

What about our religious and aesthetic education? There were in my childhood two cinemas (the Highbury and the Palace); the larger Adelphi was built later; these two changed their programmes twice a week, I think, as well as providing fare for children on Saturday afternoon (the twopenny rush), which I was only rarely allowed to patronize. My piano lesson was arranged to make cinema-going nearly impossible. I'm not sure whether this was deliberate or not, but I am quite certain that my father never entered a cinema in his life. The theatre, the Olympia, now Woolworth's, sometimes had a Christmas pantomime, and the main

Bulwell Trust, the first school that the author attended, Nottingham

song one year when I went to see *Aladdin* was "Charmaine." The radio began to bring these popular songs into the home (I remember with awe my brother erecting a huge, branch-stripped tree trunk in the back garden for our wireless), but if one had a piano one could go down to Robinsons' on the main street and buy sixpenny copies, words, and music, with ukelele diagrams, as well as more artistically produced piano scores of *In a Monastery Garden* or *In a Persian Market* by Albert W. Ketélby, complete with accent so we'd get the pronunciation right (none of your kettles), the profits from which incidentally financed Clifford Curzon, the pianist, through his musical studies. In our house we were not allowed to sing these popular songs on Sunday (there's an interesting argument in D. H. Lawrence's novel *The Rainbow* as to whether a French song learnt at school fell outside the province of secular songs and so could be sung), but I went one free day to help the art master, Mr. Hilling, at Albert Street size some of the flats, pieces of scenery, for the school play, and as we worked he sang, "When it's springtime in the Rockies / I'll be coming home to you / Little sweetheart on the mountains / With your bonny eyes of blue," and one evening during the "Pageant of Old Bulwell" at the Olympia 1929 (more of that later), I was made up for my stage appearance by a very tall, handsome, young man and his petite, vivacious wife, Mr. and Mrs. Norman Carey, the son and daughter-in-law of W. H. Carey: owner of the finishing company, who is now remembered by a road name. His factory sounded a mournful hooter (the "buzzer") over the town at seven o'clock in the morning, at noon, and so on through the day. And young Mr. Carey, as he daubed me with 5 and 9 greasepaint (and I didn't think the gentlefolk or the learned professions knew such rubbish and so was slightly shocked), sang, "O Shenanikidah, he played his guitar outside the bazaar, dee-dah, dee-dah, dee-dah."

Places of worship easily outnumbered the cinemas, but not the public houses and beer-offs. There were two Anglican churches (we went from the Trust School to see the laying of the foundation, by a bishop, no less, of the new vicarage when the curate of St. Mary's became the vicar of St. John's) as well as a kind of mission hut on St. Alban's Road. The Methodists had at least six churches, Wesleyan, Primitive, and United. There was a Baptist

There is more than one story on how Bulwell got its name: "The carving over the main entrance of Bulwell Trust shows a bull sticking its horn into the rock from which water then flowed. . . . Bull Well. Yet scholars believe 'Bulwell' derives from Bulla's Well. Bulla must have been some dweller here in Anglo-Saxon times."

church, rebuilt by the corporation when later they widened the main street, with an organ which was said to have come out of Windsor Castle, two Churches of Christ, a Salvation Army barracks built where the doctor's house once stood, so you had a wide choice. It's my recollection that the Nonconformists I knew thought they took their religion more seriously than the Anglicans (who had to live down an absentee rector in the nineteenth century, though fortunately the squire of that era was in holy orders and so able to look after their spiritual as well as bodily needs. This same squire refused to sell a piece of land to the Methodists for a chapel, but in a fine demonstration of ecumenical spirit gave them exactly what they wanted, and where they wanted it, for nothing). And there the building stands to this day,

"The back of the Old Town Hall, built in the late nineteenth century. The white building to the right is the Horseshoe Inn, and behind that is the tower of St. Mary's Church. In the foreground is the bridge that was built in A.D. 1832 over the River Leen. This bridge carried at one time the old main road from Nottingham."

in Hazel Street, dated 1811. One of the later Anglican rectors is remembered by a street name, Cantrell Road, so that justice is done, now and again. It's also my impression that each of the Nonconformist chapels (they didn't call themselves "churches" in those days, nor give themselves saints' names, but were known by the name of the street on which they stood, Vere Street, Main Street, Commercial Road, Broomhill Road) thought that it was nearer the truth of the gospel than any of the others.

One thing, however, these chapels did have in common was a large Sunday school. Their Sunday school anniversaries, which took place on set Sundays so there'd be no clash in spring and early summer, were remarkable affairs. The men of the chapel erected with scaffolding and planks enormous platforms at the front of each place of worship, so high that those suffering from vertigo were in serious trouble, and from this eminence the children, girls in new frocks,

and boys slightly more rarely in new suits, recited poems and sang anniversary hymns, in one case at least to orchestral accompaniment. These verses and hymns were, to my recollection, nearly all of no artistic merit whatsoever, but whole businesses managed to thrive on the printing and selling of such rubbish. The anniversary had, however, this advantage that it taught young children to stand up to sing or recite in public, a not insignificant acquisition. It also paid for their prizes and the Sunday school treat. The chapels were thronged on these days. You'd hear that there were extra seats rammed two deep down all the aisles. Heaven knows what the present fire authorities would have made of these arrangements. And the ministers, faced with so many fathers more used to the stimulating beverages of the four-ale bar than the milk of the gospel, were put to an annual test. What could be said to these sinners, and in front of their offspring?

And how long should it take? The conclusion amongst people I knew seemed in favour of brevity, if nothing else. The chapel I attended, now gone, on the site of the present bus station, had the sense on the Monday evening (just think, three Sunday services and then Monday night) to invite every year one of the best speakers to children I ever heard, H. H. Swinnerton, professor of geology at the university, who paid no attention at all to the adults, sinners or otherwise, but spoke only to the scholars, fetching a dull bit of rock or a blade of grass from his pocket, and blinking through his owlish spectacles, transported you, and your elders with you, to a wonderland within minutes.

On these occasions the adult choirs would be expected to perform some mighty, long-prepared anthem, the relevance or suitability of which was often hotly debated. These same choirs, if they had any pride, would deliver sacred oratorios from time to time during the year as well as versions of opera (I took part in a concert recital of Wagner's *Tannhäuser* in my teens), and perhaps even musicals. One of my early memories is of walking down Highbury Vale with my parents and passing the gate of the Conservative Club in the glamorous dark, having been to "Broomhill Road" (chapel) to see a performance of *The Desert Song*. The chapel choirs sang Gaul's *Holy City*, Mendelssohn's *42nd Psalm* as well as *Elijah*, Haydn's *Creation*, and at Easter *Olivet to Calvary*, or more rarely, as it was thought to be Anglican in bias, Stainer's *Crucifixion*. But foremost stood Handel's *Messiah*. My chapel gave a performance on one Sunday afternoon each year at the beginning of December. My brother and sister, even my father who was no musician, would be offering me trailers at home for weeks with "The people that walked in darkness" or "O thou that tellest." One soloist I remember with particular pleasure came down from London. Lucy Goodwin, a Bulwell girl, who had been schooled at the Royal Academy, made a considerable living by her singing of oratorio and by giving private recitals in the large houses of the capital. She reduced her fee for us but it still was three or four times what a skilled artisan could earn in a full week. Her soprano voice was brilliantly clear; she first made me realize that the semiquavers in "Rejoice greatly, O Daughter of Zion" could be sung as written. Later, slightly outside our period, she was joined by a young

contralto of striking appearance, not half a dozen years older than I was, who made a considerable international name as an opera singer: Constance Shacklock, happily still alive, who returned last year to give a master class in Sherwood.

The choir did not perform the whole of *Messiah*. Such choruses as "And He shall purify the sons of Levi that they may offer unto the Lord an offering of righteousness" were always omitted. This was not on grounds of theology or even ignorance, I guess, but because Handel's operatic counterpoint took too much singing. I've no idea exactly who these sons of Levi were; later English writers equated them with English clergymen, but I was never sure whether they were demoted from pure priesthood or elevated above the other tribes of Israel to a priestly role of honour. These considerations did not deter Bulwellians from handing out such

"The Church of St. Mary in Bulwell, an Anglican parish church, was built in 1850, replacing the medieval church which was built in 1300 and stood almost on the same site. It is said that a church of some sort has stood on this hill since A.D. 800."

Biblical names to their sons. I knew one Levi (pronounced Levvy), a beautiful footballer, a Eubulus who kept a shop on the main street, and an aged, saintly man whom my father used to visit called Elias Harrison. I wonder why his parents chose the Greek form of his name rather than the more common Hebrew, Elijah. And mention of Elijah brings me back to street names. Where did Tishbite, as in Tishbite Street, come from? Tishbite is an adjectival noun, like Bulwellian, derived from Tishbe, a Biblical village. Now as every schoolboy knows there were two Tishbes—one in Galilee and one in Gilead, and the second was famous as the birthplace of Elijah the prophet. So Tishbite equals Elijah. Thus the name of a nearby street, Gilead Street, is so called *not* for its famous healing balsam—"Is there no balm in Gilead?" asks Jeremiah—but for its connection with the prophet. My conjecture is given further credence with the nearby name, Cherith Street. The "water-man" who dealt with recalcitrant washers on your taps lived there in my day, to the delight of my father, who thought it specially appropriate, for Cherith was the name of the brook Elijah drank from when he was fed by the ravens. But what aficionado of the Old Testament prophet was responsible for naming those parts?

It may seem as if the Nonconformists scored over the Anglicans with their anniversaries, concerts, plays, oratorios, and recitals, but the old church more than got its own back in 1929 with the production of a "Pageant of Old Bulwell." I deliberately have not consulted the programmes, copies of which, I believe, are held in the Bulwell (Northern) Library, so that it's only my recollection I can rely on. To tell the truth I did not see much of the pageant apart from the two scenes in which I made an appearance. One piece I do remember, however, was the boisterous singing of

> Here's to the maiden of bashful fifteen,
>   Here's to the widow of fifty,
> Here's to the flaunting extravagant quean,
>   And here's to the housewife that's thrifty.
> Let the toast pass; here's to the lass
>   I'll warrant she'll prove an excuse for the
>   glass.

I greatly doubt whether such literary dactylic verses were ever sung in the Horse & Jockey or the Horseshoe (it's by R. B. Sheridan from *The School for Scandal*) but it was delivered with

such vigour in a tavern scene that I heard it but once or twice and acquired and have remembered to this day both words and tune.

The pageant was written, as far as I can make out, by the then rector, the Rev. Stanley Mortimer Wheeler. How I got involved, I do not know, but I guess it was on the recommendation of Mr. Clarke. I had a nonspeaking part in a scene about Bulwell in Anglo-Saxon times where I wore a smock and, like Malvolio, was cross-gartered. My brother carved for me in wood, so that I wouldn't cut myself, the most beautiful dagger, but Mr. Clarke appearing in the same scene thought this exquisite weapon more suitable for an adult and learnèd Saxon than for a dumb, bystanding child, and wore it himself through the week with great distinction. I came to my own, however, in a scene set in the old grammar school, Strelley House, in the nineteenth century. The schoolmaster, a Mr. Calladine, was played by the rector and I, a prize pupil, chosen perhaps on account of my clear voice or brass neck, had to stand up and recite, having blown my nose largely on a red bandanna handkerchief, not some marmoreal verses from Vergil's *Æeneid* but a music-hall ditty which went as follows:

> Her eyes were as bright as the pips of a pear.
>   No rose in the garden with her lips could
>   compare.
> Her hair hung in ring-a-lets, all beautiful and long.
>   I thought that she loved me, but I found I
>   was wrong.

This I did, to my satisfaction at least, for the whole week. I don't remember anything at all about rehearsals which must have taken place somewhere, probably in the National School. What I remember best are the fizzing limelights then in old-fashioned use at the Olympia. This was my first appearance on a real stage.

Bulwell seemed a more rural place then, without the outlying estates. One could actually paddle (or fall in, as I did) the stream at Bull Well. The Leen was much less under control than it is now. At the top of the street where I lived and the next was a very high, stone wall. I have no idea why it was built, but by my time someone had effected a breach at the top of Minerva, though Merchant was still cut off. On the other side of this wall,

"Strelley House, the oldest brick house in Nottingham, was built in A.D. 1667 by the Strelley family. Their coat of arms appears above the door. They endowed it as a grammar school. It is now a private dwelling. My watercolour of this building was used as the dustcover of my novel Catalysts.*"*

graced with what my father called gillivers, gilly-flowers, ran a dirt path alongside a hedge and allotments. The Squire's Avenue, treelined of course, was also unmade-up at this period and cut through with runnels formed by rainwater. Where the Adelphi now stands was a row of cottages; a large tree stood in front of and gave its name to Sycamore House and on Robinson's Hill one could stand at the door and watch my old Sunday school teacher Cornelius (another Biblical name) Walker at work, sparks flying, at the anvil in the forge. There were factories, finishing and hosiery companies on the Leen, and collieries with queer names like "Shonkey," and the pottery works, and the quarries, but they seemed set down in the countryside. I'm told that the women employed at Carey's used to dash onto the Forest to see to their washing hung out to dry on the gorse bushes, but that was before my time. No golf was played on the Forest on Sundays, and there the respectable of Bulwell paraded

in the afternoon in their best clothes staring out towards Annesley Church. As one approached the cricket field from the town one passed a working farm, and the field itself was bounded by ploughed land on one side and a meadow on the other. A six from the far end of the Bulwell pitch over this and onto the roof of the cowshed was greeted by a great burst of music from a spectator with a concertina. Sport played its part both winter and summer and if I could choose some ideal football match to watch on the Elysian Fields it would not be, for instance, Matt Busby's Babes vs. Herbert Chapman's Arsenal of the 1930s, but Bulwell Wesleyan Mission vs. Quarry Road Old Boys from my childhood. You'd see one or another of the footballing Mees from Forest Side in this game, probably "Rum 'un" Mee, who won this sobriquet on account of his mesmerising dribbling round bemused opponents. His brother, Bertie, at school with me, went on to become in due course manager of the Arsenal.

If one looks at old photographs of Bulwell, one is surprised at the absence of traffic. The internal-combustion engine had been invented, but not too many people of my acquaintance owned cars. Horses were used extensively. You spoke of the horse-road as opposed to the causey, the pavement. I recall a horse bolting with its iron-shod wheeled cart down the main street, and a man called Brailsford heroically trying to stop it by hanging onto the reins and being dragged along the tar-macadam road (most side streets were cobbled) bolt upright like a modern water-skier. He let go at the end of Montague Street and was flung clear; Shipstone's Brewery delivered their barrels on high carts drawn by magnificent grey horses, but kept up-to-date with steam-driven lorries, the likes of which I've not seen elsewhere. I never heard of vets, though many, like us, kept cats and dogs. If animals were ill they were taken to a very old man, said to be in his nineties, called "Prog" Roper, who drove a leisurely cart connected in some way rather inappropriately with the slaughterhouse which stood on Bulwell Green, now part of St. Mary's playground.

I am very close to the end of this essay, and I realize how much I have missed out. Nothing of shops or shopkeepers. I think of three on Main Street alone who with a different start in life would have been doctors of divinity. The son of one of them was senior tutor at a Cambridge college. And then there was a boy who started his working life as a house painter, but who gained a D.D. of London University by dissertation; his niece, who lived over the back wall from us, became vice president of the Methodist Conference. I think of the artisans, the colliers coming home from work in "their pit-muck." And what of the entrepreneurs? (The Old Town Hall didn't build itself.) Or the church organists, the choirmasters, the Salvation Army bandsmen and songsters, the music teachers one of whom became music adviser for Leicestershire and formed and trained that marvellous youth orchestra, famous all over Europe, and commissioned works from Sir Michael Tippett for it. And then there were the oddities, rather frightening; and the denizens of Martha Brailsford's doss-house on the end of Jennison Street. People in old Bulwell had their ambitions. One of my saddest memories is of a Sunday school superintendent who hung on his wall an empty picture frame for the photograph of the first missionary from his

Stanley Middleton, November 1994

school. The frame was never filled. Then there were the publicans, and the leaders of youth, the sportsmen, the allotment holders with their huts, some with fireplaces and chimneys, where they could retire from family cares for a peaceful hour. And the leaders of women's meetings and their constant organization of teas and parties and outings and processions and treats for the needy by these ladies. I realize I've said too little about the women of Bulwell. In those unregenerate days married women stayed at home; there weren't enough jobs for the men. And what did they do all day? The answer is: work. I'll instance one day only. On Monday, washday, they'd be up at six (as my mother was) to fill the copper in the kitchen and light the fire under it. The washing took all day. They laboured with wooden ponchsticks in wooden ponchtubs and wrung their clothes out on huge grim iron mangles with wooden rollers. I think of the bowl of "blue" and the bowl of starch I was sometimes allowed to make. Lunch that day was sparse. Cold meat from the Sunday table, and a watery rice-pudding in the oven all morning. A housewife was lucky to get the ironing (their irons heated before the living-room fire and tested by spitting) over and done by Tuesday. Children learnt to behave on Monday, especially wet Mondays; there were more good hidings and thick ears from harassed mothers on that day than on any other.

Nor have I mentioned the doctors, and their diseases, consumption, "captain of the ranks of death," and diphtheria, the dentists, the policemen, the trades unionists, the politicians, the elections, all important, they'd claim. You'll see some of the names of the successful recorded on foundation stones if you look about Bulwell.

There was the Bulwell Library itself; I once told David Gerard, the former city librarian, that my idea of heaven was walking into the library to change my books on a Friday night in winter. Not that children weren't sometimes regarded with suspicion there, and perhaps rightly. I learnt a great deal inside those walls.

Some years ago I lectured at Cambridge on D. H. Lawrence's *The Rainbow* for a paper called "Literature and Education." In the course of talking about Lawrence and educational processes (I thought and think still that literature and life have contacts), I told the students about something that had happened to me. A Bulwell shopkeeper, Charles Banks, one day when I was a boy suddenly put a copy of Bach's "Prepare Thyself Zion" in front of me, and asked me to play it. I had never heard of *The Christmas Oratorio* at that time. But the effect on me was very great, and led from one piece of knowledge, of enlightenment, to another and yet another. I'll never cease to be grateful for what that man did for me that evening, perhaps unknowingly. It so happened that I met Charles Banks's widow later and mentioned what I'd said about her husband in this lecture. She looked surprised, and then murmured, "He'd have been very proud to be talked about at Cambridge University," and then thought a bit and added, "Do you know what he'd have said?—You could have found something better to lecture on." This modest, awkward realism or scepticism appeals to me as typically Bulwellian.

I suppose one is usually fond of the place where one was brought up, especially if one was happy. After all, this suburb has produced two cabinet ministers since the war. But I'm not telling you it was altogether magical here, because you wouldn't believe me. In his "Ode on the Intimations of Immortality" the poet Wordsworth wrote: "Heaven lies about us in our infancy." In Bulwell? you may well ask. Well. . . .

We had been marched in a crocodile from the Trust School one bright Ascension Day, up Forest Side, over the crossings, up St. Alban's Road, had turned right by the Newstead Abbey and along Austin Street and then, as you can't now, walked the rest of the way over the fields to Church Lane and finally to St. Mary's, where the rector, the one who wrote the pageant, told us quite calmly and casually that he had, one morning, seen an angel fly across the west end of his church. Heaven lay about me in my infancy. Now and again, even when I didn't notice it. I was spellbound that morning.

I am spellbound still to this day.

This essay was adapted from a speech given at Bulwell (Northern) Library, 23 February, 1994.

BIBLIOGRAPHY

Fiction:

A Short Answer, New Authors, 1958.

Harris's Requiem, Hutchinson, 1960.

A Serious Woman, Hutchinson, 1961.

The Just Exchange, Hutchinson, 1962.

Two's Company, Hutchinson, 1963.

Him They Compelled, Hutchinson, 1964.

Terms of Reference, Hutchinson, 1966.

The Golden Evening, Hutchinson, 1968.

Wages of Virtue, Hutchinson, 1969.

Apple of the Eye, Hutchinson, 1970.

Brazen Prison, Hutchinson, 1971.

Cold Gradations, Hutchinson, 1972.

A Man Made of Smoke, Hutchinson, 1973.

Holiday, Hutchinson, 1974.

Distractions, Hutchinson, 1975.

Still Waters, Hutchinson, 1976.

Ends and Means, Hutchinson, 1977.

Two Brothers, Hutchinson, 1978.

In a Strange Land, Hutchinson, 1979.

The Other Side, Hutchinson, 1980.

Blind Understanding, Hutchinson, 1982.

Entry into Jerusalem, Hutchinson, 1983.

The Daysman, Hutchinson, 1984.

Valley of Decision, Hutchinson, 1985.

An After-Dinner's Sleep, Hutchinson, 1986.

After a Fashion, Hutchinson, 1987.

Recovery, Hutchinson, 1988.

Vacant Places, Hutchinson, 1989.

Changes and Chances, Hutchinson, 1990.

Beginning to End, Hutchinson, 1991.

A Place to Stand, Hutchinson, 1992.

Married Past Redemption, Hutchinson, 1993.

Catalysts, Hutchinson, 1994.

Toward the Sea, Hutchinson, 1995.

Live and Learn, Hutchinson, 1996.

Marilyn Nelson

1946-

Marilyn Nelson

In the Southern and black tradition, I like to start telling of myself by telling who my people are. My mother's mother was an Atwood, the eldest of a family of seven children, some of whose names are remembered in the little town of Hickman, Kentucky, even now, long after their deaths. Their parents were mulattos born into slavery; later their father, Pomp Atwood, co-owned a little grocery store in Hickman, had a coal and oil business, and sold real estate. There's an Atwood Street in a black neighborhood of Hickman. I met a woman from Hickman in California once, who told me that if anyone ever stood in my way, I should "tell them you're an Atwood woman, and go right on to the top." My grandmother's sisters and brother were teachers and preachers and darers. In the nineteen-teens, Aunt Blanche won an essay contest whose prize was a full-tuition scholarship to a major Southern university. When she showed up to claim her prize and it was discovered that she was "colored," the committee decided not to award the scholarship that year. The Atwoods fought the decision. The committee finally compromised and gave her a full scholarship to a Negro college. She taught for a while at Fisk University. For some thirty years Uncle Rufus was president of Kentucky State College. I found his name in a Negro history textbook when I was in college: he won the Bronze Star for bravery in World War I. Aunt Rose once stuck a hat pin—she always kept one in the lapel of her coat, to be used in such circumstances—into a haughty white woman who snorted something insulting when Aunt Rose sat down next to her on a city

The Atwood family: (from left) Great-uncle Rufus (president of Kentucky State College), Annisue (Mildred's daughter), Geneva, Story (in front, Mildred's husband), Annie, Mildred, Blanche, Rose, Ray (my maternal grandmother), Mabel (Rufus's wife), Julian Hale (Annie's husband), in front of the president's house, 1943

bus. The Hickman woman I met in California told me her high school graduation ceremony was interrupted when my grandmother entered the auditorium with her walker, after decades of living elsewhere teaching school. The high school principal said, "Wait; is that Miss Ray? Miss Ray, would you like to say something to our graduates?" Meema, who must have been in her late seventies then, followed her clunking walker down the middle aisle, and at the stage turned to face the audience and recited a soliloquy from a Shakespeare play. She played the piano by ear— but only on the black keys—and was so proud, the story goes, that "she was the only woman in the county who bought shoes without looking at them: she refused to lower her head in front of a white shoe salesman."

The other half of Mama's side of our family was her father, John Mitchell, who was born into slavery. His father ran away to fight for the Union. After the war he rejoined his family in Tennessee, and with his severance pay bought a piece of land to farm. Night riders attacked the farm when my grandfather was a little boy and set the cabin on fire. His mother told him to run north, and he ran away with his younger brother, Will. He lost Will; I've never heard the story of that loss. My grandfather was found by a white family, the Bryants, in Dorena, Missouri. They took him in and raised him with their own son, Cullen. They were never able to find his birth family. As a young man, he farmed with the Bryants and ran their Mississippi River ferry. One day a bunch of rednecks from out of town insulted him on the ferry, and he threw them overboard. He left town that night, on a train with a ticket paid for by the Bryants, and with farm animals they had given him as a premature inheritance. He went west, to the all-black town of Boley, Oklahoma, and farmed there for the rest of his life. Mama said he talked so often about "ol' Cull," his boyhood friend and surrogate brother, that at last her exasperated mother said he should write Cullen a letter. He did. A few weeks later they received a reply: Cullen was dead. His wife said Cullen had spoken of my grandfather often and with love, even on his deathbed. A few years ago my uncle was in Hickman, which is near Dorena, so he drove into Dorena for the first time in his life and stopped at a little department store called "Bryant's." He asked to speak with the owner, and when he did, told Mr. Bryant that he thought perhaps Mr. Bryant's parents might have raised his father. Mr. Bryant remembered hearing of John Mitchell when he was a boy; he invited my uncle home with him to meet his family, and he accompanied my uncle to our family reunion the following day. My uncle says that when I was an infant he and my mother, having received the news that their father was dying, drove with me all night from Cleveland to Boley. They got there in the morning, went into their father's room, and Mama held me up: "Here's your first grand-baby, Papa." He opened his eyes and said, "My grandbaby." He died later that day.

My father never talked much about his family. His people came from Tennessee, but Daddy was born and raised in St. Louis. His father was a cook on a paddle-wheel steamboat. Somewhere there's a photograph of the steamboat crew, in which my grandfather is wearing a long white apron and a white chef's hat. My grandmother's German shepherd once grabbed the shirt of a child who was teetering on the edge of their upper-story tenement balcony and held the child in the air until she could haul the child up. When she died, the dog lay down and refused to move or eat until it died. When my eleventh-grade history teacher told us to ask our parents about the Great Depression, Daddy's eyes filled with tears. All he said was that he used to walk along the railroad tracks, looking for pieces of coal. His parents died when he was a young man, and he attended Wilburforce College on scholarship. He had wanted to be a doctor, but wasn't able to afford medical school. He went to law school for a while, but made his career in the air force. He was in the last class to graduate from the experimental military Negro cadet school which produced the Tuskegee Airmen. His class graduated too late to fly in World War II, but they were of that first generation of Negro military aviators.

"Daddy's crew" (front row, far right), about 1954

Daddy was a navigator, and my childhood was splendid with pride in the fact that he flew, and that because he was an officer, men in uniform saluted him right and left. Our car was saluted whenever we passed the checkpoint leaving or entering an air force base, and Daddy's magisterial military bearing commanded respect wherever he went. One foggy New Year's Eve, on our way to Mexico from our home in northern California, we were stopped by a white highway patrolman. The policeman walked up to our car, shined his flashlight on us, and asked Daddy, "What do you think you're flying, boy?" Daddy, who was wearing his uniform, said with great dignity, "B-52's." The policeman looked shocked, then laughed and said, "Well, I guess you know what you're doing, then. But please be careful." They exchanged New Year's wishes and waved as we drove away.

This background provided me with the security and courage implied by the proverb which advises us to give two things to our children: roots and wings. Mama, with her proud stories of her family, gave us roots; Daddy, who used to drive

Marilyn (right) with sister, Jennifer, about 1951

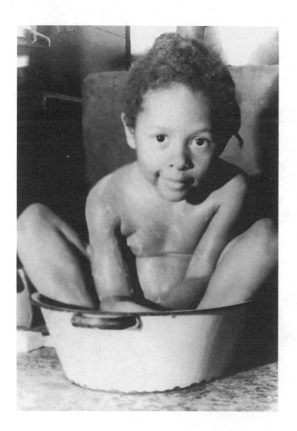

Marilyn in 1948

us out into the country at night, park the car, and point out constellations and name stars, gave us wings. They encouraged us to dream big, and they had confidence in our ability to be what we dreamed. My sister, Jennifer, is an actor/director; our brother, Mel, is a musician/composer. These are my people, and this is where I start.

Mama and Daddy met in Cleveland; I was born there in 1946. Daddy was driving a taxi and going to law school; Mama had graduated from Kentucky State and was working on a master's degree in music theory at Case Western Reserve. I foiled her plans: she didn't get her master's for another twenty years. Jennifer was born two years after I was. We lived in an apartment on, I think, Euclid Avenue. The one surviving photograph of the neighborhood shows me on a tricycle, in outsized, shabby overalls (Mama said I used to embarrass her by announcing, when someone admired my clothes, that we had bought them "to the Goodwill"). Behind me are the wooden fire escapes of a ghetto tenement. And with me are a few other children; we look like the Dead

End Kids. One of Mama's cousins, George Free-man, lived in Cleveland. We called him Uncle George; his wife, Aunt Carma, was my godmother. Their daughter, Oneida, died of childhood leukemia. Uncle George's mother, Aunt Rose (Mama's aunt, my great-aunt), lived in Cleveland, too, and was for years the housekeeper of the Jeloff family. One day Aunt Rose was talking to her minister on the telephone when the elastic in her "bloomers" broke and they fell off. She did a little dance for me, laughing with her eyes, the "bloomers" around her ankles, as she continued her serious conversation. She was my favorite aunt.

Jennifer and I shared a double bed and told each other stories or played a game we called "footsies" until Daddy banged on the door and told us to "pipe down in there!" I started kindergarten in Cleveland, but all I remember of school there is a plague of head lice (I didn't get them) and snacks of graham crackers and milk. Mama was teaching school and Daddy was working and taking law school courses, and act-

ing and taking photography classes at the Karamu settlement house, when he was recalled into the service for the Korean conflict.

He stayed in the air force for sixteen years. We lived in Waco, Texas; Salina, Kansas; Denver, Colorado; Sacramento, California; Portsmouth, New Hampshire; Kittery Point, Maine; Sacramento again; Fort Worth, Texas; Burns Flat, Oklahoma; and Sacramento again, permanently. We usually lived in base housing, which meant we lived in the "better" neighborhoods of a society which segregated officers and enlisted men. Daddy was often the only Negro officer on a base, and even when he wasn't, we were often the only Negro officer's children, and more often the only Negro children in our classes. Jennifer and I were studious to the point of bookishness, though I was more of a "tomboy" than she. We rode bicycles, roller-skated, caught frogs and lizards, and climbed trees. My knees and elbows are permanently scarred from being skinned so often. In second or third grade at an air force base near Salina, Kansas, I read all the books in the school library,

"Mama with her class at Shilling Air Force Base," 1955

and Mrs. Leibel brought in books from the high school to keep me occupied. My best friend was Tommy Avery. Tommy's mother was British; they had a little Winston Churchill statue next to their radio, and a box of teensy cigars it could actually smoke when Tommy's mother lit them. Tommy got sprayed by a skunk one day when we were out playing in a dry drainage ditch. His mother made him take off all his clothes outside and washed him with a hose. I couldn't look into his eyes for a long time after that.

In fourth grade at Mather Field, near Sacramento, California, the boy I liked best was Sammy Hartley. He had red hair and freckles, and looked like he could have been invented by Mark Twain. My best friend that year was Helene Straker, whose father had known mine when they were Tuskegee cadets. Helene and Jennifer and I had lots of slumber parties during which we pretended we were orphans lost in the woods, or made up stories about our futures. One of the few racial incidents I remember from childhood happened with Helene: we were walking in another neighborhood of base housing when a little white girl called us the N-word. Helene said, "What did you say?" The girl repeated the word. Helene hauled off and hit her with her fist, right in the middle of her forehead. A big lump formed. Then Helene and I walked on home. I guess the girl's father was an enlisted man; we never heard anything more about the incident.

My brother, Mel Junior, was born in 1956. He was just a few weeks old when Daddy was transferred to Portsmouth, New Hampshire. A few weeks later Daddy was sent to England on temporary duty, and Mama, who wasn't happy in the apartment we had found, moved us across the river to Kittery Point, Maine. There we rented a big old colonial house a block from the ocean, between Miss Lydia Pinkham, a sweet old spinster-lady, and Ed and Flossie Bayliss, an old childless couple who soon became our surrogate grandparents. There were fruit trees in their overgrown yard, and in the barn a Model-T Ford which hadn't been driven in years. Daddy convinced Uncle Ed that it should be driven, so we took them for rides in it, Aunt Flossie pointing out medicinal herbs by the roadside. A poultice of Queen Anne's lace flowers is good against psoriasis. They had a dark parlor they never used, with photographs of dead relatives, in their coffins, on the tables and mantel. Uncle Ed used to sit in their bay window with binoculars and watch the town. Once or twice he said, with his broad Maine accent, "I

Ed and Flossie Bayliss, 1959

saw you had steak last night." We were the first Negroes ever to live in Kittery Point. My sixth grade teacher, Mrs. Dorothy Gray, had never had a Negro student before. Some of the other children—temporary immigrants from the South whose fathers worked at the Kittery Naval Yard—snubbed me, but I had many more friends than enemies. My best friend that year, Ellie Mitchell, has been my friend for almost forty years.

That year was a turning point for me: our house was only a few doors from the library, and I read almost every book in it. I loved A. J. Cronin's *The Green Years,* which I read over and over. And I discovered poetry, reading anthologies of old nineteenth-century chestnuts. I decided I wanted to be a poet, and I wrote my first poem about my baby brother: "Little Sir Melvin, in knighthood is he, / Rides on a brown charger (it's really my knee)," and so on. Mama kept a copy of it, and Mrs. Gray predicted that I'd grow up to be a famous writer. I was heartbroken when we had to leave Kittery Point; I'd planned to become a Mariner Scout the next year and learn to sail.

We were transferred three times the following year, back to Sacramento, then to Fort Worth, Texas, then to Burns Flat, Oklahoma. In Fort Worth we lived in a black neighborhood called "Stop Six" and went to segregated schools. The teachers I liked best there were Miss Lee and Mr. Lee. Miss Lee taught English and read poems to us by Paul Laurence Dunbar (the school was named for him). Mr. Lee taught string quartet. Since we were only to be in Fort Worth for a short time, Mama had put the piano into storage. She told me to continue to practice, however, by fingering on my school desk the pieces I'd been learning. My homeroom teacher noticed this, thought I must be "musical," and had me put into Mr. Lee's class. He gave me the viola. Daddy made me go out on the balcony to practice: he couldn't stand the screeching. How humiliating it was to stand in the open air, scratching out scales, while the cutest boys in the school, I was sure, were watching and hearing me. But I loved the class: Mr. Lee would start the three of us girls sawing notes that must have made several great composers groan in their graves, then he'd crack us up by plucking out jazz accompaniments on his bass. I was famous in the school because I had "a California accent." Kids stopped me in the hall, asking me to talk for them. Before I could capitalize on my fame by exchanging words with the boy I'd noticed, whose first name was Major, we were transferred again, this time to Oklahoma. By now I had known and forgotten so many people that I was half convinced that they permanently disappeared after we left them. I'd learned not to look back.

On one of those cross-country trips, which we made driving all night, stopping at dusk-to-dawn drive-in theatres where Mama and Daddy snored while we children watched movies until we couldn't help giving up, Daddy drove as we slept and parked the car on the edge of the Grand Canyon. We awoke to that grandeur at dawn. Daddy was like that. He loved the sound of rain on the car's roof at night, and once or twice he invited me to sleep in the car so I could hear it. I slept in the backseat, he in the front. Rain sounds like wren's wings beating against a parked car's roof at night. Or like a cascade of coins made of moonlight. Or like a raging stampede of chipmunks. Daddy could pull coins out of our ears. I remember thinking as a young child that as long as he could do that, we would never be poor. He could also execute a standing back-flip, which for years endeared him to my friends. When

I was little, children used to knock on our door after school and ask whether Mr. Nelson could come out and play. Once or twice he drove into a midwestern farmyard because the mailbox said "Nelson." He introduced us as "Nelsons, too," and asked if we could look around. The Nelsons never turned us away. Mama was a trained and intuitive pianist with perfect pitch. She could identify all of the notes in a chord heard once, and often called from the kitchen when we were practicing the piano, to say, "Not B-flat; B-natural!" Severe storms were always a treat because when the electricity went out our neighbors came to our house, and Mama played and everyone sang along by candlelight. When the Civil Rights Movement started in earnest, Mama made up a joke: "Knock-knock." "Who's there?" "Eyes." "Eyes, who?" "Eyes yo' new neighbor." We sang and laughed and played games, driving across the country eating fried chicken and sandwiches of raisin bread and bologna.

I finished seventh and eighth grade and part of ninth at Burns Flat High School. There were three Negro students, all from air force families, in the school. Though we lived on base, the school was in town, and the high school townies made life miserable for us. The boys teased each other at lunch by calling me across the cafeteria, then pointing at each other and saying, "He says he likes you." Two of the teachers, Mr. and Mrs. Purdy, resented my presence in their classrooms. Though my grades were excellent, Mr. Purdy gave me a *D* in math. I went home in tears. Daddy said, "He's a redneck cracker, Marilyn; he knows you're better than he is. Just do the work and be proud. We'll be out of here soon." Mrs. Purdy once made me read a racist black dialect poem aloud in English class. She had the smile of a viper. But the other teachers encouraged me and treated me with respect and affection. I had three best friends: Kim McCauley, Cheryl Wesson, and John Henry Brand III. Kim and I wrote a novel, "The Case of the Fabulous Belt-Buckle Monster," passing a notebook back and forth in Mr. Purdy's class. Kim told me only years later that her mother had disapproved of our friendship. The Civil Rights Movement was in the daily news, with lunch counter sit-ins and police dogs and fire hoses. Kids whose fathers had been transferred to Burns Flat from Little Rock had terrible stories to tell. Even in Oklahoma, Negroes couldn't try on clothes in the local department stores, or eat in ice cream parlors (you had to buy your soda and drink it outside). My class voted not to take a field trip to a local movie theatre because I wouldn't have been able to sit with the class: Negroes had to sit in the balcony.

One day I was roller-skating near our house when I ran into Sammy Hartley, who had been in my fourth grade class. I'd never met a classmate from my past before, and I was stunned. Sammy's life had gone on, as mine had, and our paths had crossed twice! This changed some heavy thinking I was doing at the time, about being and—shall we say—nothingness. I was trying to decide whether I was Catholic or Mohammedan. Though my parents had been raised in black AME and CME churches, we usually attended nondenominational Protestant services in the base chapel. But after seeing *The Nun's Story* and reading a book about Albert Schweitzer, I imagined that I might someday be called, so I was reading everything I could find about saints. And, after reading an article about him in *Life* magazine, I'd developed a crush on Karim, the Aga Khan (at that time a dashing Harvard undergraduate), so I was also reading everything I could find about Islam. I spent one whole summer believing I was born to unite Christianity and Islam.

In 1958 Mama had another baby, a boy we named Peter Michael, but called Michael. When he was a few months old, the doctors informed us that he had Down's Syndrome. Daddy, who chain-smoked Salems, was flying twenty-four-hour missions for the Strategic Air Command then, and under a great deal of Cold War, Civil Rights, and family stress. One night while flying a mission he had a heart attack. After leaving the hospital, he was grounded, with a large reduction in pay, and transferred to California for retraining.

In the middle of my ninth grade year we moved back to Sacramento, to Glen Elder, the black neighborhood of tract houses in which we had lived for a short time three years earlier. After several years of financial difficulties caused by his loss of flight pay, Daddy took a medical discharge from the air force and entered civilian life. The family stayed in Sacramento, while he moved from a position as technical writer for a large corporation, then to one as technical editor, then finally to a job teaching English in a junior high school. I went to high school in Sacramento. Having lived for so long in a predominantly white world, I was a social dud in the neighborhood and with the black kids at school. I couldn't dance, I "talked white," I read books for pleasure and enjoyed studying: I was as square as they come.

But my best friend, Marjorie Gibson, was as awkward a black girl as I. Hiram Johnson High School had a substantial black student population, though the student body was predominantly white, with a lot of Chicanos and a sprinkling of Asians. We were "tracked" in three levels: most of the white and Asian students took accelerated college-prep classes; some of the whites, some of the Asians, and one or two Chicanos and blacks took the "normal" curriculum; and most of the blacks and Chicanos and a few whites took vocational classes. When I told my high school counselor that my junior high school counselor had told me that I would be put into accelerated classes, he said I must have been mistaken. I was finally accelerated in my senior year, after my father demanded to know why, since I was almost a straight-*A* student, I hadn't been given more challenging courses.

In my junior year I fell in love. He was a sophomore, an athlete; his name was Walt Slider. During our two years as a couple, Walt excelled in everything he did: he was the star of our varsity basketball team; he played third base on our varsity baseball team; he lettered in football and track, winning several second or third place medals in long jump in state-wide competitions. And he got good grades, he was funny and sweet, and more than six-feet tall and brown-skinned, with sleepy-looking eyes and a faint, downy moustache. Walt and I became one of the "campus couples," his popularity winning me a place in the coveted inner circle of high school society. We had friends in all of the racial groups at school. I was elected homeroom representative to the student council and selected for rally committee. I was yearbook editor, sang in the choir, and marched in the drill team at football and basketball games. I was in several clubs, and was our school's representative to California Girls' State. But Walt was my focus in those years. He taught me a great deal about tenderness. I wore his medal-festooned letter-sweater. We held hands in the hall. Because of him, my high school years were virtually painless. In his senior year Walt was student body president, the first black student in the history of the school to be elected to that office. He maintained a *B* average throughout high school, yet when he graduated in 1965 his counselor suggested he apply only to the local junior college.

Our youngest brother began to have spells during which he stopped breathing and turned

Marilyn (right) with her mother, sister, Jennifer (left), and brother, Mel, on New Year's Day, Mexico, 1961

blue. My years as a Girl Scout had included a first aid badge, and several times I resuscitated Michael mouth-to-mouth. When he was three years old he contracted pneumonia, was hospitalized, and died. People outside the family said it was for the best. Maybe it was. But his presence among us was one of total trust and love.

I was in civics class when we got the news about President Kennedy's assassination. In gym one rainy winter afternoon playing "floor volleyball," I suddenly realized that I was me, here, alive; that the other girls were themselves, alive and here, too; and that the meaning of life is love. It came to me suddenly and powerfully, in the midst of the noise. I graduated in 1964 and gave a commencement speech about "Today's Woman." And behind my father's back (he wanted me to go to Sacramento State College and live at home) and with Mama's blessing, I applied to the University of California at Davis. To my delight, I was accepted.

At our Lutheran church the summer after graduation, I met Drew Blackwell, a Harvard stu-

dent, a white Canadian boy in Sacramento on a summer youth project. We began to correspond. During that year I outgrew Walt and dumped him as gently as I could, though we remained close. The following summer, at a national Lutheran youth conference, Drew and I became "engaged to be engaged." Our romance lasted for four years, fed by long letters and expensive phone calls and half-fare standby airline tickets. Drew was the son of a Lutheran pastor and at Harvard on scholarship. He had been a Fabian Socialist since the age of fourteen and planned to go into politics in the Canadian New Democratic Party after finishing his studies. His studies enhanced my own, in which I was flourishing with wide-eyed wonder.

There were only five of us black American students at Davis, in a student body of approximately 12,000. We joked that I was "the English department nigger," while others were the "niggers" of their major departments. But I was in my element at Davis, with a social life in some ways more rewarding (and interesting) than I'd had in high school.

Though I loved Drew, I liked lots of other boys: I dated boys from Nigeria, Guinea, India, Australia, and Guatemala, a couple of black American students from Stanford and California Polytechnical Institute, and several white Americans, one an Orthodox Jew. I worked in the library, paying my way through college. Drew and I saw each other at holidays, sometimes in Sacramento and Davis, sometimes in Cambridge or Drew's hometown in Ontario.

We spent the summer of 1965 in Chicago, Drew at the Urban Training Center in an experiential course on poverty (in its "plunge," students were given five dollars and sent out to live for a weekend in Chicago), and I on a YMCA/YWCA summer project which placed college students with community-development projects. At the orientation for the YMCA/YWCA project, we students were asked to introduce ourselves and our interests. I told my name, and that I liked to read and write poems. The director of the program said sternly, "Baby, you gone have a hard time." Drew and I lived on the west side. Not together. He shared an apartment with a bunch of seminary students; I lived with six students from various colleges and countries in the large home of a black family. The Southern Christian Leadership Conference brought the Movement to Chicago that summer in a struggle for equal housing. We did volunteer office work, "tested" real estate agencies, handed out leaflets, and marched. We celebrated the day one of my roommates was asked to clean Dr. King's house. The city erupted with riots that summer, and with the nastiest, most virulent racism I've personally experienced. But, in a bubble of love, I wasn't afraid. Attacks and insults came from all sides. Police cars slowed, sometimes even stopped, when Drew and I walked together. When we marched with SCLC in white neighborhoods, we were spat at and called vile names. I was passing out leaflets on a corner one day, when a group of young black men circled me, jeering and hooting obscenities. Suddenly, a black man in a suit and tie said in a firm voice, "That's my daughter. Now, you leave her alone!" When I turned to thank him, he was gone.

I went back to Davis. Drew spent the year as a Student Nonviolent Coordinating Committee volunteer doing voter registration in Pine Bluff, Arkansas. I marched for equal rights and farm workers and peace, helped to organize the new Black Students' Union (the number of black students at Davis increased with Affirmative Action), was a fellow-traveler of Students for a Democratic Society, participated in activities sponsored by our activist campus ministry, learned to dance High Life at parties hosted by West African graduate students, and represented Davis as a poet at an all-University of California student artist conference. My sister had joined me at UC-Davis, and in the apartment we shared with another black girl and one white girl, we held a little on-going *"salon."* I'd started writing more seriously, encouraged by a new graduate student, Jack Vernon, who offered a poetry workshop through our student-initiated "experimental college." Jack, who is now a novelist (*Peter Doyle, All for Love*), was my first and best poetry-writing teacher.

My father had another heart attack the day after Christmas. He had taken up acting again and had played Othello at UC-Davis and many roles in the Sacramento State College theatre and various community theatres. His death came the day he returned from a whirlwind drive to Los Angeles, where he had been invited to audition for the National Repertory Theatre. He died after the celebratory party. We never knew whether he would have been invited to join the company, but he thought the audition had gone well. I felt the bottom had fallen out of my world.

I met a boy that year who made me question my commitment to Drew, but nothing happened except with our eyes, so I flew off to Cambridge,

Massachusetts, that summer, to work as a secretary at Massachusetts Institute of Technology, and live with Drew, who taught that summer in an Upward Bound program. Our Harvard/Radcliffe friends were all English majors; most of us dreamed of being writers. We had lobster feasts in our apartment on Pearl Street and roasted legs of lamb in the fireplace of a friend's room in Adams House, drinking Greek wine, reciting poetry, and talking politics. We went to Red Sox games and to the beach, we took long walks along the Charles. It was a wonderful idyll; every girl should have a summer like that. Drew and I planned to live in Vancouver on the Commonwealth Fellowship he had won (which would pay for his Ph.D. studies in any country in the British Commonwealth), while we worked toward graduate degrees at the University of British Columbia. He planned after completing his Ph.D. to run for office with the NDP. We also planned names for our two children and our Irish setter. But I was somehow numb at the center, and that numbness lasted through the following year.

"Daddy as Othello," University of California at Davis, 1963

We graduated in 1968. Drew decided that summer that we should go to Venezuela for two years, with a sort of Lutheran Peace Corps called "Prince of Peace Volunteers." He signed us up, then called to tell me. Suddenly a loud voice in my mind said, "Whoa!" I had turned down a graduate fellowship at Davis, planning to take courses at UBC. I turned to my advisor for help and wound up with a tuition fellowship at his alma mater, the University of Pennsylvania. Drew and I drove from California to Pennsylvania, then he left. I called him once from a pay phone in Philadelphia with about twenty-five pounds of quarters. But it was over between us.

In Philadelphia I lived in a one-room apartment in a running-down building in Rittenhouse Square. It was a neighborhood of expensive boutiques and fancy little dogs, and I believe I was the only black person living there. On several occasions, in the real estate office paying my rent, I overheard conversations between an agent and a black person looking for an apartment: the agent always said the only apartments available were in the ghetto. I knew there were vacancies in my building, and I wondered how I had slipped through the net. My apartment was a short walk across the Schuylkill River to the Penn campus. I mourned my father, missed the rest of my family and Drew, and floundered in required courses which seemed absolutely irrelevant to what was going on in the world. John Lyly, for heaven's sake! The only professor I got to know slightly was the poet Daniel Hoffman, with whom I studied modern American poetry. The only student who was in all of my classes was a handsome young German, Erdmann Waniek, who seemed brilliant. We met when we literally bumped into each other on the street, both of us reading and walking at the same time. Thus thrown together we rapidly became friends, then, much more slowly and with great trepidation, lovers. He passed his M.A. exam; I failed mine. At the end of the year we decided to let our brief romance become a beautiful memory. He left to work toward a Ph.D. in German at the University of Oregon. I accepted a position as lay associate in campus ministry with the Lutheran church at Cornell University. He telephoned a few weeks later, having decided to risk losing his family and his ability to feel comfortable living in Germany to ask me to marry him.

I spent the summer of 1969 teaching in an Upward Bound program at Franklin and Marshall College, with wonderful black high school kids.

Marilyn Nelson and Erdmann Waniek, 1969

I've often wondered what happened to one of them, Lance Edward Jones. He told me once that he knew he wouldn't be dead when he died, if I remembered him. Then I spent a year in campus ministry at Cornell, as a gadfly in the congregation and an off-campus housemother for the Lutheran student community. I worked with the Reverend Lee Snook, a fine, funny, and wonderfully intelligent man. I had an office on campus, in a big building which housed Cornell United Religious Work (CURW). Father Daniel Berrigan was one of our colleagues there. I counseled would-be drop-outs and pregnant undergraduates, played matchmaker, argued with born-again students, and worked for peace, racial equality, and the environment. I marched on Washington. I drove down to Penn and passed the M.A. exam. I counseled draft-dodgers. One day someone called from New York City, asking how he could avoid the draft. After a long conversation, I suggested he might talk to others in CURW. Two days later he arrived on a bus, a tall, cadaverous young man with a duffle bag, wearing a black, ankle-length coat. He looked exactly like Bartleby, the Scrivener. He wanted me to help him find a job as a librarian in Canada. He was clearly out of his mind. I turned to Lee for help. He said, "You got him here; he's yours." The other ministers and priests at CURW said he was my cross to bear. So I was stuck with him. I persuaded a Lutheran fraternity boy to let him sleep in the frat house, and he arrived at my apartment promptly at 6:00 every morning: he had to eat at 6:00, and he had to eat oatmeal. He had to have a tuna sandwich for lunch, and a large glass of grapefruit juice. I no longer remember what he had to have for dinner. He spent days in my office laboriously hand-writing job application letters to Canadian libraries, offering as professional experience the fact that he had read many library books. He never took off his coat. He never said thank you. I finally bought him a one-way ticket to Toronto and put him on a bus. I figured somebody else could carry that cross for a while.

That year, in a letter responding to a sheaf of poems I had sent him, my great-uncle Rufus asked, "Why is it that young poets nowadays don't write poems people like me can understand?" His question shook me then and has stayed with me. Uncle Rufus wasn't exactly a literary man, but he did earn a master's degree in the twenties from Iowa State, and he was, after all, a college president. Why, indeed?

Walt was killed in an automobile accident that year, shortly after his college graduation. A drunk driver hit his car from behind, and he was thrown through the windshield. He left a twenty-two-year-old widow pregnant with their first child.

After another summer at Franklin and Marshall's Upward Bound program, I joined Erdmann in Eugene, Oregon. We married that fall, in the backyard of the beautiful little house we had rented for its view of the Cascade Mountains. Erdmann took graduate courses and was a teaching assistant; I taught English at Lane Community College (LCC). We hiked, skied, walked on the beach, and went camping. We had two Irish setters, a fireplace, and homemade plywood furniture. I was appointed to a committee which was preparing a new Lutheran hymnal; periodically over the next few years I was flown to other cities to pore over mountains of hymn texts, looking for racism, sexism, and militarism. The committee edited, retranslated, or rewrote many hymns. There's a small chance that any Lutheran in America may one Sunday sing one of my words. In our second year in Eugene I taught full-time at LCC (four courses each semester) and half-time (two courses) at Reed College, in Portland. Then Erdmann finished his degree and, because he had come to the U.S. on a Fulbright Fellowship, had to leave the country. He thought life would be difficult for us in Germany. My dean at LCC wrote to some of his friends at a college in Denmark, and we were hired.

We spent a year teaching German and English at Nørre Nissum Seminarium in Jutland. During visits to his home in Germany, I got to know and love Erdmann's family. Our Danish friends were Inge and Bent Pedersen, both of them now writers, and my special friends were Niels Jacob Nielsen and Jan Holtegaard. Niels Jacob and Jan and I took a camping tour of Denmark that summer. We must have been a sight for villagers: Niels Jacob with dark-tinted glasses and a goatee; Jan with a bright red beard; and me. The owner of one campground asked us to play one night; when we asked what she meant, she asked whether we weren't a rock and roll band. *Og jeg kan taler Dansk.* On a driving and hiking vacation in Norway with Erdmann's sister and brother-in-law at the end of the year, we walked through a grocery store in a tiny, remote mountain village, discussing in English and German which meats we wanted to buy. When we had decided, I told the butcher in Danish (which is Norwegian with a mouthful of mashed potatoes) what we wanted. He wrapped our packages, gave them to us, and followed us to the cashier. The cashier asked him in Norwegian how he had known what we wanted. The butcher, pointing at me with an expression of absolute wonder, said in Norwegian: "*SHE* speaks Norwegian!"

One of my colleagues on the Lutheran Hymn Text Committee was the head of the English department at St. Olaf College in Minnesota. He wrote that there was an opening and suggested I apply. We said we could only come if there were two positions. There was an opening in German, too. We were interviewed in Copenhagen by Howard and Edna Hong, the translators of Kierkegaard. They liked us. We liked them. And who'd be crazy enough to turn down two jobs? Vowing to return, we left Denmark in the fall of 1972, though the whole country felt like home.

St. Olaf (not St. Olaf's) is a small Lutheran college in the town of Northfield, Minnesota. On its beautiful hilltop stone campus all of the students, except for a handful of black students recruited from northern cities and small towns down south, were blond midwestern Norwegian-Americans. I liked my colleagues and my students, and was delighted to have a black friend and colleague in the English department, John Edgar Tidwell. I taught composition, American literature, and black literature, and invented courses in minority literature and Native American literature. My friends, the theologian/philosophers Mary and David Pellauer, lived across the street. I nursed a sourdough starter, made all of our bread and granola, and cooked dinners for my minority literature classes, with smoked salmon and homemade bagels, corn bread and fried chicken, or roast rabbit and succotash. I had given up writing and politics and the church, and led a rather hedonistic life with Erdmann, going to parties, making fancy dinners, camping and hiking and cross-country skiing, attending the theatre, discussing books. I enrolled in graduate courses at the University of Minnesota, eventually taking a leave from St. Olaf to finish course work toward a Ph.D. in English with an emphasis on American minority literature.

I took courses in the English department and in the Afro-American and Latin American studies programs, and studied Native American culture with an anthropologist. One day, arriving at the anthropologist's office for my weekly tutorial, I was told our meeting had to be cancelled: a Sioux singer had stopped by to say hello. My professor introduced me to a tall, white-haired Indian, who looked into my eyes for a long moment, then told me to wait: he wanted to sing for me. My professor whispered that this singer was famous nation-wide; that it was a very great personal honor to be invited to be his private audience. I hung around in the hall until they had finished their conversation in Sioux, then the old singer ushered me into the office and closed the door. What followed was strange, magical, and transporting. For the next hour or so, I sat and listened as he introduced each song by its tribal origin, explained what it signified, closed his eyes and sang, shaking a feathered gourd rattle and slowly dancing from one foot to the other. Natachee Momaday, the Pulitzer Prize-winning Kiowa novelist, often writes of times when his grandmother, by telling him ancient stories, opened for him the door to the timelessness of the oral tradition. Momaday calls it being "invited into her presence." I know exactly what he means.

Erdmann and I traveled a lot, usually to spend holidays with our families in California and Germany. One summer, having heard from friends who had camped out there, we visited Churchill, a town on the southern shore of Hudson's Bay. The trip required a day of driving to the end of the highway, then a long train ride across the flat summer tundra. We arrived in Churchill in the afternoon, got off the train with our camping gear, and walked into town. Several townspeople asked whether we seriously intended to camp out *now*. It was polar bear migration season; one person after another told us polar bear stories: the size of a paw print; the time a bear

ripped out the side of a panel truck to get at the dressed goose inside. We walked around for a couple of hours in a constant swarm of biting gnats. We visited a museum of Inuit art. Then we got on the train again and went home. But we did see a distant pod of Beluga whales and a sky ablaze with the northern lights.

One year we flew to Venezuela to visit my former fiancé, Drew, and his wife and child. Drew was teaching in Caracas, at an experimental national university based on the teachings of Paulo Freire. His family and friends called him Andres. We spent several days in Caracas, then flew off to explore the rest of the country. Luckily, I'd studied Spanish in high school and college. Everywhere we went, brown and black men surrounded me to ask where I was from, or called "*Ay, negrita!*" admiringly from busses and cars. And they called Erdmann *gringo*, and threw bottles and stones at his side of our little rented car. I've often thought since that visit that I'd like someday to teach in Venezuela, at the University of the Andes in Merida. We drove there, passing almost vertical fields divided by stone walls, here and there a farmer leading a laden ox. At every place we stopped, children with runny noses and cheeks red with cold, barefoot and wearing rough-woven ponchos, ran up to the car, crying, "*Señor! Nosotros somos pobres! Danos algo!*" —"We are poor! Give us something." White children. Blond, with blue eyes. In Merida we happened, completely by chance, into an international festival of New Song, where for the first time I heard Inti-Illimani sing the rousing and tender melody of Latin American liberation: "*El pueblo unido jamas sera vencido!*"— "The people united will never be conquered!" It is as memorable and heartwarming an anthem as "We Shall Overcome." We visited a village settled more than one hundred years ago by German immigrants, where an archaic Black Forest dialect is still spoken. We flew with "Jungle Rudy" (whose age and German accent—not to mention the dueling scar on his cheek—made us wonder whether someone in Israel might be looking for him) over Angel Falls. We spent a week on the island of Margarita, watching pelicans snatch fish from the fishermen's nets, eating fish fried so fresh they retained their tropical colors, and lying in hammocks and waving the oysterman over to pull an oyster out of his bucket, open it with his knife, take a lemon from his pocket, slice it, squeeze the juice over the oyster, and sell it to us for a coin. I spent the first part of the week lying in a hammock and drinking down tart, sweet oysters. I spent the last part of the week in the necessary room.

In my last year of course work at the University of Minnesota, I gave myself a gift: though I hadn't tried to write a poem in several years, I enrolled in a graduate poetry workshop taught by Michael Dennis Browne. David Wojahn, who was also in the workshop, became a good friend; as a lark we invented a Danish poet and his biography, and David wrote fake "translations" of several of his poems, which I translated into clumsy Danish. We planned to send them to a major poetry journal, but as I remember we chickened out. Later we enrolled in a workshop offered privately by Etheridge Knight, which promised occasional visits by Etheridge's friend, Robert Bly. Under Etheridge's tutelage we sweated over drafts of our poems and regularly presented unannounced group readings at sites he picked: restaurants, bars. Bly came to a few of our readings; an approving grunt from him was a special sign of honor. One evening we were reading in a bar when a drunk held out a piece of paper and asked the poet at the microphone to read it aloud. It was a letter from his wife on the reservation, asking him to come home, saying the children missed him, promising they could make their marriage work. Our poems seemed suddenly very trivial.

Erdmann and I taught one semester in Germany at the University of Hamburg. We became friends with two other couples mixed racially and nationally like ourselves, who seemed to be perfectly content living in Germany. But when I walked alone in the city, North African "guest-workers" ran up to me to tell me that they knew, after living for some time in Germany, what it was like to be an American Negro. Germans look you up and down, and then stare right into your eyes. I know it's a cultural, rather than a personal characteristic, but it made me feel as I'd felt marching through pristine white neighborhoods in Chicago. I was several times discussing a product with a shop clerk who addressed me politely as *"Sie,"* when a Turkish guest-worker entered the shop and she turned and addressed him contemptuously as *"du."* All of the university students in Germany went on a long strike a couple of weeks into the semester, so I spent much of that period working on my dissertation and writing poems. I read *Leaves of Grass* that spring and walked in the park along the Alster River charged with Whitman's magnificence. We went

to the opera. I love Mozart's operas. I became friends with Ralf Thenior, a young German poet. I saw a rainbow which straddled the Alster with one foot on each bank.

We went to Innsbruck, Austria, during that spring, to visit my friend, Michael Ihlenfeldt, whom I had met at Cornell. Michael loaned us his old VW for a trip through Umbria, the northeastern part of Italy. We picked up a young American hitchhiker on the way, near Garmisch Partenkirchen, high in the Alps. When he was settled in the backseat, we asked him where he was headed. He said he thought he'd go to a city Erdmann knew to be far distant. Erdmann told him he'd have to get out of the Alps first. My countryman responded flatly, "Oh. Are these the Alps?" In Italy—Ah, Italy!—we visited cathedrals and museums and castles and art and art and art (My now-husband, Roger, calls such trips "the grim march through culture"). But on the other hand, Italian men called *"Ciao, bella!"* when they passed and threw me kisses. In the first part of the trip we ate pasta in workers' restaurants we'd found in *Europe on $10 a Day.* We ran out of money early in the trip, so for the rest of the time we traveled high on the hog, eating truffle-laced sauces in fancy restaurants that took American credit cards. I can close my eyes and see the morning landscapes dotted with sunlit hilltop villages sticking up over thickly misted vineyards. The Umbrian light seemed, somehow, different from any other light I've ever seen. As I walked in that light in Assisi, it seemed no wonder, I thought, there are so many Italian saints.

My commitment to writing grew steadily; poems came to me with a frequency that frightened me. I saw that the muse can be a terrible taskmaster. When we returned to Minnesota, I lived part-time in Minneapolis with my friend, Pamela Espeland, with whom I later translated several poems for children written by the Danish poet, Halfdan Rasmussen (published as a chapbook called *Hundreds of Hens and Other Poems*), and still later wrote a book of verse for children, called *The Cat Walked through the Casserole.* My time was given to writing my dissertation, going to readings, and finding my voice. I gave my first big reading in Minneapolis with Mary Karr, to a surprisingly large and appreciative audience. I sent some of my poems to Daniel Hoffman, who had been my professor at Penn, and Dan suggested I send him a manuscript, which he would submit to a publisher.

When Erdmann came up for tenure at St. Olaf, it was denied—more, we believed, because of the years-long feud he'd had with the head of his department (who once told me at a dinner at our house that it was too bad it had been made illegal to ask a candidate's race, but that he'd compensated by deciding that if a candidate's letter was ungrammatical, the candidate must be black) than because of his work. We decided to seek other positions. I felt freed. I was struggling to accept the new identity which had come with my serious commitment to poetry, and our marriage was too small to hold my emerging wings. Erdmann went one direction; I went another. Though we've both looked back, that decision was for the best.

I've been at the University of Connecticut since 1978. By the end of my first year here, I had finished my dissertation, gotten my Ph.D., had a book published, and decided to marry one of my colleagues. Milton scholars know my husband, Roger Wilkenfeld, for some essays he published when he was in his twenties. He can recite much of "Paradise Lost" by heart, and does so at most opportunities. He's a sports fan, an old-movie buff, a collector of beautiful objects, a voracious reader, and an excellent poetry critic. He has an aggravatingly intractable opinion about any topic you can name. Like most men, he's impossible. He may, as a matter of fact, be more impossible than most. Our son Jacob was born in 1980; our daughter Dora in 1986. Lest this essay dissolve into a warm bath of motherly anecdotes, I'll change its direction now and talk about my work.

For the Body was published in 1978. Daniel Hoffman, who submitted its manuscript for me to LSU Press, was its godfather. The first poem after its "Dedication" was the last one I worked on as a grad student at Penn; Dan had seen the earlier draft and written to me with suggestions. I finished it five years later and felt it might be good enough to send to him. I was, frankly, surprised that he remembered me. I'd been as colossally undistinguished a student in his class as I was in my other classes at Penn: I'd spent much of my time wondering where my next meal would come from (my fellowship paid only for tuition), and then falling in love. My book is clearly autobiographical, and anyone long-suffering enough to have read thus far will recognize people and places, if she or he has read that book. My former father-in-law, who served briefly in the German cavalry toward the end of World War II, is the

old soldier in "War-horses." "April Rape" started not with a rape, but with the whistles and cat-calls I provoked when I walked across the bridge to Penn. At that point they raised my feminist hackles; later I came to accept them with pleasure. I think now I'd be flattered to death. The Mary of several poems is Mary Pellauer, my theologian friend in Northfield. I wrote "Emily Dickinson's Defunct" after she told me she'd like to make theology out of women's poetry and asked me where I thought she should start. When I suggested Emily Dickinson, Mary said she'd always been intimidated by Emily Dickinson. I found very funny the idea that the reclusive maid of Amherst could intimidate anyone, and wrote a poem about her in which all of her intimidating features are true. "Wanda S." was my roommate, Wanda Smith, at UC-Davis in 1965. We shared an apartment in a trailer park and mailed each other long letters, although we saw each other every day. She recently moved back to the U.S. after living for a while in Chile. The young women in "Silver Earrings" and "For Karen" were St. Olaf students. I wrote "The Life of a Saint" after seeing Giotto's frescoes of the life of St. Francis in the cathedral of Assisi. "The Perfect Couple" is one of several poems I wrote during the time I first began to wrestle with the muse; it's about finally accepting that sense of being possessed. Several of the poems started with reading I was doing for my courses in Native American culture, immigration history, and speech-act theory. I wrote "Fish Poem" after a friend asked me whether I'd noticed that several of my poems contained fish and told me fish are a phallic symbol. My friend Pamela gave me a jade fish on a gold chain to remind me that my fish was a muse. "Dedication" and "The Source of the Singing" are intended to mirror each other, and to claim the body (not just the mind) as the source of consciousness and creativity.

Like most first-book poets, I fully expected my first book to catapult me to the stars. What it did instead was make me want to be a better writer.

I hoped *Mama's Promises* would be read as a book of black feminist theology. I wanted to proclaim a "Mama" God, a black working-mother God, whose stress might be greater than my own (I came up for tenure when Jacob was a nine-month-old toddler), and who might be too wrung-out (as I was every night) to answer our prayers. I had originally wanted to call Her "Mammy," remembering an offensive joke I heard a comedian tell years ago on the Johnny Carson show: an astronaut came back from orbit with good news and bad news—the good news was that he'd seen God; the bad news was that "She's black!" Unfortunately, my own life dominates the book. Our house had a very strange layout; my desk was right beside Jacob's crib. Though my self-correcting electric typewriter (God, I loved that machine!) was quiet, Jacob was a very light sleeper. We experimented, and found that just our talking about him in low voices two or three rooms or even a floor away woke him from his version of a sound sleep. Until we partitioned the space and enclosed my desk in a tiny, cork-lined cubicle study, I could only write when he was in day-care or with a baby-sitter, and even with the study I had to spend most of my not-mommying time preparing classes and grading papers. I wrote most of the poems in this book by getting up before dawn and writing for the hour or two before Jacob woke. It's good to hear the birds begin their day's business, and to watch the sun rise.

The titles of the first few poems in this book were written by Amanda Jordan, who was eight years old when we met in the public library, reaching for the same book. We discovered we were both writers; I wrote poems, and Mandy wrote titles of poems she planned to write someday. She had several notebooks full of titles; she agreed to give me some of them, and I agreed to write poems for them. For several months we had regular "writers' lunches." I have a book of poems she wrote and stapled together in a little illustrated book to give me for Christmas. The porcelain fawn in the title poem was a birthday present my friend Kim bought for me in seventh grade: just as she handed it to me, it fell and shattered; Kim was mortified. There are several dragons in this book, in my mind modeled after the dragons of Anne McCaffrey's "Pern" science fiction novels. Between 1978 and 1980 I had worked unsuccessfully on a blank-verse adaptation of Rilke's first and second "Duino Elegies," turning them into dialogues between myself and a dragon-muse. My "Dragon Dialogues" never got off the ground, but McCaffrey's fierce and benevolent flying dragons stayed with me. Roger and Pamela and Jennifer gave me dragons to wear while I was working on the book. The dragon-muse in "Levitation with Baby" flies off with my next-door neighbor, Bob Burkinshaw, who's always out working in his yard. Bob likes this poem a lot.

"It's All in Your Head" is dedicated to Deborah Muirhead, who teaches art here at the University of Connecticut. Deborah's abstract paintings explore her roots in the black South; her genealogical research inspired my own. Readers of this essay will recognize most of the names in this poem. Zilphia was the daughter of one of my grandmother's sisters; I love her name. Jamie Crowl, who is mentioned in "Mama's Murders," was from one of the southern families stationed at Kittery Yard when I was in sixth grade. At recess one day we were throwing her end of the seesaw down so that it banged against the blacktop; she realized we were trying to hurt her and tried to get off. Her arm was caught under the seat. It was an accident, but accidentally on purpose.

"I Dream the Book of Jonah" antedates the other poems in the book. I began working on it in 1977 when Pamela, who works as a freelance editor, edited a book about the Bible, and called me in Northfield to say she found Jonah very funny. She suggested I tell his story. The poem grew very slowly, as I discovered a voice for Jonah, moving from a Standard English voice through several levels of folksy colloquial ones before finally arriving at a Jonah I could see clearly. He looks like the great blues artist, Mississippi John Hurt. At that point I thought the poem was finished. But Mary Pellauer said it couldn't be finished unless I included a Blues. I wrote the last draft of the poem while visiting Pamela in Minneapolis. I was looking for a way to end the poem. Pamela and I discussed at length what I had in mind and mused over it together for several days. One morning she came out of the bathroom, took her toothbrush out of her mouth, and said the last seven lines of my poem. *Our* poem. Pamela's son, by the way, is named Jonah.

I dreamed a phrase early in the writing of this book: "Rhymed free-verse" (I also dreamed the phrase "Iago powder"), so I worked very hard making several poems rhyme. I hid the rhymes by making them slant-rhymes; they are so slant that even I can only find two or three of them now. There's not much else to say about the book, except that the cover is a portrait of me, drawn by Jacob. Note the big earrings.

Like many second-book poets, I began to realize that maybe it was time for me to learn something about poetry. I began to study traditional prosody. I had long admired the work of Marilyn Hacker, and I followed with mild interest the passionate debates in literary journals about the so-called "new formalism." I began to include Paul Fussell's *Poetic Meter and Poetic Form* as a text in my graduate workshops, and to experiment with

"With my husband Roger Wilkenfeld and our son, Jacob," 1982

fixed forms in my own work. For about a year I was busy writing a sequence of fifty therapeutic sonnets about my first marriage, modeled after George Meredith's *Modern Love,* and not intended for publication. A couple of years after they were finished, I showed some of them to my friend Margaret Gibson, who asked me if she could include them in an issue of *The New Virginia Review,* which she was guest-editing. I hesitated, but finally agreed to publish them under a pseudonym. To my astonishment and chagrin, they won a Pushcart Prize and were reprinted, still under a pseudonym, in the *Pushcart Prize Anthology.* In 1992 Emily Strayer of the Kutenai Press offered to publish a chapbook for me. I had no work at the time to give her, except the sonnets. She published fourteen of them, with two illustrations by Eric Spencer. The book, *Partial Truth,* is designed by Emily and printed with handset Californian type on Japanese Wahon paper and sewn with linen into covers of Duchene Mouchette from the Moulin du Pombie in France and endsheets of banana paper, handmade in the Philippines. The edition is limited to two hundred numbered copies signed by Eric and myself. It's a beautiful book; it even smells good. The rest of my sonnets are gathering dust.

There's not much to say about *The Homeplace* that hasn't been said earlier in this essay. The book is a family history. For several years my mother had been slowly disappearing into the fog of Alzheimer's disease; the last time I came home from visiting her in California, my husband said he thought I should go to my grandmother's hometown. I don't know what made him suggest that: I don't think I'd talked of Hickman often. But I made airplane reservations the day after I got back to Connecticut, and wound up flying to Kentucky on that reservation only a few days after coming home from my mother's funeral in Sacramento. (Entering the cemetery, the cortège passed four young white men in an open convertible. Jennifer, Mel, and I rode in the funeral parlor limousine. My eyes met those of the driver of the convertible as we passed it, and he yelled, "Good! Another dead nigger!") I spent several days in Hickman with my second cousin, Annisue Briggs, sleeping in "the homeplace" that's been in the family since 1862, and prowling through records in the county courthouse. I planned to write a book in Mama's memory, just for the family, but gradually, as far-flung relatives and local historians, black and white, eagerly gave me anecdotes and information, the book "jest growed." The first part of the book, poems about my mother's family, was much influenced by my earlier work with fixed forms.

Since I know so little about my father's family, I decided to include a section about his second family, the Tuskegee Airmen. Some of the stories I tell about them were given to me by my uncle, Rufus Mitchell, who was a member of the ground crew of the Tuskegee Airmen, or by Edward Woodward, an old family Air Force friend. Ed Woodward and my father were among the men who were almost court-martialed after the incident at Freeman Field, when black officers refused the order to use the NCO Club instead of the Officers' Club. Most of the stories came from my fortuitously meeting Bert Wilson, a black retired lieutenant colonel, formerly a pilot in the famed ninety-ninth Squadron, who lives not far from me in Connecticut. Over lunch one day Bert told me his World War II experiences; the best line in the book ("I was sleeping on his breath") quotes him directly. I did not tape record these men's stories, but I did try in the poems to capture their voices as authentically as I could.

The photograph of Tuskegee cadets, which introduces the last section of the book, came to me in such an odd way that I wrote a poem about it ("The True Magic" in *Magnificat*). But I'll tell the story again here. I had given up on finding a photograph of my father as a cadet, and settled for a photograph of three cadets I did not recognize. A few days before the manuscript was due to arrive at the press, one of my cousins, Roy Mitchell, telephoned from Ohio. He had recently joined the fraternal organization known as "The Tuskegee Airmen" and attended his first meeting. Since in order to become a member one must be related to one of the original Tuskegee Airmen, the man sitting next to Roy asked what his relationship was to the original group, and Roy told him my father's name. The man, Bob Hunter, had brought to the meeting a large black-and-white photograph of a group of cadets; he said, "Well, I guess this is for you." The photograph shows Bob Hunter second in line in a group of cadets getting ready to climb into a plane. My father is first in line, in the center of the picture, looking directly into the camera. On the phone Roy said, "Marilyn, there's no question about it: there's something divine in this."

The Homeplace was a finalist for the 1991 National Book Award, and it won the Annisfield-Wolf Award in 1992. I've been amazed by the warmth with which readers of all racial backgrounds have received the stories of my family, which I'd thought of as private and personal, as if my family were theirs.

Like *The Homeplace*, my most recent book, *Magnificat*, is a narrative made up of individual poems. When I confessed, before sending it to the press, that I was uncomfortable about the possibility that it might inadvertently reveal the identity and location of the monk/priest it presents, my friend, the poet Theodore Deppe, assured me there was nothing to worry about: nobody would believe the story anyway. And it is, I think, an extraordinary story. At the end of fall semester in 1989, as I commented on a story written by a student in my undergraduate creative writing course, I suddenly remembered the boy for whom I would have broken off my engagement when we were undergraduates. I couldn't get him out of my mind. At last I told my husband about him. I'd never told anyone the entire story, or confronted it inwardly for more than a minute or two. When we were introduced at a party, I had offered my hand for him to shake, and he had lifted it and kissed it, looking into my eyes and saying, again and again, that he would never cease loving me. I remember thinking, "Is he the one?" I looked around us, asking if someone could tell me his name. He never took his eyes off me,

"Our children, Jacob and Dora," 1989

never stopped murmuring his promise. At last I took a long look into his brown eyes, and, wishing it possible to see in someone's eyes whether he was serious or not, I promised to love him forever. He smiled at that and turned away. Then his friends surrounded him and took him home. He looked back once, and we exchanged a shy, wondering smile. Though we later became friends, we never mentioned that momentous meeting. He told me at another party that he had a strong feeling that we would someday write some books of poems together. My flirting, flippant response was to laugh and say maybe they would be pornographic. I don't think we ever had another serious conversation, though we did have one disastrous date. I've told the story in the first poem in *Magnificat* of how and why he ran away. When I told Roger about him, I hadn't seen him in twenty years, though I had heard that he had entered a Benedictine monastery some ten years later.

Roger said we had to find him. Our search lasted for almost a year, during which I pored over books about the monastic life and contemplative prayer and Catholic theology and spiritual poverty and desert spirituality and Divine Union. Roger trusted my memory of this man to be accurate enough to ensure that our finding him would bring joy to all of us. When we found him, he wrote to us that he had finished a doctorate at Cambridge University, worked for several years, then felt the call. After seven years in a monastery he had left, with the blessings of his Father Abbot, to live as a hermit and build a new monastery.

My list of acknowledgments for the book includes medievalists, Catholic and Episcopal priests, Protestant ministers, monks, and nuns. The monks are the brothers of Weston Priory, a small Benedictine community in Vermont. When I went to the Priory to find out something about contemporary Benedictinism, the brothers welcomed me like a long-lost sister. The nuns I thank are the Guadalupans, a Mexican Benedictine community, the "sister community" of the Weston Priory, with whom I participated in a two-week long "hospitality experience" in which *gringos* are invited to receive the hospitality of the poor, and which deepened my understanding of poverty and of the radical interior changes demanded by Christ's proclamation of liberation. The Weston monks (R.R. 1, Box 50, Weston, Vermont, 05161) organize several such "experiences" each year, for groups of ten or fifteen people. The several priests to whom

I turned for advice assured me that I was not doing wrong in trying to find my friend again. One told me that "You're probably perfectly matched: a mystic and a poet. To the rest of the world, you're *both* nuts!" These new connections have very much altered my life: I once overheard Dora telling a playmate that "My mom is a monk."

I meant *Magnificat* to reflect spiritual struggle and growth. The longest poem in the book, "Letter to a Benedictine Monk," tells of the beginning of humility and renunciation. I wanted to write an ode, but couldn't find a clear enough definition, so I "deconstructed" Wordsworth's "Immortality" ode, patterning my lines and rhyme scheme after his. The sequence of prayers which follows is intended to demonstrate a development from humor to seriousness, from selfish requests and gratitude for personal blessings to awe at the mysteries of time and death, and finally to compassion. The title of "The Dream's Wisdom" was left over from Mandy Jordan's notebooks. And, after, in "Gloria," I receive the first answering letter from my friend (in real life, he sent a telegram), my prayers open to profound and thankful silence.

Most of the anecdotes of the book's second section, "A Desert Father," are things that happened, more or less, the first time I visited my friend's hermitage. "A Canticle for Abba Jacob" is modeled on "The Canticle of the Soul" by St. John of the Cross. I don't think there's much else to say here about this section of the book, except that when I showed one priest a photograph of my friend, he said, "Oh! He's not a nerd-monk; he's a matinee-idol monk!" And that I hope it's read, if it's read at all, less as an impossible love story than as an invitation to understand those who choose solitude and renunciation in order to be witnesses to love, and to offer unceasing prayer.

My poem, "Payday Evening at My Desk," in the book's third section, remembers Mariano Serano Cirilo, an eight-year-old boy I met with the Guadalupan sisters in a Cuernavaca slum. I had asked Jacob, who was then eight, whether he wanted me to bring him something special from Mexico; he had written his name on a slip of paper, asked me to give it to a Mexican kid, and said he'd like me to bring him back the Mexican kid's name. I gave it to Mariano, who took it solemnly, then wrote his own name for Jacob. His grandmother was so pleased by our visit that she insisted we accept the rolls a baker had given her when the market closed earlier that day. They were the only food in her bare, clean, one-room house. This is the hospitality of the poor.

"The Sacrament of Poverty" and "Valentine for a Bride Bereaved" were written for Judy Maines-LaMarre, who is one of the "Ladymonks," my friends who committed several years ago to work together toward self-understanding and spiritual growth. Judy, a widow, had been married to her second husband for only one month when he died suddenly, while away at a conference, of a heart attack. Judy is a nurse and has given herself to working with families of critically ill babies; every year since I've known her, she has spent her vacations holding Haitian babies who are dying of AIDS, or assisting in portable eye-clinics in Honduras, or inoculating children in remote villages in Papua New Guinea.

For three years I offered a poem-to-order at the annual fund-raising auction of the local Congregational church. One year bidding for my poem was fast and furious; it was finally sold for, I think, $73.00. A few months after the auction I asked one of the women who had bought it whether they didn't want me to write their poem. They told me they were lesbians; they had found a minister willing to marry them in the church; they wanted me to write a poem to be used in their wedding. When I told Roger of their request, he said, "Boy, this one has to be *good!*" Linda and Debbie and the minister (also a woman) and I met one evening to discuss the service, which they were writing themselves. They wanted the poem to include the idea that lovers are loaned to each other by God, and that, in love, one solitude embraces another. Judy told me over lunch one day, as I was struggling with the poem, that we take such a risk in loving that it's like walking out on a tightrope into the unknown. Another of my "Ladymonks" friends, Kathy Jambeck, who is a medievalist, told me that St. Bernard once wrote something about religious people and lovers being "holy fools." The fools' song in the poem is an echo of an ecstatic poem by Rumi, whom I was reading avidly at the time. Linda and Debbie have a houseful of cats and dogs— Linda works as a dog-catcher—so I put cats and dogs into their poem. I read it—"Epithalamium and Shivaree"—at their wedding, which was very beautiful. Linda's father, who had for years refused to acknowledge their love, and who had told Linda that he would not attend her so-called wedding, gave her away with tears in his eyes.

I must confess here that I did not read Plotinus. But Roger did and copied on slips of paper passages he thought crucial or beautiful. Each of the poems of "The Plotinus Suite" started with the italicized passage from Plotinus; the poems grew around the quotes.

My life has been full of blessings. As Mama would have said, "Knock on wood." I don't think I'm a good teacher, but I have tenure. I've spent semesters teaching in M.F.A. programs at the Vermont College, the University of Cincinnati and NYU. I've studied briefly with Seamus Heaney. I've had writing time purchased for me by the National Endowment for the Arts. Since finishing *Magnificat* I've spent another two weeks in Mexico with the Guadalupan sisters and the Mexican poor, traveled in Zimbabwe (where I spent several days in Harare with an independent community of African nuns and visited the ruins of Great Zimbabwe and Victoria Falls), and lived with my family in the south of France, on a Fulbright Teaching Fellowship. I am nourished by family and friends, both old and new. Last week I legally changed my name back to Marilyn Nelson and spent $176.00 on three little jars of creams which promise to make my face twenty years younger. I'm sitting in front of my computer right now, at five minutes to midnight, on Sunday, September 10, 1995. Roger and Jacob and Dora (and Sydney, our dog) are asleep upstairs. I'll spend tomorrow running errands and preparing for Tuesday's classes. Our lakeside house is small, but there's only one small leak in the roof, and it hasn't rained here for thirty-seven days. This afternoon Dora and our neighbors' boys put on a show for us—"The Harley Davison Show," their placard read—of look, Mom, no hands bicycle-riding (one of the showpeople had training-wheels). Our dogs tussled and growled around our legs, the sky was a deep and cloudless blue.

Meanwhile, people are dying of age and illness, and killing each other and themselves, and starving, and devising new ways to humiliate and degrade each other, and making love and giving birth and being lonely and closing their eyes and wishing, all over the planet. The first time I sat in the little oratory of Abba Jacob's hermitage on my low stool to the left of the door, while he sat on his on the right side, his head bowed, his eyes closed, his hands still and relaxed in his lap, I listened to the wind in the cane and knew that we are the only way God's light can enter this darkness. I hope my poems are windows. So many people have been windows for me.

BIBLIOGRAPHY

Poetry:

For the Body, Louisiana State University Press, 1978.

(With Pamela Espeland) *The Cat Walked through the Casserole and Other Poems for Children,* illustrated by Trina Schart Hyman, Hilary Knight, Nancy Carlson and Peter E. Hanson, Carolrhoda, 1984.

Mama's Promises, Louisiana State University Press, 1985.

The Homeplace, Louisana State University Press, 1990.

Magnificat, Louisiana State University Press, 1994.

Other:

(Translator from Danish) Phil Dahlerup, *Literary Sex Roles,* Minnesota Women in Higher Education, 1975.

(Translator from Danish with Pamela Espeland) *Hundreds of Hens and Other Poems for Children by Halfdan Rasmussen,* Black Willow, 1983.

(Contributor with Rita Dove) *Poetry after Modernism,* edited by Robert McDowell, Story Line Press, 1990.

Partial Truth (sonnet sequence), Kutenai, 1992.

Contributor of numerous essays to periodicals, including *Callaloo, Gettysburg Review, Image: A Journal of the Arts & Religion, MELUS, Minority Voices,* and *Studies in Black Literature.*

Gibbons Ruark

1941-

VOICES BEHIND A DOOR: AN AUTOBIOGRAPHY OF SOME POEMS

Gibbons Ruark at Ballycotton, Co. Cork, 1989

There is a moment in Elizabeth Bishop's "In the Waiting Room," mysterious and thrilling in itself, which is also evocative for me when I try to think about how certain of my own poems made their way to the page. The six-year-old Elizabeth is sitting alone, waiting for her aunt, who is presumably being ministered to behind the inner door of a dentist's office. Suddenly, the child hears a cry which she knows to be her aunt's. She is not surprised by the cry itself, but she is thoroughly startled to realize that the very same cry has somehow simultaneously come from within *her*

as well. With that realization is set in motion the whole vertiginous seesaw ride of self-discovery and the discovery of a frightening kinship that the poem becomes.

When I was only a little older than the Elizabeth of "In the Waiting Room," my mother, who was born in the same year as Bishop, contracted a severe case of polio. She was taken abruptly to the hospital from the house we had barely moved into and was away for six months, during which time I think we children may have seen her once if at all. When she returned, it was to a different house, and

*Parents, Henry and Sarah Elizabeth Ruark,
on their wedding day, February 4, 1939*

Polio

The snore of midsummer flies at the screen,
Afternoon's tepid fog crawling my sleep.
In my unrelenting dream the fire truck
Peals round the corner, and when I wake
The sirens still confound me. From the wobbly
Room I stumble to my mother's door,
A shifting blur in the wall before me.
Her limbs are weak and rumpled on the sheet.
The empty braces glint. Their brightness hurts.
Pale pillow, damp hair, my father's shadow
Straining over her, sweat at his armpits,
Straightening, bending, straightening her leg.
Like knives her shrill cries peel the heavy air,
But he keeps at it, forcing tears back till
His eyes ache. The veins map out his anguish.
His false teeth tighten on that work of love.

I don't mean to suggest any serious parallel between an early effort of my own and a late masterwork of Bishop's, except to note that in both poems the mysterious, initiating voice comes from behind a door, is *other* than the speaker's, and then somehow *becomes* the voice of the speaker and by extension that of the poet. What I'm suggesting here, I suppose, is the existence of a kind of preliterary influence on a poet's voice, without any immediately apparent mediation through the work of another poet. If I begin to listen to those sounds made by others which enticed rather than disturbed me during my boyhood, I end up standing outside my father's study door.

When my second book of poems appeared in 1978, the jacket copy included a generous paragraph by the poet and novelist James Whitehead, in which he noted my awareness of "the inevitable personal losses we are all bound to study." Later that same year, when I met Whitehead for the first time in San Francisco, I asked him if he could guess my favorite word in his endorsement. "Yeah," he said without a flicker of hesitation, *"study."* I don't know if there is something about the word over which a southerner's tongue lingers with special pleasure. There may be. Its sound is proximate to that of another of my favorite words: *steady.* Indeed, in some parts of the South the local accent will nearly turn *study* into *steady.* Or vice versa. There's a line I love in the old mountainy song called "Cripple Creek" which sometimes sounds like, "I'm so drunk I can't stand study." One of the surest phrases of dismissal where I grew up was, "I ain't studying

she herself was, as Yeats has put it, changed utterly. She was in a wheelchair at first, and then, over the months and years, supported by various combinations of braces and crutches, until at last, and in another town altogether, she could walk again, though she had a slight residual limp and her central nervous system remained affected for the rest of her life, so that she was thereafter brought quickly to tears. But it is with the earliest days of her recovery that I am concerned here. While she remained mostly bedridden my father was obliged to perform painful exercises on her legs, and these were conducted discreetly, not to say clandestinely, almost as if they were the intimacies of the marriage bed, of which at least I as a nine-year-old hadn't a clue. One sultry afternoon I was sick with a fever and maybe sleeping so hard that my father neglected to close the door to their bedroom firmly. In that household I would never have entered a closed door without knocking. Here is the poem that, years later, came out of that afternoon:

that." One late night in Dublin several years ago Seamus Heaney and I were talking about a particular writer, and I wasn't sure what Heaney thought about his work until he said with a sly look at me, "I'm not studying him." I don't think that's an Irish locution. I think that Heaney, sensing my reservation, was being his usual empathetic self and that he might have picked up the phrase by hanging around with Tennessean Richard Tillinghast at Harvard. In any event, I have long felt that to have my own work described as at least in part a kind of study was a high compliment indeed, not in spite of but precisely because of the air of deliberate thought and even bookishness the word emanates.

To turn to the nominal form, a study is a place where one might recollect in tranquillity that "spontaneous overflow of powerful emotion" that is so often lifted out of the context of Wordsworth's remarks on the subject. One of my touchstones in poetry is the powerful closing of Robert Hayden's near sonnet for his father called "Those Winter Sundays": "What did I know, what did I know / Of love's austere and lonely offices?" As James Wright has beautifully observed, the poem is about the penchant for formality among people who have to work terribly hard, and the last word has the force to suggest a religious ceremony, especially if given the French intonation: oh-*feece*. But I like to think of Hayden as writing the poem in a study. My friend Michael Heffernan once summed up his opinion of a contemporary with the remark, "He keeps his Yeats in the office." The office is at work. The study is at home. In the right room of my dreams there is a single window looking out on nothing spectacular, maybe a beech tree in whose changes I can read from time to time the clockface of the year. There is a desk at the window with a wooden armchair pulled up to it. In one corner of the room there is a comfortable reading chair with a lamp tilted over it just so. It is quiet there, and the walls are lined with books from floor to ceiling.

*   *   *

It could be said with partial truth that I come from a family of writers. My sister has published poems in literary magazines. My grandfather and two of my uncles were lawyers, no doubt composing on the page much of the time they weren't in court. My father's first cousin Charles Murphy was also a lawyer and special counsel to President Truman and may well have been involved in the shaping of Truman's speeches. The best-known writer in the family, however, was Robert Ruark of African fame. His father and my grandfather Robert were first cousins. I never met the writer Robert, though as a boy I knew who he was, especially once when his photograph graced the cover of a national magazine. He was shown sitting in his bathtub with a revolver handy in the soapdish, and the caption read in bold lettering: "ROBERT RUARK AMONG THE MAU MAUS." During the time we lived in Laurinburg, North Carolina, in the 1950s, the news arrived that the famous writer Robert Ruark was to be in town, visiting an old friend who was the wife of a local doctor. I'm sure he had no idea we lived there. We all piled into our 1953 Ford and drove around the block to see if we could catch a glimpse of him, but all we saw was his Bentley glittering in the doctor's driveway. It was just like my quiet modest father not to make himself known to his cousin.

All of that really meant very little to me at the time, or even later for that matter, since the living writer I knew best and revered most when I was growing up was my father himself, though I don't remember ever actually thinking of him in those days as a writer. He was a highly educated and literate and articulate man who had chosen the ministry as a profession. After all, he had one older brother go for a

*In the North Carolina surf with his father,
about 1945*

doctor, as they say, and another for a lawyer, so what remained for him in the late 1920s, as the son of a Raleigh lawyer, but teaching or preaching? I don't mean to suggest that he was not a devout man or that he did not see his ministry as a spiritual calling, but he himself worried at length in a diary he kept while at Yale Divinity School that he had not had some singular and dramatic conversion experience. He had great faith, but in keeping with his mild and slow nature, that faith grew and deepened and broadened in unspectacular ways rather than overwhelming him on some Damascus road and sending him out with his voice permanently raised to carry the Truth to the benighted. He was a powerful and eloquent preacher and always an agent of wise counsel and great comfort to members of his congregation in trouble, but I think perhaps the hours closest to the center of his nature were those spent composing his sermons by hand or reading Paul Tillich or Jeremy Taylor or the *Little Flowers of St. Francis.* He was at home in his study. Sometimes the door into the rest of the house would be open, but often it was closed, of course, and we children were taught to creep by it, especially on Saturday nights when he would be working on his sermon. Memory tells me that he wrote it out in longhand first and then rather quickly typed it up, since his writing was small and crabbed and he at least claimed that he often couldn't decipher it himself once it was stale. Then he would memorize the sermon. We could hear his low voice reading it over and over, the words a mystery but their cadences carrying a meaning of some kind under the door. The next morning at eleven, not to tempt fate, he would lay the typescript on the pulpit before him, but I don't recall seeing him from my second-row vantage point ever look down at it once. His delivered sermons were vivid, but what haunts me more is the hidden murmur of the night before, the narrow gleam of light at the threshold of the door, something coming from in there which might be described by Robert Frost's phrase about birdsong in the Garden of Eden after Eve's arrival, a "tone of meaning but without the words."

In his prose Frost called such murmurings "sentence sounds" or "the sound of sense," depending on his mood. "A sentence," he once wrote, "is a sound in itself on which other

With his father on the fishing pier at Garden City, South Carolina, 1958

sounds called words may be strung." He also more than once used the figure of a closed door to convey his meaning. "The best place to get the abstract sound of sense is from voices behind a door that cuts off the words." Though he occasionally used the word *music* in discussing these matters, he stubbornly resisted any analogy between the "tune" he was hearing and bringing onto the page and the tune of actual music. "It's a music of itself. And when people say that this will easily turn into—be set to music, I think it's bad writing. It ought to fight being set to music if it's got expression in it." For my own part I have to say that although the murmur of those "sentence sounds" was probably most important for me, they were also occasionally interlaced with little snatches of actual song, pretty much tuneless but nonetheless song. Since the door was closed I have to imagine my father looking up from his work to hum or sing a little dreamily a fragment of one of the old hymns he loved, "Abide with Me" or "Come Thou Fount of Every Blessing" or some such thing. (His own mother, who outlived him and possibly even forgot who he was in her nineties there in Mayview Convalescent Home in Raleigh, had to be put in a private room at the end because her incessant hymn-singing drove her roommates crazy.) My father was aware that he couldn't carry a tune (a trait I inherited), so although he would give full voice to his unmelodiousness around the family piano, on those mornings when it was the Methodists' turn for their service to be on the local radio, he would discreetly step back from the pulpit when hymn-time came. His limitations as a singer, however, did not deter him from going to the radio station with other local luminaries (the police chief, the school principal) to sing out over the air waves in response to phoned-in contributions to the March of Dimes, which in those days supported polio research. Not long after his death years later, I moved with my wife and small daughters to an old farmhouse in southeast Pennsylvania, to which landscape we have now returned after twenty-three years in town. In the late nights there we would sometimes gather and sing the old hymns around our own piano, and my father would inevitably come to mind.

Singing Hymns Late at Night for My Father

While our mother, your dark-haired lover,
Lay paralyzed with polio,
We heard your crackling voice recover

A lost tune on the radio.
Never a singer, you nearly sang in time
"You Are My Sunshine," one more blow

Struck gladly for the March of Dimes.
Sister and I called up and pledged
Five bucks to hear it five more times.

For though on Sunday mornings you edged
Back from the pulpit microphone,
At home you offered like a cage

Of swallows your hopeless monotone.
By the old piano out of key
You sang too early, stopped too soon.

Last time I saw you, you had only
A seamy lyric in your ear,
Dandling the baby on your knee

To words you never let us hear.
If now, far from you in the close
Of night, we falter out of fear

Or out of tune or out of too much whiskey,
Bear with us, even in distress,
And when we raise the raucous noise

Of "Come Thou Fount of Every Blessing"
We will make an everlasting
Music with something missing.

Though the old hymns and the sentence sounds from under the study door have grown fainter in their particularity, it's my feeling that they have been absorbed somehow into the characteristic tilt of my listening ear, that I am somehow expecting them to rise up any minute in pretty much everything I read or hear. If my more recent poems have been typically responsive to later and more literary noises, they are, I think, still influenced in a manner that was established a long time ago, in one Methodist parsonage or sanctuary after another over the years of my boyhood. In whatever I hear, however much I love its motion toward the infinite, there is almost always something missing, and that missing element may just be what prompts this reader of poems to want to be a writer of poems as well. I have come to think that a poem which we find wholly satisfying in all its dimensions is not apt to move us to write in response a poem of our own. Everything is already there. But that very seldom happens, because what gives us pleasure in poems most of the time, I believe, is the ghost of those "sentence sounds" behind the actual words of the poem. It is *that* we respond to, that which touches the quick of our own memory and experience and makes us want to say something close to it in our own particular way. It's not so much the highly touted and anxious principle of competition at work as it is a feeling of kinship which runs between us and another writer *underneath* the surfaces of any specific words either of us might say, though, of course, it *is* the other writer's specific words, on any one occasion, which complete the electrical circuit and ground us once again in something that matters to us all. When we write a poem with another writer or talker hovering if not looming in the background, we may *think* it is form or subject matter or point of view we are learning from, but I'm convinced it is instead something prior to what has already been spoken.

*   *   *

If we have discovered in our own reading and writing any validation of Frost's notion of sentence sounds, of wordless but still expressive cadences coming from behind a door, how far are we from feeling that sounds other than those made by human voices may infiltrate and inform our poems? Perhaps a step in that direction is to realize the importance of our own involuntary noises, maybe as close as we come to animal or other "natural" sounds. Frost muses about that briefly in an exchange with Robert Penn Warren:

> FROST: And of course before all words came the expressiveness—groans and murmurs and things like that emerging into words. And some few of these linger, like "um-hnm" and "unh-unh" and "mmm" and all our groans. . . .

> WARREN: From a groan to a sonnet's a straight line.

> FROST: Yes, that's right.

And, I feel like adding from the sidelines, if the sonnet's any good it will call up in the reader straightaway something kin to the original groan.

Other poets have argued as well that the *pulse* of poetry, whether metered or not, may have its source in some inarticulate pulse like the beating of the heart or the rising and falling of the tide. If there is a significant sound behind my own poems nearly as important as those voices behind a door, it would have to be the sound of the surf, "inhuman," as Wallace Stevens said, "of the veritable ocean." Though I grew up mostly as an inlander, people on both sides of my family were from coastal places in Virginia and North Carolina, and the pull of the sea was and still is very strong for all of us. My father's family was from Southport, a fishing village at the mouth of the Cape Fear River, and an ancestor of his was a lighthouse keeper. He lived himself in Wilmington until he was sixteen, when my grandfather moved his practice to Raleigh. Various members of the family owned or regularly rented waterfront cottages at spots like Long Beach or Holden Beach all through my early years, and since our immediate family was so often moved from one town to another at the whim of the sitting Methodist bishop, those seaside gathering places, like my grandparents' houses in Raleigh and Roanoke Rapids, took on a constancy for me stronger in some ways than whatever roof we were officially dwelling under in any par-

ticular year. Even the furniture in an aunt's cottage stayed the same, while most of the tables and dressers and beds we lived among changed from one town to the next. Perhaps I should say that at least in those days a parsonage came largely furnished, with the minister's family bringing along personal odds and ends, an arrangement which may have made the uprootings we were subjected to a little more practically manageable anyway. I remember that my mother unthinkingly exclaimed on learning of my wife's first pregnancy, "Why, you're about to have a baby and you don't even own a bed!" My father gently if amusedly reminded her that she was twenty-five years married with three grown children and did not herself own a bed. Anyway, I think it's fair to say that even though we were not real coastal dwellers, one of the most familiar sounds I fell asleep to as a boy was that of the ocean backing and filling along some stretch of the North Carolina coast. It was a sound I stayed awake to also as I grew older and my father would take me as the oldest child surf-fishing with him. We also fished off piers and only very rarely from a small boat in the backwaters, but it is the surf-fishing I remember most, and we would continue that at various beaches until I was married with two daughters and he was only a year or so away from his death. I wrote about it before he died in a poem called "Night Fishing," collected in my first book in 1971, and years later, after spending some time with my brother and sister on Hatteras Island, I went back to it again in a poem published in *Rescue the Perishing* in 1991.

Leaving Hatteras

Deep summer is time forgetful of its calling,
The place a screened porch hugging the home
   Atlantic,
My brother's voice beside me: All you do is
   close
Your eyes. The surf's invisible below the dunes,
But its sound is the fallback and lift of
   memory.

After the days of heat and stillness, heat piling
Over our heads in columns ranked immovable,
The storm-cooled breezes riffle every window
   shade,
Freshness billows and flaps the air like a sail.
All I do is close my eyes. A screen door
   shudders
And bangs and a boy lights out for the water

And it is south of here by thirty years and
    more
Where the shore curls inward and the dunes
    are lower
And a boy can see his father from the water
Cleaning and oiling his tackle in a porch
    chair.
By the time he gets it right the fish will
    vanish.

One afternoon he walks as far as the shell line
Marking the tide's reach, remembers his
    scaling knife,
And goes back in and puts his feet up for a
    minute
And wakes to a plate of oysters on the table.
Now on a sleeping-porch just wavering toward
    its name
My brother and I are pulling on our road
    clothes

Halfheartedly, a sleeve or a sock at a time,
As if we were young and moving house all
    over
And not just going home at the end of
    summer.
There is a snapshot of a kindred moment
    somewhere,
More formal, though we stand there in our
    undershorts,

August in Carolina laving our faces,
The sun through stained glass dim but
    unrelenting.
It is the choir room before my sister's
    wedding,
My father reaching to help us with our cuff
    links,
His brow lit with sweat or the new
    forgetfulness.
Here what looks like water shivers over the
    screens

And we breathe deep, two of us only,
    buttoning
Our sleeves and zipping up the nylon duffel
    bags,
Unless you count the lazybones in the
    doorway,
Stretching himself and rubbing his eyes with
    his knuckles,
Blinking like a child as the room turns
    familiar.

It is a fiction, of course, that time ever
grows forgetful of its calling, but it may be a
forgivable and possibly even an honorable fiction. I leave off before the adjective *supreme*.

It is we ourselves who are momentarily and
mercifully oblivious to time's calling, whether
in those acts of mind and memory and imagination we hope will be poems, or in the beautiful lapses of time when we simply sit and
watch a minor league batter fouling off pitch
after pitch in order to stay alive; a beloved
woman tucking in the soil around a basil plant
in a summer garden; an aging father, his own
final forgetfulness well under way, patiently
untangling the knots in his fishing line. Then
when time's call comes into earshot again
("HURRY UP, PLEASE, IT'S TIME"), it is all
too audible.

It seems at least coincidentally fitting that the
last time I saw my father, in mid-February
of 1970, he was living again in a coastal town
after an inland exile of roughly forty years.
The trouble was, he loved the territory, but
he didn't really relish the job. He had been
sent to Elizabeth City, connected by the
Pasquotank River and then the Albemarle Sound
to North Carolina's storied Outer Banks, to serve
as district superintendent to the Methodist
churches of the area, the first administrative
post he had ever held. I suppose such jobs
were regarded as plums by many ministers,
because of the prestige and vestige of power
and slightly higher pay, in the same way that
many a college professor eyes a department chair
going vacant and beyond that maybe a deanship.
Had my father been a teacher, he would no
doubt have happily stayed in the classroom and
left the administration to others. He sorely missed
having a congregation and being its pastor, and
he didn't much like being located somewhere
primarily for its geographical convenience. But
the job was growing on him, and he was warming
to it, for that was ever his nature. He liked
the idea of being a pastor to pastors, and I
think eventually he came to regard the ministers of his district as his congregation, scattered as they were. And they were scattered
indeed, since the area was not heavily popu-
lated and the distances between churches were
long. They were also watery distances in many
instances, and my father loved to drive down
to some backwater church to hold a quarterly
conference and find that the local minister had
an extra rod and reel. He always loved, too,
the names of places, and sometimes he would
talk about his work mainly in order, I think,
to say aloud names like Stumpy Point and Swan

Quarter and Salvo. When I was a very small boy and we would take the drive to visit some cousin or other, we would always pass through the crossroads of a township called Deep River. As we came to the western edge, my father would say, "Deep River," and as we crossed the eastern edge about a hundred yards later, I would say, "Yeah, Deep River." He was a quiet man, and although memory is tricky, I'm convinced that on some journeys those five words would be the sum of our conversation.

Sadly, as my father's humor about his assignment to Elizabeth City improved, his health was declining, and much more drastically than any of us knew. He grew increasingly forgetful, and on my last visit took me out on an errand and forgot where he was going three or four times. He kept turning the car back in the direction of home. I remember from that ride that there were several heart-shaped red balloons drifting and bumping in the backseat, left over from a recent heart fund drive of some kind, and both of us jumped when one of them suddenly popped. It didn't seem like any kind of omen then, even though I knew my father was scheduled for heart surgery at the end of the month. His forgetfulness and uncharacteristic irritability and more and more frequent and lengthier naps at all hours had led one doctor to suggest arteriosclerosis, but he was only sixty-one, and my mother's penchant for keeping up appearances made that a diagnosis to be ignored or at least only whispered about. (Her only response to my "Polio" poem was to object to the reference to my father's false teeth, since that made him seem older than he was.) Eventually, however, he was found to have an aneurism of a coronary artery, and that was to be surgically repaired. I had come down from Delaware with my wife and daughters, even though all was expected to go well, to see him before he headed off for Duke Hospital. It was a lovely visit despite his condition. He took great pleasure in his granddaughters, then four and one, singing to them now and then in his cracked voice and saying to Emily, the one-year-old, as we were making our farewells, "Don't grow too fast." Only a close familiarity with his undemonstrative nature could make clear what a remarkable thing that was for him to say.

On the afternoon of February 25, I brought into our faculty house in Newark, Delaware, a copy of Simon and Garfunkel's album *Bridge*

over Troubled Water and spent the early evening listening to the beautiful title cut over and over. When I was out for a beer with a friend a while later, my wife called to say that I should come home immediately. I knew what that meant. She just didn't want to tell me over the phone. My father's brother, a Raleigh obstetrician who had delivered my brother and me and whom we always called Uncle Doctor, had called to say that my father had died. The surgery to correct the aneurism had been successful, but, unknown to the doctors, he had severe aortic stynosis, and his heart failed under the strain of the surgery.

John Ciardi said somewhere that a poet, since he lives by language, can be forgiven for composing the first lines of an elegy at his father's funeral. I didn't go quite that far, but I was certainly trying to write poems for my father in the months following his death. The one about singing hymns came fairly early, and I still like it well enough to have quoted it here. There are others, but from this perspective I don't think I struck the note I wanted until four years had gone by. I can't be sure about this, but I think the poem that crystallized things for me did so maybe because it was the first of my "elegies" for him that attempted to be about *him* in some way rather than being primarily about *my* grief. It was also the first of those poems that tried to bring the cadences of his own voice into its lines. He liked to watch birds. One of the last things he said to me, the last time I saw him, was simply to look out the window and name the bird at the feeder: "Rufous-sided towhee." He was a watcher of the birds, of the stars, of the skies and all their weathers.

Weather Report to My Father

You always took sharp pleasure in the
    weather,
Noting the angle of sunlight or saying
Merely to yourself as I am saying now,

Yesterday all day it failed to snow,
And now this morning fallen everywhere
The earth is six white inches nearer
    heaven.

I look beyond the vine-leaves at the
    window,
Beyond the tree-forks catching their wings
    of snow,
Beyond the acres of descending light

To a cold transparent Carolina day
For four years now accumulating nothing
But cloudless heaven breathless as the
    small boy

Waiting for you in the doorway all those
Winter evenings, who heard your only
    breath
Fall out of February like a snow.

It will come as no surprise, given what I have written so far, that one of the poems I have lodged in my memory so firmly it will not shake loose is this little eight-liner by Robert Francis:

Blue Jay

So bandit-eyed, so undovelike a bird
to be my pastoral father's favorite—
skulker and blusterer
whose every arrival is a raid.

Love made the bird no gentler
nor him who loved less gentle.
Still, still the wild blue feather
brings my mild father.

I think Robert Francis was the first real poet I knew, even before my teacher and longtime friend Joe Langland, though I met them both in Amherst, Massachusetts, in the early sixties. I had followed my wife-to-be up there from Chapel Hill in 1963 to keep her company while she began her graduate studies and I waited to go to Naval Officers' Candidate School in Newport. As it turned out, she liked graduate school about as much as I liked the idea of the navy, so we got married on October 5, I worked as a busboy (it says so on our marriage license) at the Lord Jeffrey Inn while she finished out her semester, and then she quit to put *me* through school to the completion of a master's degree I had never intended to get. But it was all a lucky accident, since while I was there I met Robert and Joe and my great friend among the poets my own age, Michael Heffernan.

After beginning our married life in a single room, Kay and I moved as soon as possible to an apartment in a sprawling old house on Churchill Street, directly across from the Congregational Church where we were married and only a block or so from Emily Dickinson's house. A fellow in a neighboring apartment discovered my interest in poetry and, having a casual acquaintance with Robert, suggested that the two of us arrange to visit him at Fort Juniper, the one-man cottage he had had built for himself at the edge of North Amherst some twenty-five years before. As it turned out, my neighbor fell ill on the day of our appointment, so I made my way out to Robert's on my own, as I was to do off and on for a number of years, even after we were long gone from Amherst. Some things that happened at Fort Juniper are so indelibly recalled in Robert's own writing, the occasional visitor may have trouble sorting out when he was really there. I've persuaded myself that I never climbed up to the roof of the cottage for an hour's talk with Robert in the sun; nor was I there to help him adjust the windscreens he set up to shield his famous visitor in earlier years, another Robert, from the capriciousness of summer air. Other moments live in a more uncertain light. I paid my first visits to Fort Juniper by cadging a lift to North Amherst Center and walking out from there. More than once I found Robert in his garden, bending to some task or other which I stood quietly by and let him finish before we went inside for tea or his homemade dandelion wine. But did I actually find him rubbing the hubcaps of his Volkswagon Beetle with a bar of soap so the birds wouldn't fly into their reflections and come to harm? It hardly seems to matter. One way or another, there are times I know I was there. Of the two times I remember most vividly, one involved not seeing Robert at all. That would have been in the late seventies, not long after Robert turned seventy-five and saw the publication of his *Collected Poems.* I had taken the train up to visit Joe, and he was occupied elsewhere for a couple of hours, so I decided to borrow a bicycle and ride over to say hello to Robert. When I got there his car was in the driveway, but when I stepped onto the porch at the house's single door and made ready to knock, I noticed a little paper pad hanging there with a pencil attached to it by a string. There was a note in Robert's hand: "MAN WORKING. PLEASE LEAVE A MESSAGE." I didn't want to leave a note and let him know a visitor from out of town had turned away, but neither was I about to disturb the seventy-five-year-old Robert Francis at work on one of his poems. So I tipped my cap and cycled back to Joe's. I don't think one can say that there were *none* of Frost's "silken ties of love and thought" going taut in the silence of that visit, but it's certainly true that an earlier afternoon and evening at Fort Juniper were more traditionally convivial. In late May of 1972, Michael Heffernan had been visiting us in the old farmhouse about a mile from where I sit writing this, and at his urging he and I drove up to Amherst to see Joe. He had continued to visit since our school days there and had become close to Joe, but this may have been the very first of my own returns. Joe took us over to the Fort in early afternoon to find Robert just winding up a lunch he had prepared for a young student poet from Wesleyan who was hiking up to Canada and had stopped to call in with an introduction from one of Robert's most admiring readers, Richard Wilbur. I think Robert may have preferred to concentrate on one or maybe two guests at a time, but he welcomed us warmly, with no suggestion that we were descending uninvited on the kind of quietly orchestrated ceremony which afternoons with him often became. It was just as well, since by that time there were five of us and the next hour was to bring two more. Tom O'Leary, who had also been visiting at Joe's but who had wandered off on some errand of his own with a promise to meet us at Robert's, arrived at the door with a can of beer in hand and joined the circle. I can't convey how out of place that beer can, emptied and then crushed, looked in Robert's living room, except to say that it had exactly the opposite effect from that of the jar Wallace Stevens placed in Tennessee. But the hour transcended it. Shortly after O'Leary's breezy entrance came the arrival of Wang Hui-Ming, the Chinese artist who had collaborated with Robert on several beautiful broadsides and to whom the 1976 *Collected Poems* would be dedicated. It was quite an afternoon. Joe speculated later that there had probably never been that many people in Robert's living room at one time. But Robert took it in stride. Much of the detail escapes me now, but I remember that Wang Hui-Ming, who had been on the Long March in China, told scarifying and sometimes hilarious stories about that adventure. Joe sang his poem about the rainbow trout. Robert recited the witty but eerie "Mouse Whose Name Is Time." I can't recall what O'Leary contributed, but I feel sure even from a distance of nearly twenty-five years that Michael said for us his fine early poem "The Apparition." The student, who was after all the only *official* visitor of the afternoon, I guess was cowed

Robert Francis at Fort Juniper, about 1975

into silence. Vanity keeps me well reminded that I recited "Singing Hymns Late at Night for My Father," which I had only recently written, and that Robert responded in a way that still touches me. (His own father had been a minister.) He said one or two flattering words about the poem and then simply sat down at the piano and played "Come Thou Fount of Every Blessing." Four or five years later I wrote a poem for him which tries to gather some of the fragments of gesture and mood and weather from a number of visits to Fort Juniper and suspend them within the boundaries of a single form. It was my good luck that he got to read it, and I even have a valued letter from him about it, but time has turned it into elegy.

Thinking of Robert Francis at the Autumnal Equinox

Clear everything out of your head but the sight
Of one man lifting his thoughtful head
To late September, in the early evening.
He moves so slowly you know he means to last.
He moves alone but his lamp may yet light
Faces of friends before the stars come clear.

Look where he moves at ease about the
  unclear
Boundaries of his summer garden site,
Look where he turns the sweetbriar to the light
And bends to gather the last fresh parsley hid
By fallen leaves. His watchfulness is a last
Signpost to turn his friends toward him and
  evening.

When they arrive sunlight and dark are evening
The odds against his cottage, whose clear
White walls and windows have withstood the
  last
Resorts of thirty winters. They know this sight
From other summers, and when he turns his
  head
And slowly as the late sun levels his light

Gaze to greet them, you are not surprised that
  light
Includes you in its welcome. The edge of
  evening
Is the flat stone lying like a little head-
Land at his single door. Then there is the
  clear
Wine of the dandelion, and the slow sight-
Reading of the gathered faces like a last

Uncertain harmony not meant to last.
He is naming over the birds that light
His windows in all weathers, naming the sight
Of the brash jay flashing his wings at the
  evening.
He is saying a poem for you in such clear
Tones, the sound alone illumines his head.

He is showing you a stone shaped like a head
And you are leaving, relishing the last
Wine on your tongue, entering again the clear
September weather where he shines his flash-
  light
Down the driveway to the road out of this
  evening
And stands there quietly watching you out of
  sight.

He waves you the last farewell of his evening,
Then sets his sights by star- instead of flashlight.
Thinking him gone, clear everything out of
  your head.

Since it was my fate to take only a single
poetry-writing class in the course of my studies, I remain grateful that its teacher was Joe
Langland. He taught with great humor and
invention and empathy, he never tried to get
us to write like him, and his by-heart com-

mand of a range of English poems from over
the centuries was a perpetual astonishment. I
got along well enough with all my classmates,
but the only one who became and has remained
a close friend was Michael Heffernan. I'm sure
I'm oversimplifying here, but I almost feel like
saying that aside from what must have been
our natural affinities, what drew me to him
was that he was the only other student not
hypnotized by the work of James Wright. I'm
sure that can't be true, but from this distance
it feels like it. My cartoon version of the class
has Heffernan off in one corner writing sonnets, me off in another writing sorry imitations
of Dylan Thomas, and everybody else looking
out a bus window in Ohio at a herd of cows.
The Branch Will Not Break, which is now one of
my favorite books, had come out in 1963. Our
class met in the spring of 1965, and the ap-
plause was still very much in the air. My stub-
bornness, which hasn't left me, obliged me to
go against whatever grain could be gone against,
so I was to own a signed copy of *To a Blossom-
ing Pear Tree* before I bought my first copy of
The Branch Will Not Break. Jim signed that copy
for me when he was distinguished visiting professor at Delaware in 1978. But that's spinning
the hands of the clock. It was *Shall We Gather
at the River* which first put me in touch with
the man himself. It was 1968, and I was in my
first year at Delaware, having been hired as
instructor on the strength of a few published
poems, mainly to teach composition but also
an occasional poetry-writing class, since the
departure of Robert Huff had left the campus
without a poet. One afternoon I was sitting in
my basement office reading with growing excitement the poems in *Shall We Gather at the
River,* which I had picked up on a whim at
the bookstore, and the chairman stuck his head
in the door and asked what poet we might
invite to read the following year. I made an
instant nomination, was given the go-ahead on
the spot, and so it was that the next November Kay and I drove to the then unrestored
Wilmington train station to collect James and
Annie Wright. It so happened that there was
to be a march against the Vietnam War the
next day in Washington, and the trains were
late and packed with traveling protesters. The
platform was crowded, and it took us a while
to pick out Jim, who had grown a beard since
the last photograph I'd seen of him. Finally, I
thought I recognized him, so I said, "Are you

James Wright?" and he said, "Yes, are you Gibbons Ruark?" I said I was, and he said, "Well, it takes one to know one." So there on that seedy railway platform (where else?) began a friendship that was to last until his death in 1980. Since I feel the weight of that friendship pulling me toward a whole separate essay, I'll make no attempt to chronicle it here. Anyway, much of it is already there in the poems themselves. I count at least ten poems scattered through my books in which he figures in one way or another, whether actually named or not, and there are no doubt others in which he seems to have stepped out of the room just minutes ago. Certainly he is looking over my shoulder in some of the poems about Italy in *Reeds* and *Keeping Company.* I can't imagine we would have gone in 1974 to spend a year in Fiesole had it not been for Jim's example and his poems. Several of the poems in *Two Citizens,* which so many readers, including Jim himself at times, relegated to the dustbin, were like lights along the way to me. I want to concentrate here, though, on a poem of my own which brings Jim Wright and Italy together, written mostly in the spring and summer of 1980 following his death in March. Kay and I had been back to Florence and several other places briefly in 1977, and once again, in the fall of 1979, thanks to the National Endowment for the Arts, we were hatching plans to return with our daughters the following summer. Jim and Annie were back in New York, after what was to be their last European journey. They came down to see us in late October, and Jim was complaining of a sore throat he couldn't seem to shake, but his doctor had recently declared him "in the pink." Then in mid-December he called to say he had cancer but that it appeared operable. We were worried about him, of course, and on December 30 Kay and I drove to New York for the day to visit with him and Annie. He seemed tired and needed to nap while we were there, but he also seemed very much himself, commenting with great humor and wonderment about one contemporary folly or another and reading to us now and then from whatever book came to hand. He kept a rack of books beside his reading chair in the living room, and though I didn't catalog what was there that afternoon, I'd be willing to bet that Orwell and Mencken were not far away. If I'm not mistaken, a passage he read to me about writers' letters came

from Edmund Wilson's *Shores of Light.* Before we left, knowing we had plans for Italy in the summer, he gave us his and Annie's map of the Adriatic town of Fano, which they had both come to love during their time there. He also told me at some point, apropos of letter-writing and Italy, that he was persuaded that it took Caesar thirty years to launch his second invasion of Britain because he sent for reinforcements by regular Italian mail.

Lost Letter to James Wright, with Thanks for a Map of Fano

Breathing his last music, Mozart is supposed
To have said something heartbreaking which
    escapes me
For the quick moment of your bending to a
    dime

Blinking up from York Avenue, the last chill
    evening
I ever saw you, laughter rising with the steam
From your scarred throat, long-remembering
    laughter,

"Well, the old *eye* is still some good, anyway."
I thought of your silent master Samuel
    Johnson
Folding the fingers of drowsing vagrant
    children

Secret as wings over the coppers he left in
    their palms
Against the London cold and tomorrow's
    hunger.
You could not eat, I think you could scarcely
    swallow,

And yet that afternoon of your sleep and
    waking
To speak with us, you read me a fugitive
    passage
From a book beside your chair, something I
    lose all track of

Now, in this dim hour, about the late
    driftwood letters
Of writers and how little they finally matter.
You wrote to me last from Sirmione (of all
    things,

Sirmione had turned gray that morning), and
    it mattered.
We were together when the gray December
    dusk
Came down on snapshots of the view from
    Sirmione,

Sunlight ghosting your beard on the beach at
    Fano.
I had thought to write you a letter from Fano,
A letter which could have taken years to reach
    you

On the slow river ways of the Italian mails,
And now I write before we even come to
    leave.
We are going to Fano, where we may unfold
    this map

At a strange street corner under a window box
Of thyme gone to flower, and catch our
    breath remembering
Mozart breathing his last music, managing

Somehow to say in time, "And now I must go,
When I have only just learned to live quietly."
Last time I saw you, walking a little westward

From tugboats in the harbor, your voice was
    already breaking,
You were speaking quietly but the one plume
    of your breath
Was clouding and drifting west and away from
    Fano

Toward the river ferry taking sounding after
    sounding.

I sent that poem to Roland Flint, who knew
Jim longer and better than I did, and he wrote
back very kindly and generously but with the
reservation that "sometimes it sounds too much
like Jim." He may very well have been right,
but I have to take refuge in a remark Jim
made to me a couple of years earlier. I showed
him a poem called "With Our Wives in Late
October," about some times he and Annie and
Kay and I had spent together, and I apologized in advance for having appropriated several of his characteristic images (not mentioning that I had also followed his cue in "Prayer
to the Good Poet" by trying to cast the thing
in Sapphics). He said, "Oh hell, Gib, don't
worry about that. That's just correspondence.
The Chinese did it all the time."

*   *   *

Jim wrote to me once in some detail about
a poem of mine called "Listening to Fats Waller

Gibbons Ruark with James Wright in the Place Contrescarpe, Paris, 1979

in Late Light." I'll resist congratulating myself in public on some of what he said, but I do want to mention, having observed his great devotion to prose writers in the references above to Dr. Johnson and Mencken et al., that he took the time to say approvingly, "The syntax [of the poem] is naturally that of prose," and then went on to quote Eliot's judgment "that the poetry of many masters is at its greatest and most memorable precisely at those points where it most resembles the language—the structure, the diction—of their prose." That letter cheered me considerably, especially because my strongest allegiances in poetry had shifted since their beginnings from Dylan Thomas to the likes of Philip Larkin and Edward Thomas, who, of course, was a prose writer almost his whole life until Frost got him to writing poems near the end.

Since I have turned out to be a poet who would really rather read prose most of the time (maybe lots of poets who *teach* poems for a living feel that way), it seems to me fitting that despite my longtime devotion to Yeats and company, it was actually a prose writer who was most immediately responsible for the increasing pull I have felt toward Ireland for nearly twenty years. For it was that long ago this spring that Benedict Kiely came from Dublin to Delaware to teach for a term, and I think now that getting to know him and reading his marvelous work helped to crack open a door onto ancestral voices I had never really known were there. A reviewer of one of my books remarked that despite my Irish name I am an American. The truth is that I myself carried that name, which is really *two* Irish surnames, for roughly thirty-five years before I realized its implications. Maybe the first time I really *felt* it was when Ben Kiely quoted for me the old Irish poem "The Woman of Three Cows," which has my name in it ("O'Ruark, Maguire, those souls of fire, whose names are shrined in story"). When I spoke with my mother about it, she told me that my grandfather Ruark used to brag jokingly that we were descended from the princes of Breffni, but I have no recollection of that. My father and both of his brothers followed the Irish habit of marrying late, but that's just one more connection that escaped me. Now, looking back, I can see it all, of course: the fishing village we came from, the family tendency to disputation falling just short of litigation, that pronounced Irish indentation

Benedict Kiely in the bar of Sachs Hotel, Donnybrook, Dublin, 1983

in the Ruark upper lip. Some of the family snapshots could have been taken at Dromahair. It was from there that Tiernan O'Rourke's wife eloped with the king of Leinster in 1152, thus setting in motion the events which would lead to the Anglo-Norman invasion of Ireland. Anyway, it was really Ben Kiely who undeliberately woke me up to all that, and my allegiances have not been the same since.

I count myself among the luckiest first-time visitors to Dublin, since, when I arrived there in late spring of 1978, it was Ben who welcomed me and stood ready to show me the town. He has done so a number of times since, every street corner and statue and alleyway stopping him in his tracks to tell a story. One afternoon in 1989, when he was slowed down by surgery, Kay and I walked with him from the Horseshoe Bar in the Shelborne Hotel to a little Italian restaurant only a block or so away, and he slowed us down to his pace by getting one of us on each side of him and hooking arms with us both. What with the slowed pace and the pauses for stories, it must have taken us forty-five minutes or so to get there. At one point, maybe as we turned into Ely Place, he said, "I want to show you something written by Brendan Behan." I half expected him to pull out of his coat pocket something in

Behan's own hand, since I knew they had been friends, but instead he pointed upward to a sign painted on the brick wall before us: NO PARKING, supposedly painted there by Behan during his day job. We saw Ben most recently in October 1995, walking over from Ballsbridge to his place in Donnybrook for a late morning glass of wine. He told us he was glad to be able to find good wine in a little shop on *his* side of the street, since he now needs a stick to get about and doesn't dare cross over to his former wine merchant. He apologized for greeting us in his dressing gown and for the redness of an eye caused by conjunctivitis, and he insisted on sitting in his desk chair and letting us have the softer and lower seats, saying that once he got down in one of those he would never get up again, but he was full as ever of delicious stories and that deep country courtesy born of County Tyrone, no more eroded by over fifty years in Dublin than his distinctive Ulster accent, which some historians say is the closest thing to the speech of Elizabethans still to be heard.

Some years ago, thinking back over several of my earlier forays into Ireland, which were always guided, even if by letter or telephone, by Ben, I put together a poem in his honor. The pub of the poem's title was not really called Flanagan's. I was probably thinking of some place like Kehoe's in Anne Street, but I changed the name to protect the guilty.

Working the Rain Shift at Flanagan's

When Dublin is a mist the quays are lost
To the river, even you could be lost,
A boy from Omagh after forty years
Sounding the Liberties dim as I was
    When that grave policeman touching my
        elbow

Headed me toward this salutary glass.
The town is grim all right, but these
    premises
Have all the air of a blessed corner
West of the westernmost pub in Galway,
Where whatever the light tries daily to say

The faces argue with, believing rain.
Outside an acceptable rain is falling
Easy as you predicted it would fall,
Though all your Dublin savvy could not
    gauge
The moment the rain shift would begin
    to sing.

They are hoisting barrels out of the cellar
And clanging them into an open van,
Gamely ignoring as if no matter
Whatever is falling on their coats and
    caps,
Though the fat one singing tenor has
    shrugged

Almost invisibly and hailed his fellow
Underground: "A shower of rain up here,"
He says with the rain, "It'll bring up the
    grass."
Then, befriending a moan from the
    darkness,
"Easy there now, lie back down, why
    won't you,"

As if the man were stirring in his grave
And needed a word to level him again.
His baffled answer rising to the rainfall
Could have been laughter or tears or
    maybe
Some musical lie he was telling the rain.

This is a far corner from your beat these
    days,
But why not walk on over anyway
And settle in with me to watch the rain.
You can tell me a story if you feel
Like it, and then you can tell me
    another.

The rain in the door will fall so softly
It might be rising for all we can know
Where we sit inscribing its vague margin
With words, oddly at ease with our
    shadows
As if we had died and gone to Dublin.

Somehow in transcribing that last stanza there came into my head a phrase of Seamus Heaney's about the Wicklow rain's "low conducive voices," but though it resonates I certainly wasn't thinking of it, maybe didn't even know it, when I wrote the poem. Though his work has been the principal gravitational force pulling American poets toward Ireland and Irish subjects, I was a latecomer to it myself. His book *North,* which I believe prompted Robert Lowell to call him "the best Irish poet since Yeats," came out in 1975, but when I first went to Ireland three years later I didn't know it existed. I had seen, I guess, a few of his poems in anthologies here and there, but I had never had a whole book of his in my hands, and I was not to own one until I picked up the Faber *Selected Poems* in Dublin in 1981. All that has changed now, of course, as I have followed his work closely since then and am glad to be counted among his admirers, though I realize that doesn't exactly make me easy to pick out in a crowd.

The most beautiful reading I've heard Heaney give was at Delaware in May of 1984. Though I had arranged for him to come down and seized with pleasure the office of introducing him, I can't of course take any credit for the power and charm of his reading, but I think I can take some small credit for the issue he kept circling around in his commentary and in some of the poems as well. I had mentioned to the audience, for better or worse, that he had questioned the validity of going through with lyric poetry in the face of such circumstances as then prevailed in Northern Ireland, and that remark seemed to prompt him toward a number of observations about the relationship between poetry and politics, between the lyric poem and history, etc. Speaking of the fourth Glanmore Sonnet, for instance, in which a train passing two fields away from his boyhood home created ripples in a bucket of drinking water, he was moved to say that he saw in that "an emblem of the relationship of lyric poetry to history. The big chundering wars go past on the rails, and someplace a little tremulous symmetrical formal event occurs, which doesn't repeat history but which registers it in some way. I say that as a defense of this poem but really the poem's about ripples in a bucket of water. Though those remarks should make us cautious about trying to suggest where poems come from, I'd still like to note here something else Heaney said that evening that may have ended up reverberating in a poem of my own. Introducing his well-known "Oysters," the lead poem in *Field Work,* he suggested that when we're in good company, when we sense the day is going to be memorable, the way we tend to *conduct* it is almost artistic, making it an aesthetic as well as a social occasion. I've always felt that Heaney, despite his clear egalitarian instincts, has a very strong sense of occasion and ceremony, and I think that sense has contributed to some of his very best poems, that the poems rising primarily out of specific identifiable occasions often seem stronger than those with more openly concentrated thematic concerns. I have always preferred, for example, the Ulster elegies of *Field Work* to the famous "bog poems" of his two earlier books, which probably did more to

Seamus and Marie Heaney in their kitchen garden in Sandymount, Dublin, 1983

solidify his reputation. At any rate, I was to recall his remarks about "Oysters" when I looked back in a more private and reflective time to a couple of days I had been fortunate enough to spend in the excellent company of the Heaneys. In 1983 I flew into Dublin early on the morning of June 16, which I hadn't had the wit to realize was Bloomsday, when the Joyceans would be out in force. Seamus and Marie had the good sense to wait until at least some of the smoke had cleared, so they arranged to collect me at Lincoln's Inn near Trinity around six, knowing that the long Irish summer evening would still give us plenty of time for sightseeing. They took me on an unforgettable (at least for me) literary tour of Dublin, stopping into a pub now and then to refuel. The names and locations of the pubs have long since left me, but not the other places. We went and sat together on the memorial bench to Patrick Kavanagh by the Grand Canal, we went to see Yeats's birthplace in Sandymount Village, and we went down to the Martello Tower at Sandycove at just the right moment, when the Joyce museum had closed and the dark was falling and we had the place to ourselves. Several years later I sent them a thank-you note more formal and detailed than even my mother had taught me to write.

With Thanks for a Shard from Sandycove

Late afternoon we idled on a bench
In memory of the man from Inniskeen,
The slow green water fluent beside us,

High clouds figured among leaves on the
    surface.
Then down along the strand to Sandycove
And the late-lit water, the sun emigrating

After a parting glance, the distant ferry
Disappearing soundlessly toward Holyhead.
We were laughing, riding the crest of
    company,

Your beautiful laughing wife and you and I,
When suddenly you tired of hammering
With a pebble at a stubborn boulder

And lifted it and dropped it on another
And handed me the chip that broke away.
I thought of the brute possibilities

In those farmer's hands, the place they
    came from,
What they might have done instead of
    simply
Dropping one stone on another to give

This pilgrim a shard of where he'd been.
You lifted that heaviness handily,
Keeping it briefly elevated in the air

As if more nearly the weight of a bowl
Of sacramental lather than the capstone
Of a dolmen in some field near
    Ballyvaughan.

Guilty as charged with a faithless penchant
For the elegiac, shy of the quick-drawn
    line
In the schoolyard dust, we prayed for
    nothing

Less than calm in the predawn hours and
    the laughter
Of disarming women when the hangman
    comes.
The sea grew dark, and then the dark was
    general

Over the suburbs, the window where I
    slept
Thrown open on the moon picking out
    the angle
Of a spade left leaning in a kitchen
    garden,

Shining like something prized from
    underground.

I had with me among my gear on that visit a fine nubby brute of a blackthorn stick I had found in a curio shop in the city. I was especially pleased that it was its natural color and had escaped the vats of black lacquer into which nearly every blackthorn for sale in Ireland has been dipped. I also liked it that some of the bark on its natural handle had been rubbed away through long use by an unknown hand. When I took it into the Heaneys' place in Sandymount, Seamus looked it over and hefted it admiringly and then with his usual grace let a decent interval pass before going upstairs and returning with a walking stick of his own. It had belonged to Parnell, he said, and then had passed to a blacksmith in Wicklow who had made Parnell a new ferrule for it now and then. It then came into the keeping of Brinsley MacNamara, who handed it on to Conor Cruise O'Brien with a paper testifying to its provenance and the stipulation that O'Brien and each succeeding trustee of the stick was to pass it down to a younger Irish writer who seemed deserving. O'Brien had given it to Seamus. I left for County Monaghan the next day with my own prized blackthorn, feeling somehow that a proper sense of *scale* was inherent in the differences between Seamus's walking stick and mine. Another stick turns up in Seamus's "Harvest Bow," still another in "The Ash Plant," and then there's a moving haiku-length piece in which he contemplates yet another icy January in Cambridge, the difference being that this time he is differently armed, having inherited his father's walking stick.

Recalling those poems turns me back to my father again, and toward the end of this essay. It seems strange to me that of the poems of mine quoted here, my father lived to see only the earliest one, "Polio," and I don't remember what if anything he said about it. I did show him several other poems written in my early twenties, including one or two which made their way into the little magazines, but I

With his daughters Emily (left) and Jennifer on the ferry from Hatteras to Ocracoke, 1987

never waited around for his reaction, which would probably have been what he said when anybody showed him something in the hope of pleasing him ("That's nice"), but I once lingered in the hall outside his study after giving him a poem about his own father, dead for some years, and I watched him read it and then put his head on his desk. When the news had come by telephone of my grandfather's death, I had happened by my father's bedroom door just as he was replacing the receiver in its cradle, and I saw him soundlessly kneel down beside his bed and put his head in his hands. He had a warning heart attack himself several years before he died, and the doctor told him to walk as much as possible. He found he needed a stick to ward off bothersome dogs, since he was advised not to break into a run, and a friend brought him down a wonderful piece of laurel from the Carolina mountains which he polished until it was smoother than glass. It is now the centerpiece of a loose bouquet of sticks I keep in an umbrella stand near the door, and when she was in college my older daughter Jennifer wrote me a poem about it and

several of the other sticks I have collected here and there. I suppose the autobiographical license of this essay would permit me to quote it here even if I loved its sentiment but questioned its literary merit. But she did after all win a prize for it, and I have passed on to her an admiring letter from no less discerning a reader than Heaney himself, who found the poem's "*tendresse* and technique all at one."

Walking Sticks

There is a comfort in walking,
the easy rhythm of one foot
falling solidly to earth
and one foot surely following.
And with your newest walking
stick, a third beat, tapped out
by the shiny tip on the end
of a slender Irish blackthorn.

You left by the back door, pulling
it from the bright brass can,
shifting it in your hand
as you set out, to find
the proper place it held.

Your first one is still your favorite:
your father found
the root of a mountain laurel
with a natural grip,
worked it smooth
and polished it.

Now in the backs of dusty shops
you discover birch, maple and walnut,
some cool and clean as marble,
bits of light wood fit with dark,
others with the nub-ends of smaller
branches still attached,
and even one with a solemn-headed owl,
ivory carved to make a handle.

Now one by one you gather
them, but none like the first from your
   father;
walking with it you remember
one hand fitting into another.

What would you be up to this April morning?
Muttering to yourself, looking high and low
For the good stick fashioned out of laurel?
I have it with me.

Patience. Lean back and light another Lucky.
Whatever will kill you dozes in your rib cage.
Read a few more pages in the *Little
Flowers of St. Francis,*

Then throw a window open on the fragrance
Of even this, the northernmost magnolia.
By now the child you lifted in your arms has
Slipped from their circle

To cherish and polish your crooked old stick
Into a poem of her own so tender and deft
I can hold its wrong end and reach you the
   worn
Thumb of its handle.

—Gibbons Ruark

Jennifer gave me that poem in 1986, and it was not until the northern spring of 1993 that I was able to thank her (I hope properly) in one more poem addressed to the ghost of my father. We had great glossy-leafed magnolia trees in the towns of my boyhood, one in a churchyard somewhere big and leafy enough for me to climb up into it and hide in one of its crotches to escape having to go to Sunday school. There's nothing like that tree around here, but there are others.

Hybrid Magnolias in Late April

You bent to whisper to a small grand-
   daughter,
Exposing the bald priestly back of your head,
Lifting her then and handing her to me:
See you in April.

Never the same, these northern magnolias,
As the great starred candelabra ghosting,
Even before I left them, the deep-shaded
Lawns of my boyhood.

And yet these too break wholly into blossom,
What somebody called the early petal-fall:
I walk out one day and the limbs are bare;
Then they are burdened

With the flared tulip shapes of opening
   blooms.
Two rainy indoor days in a row, then out,
The sun is out, and a fallen constellation
Litters the grasses.

*Kay Ruark on the grounds of Gregans Castle,
Ballyvaughan, Co. Clare, 1992*

BIBLIOGRAPHY

Poetry:

A Program for Survival, University Press of Virginia, 1971.

Reeds, Texas Tech Press, 1978.

Keeping Company, Johns Hopkins University Press, 1983.

Small Rain, The Center for Edition Works, State University of New York at Purchase, 1984.

Forms of Retrieval (chapbook), Yarrow, 1989.

Rescue the Perishing, Louisiana State University Press, 1991.

Contributor:

American Literary Anthology #1, Farrar, Straus, 1968.

Lionel Stevenson and others, editors, *Best Poems of 1968,* Pacific Books, 1969.

X. J. Kennedy, editor, *Messages,* Little, Brown, 1973.

Lionel Stevenson and others, editors, *Best Poems of 1974,* Pacific Books, 1975.

X. J. Kennedy, editor, *Introduction to Poetry,* Little, Brown, 1982.

X. J. Kennedy, editor, *Introduction to Literature,* Little, Brown, 1983.

1984 Anthology of Modern Poetry, Monitor Book, 1984.

Dave Smith and David Bottoms, editors, *The Morrow Anthology of Younger American Poets,* Morrow, 1984.

Leon Stokesbury, *The Made Thing,* Arkansas, 1987.

Robert Richman, editor, *The Direction of Poetry,* Houghton, 1988.

Robert Wallace, *Vital Signs,* Wisconsin, 1989.

Other:

(Editor with Robert Watson) *The Greensboro Reader,* University of North Carolina Press, 1968.

Alan Shapiro

1952-

Alan Shapiro, in college, 1971

EDITOR'S NOTE: *Alan Shapiro's essay "Fanatics" will appear in his autobiographical collection* The Last Happy Occasion, *to be published by the University of Chicago Press in the fall of 1996. "The Last Happy Occasion," writes Shapiro, "is a book about the intersection of life and art. The subject, I guess, is poetry, but not as a craft isolated from the current of experience but as something deeply interwoven with the fabric of daily living and personal growth. Each essay in its own way focuses on situations that illustrate the truth of what Eugenio Montale calls the second life of art, the life that art acquires in us as we go from the theatre, museum or book back into the world which the art mirrors and from which it arose. In six overlapping autobiographical essays, essays that follow an interrupted but roughly chronological narrative, I explore the expected and unexpected consequences of a life devoted to poetry, how certain poems have taught me over time to read my own and other people's lives, and how those lives, in turn, have shaped my understanding of certain poems. Part memoir, part meditation,* The Last Happy Occasion *attempts to trace the circulating current of that interaction."*

Fanatics

When Billy "the Kid" Lazarus called me to announce that he'd converted to Hasidic Judaism, I thought, okay, so Billy "the Kid" is now Billy "the Yid." What else is new? I wanted to see this fresh turn his life had taken as no different from the others: like his sudden craze for weight lifting in high school, for cars in college, like his brief stint as a Jew for Jesus the previous summer when he visited me and my first wife, Carol Ann, in Ireland. So what if Saul, after an interlude of being Paul, was Saul again, but in a purer way. Yet as I listened to him happily describe his life as a Lubavitcher, the long hours of study, the arduous yet joyous dedication it required, the heady sense of chosenness, the mystical connection to the Torah, to the Jews he lived among, to Yawveh himself, his voice now inflected with the Yiddish intonations of our elders, I wondered if all his other passions weren't just so many dress rehearsals for this last big fling. Anyway, this was 1978, just after the mass suicide in Guyana of the followers of Jim Jones, whose cult, the People's Temple, had originated in San Francisco, just miles from where I was living at the time. Even more so than the rest of the country, the Bay Area news was all abuzz with cults and sects, and the evils of fanatical devotion. There was nothing evangelical to Billy's faith in Jesus as his personal savior. He never tried to proselytize. He was quite happy to be the only one among his friends who wasn't damned. But Yawveh was a jealous God. And now, as a Lubavitcher Hasid, a member of the evangelical wing of Jewish Orthodoxy, wasn't Billy, or Shlomo as he now called himself, obligated to bring all Jews back into the fold? Wouldn't he be especially solicitous of me, his oldest friend?

My worst suspicions were confirmed when, just before hanging up, he mentioned that he'd be spending Chanukah with a fellow Lubavitcher whose parents lived in Oakland. He planned to visit me (just me, not me and Carol Ann) shortly after he arrived. And he prayed to *HaShem,* blessed be his name, that I would listen with an open mind to what he had to tell me.

Only after we hung up did I realize that Billy had done all the talking. It was almost a year since we had seen each other, yet he never once asked me how I was doing, what was new, how Carol Ann was. He'd always been extremely interested in my career. Though he himself had no artistic inclinations (in college he was a pre-med major), he'd always taken a kind of sentimental pleasure in my poetry, proud in an almost fatherly way that someone so close to him could do and succeed at what seemed so foreign to his interests. In the years I'd been at Stanford, first as a fellow in the writ-

ing program, then as a lecturer, he'd always made a point of asking me what I was working on, or if anything I'd written had appeared in magazines he might have heard of. He liked to brag about me to our old friends. But God apparently (being the jealous God he is) had claimed whatever interest Billy used to take in this side of my life. My wounded vanity aside, what troubled me most about our conversation was the sheer relief, the stainless-steel serenity his voice possessed. How free his speech now seemed of that congenital yet touching urgency that used to make his words stumble and trip over one another in their hurry to get said, the sense anxiously running ahead of the sentences, which often spilled out in a pell-mell rush of fractured syntax, malapropisms, and comically mixed metaphors. He once told me that he hated to be in a car that someone else was driving because he didn't like to put his life in someone else's foot's hand. He used to say things like "mea capo" for "mea culpa," "negligee" for "negligent" ("Hey, so, you know, so I was a little negligee, so sue me."), and he once bemoaned how he had squander his four years at college, adding, "For all *intensive* purposes I have no education." This new voice was clear, unstrained, and eloquently simple. The sentences flowed from his tongue so gracefully they almost seemed to speak themselves.

The more I brooded on how differently he sounded, the more I could see Billy as he used to be, not just in college and high school, but in grade school as well, and even earlier. I could see him in that third-floor apartment where he was raised—the small flat made even smaller, more claustrophobic, by his two stepsisters on whom his parents doted, his obese often out-of-work musician stepfather, and his mother, who looked like a human thimble in her faded housedress, somehow both diminutive and dumpy at the same time, yet who compensated for her small size with titanic fury as she cooked and cleaned. Billy's biological father died in the Korean War. Since my father had been a mess sergeant during World War II and never killed anything but cows, I admired Billy for having a dead war hero for a dad. Even though he never knew him, Billy talked about his father all the time. He even carried around a crumpled photograph of him in uniform. Unlike his stepfather, who mostly sat around the house all day picking on Billy, his "real" dad (that's how Billy would refer to him) had been brave, hard working, handsome, and fun to be around—"a regular prince" he used to say, mimicking his mother. Billy's obsession with his "real" dad (not to mention that most of what the family lived on came directly from his "real" dad's army pension) must have fueled his stepfather's low-grade continuous hostility. In any event, he couldn't see Billy without complaining: Why can't you clean your room the way your sisters do? Why do you have to be so noisy? What are you made of—wood? Do I have to tell you everything a thousand times? Invariably, Billy would talk back, and the fight would escalate, his mother cleaning furiously all around her son and husband while they went on shouting at each other until her son was finally shut up in his room.

If you can call it a room. Just off the kitchen, windowless, no bigger than a jail cell, it had probably been a pantry once. One wall of it was brick. The room held nothing but a bed, a tiny dresser, and the baseball bat that Billy kept under the bed. More a pressure cooker than a room, in which for eighteen years Billy seemed to boil up more than grow up, jittery, high-strung, breathless, with angers and appetites the small apartment and his room especially seemed to intensify by cramping. There he would steam and simmer for hours at a time, until he'd finally get the bat out and beat the brick wall with it, his explosive anger reflected in the thousands of tiny brick shards that were always peppering his sheets.

By the time he left home, his appetites and desires lived in his body the way his body had lived in the room. It was as if whatever limits, forms, proprieties, or expectations he encountered became another incarnation of the room itself, each impulse another bat to beat the brick wall with.

It saddens me to think that the very qualities I loved in Billy might have been the ones that most tormented him. His wild impulsiveness, his ever restless hunting after more and better, the edgy speed with which he gobbled up each pleasure as if some unseen hand were poised to snatch it from him if he didn't eat it quickly—the very things that made him, in my eyes, fun and sometimes dangerous to be around—were, I see now, the very residue of thwarted need, ancient trauma.

Of course, even back in college I knew that Billy was a problem to himself. But in those days, who wasn't? Seeing him through the lens of my timidity and inhibition, I envied his honesty, his courageous refusal to abide by codes of behavior I disparaged in superficial ways but with which I was enthralled in all the ways that mattered. As someone often paralyzed with self-consciousness and doubt, I found Billy's impetuosity exhilarating. If most of us, in theory anyway, were anarchists, abstract celebrants of openness and spontaneity, enemies of constraint and inhibition, Billy seemed to be the thing itself. And I admired him for it.

I remember early in my freshman year taking Billy to an open-mike poetry reading in the student center. I at the time was too shy to read myself. But I was curious about the poetry the other campus poets wrote. Billy, the pre-med major, had no interest in anybody's poetry but mine. His overheated nervous system, however, ill-equipped him for the concentration and discipline pre-med demanded. In fact, the grind itself aroused in him from the start the impulse to rebel, which was probably why he chose that onerous course of study in the first place. He was always on the verge of flunking out. That he managed not to, given how little he studied, was a measure of his natural ability. In any event, the more he fell behind in his studies, the more vulnerable he was to anything, even a poetry reading, that might distract him from the work he was supposed to be doing.

There were twenty or so kids in the room, a few genuinely attentive, but most just pretending to be, lending an ear to other people's poetry so other people in turn would lend an ear to them (with interest) when they got up to read. Each reader sat in a chair at the front of the room. The first poet gave a rather long introduction to his poem, saying, "I was walking back to my dorm from the library the other day and saw the sun setting, dropping down behind the treetops and I realized now that I'm older and busier that I never stop to watch the sunset anymore, I never just let go and groove on the moment like I used to when I was younger, so I went back to my room and wrote this poem." Then he started reading: "I was walking back to my dorm from the library the other day and saw the sun setting, dropping down behind the treetops and I realized. . . ." I remember another kid reading a sort of Ashberian montage, full of abrupt shifts in tone and diction, ironic undercuttings and deflations. The end went something like this: "The almost misting of your violent nuance now at last drains you from the source they told me you could never find. So it is all weather, news, laughter, a dog barks, someone is eating yogurt, I wish I were dead, or fucking, I guess." Billy sat beside me like an engine whose idle had been set too high, with one knee trembling, one finger fiddling with his moustache, his big jaw twitching. The last reader was a cross between Rilke and Jughead. His black beret, black shirt, and black trousers made his complexion seem paler and more ravaged than it was. I don't remember much about his poem except that it was long and hard to follow, an interminable smear of sensibility in which vagueness masqueraded as profundity. I thought it was terrific. I was so entranced by the way the poet swayed and chanted that I didn't notice till the poem was nearly over that Billy had crossed the room and was now standing right in front of the poet, looking down at him as he intoned the final lines: "I, too, have known the joys of rum. I have walked down what other men call sidewalks." The room was hushed. The bard looked up at Billy. Billy, smiling, stuck one finger up into the bard's nose, one finger nearly lifting him by the nostril off his chair. "Well, asshole," he said before he let him go, "I pick what other men call noses."

As we hurried from the room, all I could say was "Jesus!" Billy just shrugged. He seemed as startled as I was by what he'd done. That's how he always was after doing something outrageous, like a sobering drunk only dimly aware of what he might or might not have said the night before. He felt bad about embarrassing the poet. I said something encouraging like, "Don't worry, Bill. By the turn of the century no one'll remember this had ever happened." Then, because he really did feel bad, I added, "Anyway, I guess it was a shitty poem, after all." He shook his head sadly. "Yeah, I know, but it wasn't just the poem, Al." But whatever else it was that made him do what he did he couldn't say.

Just as he couldn't say a few months later why he hurled the baseball through the plate-glass window of the dining hall. We were playing catch in the quadrangle. It must have been around exam time for in my memory the quadrangle was entirely deserted, everyone else holed up cramming in their rooms or at the library, only me and Billy throwing the ball back and forth, each of us chanting "Hum baby lotta fire, lotta fire" as the other threw. The dining hall, too, was empty. Only the tables and chairs nearest the massive window were visible within the gloom. After a half hour or so, I said I'd had enough, threw the ball to Billy, and started back to the dorm. Billy was standing before the plate glass. He was flipping the ball in his hand, up and down, up and down, staring at his reflection as if admiring himself. I heard the shattering boom. The window was a panicky spider web of cracks around the jagged black hole where Billy's face had been. Billy just stood there, peering with a look of puzzlement into the shadowy room beyond the glass at whatever it was his reflected face had been obscuring. "What are you crazy or something? You wanna get suspended?" I asked. But he just kept on staring, oddly calm, at ease, as if a spring that had been tightening inside him had suddenly been sprung, though I could sense that it was already tightening again as I anxiously rehearsed the story we would tell—that it was all just an accident, that we were playing catch, that the ball just got away from us, and . . . "Al," he interrupted, "no problem. I'll handle it." Then he walked back toward the dorm, saying we probably ought to hit the books.

Billy looked pretty much as I expected him to look: fedora hat, full beard, black suit, white shirt unbuttoned at the collar. If I was somewhat ready, though, for his appearance, I was wholly unprepared for how he greeted Carol Ann. It had been only a year since he had spent two months working on her father's farm in Ireland. During his stay there, he and Carol Ann became good friends. With her long brown hair, pale skin, green eyes, and slender figure made more shapely by the tight-fitting clothes she liked to wear, Carol Ann was every Jewish mother's nightmare. Billy was drawn to women, any woman, with a kind of animal urgency he was unable to disguise. Some women were repelled by this, but some found it irresistible, enough anyway so that he always had a girlfriend. But the girlfriend he had on any given day never turned out to be the one he wanted. It almost seemed he was compelled to sleep with any and every woman who attracted him in order not to think about her anymore. In any event, whenever a pretty woman passed him

Billy Lazarus, in college, 1971

in the street, especially the ones with other men, he'd stop dead in his tracks and gawk with such frank longing you'd think that she was paradise itself, and that without her he would hate his life. Carol Ann was charmed by his gruff directness. And he in turn was charmed by her gentle mockery of it. Their devotion to me made it safe for them to flirt and banter. And by the end of the summer they were pals. Or so Carol Ann thought.

Billy turned away as she came up to embrace him. He wouldn't look directly at her. She asked how his family was. Fine, he said— to me, as if *I* had asked the question. She asked him if he had seen a mutual friend of ours, and he said no, again to me, not her. Would he like something to eat or drink? No thanks, he replied, looking again in my direction as if an invisible harness strapped around his head was pulling it away from Carol Ann whenever she would speak. After a few minutes of this, visibly hurt and angry, she left the room. I asked him, what's up? How could he treat Carol Ann like that?

He ignored the question. Or rather he answered it by saying that the fate of the Jewish community as a whole, and beyond the Jewish community, of mankind itself, is tied to the particular fate of every individual Jew, believers and unbelievers alike. He talked about the 613 *mitzvot* (commandments), which govern every aspect, every moment, of a Hasid's life, and how a life lived according to the law infuses everything—love-making, eating, even bodily functions—with holiness and joy. Billy *davened* as he talked, his upper body swaying back and forth as if in prayer, the way the old Jews used to in the synagogue I went to as a child. The more I watched him, the more it seemed that the holy joy he felt (and I had no doubt that he felt it) was not a personal joy but the joy of personal extinction, the joy of the body transformed through ritual and unremitting discipline into a transpersonal vessel for the holy spirit, the living God. Wasn't that the purpose of the black suit, the ear locks, the beard, the *teffillin*, the Hasid straps to his hand and forehead once a day? Not just a way of saying that the self is this, not that, Jew not Gentile, Hasid not mere Jew, Lubavitcher Hasid not mere Hasid, but also a way of saying that the self has no identity except that corporate one. Not just a way of saying this transcendent unity has been achieved, but also a reminder that only with great and constant vigilance is it sustained, is it preserved. Implicit in the uniformity of dress and the ritual circumspection of every single moment of the day is the recognition of anarchic appetite, unexpungeable violence, unbridled selfishness and egotism that require an equally violent or comprehensive set of rituals to be kept in line. Yawveh wouldn't be such a jealous God if his children weren't so easily distracted. If we weren't so forgetful of his word, he wouldn't need to repeat himself so often, constantly reminding us to love "the Lord your God with all your heart, and with all your soul, and with all your might."

It was no surprise that Billy seemed most like his old self when he described the terrible and never-ending struggle he endured to purify himself, to square his earthly nature with the heavenly rule of law. Sexual abstinence was especially difficult, he said. Since his conversion eight months earlier, he'd hardly so much as looked at a woman. In the Hasidic culture, unmarried women and men are carefully segregated. And what contact they do have is carefully monitored. Unlawful sexuality, even sexual thoughts or impulses of any kind are so proscribed that the Hasid guards against them even while he sleeps or prays. For instance, during prayers he wears a *gartel*, or belt, the purpose of which is to cordon off the upper more spiritual part of the body from the lower more earthly part, so that no profane thoughts might interrupt, contaminate his heavenly communion. Some yeshiva students (and Billy was one of them) sew shut the pockets of their pants so there's less temptation to masturbate while studying. It was also moving to hear Billy describe how embarrassing he found the jeering and taunts his dress and appearance usually elicited from people on the street. That he felt any mortification whatsoever only proved, he said, how entangled he still was in the snares of the ego, how far he had to go to reach the serene detachment and selfless devotion that genuine piety required.

If Billy was intent on extinguishing the ego, I, in my life and work, at least from his point of view, was reveling in it. For Billy, there was no such thing as a career or the personal gratifications and excitements that a career entails. There was devotion to God, and the God-given laws by which that devotion is achieved. The rest of life had value only insofar as it enabled or didn't interfere with that devotion. I was equally single-minded in my devotion to the art of poetry and to establishing a life that would enable me to do the work I felt compelled to do. But to think that there was anything worth writing or reading that didn't glorify the Creator or the life that he demanded we, as Jews, should live, was to Billy's way of thinking at best deluded *chutzpah*, at worst unimaginable blasphemy.

I listened as Billy calmly, righteously, went on hammering away at everything on which my life was built. I wasn't angry or offended. Armed with my own unassailable pieties, I listened with superior, somewhat contemptuous amusement. For I, too (though I didn't recognize this then), was a true believer, and the faith I clung to with no less fervor not only had its sacred doctrine replete with clear and definitive prescriptions and proscriptions, but it also had its spiritual leader. Billy's was Menachim Schneerson, the rebbe of the Lubavitcher movement; mine was Yvor Winters, the late rebbe of the Stanford Creative Writing Program.

Winters had died in 1968, six years before I came to Stanford. But he was still very much a living presence to me and the other students in the writing program. As aspiring writers who had yet to publish (not for lack of trying), we identified with his outsider status in the literary world. Early in his career, Winters had abandoned many of the modernist techniques and assumptions that had governed the work of his contemporaries and that still governed to some extent much of the work of mine. His poetry and criticism (*In Defense of Reason* especially) were our sacred texts, our Torah and Talmud. Just as Billy believed that the Torah was not only the law of the Jewish people, but the cosmic law of the universe itself, so we believed that Winters's definitions and prescriptions were true not only for the poetry he wrote and admired, but for any poetry at all that aspired to be deathless and universal. By dividing all poets since the eighteenth century into sheep and goats—into those enlightened few whose procedures were essentially rational and metrical, and the unenlightened predominantly romantic many for whom poetry was emotional release, immersion in irrational nature—Winters gave us, ignorant as we all were then and insecure about our ignorance, a heady sense of mastery over everything we didn't know. We read the poets Winters recommended and ignored the ones he claimed provided only a dangerously incomplete account of what it means to be alive—dangerous because if you took the ideas seriously, if you put them to the test of experience, then you would either change your way of thinking and writing, as Winters had, or like Hart Crane, Sylvia Plath, and John Berryman, go mad and kill yourself. That most poets of the irrational did not go mad or kill themselves only proved that they had isolated the poetry they wrote from the lives they led, trivializing both in the process. Like Crane, Plath, and Berryman, we, too, had the courage of our convictions, but our convictions were life-enhancing, not life-threatening. For us, the act of writing and reading had all the urgency of a morality play in which the self heroically confronts the brute facts of irrational nature and, in the confrontation, renews, strengthens, and extends the fragile boundary of human consciousness.

This is not to say we lived exemplary lives. Far from it. In the bars, in the streets, in each other's bedrooms, we caroused and rioted, while on the page we moralized about the dangers of excess. We lived like Rimbaud even while we wrote like Jonson. In fact, I sometimes wonder now if the almost magical power we ascribed to metrical control didn't in some way license and legitimize, not restrain, the chaos of the life we led. So long as our poems scanned, so long as we made rationally defensible statements, in meter, about what happened to us, so long as we believed that we had understood and mastered our experience, we were free to do whatever the hell we wanted.

I don't mean to condescend to who I was back then. Like new converts to any faith, I was more Wintersian than Winters himself, certainly more Wintersian than my teachers, Donald Davie and Kenneth Fields. But even that simplified Wintersianism was incredibly valuable. Through his anthology *Quest for Reality,* which I read constantly, I was introduced to many wonderful poets I otherwise might not have read—poets like Fulke Greville, Frederick Goddard Tuckerman, Mina Loy, Elizabeth Daryush, Janet Lewis, and Edgar Bowers. Because I learned

from Winters that great poems are written "one by one / And spaced by many years, each line an act / Through which few labor, which no men retract," I gave myself the freedom not to worry overmuch if this or that poem I was writing was even very good; even the bad poems were necessary preparation for the good ones up ahead, the good ones necessary for the great ones. As a result, I learned how to be patient and persistent, to go at my own pace. If my Wintersianism helped inflate my long-term expectations for what I might achieve, at one and the same time it helped deflate my short-term expectations so I could go on learning as I wrote. Even the more juvenile expressions of that enthusiasm were exhilarating and necessary. The circular logic that came with believing I was writing against the spirit of the age gave me what all young poets need—the stubborn arrogance to go on writing no matter how discouraging my prospects were, no matter how much the world (literary or otherwise) was telling me it had no need or interest in anything I wrote. Wasn't I, in this respect, like Billy, too? For in the same way that persecution and suffering for the Hasid are a sign of divine election, of God's interest in his chosen few, so that the more he suffers, the more assured he is of his salvation, so I believed the health of poetry depended on the metrical poems I and my fellow students were writing in defiance of the barbarian, nonmetrical hordes. The very fact that we had trouble publishing our poems only confirmed their value. The more the literary world neglected us, the more convinced we were that only through our poems could the literary world be saved.

That afternoon I couldn't have acknowledged, much less have seen, any of these similarities between me and Billy. My allegiance, after all, was to rational control, intellectual judgment, moderation of feeling—qualities you couldn't have too much of, could you? Hasidism, on the other hand, was the Jewish Orthodox equivalent of romantic excess. Moreover, didn't Hasidism and romanticism both arise at roughly the same time in the mid-to-late eighteenth century? And like romanticism in the arts, didn't the Hasidic movement favor energy over order, enthusiasm over learning, mystical release over rational control? Wasn't Hasidism pantheistic in its root assumption, that God was everywhere, in everything? And didn't the Hasid strive for dissolution into what Gershom Scholem calls "the everlasting unity"? Never mind that this is a highly distorted and reductive picture of both Hasidic mysticism and romantic art, created by a highly distorted and reductive understanding of Yvor Winters. What this picture enabled me to do, though, was sit back and listen to Billy in a luxuriously condescending mood of pity.

Poor Billy, I thought, with his black suit, his arcane ritual observances, his dietary restrictions, his 613 laws, his new Old World voice—what did all this mean but that he now had turned upon himself, his body, his very being, the restless fury he once directed at his bedroom wall and, later on, at the conventions by which people tried to make him live. Wasn't he, at every moment of every day, hammering away at any impulse, desire, look, or thought that didn't fit the impersonal mold of perfect piety? So what if he seemed happier, calmer, less edgy than I'd ever known him. He paid too steep a price for that serenity. All he'd done, I remember thinking, was exchange a universe of accident, surprise, doubt, and adventure for one in which nothing happens—no common cold, no massacre, no rape, no child abuse, not the slightest blink of an eye—that isn't tied directly to the Lord our God, Lord of the universe, blessed be his name. Billy had escaped the bad dream of his independence and autonomy into the womb of *Yiddishkeit*, and what I imagined he had found there was what his family never gave: absolute unbreakable connection to the lives of others, and a sense, too, that as a member of the tribe he had an absolute importance, that the very structure of the moral world depended on him and his devotions, his every action as a Jew. Thus, the very thing that extinguished his profane existence, the merely personal ego, at the same time greatly magnified his Jewish soul. But more than this, in Rebbe Schneerson, didn't his new family also give him back his dead but perfect father? Didn't it give him back the opportunity to be the perfect son?

My pity, however, immediately turned to scorn when Billy began extolling Rebbe Schneerson's supernatural powers. He was telling me how the rebbe, being more pious than others and therefore closer to God, can work miracles through prayer. Billy knew of several people—a woman with breast cancer, a couple unable to conceive a child, a father whose son was straying from the faith—who, after asking the rebbe to intercede with God on their behalf, had soon found that their problems had been miraculously solved: the woman's cancer went into remission, the couple conceived, and the prodigal son came back into the fold.

"Billy," I said.

"Shlomo, please," he interrupted.

"Okay, Shlomo, you gotta be joking. I mean, you make the rebbe sound like Jim Jones." I knew as soon as I had said it that the comparison was unfair. But as I mentioned earlier, Jones and his deluded followers had only recently imbibed their dixie cups of poison Kool-Aid. I wanted to dramatize to Billy how irrational and superstitious he was being, how dangerous it was to deify a man. I quoted Montaigne's famous line about puritanical zeal: "They want to get out of themselves and escape from the man. That is madness: instead of turning into angels, they change into beasts." "How can you say such a thing?" is all he said, more wounded than offended. I stammered something back about the arrogance of thinking God would take a personal interest in your problems over anybody else's. What about the starving children in Biafra? I asked him. Did God ignore their prayers? What about the Holocaust? Didn't the Jews in Auschwitz pray? Were they punished because the rebbe wasn't there to intercede for them?

"All that shows," he said, now leaning toward me, pointing his finger like a gun directly at my temple, "is what can happen when a Jew neglects his Jewishness, when a Jew forgets."

"What are you saying, that Jews caused the Holocaust? That they deserved it?"

"Who knows why *HaShem*, may his name be praised, does what he does? All I'm saying is that it's no accident that the German Jews were assimilationists."

"You can't be serious," I said.

"No, Al, you, you're the one who can't be serious, living in ignorance like this . . ."

"I beg your pardon."

"Ignorance and filth. No better than a goy. Betraying your own people."

Both of us were standing now. I asked him who he thought "my people" were. I said I didn't have any "people," only individuals I loved, many of them the goys he hated. "We don't hate the *goyim*," he said. "We even encourage Jewish women who turn out to be barren to divorce and marry goys, so they don't waste

Jewish sperm." "Gosh," I sneered, "how ecumenical." He didn't come here, he said, to be insulted. He came here as a *mitzvah* to me and to my parents because I was his oldest friend, because he couldn't stand to see me ruining my life. My marriage to Carol Ann was a sin against myself, my family, the Jewish community itself. And he hoped that someday, sooner than later, please God, I would come to my senses and put an end to this abomination. He said he would continue to pray for me. He said he would ask the rebbe to pray for me. Since I obviously hated who I was, however, we had nothing else to say to one another. He went to the door. Then he abruptly turned around. He was holding out a dollar bill. It had been blessed by the rebbe. Take it for good luck, he said, and give away another dollar bill to charity.

That was sixteen years ago. I have not heard from Billy or spoken to him since. Six years later, though, he visited my parents with his wife, a South African Jew, and their four young children. He spoke only Yiddish with my parents. He told them that his marriage had been arranged. He and his wife became engaged, he said, after spending only an hour or so in each other's company. After the wedding, they moved to South Africa where Billy became a rabbi. He hoped that soon he and his family would be moving to Israel. He didn't ask about me, and my parents didn't offer any news. The news, however, surely would have pleased him. Carol Ann and I broke up a year or so after Billy's visit. Even at that time our marriage had been on rocky ground, though I didn't want to give Billy the satisfaction of knowing anything at all about our problems. She hated living in America, and I refused to live in Ireland. She missed her family, her four sisters especially, her homesickness made more acute by her complete dependence on me and my friends, all of whom of course were writers, for what community she had. At dinner parties, at bars, at any social functions, she often felt ignored or condescended to. "You're always talking shop," she'd frequently complain. "Listen," I'd joke back, "just be thankful we aren't gynecologists." Carol Ann was not amused. Her loneliness made her that much more impatient with what she called my fanatical devotion to poetry. I worked ten hours a day, seven days a week. Not wanting to let anything interfere with my daytime regimen of writing and reading, I balked whenever she would want us to do something together, just the two of us, go somewhere, have fun, relax. God forbid. She'd accuse me of caring more for poetry than I cared for her, which of course was true, though I denied it. Being with her, just living, ordinary life itself, was a chore for me, she'd say, an obstacle, something to get out of the way so I could go back in good conscience to my desk. I told her it was poetry that kept me sane, that it was poetry that enabled me to be as loving to her as I was. Well if that's the case, she'd say, then maybe I should try some other form of writing because she didn't feel loved at all. Eventually she returned to Ireland and we divorced.

I also had a more amicable parting of the ways from Yvor Winters. Around the time that Carol Ann and I split up, I began to feel constrained by the Wintersian injunction to "write little, do it well." To chisel every word of every poem as if in stone became, for me at least, a recipe for writer's block. What little I wrote, for all my patience and persistence, turned out to be pinched, narrow, bitten back. If not for Winters himself, then for many of his ardent followers, writing as if Ben Jonson were looking over their shoulder placed too great a burden on each and every line they wrote. Meter for them, moreover, seemed more a cage than a technique of discovery. And whereas Winters did in fact have a lion inside him that required caging, the poems by his epigones were lion cages holding pussycats. Around this time as well, I began to read many of the poets Winters dismissed or disapproved of: Wordsworth, Coleridge, Whitman, Williams (not just the few short lyrics Winters did admire), Eliot, and Pound, and a host of more contemporary poets who were decidedly un-Wintersian: poets like Elizabeth Bishop, C. K. Williams, Frank Bidart, James McMichael, and Robert Pinsky (the last two, ironically, were students of Winters in the early sixties). And the more I read, the more impatient I became with what I felt was Winters's moralistic austerity of taste and judgment, his finicky rankings, his violent distrust of less rational, less rigorously orchestrated ways of writing. And unlike the neoformalists who were frequently invoking Winters's name, I no longer thought that accentual-syllabic meter was the only legitimate form of verse, the only road to genuine achievement.

Alan Shapiro

Over the years, I've often thought of Billy. What would we say to one another if we saw each other now? I know I'd be no less uneasy with his absolutist thinking, his fundamentalism, his iron-clad assurance of divine approval for everything he and his fellow Lubavitchers think and do. His total rejection of the secular world in favor of such a narrow and repressive Orthodoxy still seems bizarre in the extreme. At the same time, when I think how transient my life has been, how often in the last sixteen years I've had to move, change jobs, rebuild a new life in a new place while the centrifugal pressure of professional commitments scatters old friends and family farther and farther from me, I can't help but envy Billy the fixed attachments that pervade his life. The image of a congregation worshipping together— freed from the daily drudgeries of getting and spending, from profane worries and ambitions and petty egotisms as they fix their minds as one mind upon sacred matters, ultimate mysteries, upon being itself—is an image I find more and more attractive. Though in my imagined congregation, the men are not all wear-

ing black, the women are not segregated, and no longer does this act of worship seem, as it might have once, an image of irrational superstition but of reason, to quote Wordsworth, in its most exalted mood.

I have no doubt, too, that Billy would regard my life and work as pitiably flat and empty, rudderless in the most essential ways. At the same time, maybe he would have to think that, to some extent at least, his and the rebbe's prayers on my behalf were answered. A few years after leaving Stanford I remarried, this time to a Jew. We are not believers. We don't keep a kosher home. We don't observe the sabbath. And we don't belong to any congregation. If we follow any of the 613 *mitzvot,* it's quite by accident. Moreover, as I was sixteen years ago, I'm no less obsessed with poetry, no less compelled to work and study every chance I get (which isn't all that much with two young children to take care of). But while I'm still prone to the feeling that ordinary life is an impediment to my real life as a writer, I have grown up enough to know that that feeling needs to be resisted, not indulged. I'd like to think that Billy would be relieved to know my wife and I are eager to give our kids a Jewish education of some kind or other, not just to teach them something about where they came from, who they are, but also to give them a defense against the sound-bitten, crass, increasingly homogeneous mass distractions that pass for contemporary culture. I'd like to think that Billy would be pleased, if not entirely satisfied, with my spiritual development. But I know that he would not be pleased. For Billy, or rather Shlomo, anything less than complete commitment to the rigors of Hasidic faith, to each and every one of the 613 *mitzvot,* would be more contemptible than outright heresy, a more insidious betrayal. As a Hasid, he would view my emerging but still tempered sense of Jewishness as a shamelessly self-serving way of turning the most sacred matters into sacred fripperies designed to prettify an essentially secular existence. Because he thinks that being insufficiently Jewish is to make a mockery of what it means to be a Jew, because he couldn't ever be *entirely* satisfied with how I live my life, Shlomo would not be pleased at all. Shlomo would still be praying, angrier than ever, for my lost soul.

BIBLIOGRAPHY

Poetry:

After the Digging, Elpenor Books, 1981.

The Courtesy, University of Chicago Press, 1983.

Happy Hour, University of Chicago Press, 1987.

Covenant, University of Chicago Press, 1991.

Essays:

In Praise of the Impure: Poetry and the Ethical Imagination: Essays, 1980–1991, Northwestern University Press, 1993.

Richard Tillinghast

1940-

Minnie and Adoniram Judson Williford and their sons Staley and John in 1900, two years before the birth of their daughter, Martha Williford, Memphis, Tennessee

Everything I have lived has, usually in some reimagined or sublimated form, gone into my poetry. In what follows I try to tell about those circumstances and events that have formed me as a poet.

We lived in an old house in Memphis that my grandparents had bought in 1890. In the early years of their marriage, South Cox Street was outside the city limits in a little community called Lenox, which had its own station on the L&N railroad line running east from downtown Memphis through what I have called the "whitewashed towns and sparse farms" of West Tennessee. My grandmother's people came from the farming community of Allen's Station,

near Brownsville, where the family gathered every year to celebrate Thanksgiving. While the women prepared the feast, the men went out quail hunting through harvested fields where tufts of cotton that had eluded the pickers' hands clung to the ragged plants, and faded cornstalks creaked in the wind. My father shot left-handed and was known as a crack shot. I loved the smell of the spent shotgun shells. One Thanksgiving it snowed, and all of us cousins and aunts and uncles had to bed down overnight in the farmhouse.

My grandfather, Adoniram Judson Williford, farmed near Bartlett, Tennessee, which at one time was the county seat of Shelby County. At some point he took up the law and moved to Memphis, where he was active in Democratic Party politics. Eventually he became a judge, and for obscure reasons the people in the neighborhood called him "Squire." In a field next to the house he grazed his horse, which was named "Our Bob," after Robert Love Taylor, a popular governor of Tennessee and grandfather of the Memphis novelist Peter Taylor.

A. J. Williford died in the influenza epidemic that swept the country right after the First World War. Because I never had the chance to know him, he became a figure of mystery for me. As a child I used to dress up in his top hat and Chesterfield coat from the attic or poke through his legal papers, which were kept in a big trunk stenciled with the initials A.J.W. I have his pince-nez and wear his Masonic ring, made of old gold with a reddish tint. The emblem on it is now worn away beyond recognition. He was not a churchgoing man. When my grandmother, who was, brought the Baptist preacher to see him on his deathbed—this was during Prohibition—he asked the preacher to go out and find him a bottle of beer. "You're probably the only man in Memphis who could get me one," he said by way of explanation. My grandmother always used to say that I was "a true Williford," by which I think she meant I was proud, had a sense of humor, and was subject to grandiose notions.

My mother graduated from Tennessee College in Murfreesboro, where she majored in classics. In an old scrapbook I recently found a one-inch item from a *Memphis Commercial Appeal* of the 1920s that reads, "Miss Martha Williford, daughter of Mrs. A. J. Williford, 190 Cox Street, who is a member of the faculty at Snowden School, sailed yesterday from Montreal for Europe. She will visit several countries and will study in Paris, returning about Sept. 1." She remembered this trip fondly and used to tell my brother and me about her little hotel in Paris on the rue Madame next to the Luxembourg Gardens. It's curious to think that Mama was in Paris at the same time Hemingway, Joyce, and Fitzgerald were flourishing there. For the first few years of my life she taught French and Latin at Miss Hutchinson's, a girls' school near our house in what, as the city has grown and spread out eastward, has come to be known as Midtown. I remember her walking me to kindergarten on her way to her teaching job.

Raymond Charles Tillinghast, 1902–81

The little French I still have, I speak with a Southern accent.

I went to grammar school at Lenox, an imposing brick structure with big granite eagles perched on the cornices overlooking its main entrance, four houses down the street from where we lived. Our family took pride in the school because my grandfather was one of the men responsible for its having been built. Lenox has now been turned into condominiums, but whenever I am in Memphis I visit the school and go round to the spot where my grandfather's name is chiseled into a stone tablet next to the front door.

My father was from Great Barrington, Massachusetts—the descendant of Pardon Elisha Tillinghast, who left East Anglia and settled in Providence in 1640. In England the Tillinghasts were Dissenters who went to Cambridge University and wrote contentious books about religion and politics. They opposed the monarchy, and some of them may have been among the Regicides. Daddy came to Memphis in the early thirties to work for Proctor & Gamble, met my mother, and lived in the South for the rest of his life. He was an inventor who developed several new machines for the cotton business, including a new cotton compress that he was only partially successful in convincing people in the industry to adopt.

My parents were married in 1932. Many times during my youth I would hear how, the month after they were married, my father's paycheck was reduced by half. Readers of my poems "R.C.T.," "The Knife," and "Father in October" will know him as a straightforward man of integrity. His New England temperament—and accent—differed greatly from anything else in my experience. My brother David and I thought expressions of Daddy's like "up attic" and "down cellar" were very amusing. America has become so culturally homogeneous now, it's hard to appreciate that in the 1940s a Southerner and a New Englander—my parents, for example— were practically citizens of two different countries. As I grew up, particularly after I got to know New England better, I came to see this mixed cultural heritage as the source of certain conflicts within my own character, and then later, as a strength.

Today it is also hard to appreciate the hold that the Civil War exercised on the imagination of the South as recently as the 1940s. Barry Pickett, a classmate of mine in junior high school, was a descendant of General George Edward Pickett, who led the Confederates' heroic and catastrophic charge at Gettysburg. Fully half of our American History class in junior high school was spent studying "the War of Northern Aggression." While considerable historical reading—as well as insight into the psychological effects of enslavement gleaned from books like Toni Morrison's novel *Beloved*—has brought home to me the unspeakable evils of slavery, I still regard the Southern struggle as heroic. The threadbare, daredevil troops who followed Lee and Jackson and Forrest into battle won an ineradicable place in Southern hearts. While knowing and accepting most of the reasons I should not love the Confederacy, still, as I wrote in *Sewanee in Ruins,* my long poem about the aftermath of the war in a small Tennessee community,

> my thoughts are with men I have heard of
>   and read of
> who, possessed by a fatal romanticism,
> killed at fourteen,

> ate corn burned in the field,
> and wore the dead enemies' shoes
> in 1865, when everything burned
> but the brick chimneys
> and a way of talking.

I will confess to getting a lump in my throat when I hear "Dixie." A widely held view of American history has succeeded in defining the Civil War as a contest for or against slavery, but for the white South it was also, and more importantly, a war that tested our ancestors' loyalty, courage, and willingness to fight bravely against impossible odds. That said, I reluctantly no longer have the Confederate flag hanging on the wall of my study, because racists have, sadly, defined it as a symbol of bigotry.

A statistic I cited in *Sewanee in Ruins* is that in 1860 only 3 percent of Tennesseans owned slaves. And though my maternal ancestors were among that 3 percent, I still see the Southern cause as a fight to defend the homeland. A story passed down in our family tells of deaf Uncle Joe in Bells, Tennessee, who did

Martha Williford Tillinghast, 1902–86

not hear the Yankee soldier call out "Halt!" and was shot in the back while riding out of town one day in 1864. I have his watch, a solid gold Elgin with a hunting case.

Shelby Foote, whom I interviewed for the Southern edition of *Ploughshares* that George Garrett and I edited in 1983, summed up the rationale of the average Southern soldier. "This is a rich man's war. You don't have anything to gain from it," a Union soldier called out to a Rebel across the line of battle. "Why are you fighting?" The ragged, hungry Southern veteran unhesitatingly shouted back, "'Cause y'all are down here!" Does this mean I wish the South had won the Civil War? Of course not. I would not like to contemplate what the Confederacy triumphant would have been like. But in the time and place where I grew up, the war lives in memory as the quintessential Lost Cause.

When I was one year and twelve days old the Japanese attacked Pearl Harbor. And though I had not quite turned five when the Second World War ended, I have discovered as an adult what a hold the images and emotions of those years have on me. I stress "images" here. Before I could read, my grandmother—no doubt in an effort to keep me occupied—had me cutting pictures out of magazines like the *Saturday Evening Post* and pasting them into scrapbooks. Pictures of fighter planes, aircraft carriers in the South Pacific, the American flag being raised over Iwo Jima—images which were everywhere during the war—implanted themselves in my consciousness. While writing the title poem of my fourth book, *Our Flag Was Still There,* these images, mixed with memories of my own not derived from external sources, came rushing to the surface. Some are seriocomic, like this picture of "Chessie," the Chesapeake & Ohio's advertising mascot, taken from the *Post:*

One paw bandaged.
A Congressional Medal of Honor
red-white-and-blue-ribboned around his neck.
As convincingly at attention as a military-style,
family-oriented cat can be in a pullman car.
On his well-groomed chest, rows of campaign
    ribbons.
A dignified, "can do" look
hovers about his muscled smile.

The generation of men who won the war for us represented authority and security for me as a young child. The affection I feel toward that generation is related to the sense of security I derived from images of our victory in World War II:

Against a backdrop of blue sky and
    innocent clouds,
a line of six blunt-nosed P-47 fighters—
boxy and powerful like the grey Olds
we bought after the War
and drove to the Berkshires for the
    summer—
flew off on a mission to Corregidor.

I see in my poetry a continuing involvement with history and politics, as well as a strong inclination to let images carry much of the meaning. Looking back, it seems that I arrived at both of those qualities very early on.

As a boy I spent a lot of time drawing. My perusal of the *World Book,* our family encyclopedia, led me to become knowledgeable about the Napoleonic wars. Like Robert Lowell, the man who would become my writing teacher and most influential mentor when I was in graduate school, I could rattle off the names of Napoleon's generals at an early age. Some of my earliest drawings showed the confrontation at Waterloo between the phalanxes of British infantry and the French cavalry. All through my youth, until I went away to college, I took Saturday, summer, and sometimes evening classes at the Memphis Academy of Art, which in those days was housed in two wonderfully decrepit Victorian mansions in a down-at-the-heels part of town. Learning to draw, painting still lifes, sketching the models who posed for us in what had been the parlors of an Italianate mansion built by the Lee family, who had made a fortune from Mississippi riverboats, I thought that one day I would be a painter. Though I have not made a career in the visual arts, I can see now how important that training has been to my image-making ability as a writer.

My freshman year at Central High School, playing drums in the marching band looked like a good alternative to being a cadet in our school's Reserve Officers Training Corps. Our band played for weekly military exercises when the cadets marched from Central to their parade ground. My fellow percussionists and I were a mischievous bunch of rebels. We delighted in speeding the beat up to unmarchable levels or substituting for the straight, military 4/4 rhythm an improvised samba beat we were

The author with Santa, Memphis, 1940s

pretty good at. The cadets would trip over their brogans and their M-1s trying to keep up with what we were playing, until the order inevitably came for us to bring the beat back to what the sergeant considered acceptable.

My first two jobs were bagging groceries down at the local supermarket and shelving books at the public library. From my earnings my first two purchases were a drum set and a tuxedo. Throughout high school I played in bands: jazz, rock 'n' roll, and country and western. The fifties were an exciting time to be playing music in Memphis. My brother played the banjo and I played the guitar, and we learned folk songs from singers in the Ozarks, where we camped and fished and went canoeing in the summers, as well as from the Weavers records and Alan Lomax folk music collections we got from the public library. When we took our instruments to parties for the employees at my father's plant in North Mississippi, there were singers among the black workers who would plug in their amplifiers and play the blues in that Delta style that had been making its way north to Chicago. At country club dances white band leaders like Colie Stoltz would sometimes bring on an old bluesman to play a set.

Rockabilly was in its prime. Elvis Presley, Roy Orbison, and Carl Perkins were popularizing an eclectic style that brought a rock 'n'

roll beat to country and western lyrics. Everyone my age listened to Dewey Phillips's "Red Hot and Blue" show on WHBQ, and rhythm and blues was the music we danced to and played in our own bands. The hippest among us listened to jazz; Marvin Stamm, first trumpet in the band at Central High, is now well known in the world of jazz.

The jazz and rock gigs we played were fairly conventional parties or dances attended by middle-class kids like the ones I went to school with. The country-and-western gigs were something else entirely. I played in a band with three truck drivers, and we were booked into low-life nightclubs, most of them on the outskirts of town, the very existence of which I'm sure my parents were unaware. Memphis has been called the capital of Mississippi; it also acts as a magnet to the surrounding countryside in West Tennessee and across the river in Arkansas. Some of the roughest nightclubs are to be found on the highways that run into town from Millington or Bolivar, Tennessee, or from Mississippi. I remember playing gigs at a dive called the Rodeo Club, halfway out into the county. We would set out for a gig with the piano player driving his old Chrysler, my drums in the trunk, and the bass fiddle filling most of the passenger space—the butt of it resting on the ledge behind the backseat, the fiddlehead resting on the dashboard right under the rearview mirror. The Rodeo Club was famous for its bare-knuckle brawls that would clear the entire club about once every Saturday night. The drum set offered protection when these fights erupted. When somebody broke the neck of a beer bottle on the edge of the bar and went after somebody else, I would get down behind my bass drum and watch the action unfold.

The guitar player would arrive in his '48 Buick four-holer with his wife and kids in the car. They would sit out in the car while we played. The guitar player was really hot, but he drank. At some point during every gig he would pass out while playing. The biggest problem with this was that when he blacked out he would fall backward onto my drum set. I would listen carefully to how he played and try to anticipate the precipitating moment. When it happened I would leap up and grab him before he hit the cymbals. Then we would carry him out to the Buick, where he would be revived and sent back in to play the next set.

No greater contrast can be imagined than between the Saturday nights I spent at the Rodeo Club and my undergraduate days at the University of the South in Sewanee, Tennessee. As a freshman I was already a reader of Southern writers, including William Faulkner, Robert Penn Warren, and John Crowe Ransom. The sense of the South as a land of mythic dimensions had a strong purchase on my imagination. The small towns of Tennessee, with their white clapboard houses, big shade trees, and memories of guerrilla raids by Nathan Bedford Forrest, took on the dignity of literary distance in Ransom's poems. As I read Warren's *All the King's Men* on the bus during the high school band's tour of Louisiana, the novel's straight slab of highway blended in my mind with the actual road we were traveling. That the real-life setting for William Faulkner's Yoknapatawpha County was only eighty miles from Memphis encouraged me to believe that I too could make something solid and lasting in words from my life in the same part of the country. Witnessing the transubstantiation of place through the written word has remained for me a thrilling and almost holy experience.

In his memoir, *Lanterns on the Levee,* William Alexander Percy writes of Sewanee—which graduates of the school call "the Mountain"— as Arcadia. It was that and more for me. Dreams of myself as a future artist or musician melted away. Poetry became everything for me; I wrote constantly. The Victorian Gothic fantasy of the college's architecture, the steep limestone cliffs with their views over the surrounding lowlands, the vivid autumns and startling springs—which could begin in February and keep going through May—all of this was like a waking dream for me. I was also caught in the throes of a tragic teenage romance, which in time-honored style contributed to the sweet sorrow of my first year on the Mountain.

Sewanee is an Episcopal college, and in those days chapel was compulsory. My time there predated the recent adulteration of the *Book of Common Prayer,* so I heard the stately cadences of Cranmer's prayer book along with the King James Bible on a daily basis. An enduring sense of the greatness of the English language seeped into my awareness. Our professors were our idols, however much we might parody them and chafe against their authority. Of all the fortunate things that have happened to me, the experience of studying Shakespeare

with Charles T. Harrison, English history with David Underdown, Victorian prose with Abbott Cotton Martin, political science with Arthur Dugan, and modern poetry with Monroe K. Spears was one of my great pieces of luck. Monroe Spears also published a dozen poems of mine in the *Sewanee Review;* these were my first publications.

In the fall term of sophomore year my habits of staying up all night, smoking heavily, and otherwise neglecting my health caught up with me. The doctors diagnosed my hacking cough, which wouldn't go away, as acute bronchitis. Early during Christmas vacation that year I went into the hospital, where about a third of my right lung was removed. When a staphylococcus infection developed in the operation scar, things started to look grave. At the time I drifted in the somnolent euphoria induced by shots of pain-killing drugs, but I later found out that I came close to dying. I actually enjoyed being in the hospital: I listened to music a lot—Gilbert and Sullivan in particular, for some reason—and sketched and wrote. Nowadays I loathe hospitals, but then the place easily replaced the reality of the outside world.

My hospital stay amounted to two months, and then I sat around the house recuperating for some time more. My mother took me to Florida for a while. This experience barely got into my poetry, except in one called "Less Than Yesterday, More Than Tomorrow," which I wrote eight years later while spending a month in Amsterdam. In the poem I recapture the convalescent's sense of fragility:

> Rising from sickness
> my bones thin, bending, tender to the touch,
> a lightness in the inner ear
>
> Things seem to rush at me.
> I huddle away from them, my mother driving—
> the street is shocking to the wheels.

The poem, influenced by Sylvia Plath, succeeds pretty well in rendering how strange it felt to leave the hospital, where I floated in a comfortable passivity, feeling very little. The poem closes almost brutally, with the brittle coldness of my adolescent indifference toward my parents:

> Less and less I feel I am falling forward.
> My mother is less patient,
> my father will send me to Florida.

For them I am closing the door to the place
where the dead children are stored,
where the pets have gone to Heaven.

From an emotional standpoint, that ending appalls me today. Perhaps my having, in 1966, fallen temporarily under the spell of Sylvia Plath's weird, thrilling, inhuman bravado partially explains my attitude then. Now that I have children of my own, I have a hard time recognizing the young man who could turn such a cold shoulder toward his mother and father, who had gone through the deepest grief during my illness.

Though weakened and subsequently susceptible to colds and bad coughs, I recovered from the operation and infection. Back at Sewanee I was picked to be captain of our College Bowl team. The flight from Chattanooga to New York was the first time I had flown, and I can still feel the surge and liftoff as our jet ascended from the airport. New York was a revelation. Just as I had enjoyed the sense of suddenly being taken seriously as an adult, with ideas and talent, upon arriving at Sewanee, in New York I luxuriated in having left Tennessee behind. Plus, my girlfriend, Nancy Pringle, whom I would later marry, was at Bryn Mawr and could join me for weekends in the Village. Our team did well in the contest, and that meant four free trips to the city. One moment on the quiz show showed me the extent to which I, as the novice intellectual, was still the teenaged rock 'n' roll drummer from Memphis. When asked to give bonny Prince Charlie's other sobriquet (the Young Pretender), I sounded the buzzer and called out, "The Great Pretender!" (For readers who are unfamiliar with rhythm and blues, that's the title of a song by the Drifters.)

When Andrew Lytle came to the Mountain to edit the *Sewanee Review,* he hired me as an editorial assistant during my senior year. Also during my senior year I began to spend time at the nearby Highlander Folk School, where the first stirrings of the civil rights movement were in motion. Folk music became protest music. With a small group of professors and friends, I became gradually aware of the injustice of racial segregation. My attitude toward Southern tradition soured. We had our own, rather genteel demonstrations on the Mountain, and Sewanee was officially integrated. I was suddenly a student radical and couldn't wait to leave the South. I lost the election for editor of the *Sewanee Purple* because of the stand I took against a racial incident on campus. Graduate school at Harvard was the logical next step.

Like the alma mater that she is, Sewanee gives her favorite sons and daughters a high opinion of themselves that is not always completely justified. Robert Lowell's poetry-writing class at Harvard, which I took side by side with my English Lit courses, opened me to unfamiliar writing styles and introduced me to some very good poets my age and younger.

Sewanee had one of the best English departments in the country, but it was satisfying to get the graduate education in literature that Harvard's solid, unflashy English department was equipped to give. To read Chaucer line by line in Middle English in B. J. Whiting's class, to get a thorough grounding in eighteenth-century prose in Walter Jackson Bate's course on Dr. Johnson, to study the literature of the English Renaissance with that dry Texan, Herschel Baker, who smoked a pipe and delivered his wry observations out of the other side of his mouth—graduate education at Harvard was a revelation of good sense and unhurried reading. Most satisfying to me was the exposure to Old English I got from William Alfred's class. As soon as I heard him read aloud from *Beowulf,* "The Wanderer," and "The Seafarer," I knew I had stumbled onto a poetry that would remain a touchstone for the rest of my writing life.

My one source of discomfiture was my Southern accent. This was the heyday of Northern awareness of the civil rights movement, and the sound of a white Southern voice was enough to throw one's fellow Harvard students into attack mode. There was a certain irony to this. While most of them had come no closer to the struggle than the nearest television set, I had participated in sit-ins, had confronted the vice-chancellor at Sewanee over his refusal to let Pete Seeger sing on campus, had carried protest signs in Atlanta, had been threatened by rednecks in bars, and had been called names I choose not to repeat. In trying to explain the South to them, it was hard to know where to start.

Meeting Robert Lowell, though, was *the* experience of my years in Cambridge. Lowell had a genius for friendship. He liked Southerners, and he saw a kind of symmetry in our literary migrations. While he as a young New England poet had gone to Tennessee to study with John

Crowe Ransom and Allen Tate, I as a young Southern poet had come to Massachusetts to study with him. Lowell had recently published his breakthrough book, *Life Studies,* in which, for most readers, he had left the Paleface stockade by cover of night and joined the Redskins. All true in a sense, but not for those who could appreciate the subtle intermingling of rhyme, meter, and free verse in his new work. While I was learning about free verse from other poets in Cambridge, Lowell was clearly pleased to discover a young poet who could construct a decent stanza. He would read aloud one of my elaborate ten-line stanzas from a poem like "Enter Your Garden" and challenge the other students: "Could you write something that well constructed?" "No, and who gives a damn?" they were likely to say. But the fellow feeling that came from a shared understanding of the craft, as well as some of the familiar Southern ways, bound us together as friends. Through Lowell I renewed my acquaintance with Peter Taylor, whom I had first met at Andrew Lytle's house in Monteagle, Tennessee.

A Lowell poem was not written but *built.* This was true of his own poems as well as those by writers he admired, like Thomas Hardy, Gerald Manley Hopkins, George Herbert, John Milton, John Crowe Ransom, Elizabeth Bishop. Lowell taught taste, probably without even intending to do so. I define taste—much derided at this particular moment in time—as earned opinion. As the convicts at San Quentin, where I taught in the mid-seventies, liked to put it, "Opinions are like [anal orifices (to euphemize)]. Everybody's got one." Taste has a bad name because it is, understandably, associated with snobbery. But without cultivating taste, an artist cannot grow. Lowell lived and breathed poetry. His attention to the art was thorough and unwavering. Like Elizabeth Bishop's "Sandpiper,"

His beak is focussed; he is preoccupied,
looking for something, something, something.
Poor bird, he is obsessed!

To those of us who were lucky enough to sit around a seminar table or, later, to drink pitchers of vodka martinis with him at the Iruna, near Harvard Square, this single-mindedness was the gift Robert Lowell transmitted.

Working with Lowell was only one of many things that were happening to me during the mid-sixties. In 1964 I became editor-in-chief of

Tillinghast aboard ship, Ionian Sea, 1967

Let's Go: The Harvard Student Travel Guide. This editorship financed a trip or two to Europe and gave me my start as a travel writer. My parents had sent me to Europe in 1961; just as had happened the first time I went to New York, in Europe I encountered a culture that impressed me as being aligned with the things that were important to me. At least half the poems in the last section of my first book, *Sleep Watch,* were written in Europe—the genesis of an important circumstance in my writing life. Being on non-native ground, breathing different air, seeing unfamiliar landscapes and buildings, all this gets poems going. Having grown up feeling inwardly alienated from most of the people around me, I came to feel most at home when away from home. I first saw Istanbul in 1964. The exotic atmosphere of the city struck some chord, and I have returned there five times since.

In 1965 I married Nancy Pringle in Charleston, South Carolina. She studied classics at Boston University while I did my graduate work. A Sinclair–Kennedy travel grant from Harvard allowed us to spend the academic year 1966–67 in Europe. We sold the new car my parents had given us as a wedding present and bought a new Volkswagen at the factory in Wolfsburg. The way we handled the grant enabled us to see a lot without feeling we were rushing about like tourists. We spent two or three months in Paris, London, Amsterdam, and Rome, toured Burgundy, Tuscany, the south of Italy, and Greece—including several islands—and made a short trip to Istanbul.

Wherever we stayed we met young Europeans and expatriate Americans. Their way of life, their intellectual and artistic ideas, again broadened my sense of my own possibilities as a writer and gave me confidence to rise above what I considered to be the limitations of American culture. A bohemian culture, the beginnings of what would become "the counterculture" in America, was thriving in Paris and London. We lived in the City Hotel on the rue Monsieur-le-Prince in Paris, where, after we had breakfasted on the boulevard St. Michel, I would write poetry during most of the day. Then we would go out to the cafés at night. A friend was studying anthropology at the Sorbonne with Claude Lévi-Strauss—my first exposure to making comparisons between different cultures, a practice that would become part of my thinking from then on. After a psychedelic experience in the apartment of my friend Henry Wolff on New Year's Eve 1966, I wrote my first long poem, "The Old Mill," which took me back mentally to the amusement park at the fairgrounds in Memphis to find a metaphor for the experience. On our way back to the United States, passing through Brussels, Nancy and I bought a copy of a new LP called "Sgt. Pepper's Lonely Hearts Club Band."

Perhaps during our year in Europe we were exposed to too much that was new. This was the beginning of what has come to be called "the sixties," and its appeal to me was enormous because it seemed to offer liberation in every part of one's life: psychic, sexual, political, literary. Nancy and I separated during the fall of 1966 (to be legally divorced in 1970), and I moved into digs in Kirkland House at Harvard, where I was a tutor. Many of my friends thought I was slightly out of my mind, and they were probably right. But it's hard to tell how much freedom one needs, and at that time I needed all the freedom I could get. The breakup of my marriage, though that was what

I wanted, wounded me deeply, and the wounds took a long time to heal. Anyone who reads poems like "Come Home and Be Happy," "The Same Bird Again," "Everything Is Going to Be All Right," and "A Letter" from *Sleep Watch* will know how deep the pain went.

Up to that point I had done my course work in the English Renaissance, but now that seemed too—what? Too hidebound, too English, too tradition-bound. I decided to write my dissertation on Robert Lowell's poetry, about which very little criticism had been written at that time. Over the next couple of years I enjoyed going over Lowell's poetry carefully, one line at a time. Later, when I had finished the thesis—in Berkeley in 1969—I never wanted to see it again. But it laid the groundwork for the critical memoir of *Robert Lowell* I would write later.

I was wild to go to California, where everything seemed to be happening. Academic jobs were plentiful in those days, particularly for someone with a Harvard Ph.D. When the chairman of the Berkeley English department came to Cambridge, I showed up for the interview wearing motorcycle boots and my best suit, which I had had made on Savile Row a few years earlier. As it happened, my interviewer was wearing the same kind of suspenders ("braces," we Anglophiles call them) I was wearing. We had got them at the same shop in the Burlington Arcade. Clearly we had something in common, and soon I found myself with a job offer from Berkeley.

I had never been to California before. I had only the vaguest idea what it even looked like. But I loaded my Volkswagen full of my few possessions and took off for the West Coast. The poet Bob Grenier and his wife Emily, friends of mine from Harvard, invited me to share a house with them near the UC campus. My years on the faculty at Berkeley are a bit of a blur. I have kept up with only a handful of my colleagues from the English department there: the historical novelist Thomas Flanagan and his wife Jean; Seamus Heaney, who was at that time a little-known visiting poet; Bob Tracy and his wife Becky, whom I see in Ireland every summer; and until his death, Tom Parkinson, the critic and godfather to the Beats.

The late sixties and early seventies were heady days in Berkeley. The campus was the scene of one demonstration after another. The pattern was: a campaign of campus demonstrations, followed by police intervention, tear gas, and police charges, with picketing, singing, and rock throwing by the crowd of students, sympathetic faculty, and *lumpenproletariat* from the Berkeley streets. At this point the faculty would decide to go on strike, which meant that you would be manning the barricades with your students, or else the class would be meeting off-campus at your apartment so as not to violate the strike. None of this was particularly good for formal education, but it was exciting and liberating in many ways, I suppose. We learned a lot—though some of what we learned would make our later reentry into "straight" society difficult.

Part of what we learned was an attunement to wilderness—the environmental movement was in its infancy. My friends and I made frequent backpacking trips to the Sierra Nevada, only a few hours away. And in the San Francisco Bay Area you are never far from beaches and parkland. I was also spending a lot of time with friends who were students of a Sufi master from San Francisco; I was gradually becoming involved in the "spiritual" subculture, taking yoga classes, learning to meditate, going for weekends with Tibetan lamas, and so on. My English department colleagues were not thrilled when I proposed to offer an experimental class that would bring some of these practices to the study of works of literature like *Walden,* the poetry of Wordsworth, Allen Ginsberg, Gary Snyder, and the Don Juan books of Carlos Castaneda. My chairman decided we would call the course "Literature and Transcendent Experience," which had a respectable ring to it.

Every Thursday afternoon my students and I would drive up to my cabin in Sonoma County and spend two days together reading and discussing books, meditating, doing Sufi dancing, and sleeping out under the redwoods. That cabin near Freestone provides the setting for the first two poems from *The Knife and Other Poems:* "Return" and "The Thief." In memory the place is drenched with an atmosphere of redwood forests and incipient mysticism. I meditated and did yoga for hours on my deck, which overlooked an apple orchard. Suzy Papanikolas, a friend I had met at the Highlander Folk School and traveled with in Europe years before, lived just down the road and taught me a lot about Zen.

For three summers in the early seventies I camped out and taught meditation at the Camp des Aigles, an international school run by the Sufi master Pir Vilayat Inayat Khan in the French Alps near Chamonix, precariously perched on the side of a mountain, with a stunning view across the valley to Mont Blanc. Most of the people who came there were my age or a little younger, and most of them were from France, Britain, the Netherlands, Germany, and the United States. We improvised madly. We turned a shepherd's hut into our kitchen, ran a Honda generator for electricity, slept and meditated in army surplus tents that flooded when it rained—as it almost always did. My poem "Legends about Air and Water" from *The Knife* attempts to capture some of the atmosphere of that mountain retreat.

Pir Vilayat, who taught an eclectic brand of meditation drawn from all the world's spiritual traditions, lectured alternately in English, French, and German. Like most New Age gurus, he slept with his female students, though most of us didn't know that at the time. He also had a wife in Paris and would later have another in California. When I discovered that side of the man I regarded as my spiritual teacher, I felt he had deceived us. Looking back on it, I may have been a bit narrow-

Richard and Mary Graves Tillinghast, shortly before their marriage, Mill Valley, California, 1973

minded. I treasure the mad gleam that came into his eyes when in the midst of a spectacular Alpine thunderstorm he would play a mass by Josquin des Prez on his big reel-to-reel tape player—the generator cranking away not quite beyond earshot—and urge us to contemplate the heavenly orders that were so clear to him and so hazy to me. The "spiritual hierarchy"— that invisible government that, in Pir Vilayat's Zoroastrian view of things, fought the everlasting battle of good against evil—had, I now see, some relation to the noble warriors of the Confederacy. If the armies of the masters, saints, and prophets ever need reinforcements on the plain of Armageddon, I'm sure they can count on the astral shades of Generals Lee and Jackson.

In addition to introducing me to the arcane astral worlds that existed perhaps only in his own noble and contradictory mind, Pir Vilayat inspired me to make the pilgrimage to India. On sabbatical leave from the University of California in 1970, after spending most of the summer at the Camp des Aigles, I set out on the overland trip east. This pilgrimage turned out to be even more inspiring, frustrating, comical, and unforgettable than my years under the tutelage of Pir Vilayat.

In 1970 one could travel unhindered overland from Europe to the Indian subcontinent. On the train from Geneva to Istanbul I met an English teacher from Tabriz in Iran who was bringing home boxes of consumer goods, including a television set he had bought in Amsterdam. He taught me some Turkish and Persian phrases, and I kept an eye on his possessions whenever he had to leave the train compartment. I remember the two of us wandering around Sirkeci in Istanbul carrying the TV and the boxes, looking for a cheap hotel, and then having to move from one hotel to another because of the bedbugs.

After putting him and his boxes on an eastbound train a few days later, I went to Konya, headquarters of the Mevlevi dervishes, with a friend from the Camp des Aigles. In Muslim, Hindu, and Buddhist countries the spiritual life of the community centers on some holy place, often a saint's tomb, called a *türbe* in Turkish, around which a shrine has grown up. We spent our first evening in Konya at the *türbe* of Mevlana Celalettin Rumi, a place with a very light, inspiring atmosphere. Mevlana—

or Rumi, as he is called outside Turkey—was the founder of the Mevlevi order of dervishes, known for their ecstatic music and dancing. My friend and I happened on the building where the dervish musicians were rehearsing and sat on the ground underneath the windows for hours listening to them play haunting music on their stringed instruments, hand drums, and wooden flutes. Inside these shrines rest the massive biers of the leaders of the Mevlevi order, covered in green cloth—green being the sacred color of Islam—with the departed man's massive turban coiled and resting over the head of the long box. Pilgrims walk around the shrine with their palms raised upward in the Muslim prayer posture to receive the blessings of the place. The writings of Pir Vilayat's father, Hazrat Inayat Khan, speak of developing the capacity of attuning oneself to the atmosphere of holy places like the shrine at Konya, and for me this traditional Sufi practice is not that far from the famous sense of place that Southerners are supposed to have. I pay tribute to Mevlana in my poem "Eight Lines by Jalal-ud-Din Rumi," which appears in *The Knife*.

Visiting prerevolutionary Iran, I was taken aback by the hostility I seemed to arouse everywhere I went. Boys in a bazaar once threw stones at me. At first I thought it was because I wore my hair long and sported a big bushy beard, but later I concluded it was because I was a Westerner. The shah was spending millions of dollars celebrating the one-thousandth or some other equally fantastic anniversary of the Pahlavi dynasty—a ludicrous exercise, since in reality he owed his throne to American backing, a brutal secret police, and his father, a petty general who had seized power from the democratically elected government with help from the CIA. The country bristled with soldiers. I have never seen such a display of force on the streets of any country in the world. I wanted to visit the meetings of the Kalendar dervishes in Turkestan, but they had been canceled by the government for the duration of the shah's celebration because the Kalendar rites, in which the participants would go into a trance and run metal skewers through their cheeks to prove the power of spirit over flesh, were considered too barbaric for Western eyes.

Who can explain the appeal of travel and of all that is exotic? I was particularly taken with Afghanistan, my next stop east of Iran. This was before the Russian occupation, the

Tillinghast with daughter Julia, nine months old, in "the stone and shingle house at Morgan's Steep" (from Sewanee in Ruins), *Sewanee, Tennessee, Christmastime, 1979*

war to drive the Russians out, and the civil war that followed, reducing this mountainous home of fierce tribesmen to a wreckage of charred rubble. It seems that every other person walks on crutches in Afghanistan now or is missing an arm or an eye. Twenty-five years ago I saw ancient mosques and adobe forts that dated from the days of the Silk Route caravans and the conquests of the Mongols. I was amazed by Chinese-looking faces out of which peered the bluest of blue eyes—the inheritance of centuries-old racial intermingling. Statues and murals in remote caves spoke of a time when this part of the world had been Buddhist. The history I had imbibed in my own native region went back no more than two hundred years. Here I felt part of historical currents that dated back to wars, migrations, and spiritual and cultural movements that were as old as the human race.

In Herat, where I spent most of my Afghani days, I bargained for Baluchi rugs in the bazaar and learned pidgin Hindi from other so-journers who had preceded me to India. Then on to Pakistan, where I lived in a Sufi *khankah* and practiced the Islamic rituals surrounding the observance of Ramadan. The sheikh of the Khankah had a tailor sew me up a suit of the local clothes so that I would not stand out so much in a crowd of Pakistanis. In the Lahore museum I saw art from Bokhara that blended Russian and Central Asian Islamic motifs, once again sharpening my appreciation of the fluidity of cultural traditions in this part of the world. I was overwhelmed by the hospitality of people to whom I had been provided invitations by Pir Vilayat and other fellow travelers on what we called "the spiritual path." Islam fosters a sense of brotherhood unlike anything I have ever seen.

Eventually, though, I wanted to move on to India, the source of my pilgrimage. War was threatening between Muslims and Hindus on the subcontinent. From the hotel where I had moved at the end of Ramadan I could see crowds demonstrating on the streets of Lahore, calling for confrontation with India. It was in that climate that I crossed the border between the two countries. My first day in India, two things happened: war was declared, and either I lost or someone pinched the pouch that held my passport, my shot record and other travel documents, and eight 100-dollar bills. I arrived in India broke and without any legal identity.

Mysteriously, the pouch turned up in a small town eighty miles from Delhi. Word from the chief of police in the town reached me where I was staying in Delhi, and I took a car there. The chief of police, whose name told me he was a Muslim, invited me to his house, where a good lunch was served on the lawn. Then, as I watched in amazement, he handed over everything from the pouch, including the hundred-dollar bills, whose serial numbers he wrote down on an official form that he asked me to sign. I returned to Delhi feeling as if some strange morality play had been acted out for my benefit.

The whole time I spent in India seemed equally marvelous and unreal. With David Freidberg, a friend from California with whom I was traveling at that time, I visited holy men of all persuasions, as well as ashrams, shrines, and temples all over northern India, with results that were sometimes mind-boggling, sometimes laughable. We bathed in and drank water from the Ganges with no apparent ill effects. We roamed the hills above Rishikesh conversing with *saddhus,* who kept little retreats in the forest. I experienced a startling moment of awakening when we were meditating with an obscure holy man in a small temple in the Himalayan foothills. We were debating some point from the *Bhagavad Gita,* which I had learned Sanskrit in order to read, when he unexpectedly called out, "Do you understand!?" at the same time striking me on the forehead with his bony, ascetic hand. And then, yes, I did understand.

There is much else to tell about that journey but little room here in which to tell it. Using Kathmandu as a base, I went trekking by myself in Nepal, carrying only a small pack. I would buy food along the way or eat rice

The Tillinghasts—Andrew, Joshua, Charles, Mary, Richard, and Julia, Portland, Maine, 1986

Josh Tillinghast, age eighteen, salmon fishing, Pere Marquette River, Michigan, 1992

and *dahl* in the little inns to be found along the path in the mountains. In 1970 and 1971 trekking had not become as popular and well organized as it would be later. I met other Americans and Europeans occasionally and sometimes hiked with them for a day or two, but mainly I was on my own in a meditative solitude where I was often lonely and introspective, at other times thrilled by views of Annapurna and the other high peaks above where I was hiking.

As I have suggested, this is a part of the world where out-of-the-ordinary things are likely to happen. I was staying at an inn on the Tatopani River in the Kali Gandhaki Valley in western Nepal when something else happened to me that I still regard with wonderment. The Tatopani has hot springs that bubble up in places along its bank, and I was alone, bathing and washing my clothes, recovering from a day during which the trail had climbed two thousand feet and then descended two thousand feet. Sitting in one of the hot springs,

writing in my notebook, I suddenly realized that I would return to America, get married, and have a family. This realization came in a quick series of mental images. I even sketched a little picture of the house we would live in.

Soon my sabbatical time ran out and I was back at Berkeley. To no one's surprise, I was not given tenure, and returned to the hippie life most of my friends were living, unhindered by gainful employment. If there is anything I regret about the sixties (for most of us it began in the mid-sixties and lasted into the late seventies) it is the excessive emphasis on the nonverbal. In addition to my pursuit of that *ignis fatuus* called "enlightenment," I took up drumming again in the early seventies and wrote song lyrics. It was possible to draw unemployment and live on my savings for a few years, but eventually it occurred to me that I would have to earn a living. For one who had followed Timothy Leary's advice to "tune in, turn on, and drop out," it came as a hard lesson that, while dropping out was easy, clawing my way back in took every ounce of will, resourcefulness, and determination that I could muster.

Shortly after returning from India, I met and fell in love with Mary Graves. We married in 1973, and our first child, Joshua, was born in 1974. Josh is a professional bass player, and I attribute his excellent sense of time to his having heard me practicing my drums on a daily basis while he was in the womb. I kept my drum set in our big bedroom in the communal house where Josh was born in Mill Valley. Josh's birth was the most intense experience of our lives to that point. Becoming the father of a son touched off strong feelings about being a man. In "The Knife," which was triggered by Josh's birth, that object, which is not a weapon but a tool, provides a connection between three generations: my brother and me, our father, and my firstborn son.

> I see in its steel
>   the worn gold on my father's hand
>   the light in those trees
>   the look on my son's face   a moment old
>
>   like the river   old like rain
> older than anything that dies can be.

With the pride of parenthood came an impulse to provide for my family so strong I am tempted to call it an instinct. I have observed it in other young fathers. One of my first jobs was doing carpentry work for a small outfit; all of us who worked on the job were musicians. At this time I also maintained and repaired a succession of Volkswagens, and though it was often frustrating, at the same time I found physical and mechanical work satisfying. I had never done any before. This feeling developed into a respect for hard work that I had never felt before, and I began to work very hard on my poetry. I had a small workroom above our garage, and I scotch-taped drafts of poems to the walls. My new book came to life within the four walls of that room. I was still a hippie, though, and Mary and I played in a rock/soul music/reggae band called Beauty and the Backbeats. Playing alongside the bass player Leroy Shyne, I experienced the rocksteady fusion of a tight rhythm section.

Out of many grease-stained, knuckle-bruising hours solving problems and doing work that my study of English literature had not prepared me for, I earned the long poem called "Fossils, Metal, and the Blue Limit," a somewhat comical meditation on automobiles, fishing, ecology, and much else. During the days I spent working on cars I also gained new appreciation for my engineer father and the tradition of inventors and machinists he came out of. "Fossils, Metal, and the Blue Limit" approaches that tradition obliquely, from the point of view of the frustrated amateur mechanic:

> Were days like this foreseen
> in the Platonic heaven of machinists?—
> or by the generations of men,
> with boots and soiled caps and wire-rimmed
> eyeglasses
> and daughters and sons,
> who brought iron ore out of the earth,
> learned to smelt it, and formed it into steel.

Eventually, in 1976, I started teaching again—in the college program at San Quentin Prison. If carpentry and automobile mechanics had not been part of my upbringing, the criminal world of my convict students was another world altogether. At first prison scared me, with its steel and concrete, its tattooed heavies in their mirrored sunglasses and black watch caps, the armed guards, the gut-freezing clang of the gate that slammed behind me as I entered San Quentin every night. It was the hardest work I have ever done, teaching three-hour classes two or three nights a week. After about six months I became what they called "conwise" and lost the romanticized view of prisoners I had learned in the demonstrations at Berkeley. A lot of the soul and suffering, passion and tragedy, of those men's lives found its way into what may be my best poem, "Lost Cove & The Rose of San Antone." I perform it in almost all my readings, and it never fails to thrill me as I read aloud the lines about this imaginary outlaw, based on the lives of many of my friends from San Quentin:

> The fiddles and autoharp fill up the dark room
> and push out through paint-blackened screens
> into black oaks that press against the house.
> His face hurts me. It doesn't look right.

I felt a bond with these men, some of whom were fellow Southerners. Some came out of the same counterculture I had been living in. My sympathy for Islam helped me with the Black

Sons Andrew, fourteen, and Charles, eleven, at a book party for The Stonecutter's Hand, *Ann Arbor, Michigan, 1995*

Muslims, and a shared love for music brought all of us together. At the same time there were evil men there, men whose cruelty and willingness to hurt and victimize could not be explained away by cloudy indictments of that receptacle for all blame, "society."

Our daughter Julia was born in 1979, and finally, six years after leaving the University of California, I was offered a full-time teaching job at Sewanee. It was only for a year, but now I was back inside the academic profession. Mary, who cried over leaving her friends in California, took to life in Sewanee like a native. She was soon involved in a quilting group there. We lived in a great big stone-and-clapboard house at Morgan's Steep on the edge of a cliff overlooking the valley, and I did research for my long poem *Sewanee in Ruins,* handsomely printed two years later, with drawings by Ed Carlos—who teaches art at the University of the South—by Sewanee's university press; the job was overseen by my friend Arthur Ben Chitty. Andrew Lytle used to talk about the generation of men who had fought for the Confederacy, how they had come home from the war bone-tired and wounded. The poem explores the 1870s, that defining but often ignored decade when the defeated Confederacy attempted to recover from its losses.

The year 1980 saw the publication of *The Knife and Other Poems,* as well as our move to Cambridge, Massachusetts, where I was offered a three-year Briggs-Copeland lectureship at Harvard. This move reinforced the sense that my career had moved in one enormous circle, starting in Tennessee, moving to New England, then to the West, and now circling back to Harvard again by way of Sewanee. I read Robert Lowell's letters and papers at Houghton Library, and I finished *Sewanee in Ruins* in the little upstairs office at 34 Kirkland Street, where Seamus Heaney had an office down the hall.

I was once again able to have long conversations with my old friend William Alfred at his house on Athens Street; to drink single-malt Scotch with Stratis Haviaris, who ran the Poetry Room at Lamont Library; to discuss poetry with old friends Frank Bidart, Gail Mazur, DeWitt Henry, and Lloyd Schwartz; to haunt the Grolier Bookshop, now in the hands of Louisa Solano and her little dog Pumpkin; to carouse with my old friend Peter O'Malley, one of the founders of *Ploughshares,* of which I be-

came an editor. Harvey Shapiro called me from New York and asked me to start reviewing poetry for the *New York Times,* something I have been doing once or twice a year ever since. I ran a low-budget reading series at Dunster House, where Robert Bly, Stephen Sandy, Derek Mahon, Jayne Ann Phillips, and other writers appeared and read their work for pennies.

I recall fondly two great parties, both held out-of-doors. One was the lamb roast and christening party for Elektra Haviaris; the other was a Derby Day barbecue Mary and I gave at our house in Watertown, when we served ribs and mint juleps to what seemed like the entire Cambridge literary community. Robert Fitzgerald was kind enough to let me audit his versification class, and I learned from him everything about rhyme and meter that I would later deploy when I returned to that discipline.

After three years at Harvard I was offered a tenured position in Ann Arbor. George Garrett had been brought to the University of Michigan to start up an MFA program, and he brought me on board. This was an offer I was very glad to get. Our sons Andrew and Charles had been born in 1981 and 1983, and our family of six needed some financial security. Charles was two weeks old when we once again moved. We bought a two-story stucco house with four bedrooms, a good fireplace, a porch, and a deck in Burns Park, inhabited by station wagon-driving, softball-playing, PTO-attending, *New York Times*—reading folk, many of whom are my colleagues at the university. I took up gardening seriously for the first time. After my father died in 1981 and my mother had moved into a nursing home, my brother and I had to sell the house in Memphis. One December morning in 1984 we drove off from 190 South Cox Street in two 24-foot U-Haul trucks, transporting the furniture we had grown up with to our separate homes in Michigan and South Carolina. Our house here has a Victorian feeling to it, and I like sleeping in the bed my parents slept in, using their table silver, hearing, as I write these words, the tick of the Seth Thomas shelf clock from our kitchen in Memphis.

Our Flag Was Still There, incorporating *Sewanee in Ruins,* was published in 1984. These new poems concerned themselves with war, with technology, with popular American culture. While preparing the manuscript I had an inspiration: I would write a poem about America during and after World War II, contrasting the generation who fought that war with my own sixties generation, and I would call it, quoting from the national anthem, "Our Flag Was Still There." This look at postwar America would resemble what I had earlier chronicled about Tennesseans during the aftermath of the Civil War. It was the first time the title of a poem had come first as a concept, and it was certainly the first time I had set out purposely to write a poem that would solidify the theme of the entire book.

In the late eighties I took a swerve off my path as a poet and wrote a long work of fiction called "Paint It Black." I wanted to prove to myself that I could write a novel. Writing it was enjoyable—which should have been a tipoff to me that the results might not be so satisfying. The book is a thriller, travel book, and love story, with elements of academic satire. The hero is a poet who has to solve a mystery. The agents to whom I showed it thought it would be hard to place, so I gave up on it and returned to poetry. Parts of the book are set in Turkey, and on impulse one summer night in 1987 I decided I would learn Turkish. This spinoff from the project of writing a novel turned out to be endlessly fascinating. Turkish is so hard, so different from English, the mentality so different from our own. I have translated some contemporary Turkish poetry, and in the summer of 1990 I got a fellowship from the American Research Institute in Turkey to take an advanced Turkish conversation class at the University of the Bosphorus. This gave me a chance to reacquaint myself with the city that has intrigued me since I first went there in 1964. And that renewal of acquaintance allowed me to write poems like "Pasha's Daughter, 1914," which was included in my new book, *The Stonecutter's Hand.*

The best thing that has happened to me in the last decade, though, was the year (1990–91) my family and I spent in Ireland, thanks to a travel grant from the Amy Lowell Trust. This is a grant given to an American poet every year, the only stipulation being that you live outside America for twelve months. When the Turkish course was over I flew home from Istanbul, and less than twenty-four hours later the six of us took a plane to Ireland, where we had rented a house in Kinvara, a fishing village on Galway Bay. The grant was just enough

The author with a large trout,
Pere Marquette River, 1993

to live on, and we gladly did without a television, a telephone, and a car. The children went to local schools, and Mary pursued her interest in traditional Irish music and became close friends with the other women her age in Kinvara. I had the great luxury of being able to write every day.

I have celebrated the village in more than one poem, including "A Quiet Pint in Kinvara," which I wrote right around my fiftieth birthday and dedicated to my friend the journalist and historian Jeff O'Connell. I love Kinvara's weather, its people, and its architecture:

        the broad-shouldered gravity
Of houses from the eighteenth or nineteenth
    century—
Limestone, three storeys, their slate roofs rain-
    slick,
Aglow with creeper and the green brilliance
    of mosses.
No force off the Atlantic
Could threaten their angles or budge their
    masses.

They rise unhurriedly from the strong cellar
And hold a fleshy palm, palm outward,
  against the sea,
Saying "Land starts here. Go peddle your salt
  airs elsewhere."
From farms down lanes the meat and milk of
  pasture,
Root crops and loads of hay,
By hoof or wagon, come down to Kinvara
  quay.

I wrote most of *The Stonecutter's Hand* in Kinvara. I would work at a big table, given me by Jessie Lendennie of Salmon Press in Galway, set before a south-facing window in our bedroom. Or I would hitchhike into Galway and work at a table in Bewley's coffeehouse there or in a snug at one of my favorite pubs: Naughton's, Mick Taylor's, or The Quays. Galway is a medieval city with a Georgian overlay. Its streets still follow the curves and digressions of the medieval lanes and alleys. Fragments of old stonework may be seen here and there if you know where to look. Every writer, I suppose, has particularly lucky times in his career when a bit of writing time presents itself just at the moment when he wants passionately to practice his craft. That happened to me in Ireland. "I had my innings there," I wrote in "A Backward Glance at Galway":

            hitching the coast road
Through salt meadows saturated and green,
Then walking up from the quays—a wind at
  my back
With the North Atlantic behind it, that
  thinned the coalsmoke
And refreshed with raindrops the chiseled
  limestone.
I would hole up in Naughton's pub with my
  notebook
Ferreting words from a secondhand thesaurus,
Sounding out rhymes in a snug with a pint
  of Guinness.

Also in Kinvara I started writing literary essays, often for the *New Criterion,* the conservative New York monthly, one of the few places in the country that publishes literate, jargon-free essays of an ample length and also pays well. Beginning during the year in Ireland, I have written on Rebecca West, William Trevor, Brian Friel, Elizabeth Bowen, W. H. Auden, Somerville & Ross, Bob Dylan, and the Grateful Dead for the *Criterion,* the *Gettysburg Review,* the *Sewanee Review,* and other periodicals. Somerville & Ross

were two Anglo-Irish second-cousins who wrote the Irish R.M. stories around the turn of the century. Edmund Wilson is my model for these essays: I like the task of reading deeply and widely into a favorite author and then writing up my sense of that author for like-minded, nonspecialist readers.

Mary and I spent many nights in Kinvara's pubs listening to traditional Irish music, and it occurred to me that the *New York Times* might like an article on the experience. They did, and since then I have written often for the travel section—on Georgian architecture in Dublin, driving across Ireland from Dublin to Galway, old churches in Charleston, South Carolina, the Museum of Appalachia in Tennessee, Michigan's wilderness island Isle Royale, Memphis barbecue, and other subjects. This writing combines my love for travel with a way of financing it.

Two weeks after I finish this piece my critical memoir, *Robert Lowell's Life and Work: Damaged Grandeur,* is coming out. It's a way of paying homage to the poet who taught me much of what I have learned about the art. I have nearly finished a new book of poems. I continue to travel around the country giving poetry readings. My wife and I will celebrate our twenty-fifth wedding anniversary in a couple of years. Every day I look around in wonder at the four flourishing lives Mary and I have brought into this world. In my fifties I am doing my best writing, bringing a passion and exactitude to it that I seem to have built up to only slowly during forty years of working at it.

BIBLIOGRAPHY

Poetry:

Sleep Watch, Wesleyan University Press, 1969.

(Contributor) *Ten American Poets,* Carcanet Press, 1974.

The Knife and Other Poems, Wesleyan University Press, 1980.

Sewanee in Ruins, illustrated by Edward Carlos, University of the South, 1981.

Fossils, Metal, and the Blue Limit, White Creek Press, 1982.

Our Flag Was Still There (contains *Sewanee in Ruins*), Wesleyan University Press, 1984.

A Quiet Pint in Kinvara, Salmon Publishing/Tir Eolas (Galway, Ireland), 1991.

The Stonecutter's Hand, David R. Godine, 1995.

Memoir:

Robert Lowell's Life and Work: Damaged Grandeur, University of Michigan Press, 1995.

Also contributor to numerous periodicals, including *Antaeus, Atlantic Monthly, Boston Globe, Boston Review, Crazy Horse, Critical Quarterly, Georgia Review, Harper's Bazaar, Harvard Advocate, New Republic, New York Times Book Review, Paris Review, Partisan Review, Ploughshares, Poetry, Sewanee Review, Shenandoah, Southern Review, Washington Post,* and *Yale Review.*

Cumulative Index

CUMULATIVE INDEX

The names of essayists who appear in the series are in boldface type. Subject references are followed by volume and page number(s). When a subject reference appears in more than one essay, names of the essayists are also provided.